Living with Nkrumahism

NEW AFRICAN HISTORIES

SERIES EDITORS: JEAN ALLMAN, ALLEN ISAACMAN, AND DEREK R. PETERSON

David William Cohen and E. S. Atieno Odhiambo, *The Risks of Knowledge*

Belinda Bozzoli, *Theatres of Struggle and the End of Apartheid*

Gary Kynoch, *We Are Fighting the World*

Stephanie Newell, *The Forger's Tale*

Jacob A. Tropp, *Natures of Colonial Change*

Jan Bender Shetler, *Imagining Serengeti*

Cheikh Anta Babou, *Fighting the Greater Jihad*

Marc Epprecht, *Heterosexual Africa?*

Marissa J. Moorman, *Intonations*

Karen E. Flint, *Healing Traditions*

Derek R. Peterson and Giacomo Macola, editors, *Recasting the Past*

Moses E. Ochonu, *Colonial Meltdown*

Emily S. Burrill, Richard L. Roberts, and Elizabeth Thornberry, editors, *Domestic Violence and the Law in Colonial and Postcolonial Africa*

Daniel R. Magaziner, *The Law and the Prophets*

Emily Lynn Osborn, *Our New Husbands Are Here*

Robert Trent Vinson, *The Americans Are Coming!*

James R. Brennan, *Taifa*

Benjamin N. Lawrance and Richard L. Roberts, editors, *Trafficking in Slavery's Wake*

David M. Gordon, *Invisible Agents*

Allen F. Isaacman and Barbara S. Isaacman, *Dams, Displacement, and the Delusion of Development*

Stephanie Newell, *The Power to Name*

Gibril R. Cole, *The Krio of West Africa*

Matthew M. Heaton, *Black Skin, White Coats*

Meredith Terretta, *Nation of Outlaws, State of Violence*

Paolo Israel, *In Step with the Times*

Michelle R. Moyd, *Violent Intermediaries*

Abosede A. George, *Making Modern Girls*

Alicia C. Decker, *In Idi Amin's Shadow*

Rachel Jean-Baptiste, *Conjugal Rights*

Shobana Shankar, *Who Shall Enter Paradise?*

Emily S. Burrill, *States of Marriage*

Todd Cleveland, *Diamonds in the Rough*

Carina E. Ray, *Crossing the Color Line*

Sarah Van Beurden, *Authentically African*

Giacomo Macola, *The Gun in Central Africa*

Lynn Schler, *Nation on Board*

Julie MacArthur, *Cartography and the Political Imagination*

Abou B. Bamba, *African Miracle, African Mirage*

Daniel Magaziner, *The Art of Life in South Africa*

Paul Ocobock, *An Uncertain Age*

Keren Weitzberg, *We Do Not Have Borders*

Nuno Domingos, *Football and Colonialism*

Jeffrey S. Ahlman, *Living with Nkrumahism*

Bianca Murillo, *Market Encounters*

Laura Fair, *Reel Pleasures*

Thomas F. McDow, *Buying Time*

Jon Soske, *Internal Frontiers*

Living with Nkrumahism

Nation, State, and Pan-Africanism
in Ghana

⌇

Jeffrey S. Ahlman

OHIO UNIVERSITY PRESS ⌇ ATHENS, OHIO

Ohio University Press, Athens, Ohio 45701
ohioswallow.com
© 2017 by Ohio University Press
All rights reserved

Printed in the United States of America
Ohio University Press books are printed on acid-free paper ⊗ ™

Cover photo of Kwame Nkrumah by Mark Kauffman/LIFE picture collection/Getty Images.

27 26 25 24 23 22 21 20 19 18 17   5 4 3 2 1

The following material has been previously published in a different form.
Ahlman, Jeffrey S. "Managing the Pan-African Workplace: Discipline, Ideology, and
the Cultural Politics of the Ghanaian Bureau of African Affairs." *Ghana Studies* 15/16
(2012/2013): 337–371. © 2013 by the Board of Regents of the University of Wisconsin
System. Reproduced courtesy of the University of Wisconsin Press.

Ahlman, Jeffrey S. "A New Type of Citizen: Youth, Gender, and Generation in the
Ghanaian Builders Brigade." *Journal of African History* 53, no. 1 (2012): 87–105. ©
2012 by Cambridge University Press. Reproduced with the permission of Cambridge
University Press.

Library of Congress Cataloging-in-Publication Data
Names: Ahlman, Jeffrey S., 1982- author.
Title: Living with Nkrumahism : nation, state, and Pan-Africanism in Ghana /
 Jeffrey S. Ahlman.
Other titles: New African histories series.
Description: Athens, Ohio : Ohio University Press, 2017. | Series: New
 African histories
Identifiers: LCCN 2017036212| ISBN 9780821422922 (hc : alk. paper) | ISBN
 9780821422939 (pb : alk. paper) | ISBN 9780821446157 (pdf)
Subjects: LCSH: Nkrumah, Kwame, 1909-1972–Influence. | Ghana–Politics and
 government–1957-1979. | Ghana–Politics and government–1979-2001. |
 Decolonization–Ghana. | Pan-Africanism.
Classification: LCC DT510.62 A35 2017 | DDC 966.705–dc23
LC record available at https://lccn.loc.gov/2017036212

To KT and Emmanuelle

Contents

Illustrations

Acknowledgments

I first traveled to Ghana in December 2004 as part of a study abroad course run by the University of Illinois at Urbana-Champaign's Center for African Studies. As one of the directors of the course, Jean Allman helped introduce me to Ghana and the study of its history. Ever since, she has continued to support me and my research with her wise counsel and critical eye. At the University of Illinois, I also benefited from the insights and guidance of James Brennan, the late Donald Crummey, Behrooz Ghamari-Tabrizi, and Charles Stewart. Kwame Essien, Bruce Hall, Erica Hill, Abdulai Iddrisu, Ryan Jones, Alice Jones-Nelson, Lessie Tate, Habtamu Mengistie Tegegne, and Brian Yates further provided a rich intellectual community and support system during my time there. The seeds of this project can also be found in my time at the University of Nebraska–Lincoln, where Walter Rucker introduced me to the study of Nkrumah and pan-Africanism, and James Le Sueur encouraged me to think more critically about the challenges of historicizing decolonization.

In Ghana, my utmost gratitude goes to those who graciously took the time to sit down with me (formally and informally) to talk about their experiences living with Nkrumahism. Furthermore, Abdulai Iddrisu and Emily Asiedu each provided me with homes when needed during my travels. In 2009, Kofi Baku kindly provided a forum for me to present my research in the University of Ghana's Department of History. In Ghana, I also enjoyed the wisdom and guidance of the staffs of the George Padmore Research Library on African Affairs and of the various branches of the Public Records and Archives Administration Department I visited. In particular, Edward Addo-Yobo and James Naabah at the Padmore Library truly made this project possible by introducing me to the Bureau of African Affairs files held by this wonderful and unique repository. In the United States, their counterparts at the Howard University Moorland-Spingarn Research Center, the Smith College Archives, the Mount Holyoke College Archives, the Yale University Archives and Beinecke Rare Book and Manuscript Library, the Princeton University Archives, and the New

York Public Library Schomburg Center for Research in Black Culture were similarly inviting and helpful during my and my research assistants' visits. I also want to thank Kwesi Asiedu and Ben Cudjoe, who each aided me with the interview and transcription process.

Among Africanists, Jennifer Hart and Bianca Murillo have long helped me think through the challenges of this project and, over the years, each has generously read and commented on significant portions of the work, answered questions, and offered guidance and friendship. Emily Callaci and Priya Lal were also kind enough to offer their time and energy in commenting on portions of the book. Craig and Sarah Waite added to my sense of community while researching the book. Between 2009 and 2012, I was fortunate enough to receive fellowships from the University of Virginia's Carter G. Woodson Institute for African-American and African Studies and the Johns Hopkins University's Center for Africana Studies, which further enriched my network of colleagues interested in African and pan-African studies. Among those who I had the privilege of working with and learning from at these institutions were Sara Berry, Tshepo Chery, Julia Cummisky, Adam Ewing, Ben Fagan, Jonathan Fenderson, Roquinaldo Ferriera, Bukky Gbadegesin, Anatoli Ignatov, Isaac Kamola, Pier Larson, Joe Miller, Anoop Mirpuri, Cody Perkins, Noel Stringham, Alice Wiemers, and Thabiti Willis. Joe Miller in particular expanded the ways in which I thought about and understood the African past. Sara Berry was similarly generous during my year at Johns Hopkins and afterwards. Likewise, in Baltimore, Elizabeth Schmidt—whose studies on Guinea have long inspired my own thinking about African nationalism, decolonization, and Cold War politics—served as a mentor, helping me navigate the project's conceptualization as a book. More broadly, David Amponsah, Lacy Ferrell, Harcourt Fuller, Frank Gerits, Leslie James, Keri Lambert, Liz McMahon, Stephan Miescher, Nate Plageman, Jeremy Pool, Naaborko Sackeyfio-Lenoch, Paul Schauert, Ben Talton, and Meredith Terretta all provided support, guidance, and friendship as I pursued this project.

Since 2012, my institutional home has been Smith College. It is hard to imagine a more welcoming and intellectually stimulating community of scholars and students than those I have had the pleasure of working with in the college's History Department and African Studies Program. Through a writing group started in 2013, Reem Bailony, Josh Birk, Sergey Glebov, Sarah Hines, Liz Pryor, Shani Roper, and Nadya Sbaiti have read and commented on nearly every aspect of the book. Likewise, in taking on the burden of running a History Department overrun by assistant professors, Marnie Anderson, Ernest Benz, Darcy Buerkle, Jennifer Guglielmo, Richard Lim, Lyn Minnich, and Ann Zulawski have selflessly created the space for all of us assistant professors to succeed, while also serving as invaluable mentors. Elliot Fratkin, Katwiwa Mule, Greg White, and Louis Wilson have played equally generous roles in the African Studies Program. Pinky Hota and Christen Mucher have always been available to talk through ideas and strategize. Furthermore, one of the true joys of working at a place like Smith is the institutional commitment to bringing undergraduates into one's research. As research assistants, Jona Elwell, Elizabeth Hoffmeyer, and Freda Raitelu have each contributed to this book in profound ways.

Several institutions have also made this book possible through their generous funding. The University of Illinois and Smith College have provided significant support for my research. Likewise, it is hard to imagine a fellowship opportunity that could offer as enriching an experience as that offered by the University of Virginia's Woodson Institute. My tenure at Johns Hopkins University was similarly fulfilling. Furthermore, the Council on Library and Information Resources' Mellon Fellowship for Dissertation Research in Original Sources, the American Historical Association's Bernadotte E. Schmitt Grant, and the West African Research Association's Pre-doctoral Fellowship all made the fieldwork and archival research for this project possible. Furthermore, Cambridge University Press and the University of Wisconsin Press kindly allowed me to use adapted and revised portions of articles I previously published in the *Journal of African History* and *Ghana Studies* in this book. Additionally, Kristy Johnson provided valuable copyediting assistance at various stages of the project, as has Ed Vesneske, Jr., to the final manuscript. At Ohio University Press, I want to thank Gillian Berchowitz, the staff who designed the book, the two anonymous reviewers of the manuscript, and the trio of editors of the New African Histories series—Jean Allman, Allen Isaacman, and Derek Peterson—for their enthusiasm for the project and help in sharpening my writing and arguments as I sought to turn a manuscript into a book.

Lastly, I would like to thank my family in Nebraska and Massachusetts. My parents, Roger and Julie Ahlman, have long encouraged me, as have my sisters, Sarah Hoins and Laura Ahlman. My grandparents—Donnie Dyer, Marean Dyer, and Marjorie Ahlman—have always been there for me. Likewise, Gene, Michelle, and Allison Hasenkamp have kindly adopted me into their family. Furthermore, Michelle's generosity in helping with childcare was invaluable in helping me finish the book. Finally, for sixteen years, Katie Ahlman has been my closest friend and companion, living with (and enduring) this project in all its incarnations. It is nearly impossible to thank her enough for her support, encouragement, and patience. At five now, our daughter, Emmanuelle, has provided the fruitful distractions required for moving this project forward.

Abbreviations

AAC	African Affairs Centre
AAPC	All-African People's Conference
ADM	Administrative Files
ARG	Ashanti Regional Archives
ARPS	Aborigines' Rights Protection Society (Gold Coast)
BAA	Bureau of African Affairs
BRG	Brong Ahafo Regional Archives
CAB	Cabinet Papers
CIAS	Conference of Independent African States
CO	Colonial Office
CPP	Convention People's Party
CYO	Committee on Youth Organization
DO	Dominions Office
GCP	Ghana Congress Party
GPRL	George Padmore Research Library on African Affairs
FRUS	Foreign Relations of the United States
KNII	Kwame Nkrumah Ideological Institute
MAP	Muslim Association Party
MNC	Mouvement National Congolais
MSRC	Moorland-Spingarn Research Center (Howard University)
NASSO	National Association of Socialist Students Organisations
NCGW	National Council of Ghana Women
NLC	National Liberation Council
NLM	National Liberation Movement
NYPL	New York Public Library

PAF	Pan-African Federation
PDA	Preventative Detention Act
PDG	Parti Démocratique de Guinée
PP	Progress Party
PRAAD	Public Records and Archives Administration Department
PREM	Prime Minister's Office Files
PUA	Princeton University Archives
RDA	Rassemblement Démocratique Africain
RG	Record Group
RLAA	Research Library on African Affairs
SC	Special Collections
SCUA	Special Collections and University Archives
SSC	Sophia Smith Collection
UI	University of Iowa
TANU	Tanganyika African National Union
TNA	The National Archives of the United Kingdom
TUC	Trades Union Congress
UGCC	United Gold Coast Convention
UMASS Amherst	University of Massachusetts, Amherst
UN	United Nations
UP	United Party
WANS	West African National Secretariat
WASU	West African Student Union
WAYL	West African Youth League
WRG	Western Regional Archives

Introduction

Decolonization and the Pan-African Nation

Our Independence means much more than merely being free to fly our own flag and to play our own national anthem. It becomes a reality only in a revolutionary framework when we create and sustain a level of economic development capable of ensuring a higher standard of living, proper education, good health and the cultural development of all our citizens.

—Kwame Nkrumah, undated speech[1]

In the building of a new society on liberation socialist lines, the people must be taught to help themselves.

—Report by George Padmore, 1952[2]

IN MARCH 1957, the relatively small West African country of Ghana— previously known as the Gold Coast—attained its independence. It was the first sub-Saharan colony to emerge from European colonial rule.[3] The world into which the young Ghanaian state entered was one of transition. Much as the First World War had done a generation earlier, the Second World War had had a devastating impact on each of Europe's major powers. In doing so, it threatened an international political order constructed around European imperial power. In Great Britain and France in particular, Europe's two most dominant imperial powers, the governments of both states struggled in the war's aftermath to make sense of the changing political world. Burdened with the obligation of paying off their war debts and the need to rebuild, they each scrambled to find ways to balance pressures at home with the maintenance of their massive empires abroad. Furthermore, the war's end also ushered in the seemingly unchecked rise of the American and Soviet superpowers and of the bipolar world they would spend the greater part of the next half century constructing. Meanwhile, in Africa and Asia, the postwar story has long been one of a rising set of demands for colonial reform and agitation, shifting to a period of nationalist

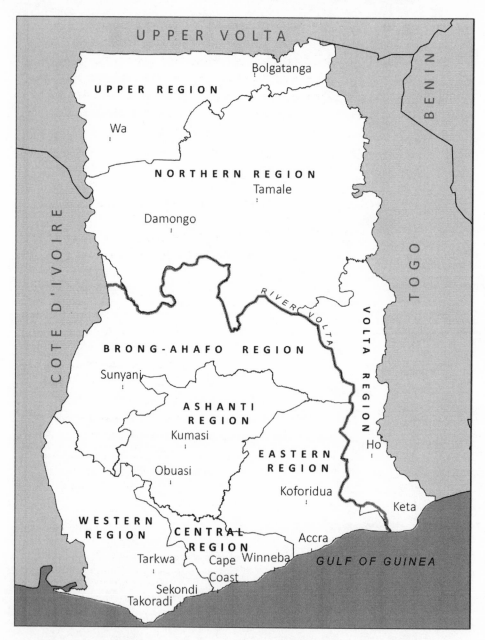

Ghana, ca. 1960. Produced by the Smith College Spatial Analysis Lab.

mobilization, followed by independence and, in many cases, postcolonial decline. The narrative that arose in these world regions was therefore one centered on not only the foundation of the twentieth-century postcolonial nation-state, but, just as importantly, its political, economic, and civic demise.

In the decade following Ghana's independence and beyond, many sought to position the Ghanaian story within this prototypical narrative structure. However, through much of the 1950s and even into the 1960s, few inside or outside the country took such a narrow view of the country's independence and the experiences of self-rule. Both locally and internationally, Ghanaian independence came to represent more than the simple addition of another nation-state to a rapidly growing postwar international community. Rather, to many, Ghana was to be the harbinger of the next phase in Africa's political, social, and historical development. For them, the Ghanaian path to self-rule and postcolonial development was often envisioned as *the* African path. Describing this sentiment in a circa 1957 essay, for instance, the American journalist and novelist Richard Wright portrayed the newly independent Ghana as "a kind of pilot project of the new Africa."[4] Ghana's status as the first postcolonial state in sub-Saharan Africa was of particular importance in cultivating such an image. In breaking the country's bond to Great Britain, Ghana was perceived as leading the way for the rest of the continent. In doing so, many viewed the new country as unleashing a wave of transformation in Africa that would guide the rest of the continent not only to independence, but, just as importantly, to a seat at the table in the emerging postcolonial international community. This transformation, however, was not simply to be political, but rather was to effect a wholesale political, social, cultural, and economic revolution in Africa. Moreover, it was also to be as much a personal project as it was to be a national or continental one, for at its core was a consciousness-raising enterprise guiding Ghanaians and Africans individually and as a whole toward a shared nation- and continent-building project.

Throughout the 1950s and 1960s, the figure of Kwame Nkrumah as an individual and as a symbol stood at the center of these imaginings in both Ghana and Africa at large. Drawing on his organizing experience in the United States and Great Britain, Nkrumah—starting even before he came to power in 1951—had long celebrated both what he and others viewed as the shared struggle of African liberation and the Gold Coast's/Ghana's perceived leadership role in that struggle. In 1957, independence would offer Nkrumah and the Convention People's Party (CPP) government he led new opportunities for exploring this shared struggle, providing them with the political and institutional space from which to advance their own continentally collaborative model for African anticolonial activism. By early 1958, the exploration of this space had come to include the convening of the first of a series of pan-African and intra-African conferences in the Ghanaian capital of Accra. These conferences both revived and redefined the pan-African tradition of the early twentieth century by providing a space in which African politicians, activists, and others could adapt this early pan-African tradition to African postcolonial realities. Likewise, as 1958 came to a close, Ghana would again take the lead in the testing of African postcolonial possibilities as it came to the aid of Sékou Touré's fledgling republic in weeks-old independent Guinea. Albeit fraught with its own set of contradictions and administrative inconsistencies, the resultant Ghana-Guinea Union represented independent Africa's first postcolonial, supraterritorial confederation, a confederation whereby each member state was to cede portions of its sovereignty to the greater union. By the end of 1960, the union would also include Modibo Keita's Mali, while Nkrumah claimed that he had also signed a similar agreement with Patrice Lumumba prior to the Congolese leader's assassination.[5]

In Ghana itself, Nkrumah and the CPP positioned decolonization and the mechanisms of postcolonial rule at the center of both a new type of disciplined, socialist, modern, and cosmopolitan citizenry and the "Nkrumahist" ideology constructed to support it. In doing so, they simultaneously, and often contradictorily, looked back to and distanced themselves from a long tradition of anticolonial agitation with deep roots in the Gold Coast and elsewhere, as they turned to a range of party- and state-sponsored institutions in the cultivation of this Nkrumahist ideal. For many Ghanaians living in the heady days of the 1950s and 1960s, this experiment in postcolonial reinvention became a defining part of their political and social lives. Not only were they asked to join—or, in some cases, charged into—the civic initiatives of the Nkrumahist government; but, more importantly, their experiences—as interpreted by the CPP governmental apparatus— became the vehicles through which the CPP and its allies inside and outside Ghana read the successes and shortcomings of the Nkrumah-led postcolonial project on the Ghanaian and continental stage. If, for the CPP and its allies, Ghana was to be Africa's "city upon a hill" replete with modern cities, rapid industrialization, and a politically and ideologically disciplined citizenry, this book argues that Nkrumahist ideology and the massive changes that followed from it emerged as terrains of negotiation in themselves for those living through this transition. Moreover, the book also argues that these terrains of negotiation were fundamentally tied to the intersections of both the citizenry's aspirations, ambitions, and frustrations with the promises of life in a new world partly forged by an independent Africa and the often tragic realities of a world the CPP itself understood as still intimately rooted in the legacies of capitalist imperialism. The result was a state-citizenry relationship, premised on hope and ambition, that was often constrained by and filtered through the realities and politics of the postcolonial state itself. It was also a relationship that, over the course of the 1950s and 1960s, became increasingly uneven.

This book is about postcolonial visions and the popular reactions to them. The book thus counters a literature on African decolonization overrun by the pessimistic hindsight of the last four to five decades of African self-rule. The pessimism of this literature is not unique to the Ghanaian case, but instead has framed much of the way that both scholars and the public have engaged with the idea of an independent Africa. In contrast, *Living with Nkrumahism* celebrates the ambiguity and contradictions surrounding the continent's transition to self-rule, as it centers the tenuousness of the decolonization process and Africa's uncertain place in the postcolonial Cold War world in a broader reflection upon, to borrow from Frederick Cooper, the "possibility and constraint" that characterized the first decade of African self-rule.[6]

In this respect, "Nkrumahism" plays multiple roles in the text. Foremost, it stands as a philosophy of decolonization developed out of a worldview blending ideologies of African socialism, global anti-imperialism, and the promises of African unity—a version of pan-Africanism. However, within this book, Nkrumahism also acts as a historically contingent term, one rooted in a shifting array of contested, experimental, and often contradictory ideas, practices, and policies put forward by Nkrumah and the CPP—a term that therefore belies a consistent and, at times, even clear definition. Historically, it is a term that, throughout the decade and a half of CPP rule, was in constant development and continuous negotiation among individuals and groups, including Nkrumah, local and national party officials, the intellectuals and journalists operating the state-run press, the diverse community of expatriate activists who made Ghana home during the 1950s and 1960s, and even segments of the populace at large, albeit most often filtered through the instruments and discourse of the state.

More than a term, "Nkrumahism" provided a language with which Ghanaians and others could talk through and proactively and reactively address the changing role of Ghana and Africa in the construction of the postcolonial international community. As such, threats of neocolonial subversion, Cold War intervention, alternative nationalisms, and internal dissension were much more than challenges to a particular set of political ambitions in midcentury Ghana within the CPP imagination. They imperiled a worldview. They also reflected the intrinsic diversity of the political, social, cultural, and economic realities in which that worldview operated. *Living with Nkrumahism* thus offers a historical deconstruction of this particularly vibrant moment in Ghana's recent past. However, it does so by framing its analysis of Nkrumahism not simply as an intellectual history of Nkrumah's and the CPP's thought. Much more importantly, the book argues that Nkrumahism served as the epistemological backdrop for many of the contestations surrounding Ghanaian political and social life in the Nkrumah era. To this end, I take seriously the aims of Nkrumah and the CPP, on their own terms, as well as the interpretations of those aims on the popular level. As a result, in a political sphere in which Nkrumah and the CPP ultimately saw themselves as creating a new world, one in which Africa and the rest of the formerly colonized peoples of the world would have an equal seat at the table in the emerging postwar community of nations, key aspects of everyday Ghanaian life—work, family, community—became subsumed in the transformative and disciplining project of creating this postcolonial world.

NKRUMAH AND THE GOLD COAST

The political and academic fascination with Nkrumah, the Gold Coast, and the CPP began almost as early as Nkrumah's 1947 return to the colony. Descending upon the colony in the early 1950s, prominent activists and intellectuals, including George Padmore and Richard Wright, joined early Africanist scholars like Thomas Hodgkin, David Apter, and Dennis Austin in the Gold Coast's towns and cities as they sought to make sense of the uniquely successful message and politics of the CPP.[7] Hodgkin, for his part, presented the CPP as a party of firsts, foremost emphasizing the party's unprecedented ability to mobilize at a national level. As early as 1951 he predicted that the CPP's success would force both Africans and Europeans to turn their attention to what just half a decade earlier colonial officials had considered to be Britain's "model colony."[8] By the middle of the decade, Hodgkin would incorporate what he observed in the Gold Coast into his broader study of the sociology of postwar African nationalism.[9] Likewise, political scientist and modernization theorist David Apter held the CPP and the Gold Coast up as models of African modernization.

In one of the first monograph-length academic studies of the postwar Gold Coast political order, Apter constructed a narrative around the Gold Coast that positioned the decolonizing colony as well along the path toward a form of parliamentary democratic governance. Key for Apter was a reading of the CPP's electoral and legislative successes that, in his mind, exemplified the Gold Coast's gradual move away from what he presented as a complex array of ethnic allegiances and institutions, toward the national.[10] The result was the emergence of a political and intellectual milieu, where an often externally driven set of narratives were infused within the particularities of the CPP and the Gold Coast political scene. Moreover, this milieu was one that Nkrumah and the CPP rarely felt shy about further cultivating themselves.

Nkrumah's own story helped advance much of the early fascination with midcentury Gold Coast politics. Born in the far western Gold Coast village of Nkroful, Nkrumah was among the first to attend Accra's famed Achimota Secondary School upon its opening in the late 1920s, from which he graduated in 1930. Later, he would travel to the United States to study at the historically black Lincoln University and the University of Pennsylvania before leaving for the United Kingdom in 1945. Working in the anticolonial and pan-African circles associated with George Padmore during his time in the United Kingdom, Nkrumah would play an integral role in the organization of the fifth Pan-African Congress, held in Manchester in 1945. Following the congress, he would align himself with the radicalism of the West African National Secretariat (WANS), of which he would become the organization's secretary. Through the WANS, Nkrumah joined an array of West African activists with direct ties to the Gold Coast—most notably including I. T. A. Wallace-Johnson and Kojo Botsio, who would become the future CPP's first general secretary—in reiterating the Congress's call for an immediate end to colonial rule in Africa, while also putting forward their vision of a united, socialist West Africa. However, as J. Ayodele Langley points out, for Nkrumah specifically and for those aligned with him in the WANS, the foremost mission of the Secretariat rested with the organization of the masses. All else was to follow.[11]

Nkrumah's ability to swiftly adapt his message and strategies to the political and economic realities of the Gold Coast following his return to the colony only further burnished his radical reputation in the late 1940s. Politically and economically, the immediate postwar years were a time of rapid transition and increasing uncertainty for the Gold Coast, both triggering and fed by widespread reforms in the colony. These reforms included the extension of male suffrage in municipal elections, an increased governmental commitment to the Africanization of the civil service, and the further centralization of colonial governance with the full integration of Asante into the colony's legislative apparatus.[12] Meanwhile, popular support for the war effort had overshadowed a volatile economy that would come to a head in the last half of the decade. Between 1939 and 1947, for instance, the urban cost of living had more than doubled, with prices for locally produced items rising to nearly twice their prewar levels. The inflationary pressures were even more extreme for many imported goods, which saw price increases in the neighborhood of five to eight times their prewar levels during the same period. As the 1948 Watson Commission reported, the bulk of these price increases had occurred in 1946 and 1947 alone, further adding to the immediacy of the economic pressures felt by the Gold Coast populace.[13]

In Accra, the economic pressures brought by rapid inflation raised the ire of the city's residents throughout late 1947, culminating in a month-long boycott of European and Levantine firms in January and February 1948. Organized by Nii Kwabena Bonne II, an Accra chief and businessman, the boycott emerged independent of the nationalist activists who would later try to coopt it, as Nii Bonne and his allies mobilized against what they considered the predatory pricing practices of the colony's foreign firms.[14] As Nii Bonne reportedly explained to his audiences during the boycott, white sellers had made themselves adept at manipulating the market so as to generate profits often well in excess of what it cost to produce the goods they sold.[15] Nii Bonne's message quickly gained the support of many chiefs, who, to the frustration of colonial officialdom, constructed "a system of fines" for punishing those who broke the boycott.[16] By late February 1948, just as many of the Gold Coast's African sellers were also beginning to feel the effects of the boycott with shortages in their own shops, Nii Bonne and his allies declared victory. In doing so, they touted their success in securing (temporary) concessions from many of the colony's foreign firms in their pricing and profit structures.[17]

As the boycott ended in late February, the colony's military veterans—many of whom had been left unemployed with the Second World War's conclusion—set out to march on the seat of the colonial government at Christiansborg Castle. As with the boycotters, it is difficult to argue that most ex-servicemen were driven by nationalist political ideals in their protests, as they too emphasized economic issues—back pay, the status of their pensions, postwar inflation, and a lack of employment opportunities—in their protests and petitions as opposed to nationalist concerns.[18] The march on Christiansborg was thus foremost to be an assertion of their rights to that which was owed to them as veterans of the war effort. As the marchers proceeded to Christiansborg, the colonial police stopped the ex-servicemen and their supporters and ordered them to disperse following the protesters' deviation from the government-approved route. After a baton charge and the release of tear gas on the crowd, the police opened fire on the unarmed crowd, killing two. Riots quickly broke out in Accra and then spread throughout the colony, with deaths and injuries reported in Kumasi, Koforidua, and elsewhere.[19] Meanwhile, in Accra, many of the major European firms that had been the focus of the boycott became the primary targets of the rioters, as emotions brought on by the police killings and boycott erupted throughout the city's commercial district.[20]

For Nkrumah in particular, the volatile nature of the Gold Coast's postwar political and economic realities provided an opening upon his return to the colony. Invited back to serve as general secretary of the newly created United Gold Coast Convention (UGCC), Nkrumah attempted to bring the lessons of Manchester to the Gold Coast. Specifically, in his writings and organizing he presented the colony and its struggles as part of a larger colonized world decimated by European imperial rule and global capitalism.[21] As he had pursued with the WANS, the goal Nkrumah envisioned for the Gold Coast was the organization of the masses—the colony's youth, workers, peasants, market women, and others. Only through such mobilization, the future Ghanaian president would argue throughout the late 1940s and well into the 1950s, could Gold Coasters and Africans more broadly escape the exploitative and extractive trap of capitalist imperialism. Moreover, as his compatriots in Manchester did just a few years earlier, Nkrumah insisted that at the heart of this path to liberation had to be immediate self-government.[22]

Over the course of the rest of 1948 and the first half of 1949, a UGCC-affiliated Nkrumah drew support from wide-ranging groups of Gold Coasters with his message of self-government. In doing so, he and the group of young men, market women, school leavers, returnees from abroad, and others who joined his organizing efforts attracted the ire of both the colonial administration and the UGCC's largely middle-class leadership as they established their own schools, "party" offices, newspapers, and, ultimately, a radical wing—the Committee on Youth Organization (CYO)—under the UGCC umbrella. By July 1948, historian Richard Rathbone argues, Nkrumah and his allies had become so emboldened by their successes that the Nkrumahist wing of the UGCC increasingly operated as its own "party within a party."[23] The formal break between Nkrumah and the UGCC would occur nearly a year later in the coastal town of Saltpond. There, before a purported crowd of sixty thousand, Nkrumah announced the inauguration of the Convention People's Party under the uncompromising banner of "Self-Government Now."[24] By 1951, the CPP would win its first major electoral victory, nearly sweeping the colony's first popularly contested election and taking control of its Legislative Assembly. In doing so, the CPP formed the Gold Coast's first African-led government, with Nkrumah taking the mantle of "leader of government business." By 1952, he would gain the title of prime minister, while he and the CPP maintained wide-reaching powers over the colony's internal affairs in a diarchic CPP-British power-sharing agreement at a time in which the details of the colony's transition to self-rule were being worked out.

As will be seen, the realities Nkrumah and the CPP confronted in the Gold Coast were much more complicated than both the future president's worldview and even the CPP's organizing successes indicated. Throughout the decade and a half of CPP governance, competing loyalties of class, ethnicity, generation, and occupation simmered underneath the popular responses to the anticolonial imaginings articulated by Nkrumah and the party he led. Moreover, even as wide-ranging groups of Gold Coasters gravitated toward the CPP's message of self-government, tensions quickly arose within the colony surrounding not only the mechanisms by which to formally achieve and then administer the CPP's proclaimed goal of self-government, but also the long-term meaning of self-government itself. For many of those scholars and activists writing about the Gold Coast experiment in the 1950s, it was this tug-of-war—often cast as a struggle between the "modern" and the "traditional," in the case of modernization-minded figures like Apter and Wright, or as one of revolutionary versus reactionary, as portrayed by individuals like Padmore—that drew them to the Gold Coast. To them, the Gold Coast and the successes and pitfalls of the CPP provided the means for understanding the prospects for Africa's decolonization as a whole. Even more importantly, it would give others a narrative through which to theorize the decolonization process itself.

DECOLONIZATION, MODERNITY, AND POSTCOLONIAL IMAGININGS

Among scholars and activists at both the local and global levels, decolonization was envisioned as a moment of opportunity and redefinition. The question that arose in the mid-twentieth century was that of what decolonization and, by extension, independence was to look like both locally and globally beyond the actual granting of self-rule. Among those who would begin to theorize the meaning of decolonization in the 1950s, decolonization and independence had to be understood not as singular events, but rather as a set of processes aimed at renegotiating the colonized's place in the world. For some, it even included a reorientation of the colonized individual him- or herself. It was in this vein that Frantz Fanon argued in 1961 that "decolonization is the veritable creation of new men."[25] The transformation implicit in decolonization, at least according to Fanon, was as much ontological as political. It was to be a restorative process that, through the actions and mobilization of the colonized, erased the realities and legacies of the colonial situation and the epistemic and systematic violence, exploitation, and racism embedded within them. The result was envisioned to be the birth of a new civilization freed from the legacies of colonial rule and capitalist extraction; it was also to be a civilization bound to the will of decolonization's new social order.[26]

Historians of decolonization have tended to shy away from the Manichean historical and theoretical models put forward by figures like Fanon.[27] However, throughout the 1950s and into the 1960s, Fanon was not alone in propagating such a vision of decolonization. Neither was Nkrumah, who, not entirely dissimilar from Fanon, advocated for a theory of decolonization rooted in a dialectic of destruction and rebirth.[28] Such attempts to theorize the process of decolonization in turn reoriented discussions around African anticolonialism away from perspectives that characterized independence as the imagined end result of decolonization. What was put forward instead by the likes of Nkrumah, Fanon, Amilcar Cabral, and others was a set of anticolonial imaginings that did not simply seek to replace a generically conceived colonial infrastructure with an African alternative. Much more significantly, they each sought to emphasize the emergent—incomplete, yet transforming—nature of the liberated, decolonized individual and society. For those with a state-centered orientation like Nkrumah, mass institutions like the CPP thus carried a special responsibility that extended beyond that of the organization of the populace. For, just as fundamentally, they also had the additional duty of creating the political, social, economic, and cultural conditions necessary for bringing about the process of collective growth, emancipation, and renaissance at the envisioned root of the decolonizing process. At least in Ghana, such a framework for thinking about decolonization would come to have wide-reaching effects on the lived experiences of many of the country's peoples over the course of the first decade of self-rule.

The extended timeframe between the CPP's 1951 electoral victory and Ghana's 1957 independence in many ways ensured the development of a procedural notion of decolonization within the Gold Coast/Ghana and particularly in the CPP. As the CPP entered into official negotiations with the British about the transfer of power to an independent Ghana in the early 1950s, the Nkrumah-led party took to its press and public meetings in its attempts to reframe its seemingly straightforward ultimatum of "self-government now" as more than a political demand. Instead, self-government became a first step in an envisioned civic project that, at its essence, required a new type of citizen. Through such a formulation, the CPP created for itself an obligation to bring about the conditions not only for the establishment of the independent country, but, more importantly, for that country's ability to grow and prosper in a highly competitive and often uncertain international environment. At one level, this required a commitment to such infrastructural projects as the rise of new planned cities, hydroelectric power, industrialized manufacturing, advanced communication and transportation systems, social welfare projects, and the wide-ranging extension of government-sponsored social services, most notably in education and healthcare. Each of these, the CPP insisted, was essential to the operation of a modern, independent country. Just as importantly, though, the party would argue, the citizenry itself had to be reoriented, if not modernized, so as to meet the assumed realities of the postwar world. Here, the labor movement, the nature of work itself, family and gender relations, youth culture, ethnicities, and relationships between urban and rural life, among others, all came under the purview of the CPP's long view of decolonization. At the same time, these political and social phenomena also tended to reflect longstanding traditions of political and economic contestation within the Gold Coast. As a result, the CPP found it necessary to consistently return to and redraft as its own everything from the colony's vibrant history of anticolonial and nationalist agitation to the colonial government's own developmentalist ideology and traditions, to the eclectic compilation of ideas, networks, and movements Nkrumah himself had sought to connect to during his decade-plus abroad.

The CPP's civically focused decolonization project only intensified as the party and government consolidated their power and sought to stem off an array of opposition movements over the course of the 1950s.

Independence forced a slight shift in the focus of the CPP's decolonization project and in its vision of decolonization, as it highlighted an independent Ghana's vulnerability on the international stage. Whereas prior to 1957 the concern was how best to bring together the colony's diverse peoples and constituencies in the shared political and social project of achieving self-government, the postindependence project was one of acceleration and adaptation to what were increasingly perceived as the dangers—internal and external—of the postcolonial condition. Here, fears of political disorder and subterfuge, neocolonial intervention in the activities of the state, and extranational allegiances threatened to cast a pall over the hopes and ambitions embodied in the sense of new beginnings—nationally and continentally—ushered in with Ghana's independence. Nkrumah and the CPP in turn presented it as their obligation to protect Ghana and, by extension, Africa from these challenges. For them, the issue was about more than just Ghana's or Africa's political independence. The real concern was a potential backslide into what they perceived to be a colonial mentality that would have ripple effects on deeper issues of African social, economic, and cultural independence.

Key to this framing of both Ghana's and Africa's decolonization was an emphasis on the emergent or burgeoning nature of Ghana as a country and Africa as a continent. A necessary optimism was embedded in this idea of emergence. Furthermore, for many inside and outside of Africa, this view of an emergent continent in the 1950s and 1960s was not a question; as James Ferguson has suggested, it was an expectation.[29] What needed sorting out, then, as Jean Allman later noted in her analysis of Ghanaian antinuclear activism, were the details. As Allman presents the expectations of the period, at the time, they did not represent the "pipe dream" they seem to do today or even did by the end of the 1960s. Rather, in the late 1950s and early 1960s, they appeared to many as simply "a plan just shy of a blueprint."[30] As Allman's analysis illustrates, such a framework for thinking about the ambitions of the decolonization moment provides a lens through which to map the histories of Ghanaian pan-African and anti-imperial politics onto the larger landscape of transnational anticolonial and anti-imperial histories that dot the broader global historiographical terrain—many of which only pay lip service to African experiences and perspectives. Even more importantly, such a method for thinking through Africa's decolonization opens the space through which we can begin to historicize alternative African postcolonial futures. As Allman, Meredith Terretta, Kevin Gaines, Klaas van Walraven, and others have shown, it was this sense of opportunity and innovation that, throughout the 1950s and into much of the early 1960s, drew activists, freedom fighters, journalists, and the curious, among others, to the country.[31] Figures including Fanon, who had served as the Algerian Front de Libération Nationale's ambassador to Ghana until his cancer diagnosis in 1961, George Padmore, Richard Wright, Robert Mugabe, W. E. B. Du Bois, Shirley Graham Du Bois, Patrice Lumumba, Che Guevara, Malcolm X, Félix Moumié, and many others, all, at various times, converged upon the country during the period.[32] Furthermore, many of them—none more important ideologically than Padmore—played a key role in helping to shape the policies and ideological agenda of the CPP both continentally and within Ghana itself.

As Padmore would argue in his published works on the Gold Coast and in his communications with Nkrumah and others in the CPP, Ghana's ultimate success depended upon its ability to construct a modern society independent of European imperial and capitalist subversion. For Padmore in the 1950s, this ultimately entailed a model of pan-Africanism that blended "black nationalism plus socialism."[33] Over the course of the 1950s, aspects of this message seeped into the CPP's own local imaginings as it was framed and reframed by Nkrumah himself, contested in the CPP-led government's various development projects, and reflected in the expectations and ambitions of those Ghanaians responding to the promises of decolonization's new society. Here, the CPP rooted its political, social, and economic programs in a midcentury modernism that held up the industrialized West—absent its capitalist extravagances—as the developmental model toward which a decolonizing Africa should strive. In at least one sense, Nkrumahism was very much a form of anticolonial modernism. It was also not alone in promoting such an ideal, with similar ideological projects playing out in Egypt, India, and elsewhere.[34] At the root of such thinking, Donald Donham has remarked in reference to revolutionary Ethiopia, was a teleology that placed countries, continents, and peoples on an imagined ladder of modernity.[35] Ferguson goes even further in his reflections on midcentury modernism, as he argues that such teleological thinking not only infected governments and politicians, but also the social scientists and technocrats brought in to study and interpret the successes and failures of African postcolonial modernization.[36] Likewise, political scientist Leander Schneider, writing on Tanzania, emphasizes the importance of the machinations of government, at least in its imagined state, in guiding a particular country up this ladder.[37]

In the Ghanaian case, Schneider's emphasis on the centrality of government in the modernizing process is particularly instructive. For Schneider, working with the Foucauldian notion of governmentality, it was through an intricate analysis of the practices of government—the actions, decisions, and logics—that scholars could come to understand not just the objectives of the development enterprise, but also how the practices themselves produced and reproduced the authority of the government.[38] The specificities of the Tanzanian experience with villagization frame Schneider's analysis. In important ways, though, the concerns driving the Tanzanian government's and specifically Julius Nyerere's advocacy of villagization were similar to those guiding Nkrumah and the CPP in Ghana. For both Nkrumah and Nyerere, the exploitative and extractive dimensions of colonialism were undeniable. Moreover, they insisted that the effects of colonial exploitation had major political, social, and cultural ramifications on African life. Self-government thus unleashed for both leaders and their governments a responsibility for, in Schneider's words, creating "a free, egalitarian, and more prosperous society" in colonialism's wake.[39] Whereas Nyerere focused on an updated, rural communalism in Tanzania, Nkrumah and the CPP emphasized the urban, industrial, and mechanized in Ghana's postcolonial development. However, as in Tanzania, Nkrumah and the CPP viewed it as the obligation of the government and party in Ghana to create the conditions necessary for this developmental and liberation model to come into being. In doing so, though, they did not simply seek to reinforce the power and authority of the emergent state. Rather, at the same time, they also sought to create an environment where all other alternatives could be cast as unmodern, un-African, or neocolonial.

Yet, at least in the Ghanaian case, it is too simplistic to merely frame the Nkrumah-era decolonization and postcolonial projects, if not worldviews, as another example of what James Scott has referred to as the high-modernist view of "seeing like a state."[40] In contrast to Scott's model, the Nkrumah-era programs and worldviews were historically contingent and site-specific. In other words, they necessarily reflected the changing realities of a world in transition and the wide-ranging aspirations and anxieties of an independent Africa's place in that world. The postcolonial imaginings and projects coming out of Ghana during this time—in all their inconsistencies, incongruities, and, at times, seeming pie-in-the-sky nature—cannot be taken out of this context. Fears of neocolonialism were real. Anxieties over the implications of the country's and continent's continued dependency on foreign markets were also real. Similarly, concerns over the solidification of African backwardness in relation to the Global North weighed on those inside and outside the CPP government committed to envisioning Ghana's and Africa's postcolonial future. Moreover, deep-seated questions existed as to what forms of governance were wanted and needed in order to meet the realities of the postcolonial world. For Western scholars like Apter in the mid-1950s, projecting negotiated constitutional formalities onto the society writ large, the apparent answer was an African-born parliamentary democracy.[41] Three decades later, Michael Crowder would ponder the implications of assuming that what Africans strove for with independence were such liberal democratic institutions.[42] A historicized emphasis on Nkrumahism ultimately allows for reflection on what the alternatives may have looked like at the time and how they may have changed and been contested over the course of the 1950s and 1960s, linking both local and international idioms of nation, nationalism, modernity, development, decolonization, and liberation, among others, into a vibrant analytical framework.

VISIONS OF NKRUMAHISM

The challenge of writing such histories of Nkrumahism rests in the nature of the CPP's decolonization project itself. Few things did more to cloud the political, social, and cultural dynamism of Nkrumah-era Ghana than the actions and rhetoric of the Nkrumahist state. Like the nation the CPP viewed itself as representing, the state as the governmental embodiment of the nation was also envisioned as an entity under constant construction. In the 1950s, as the CPP and the British entered into a period of shared governance, the key question facing the CPP was how best to create the institutions, policies, and procedures necessary for a burgeoning Ghana to ensure a smooth transition to self-rule. As alluded to earlier, in their negotiations with the British, Nkrumah and his new collection of ministers and advisors had little choice but to cede to the logistical and bureaucratic constraints put on them by the British and the realities of administering a modern government. Most importantly, these included an acceptance of the liberal democratic institutions celebrated by Apter, along with a slowed Africanization of the Gold Coast/Ghanaian civil service and the maintenance of a postcolonial British governor-general in the newly independent country. Outside the formal mechanisms of government, the concern over how best to prepare for self-rule moved to the qualities of the citizenry itself. Here, the CPP promoted not only a continued "mobilizing of the masses," to borrow Elizabeth Schmidt's phrasing, but, more importantly, the coalescence of the citizenry around a very specific CPP-defined idea of the Ghanaian nation.[43] In this regard, the party press, exemplified by the Nkrumah-founded *Ghana Evening News* (previously the *Accra Evening News* and later the *Evening News*), sought to cultivate a sense of nationhood that civically centered on the party itself. Party rallies and public awareness campaigns further promoted such a party-centered idea of the Ghanaian nation, while, along with the press, mapping for the nation the envisioned centralization of political power in the Accra-based, CPP-run government.

Independence and, even more so, the 1960 inauguration of the republican constitution only intensified the process of CPP centralization. Even more importantly, the freedoms manifested in independence provided the CPP with the room necessary to test and invest in new forms of institutions designed to cultivate the type of citizenry it believed was required for meeting the needs of the postcolonial world. Here, ideals of discipline, order, political and civic awareness, and collective national and continental development combined with a socialist and pan-African ethos rooted in a transnational anti-imperialism. As in the 1950s, the party press—the *Evening News*, the *Ghanaian Times*, the *Ghanaian*, the *Spark*, and other publications—took the lead in articulating and theorizing this envisioned citizenry. Moreover, as the CPP consolidated its influence over the press in the early 1960s—taking over or shuttering most newspapers that deviated from the party line—the party- and state-run press largely became the only publications in which interpretations of the postcolonial citizenry and nation could be publicly debated.[44] Journalists, authors, editors, letter writers, politicians, petitioners, and others had little choice but to write within the epistemological constraints imposed on them by what was increasingly emerging, from within the party itself, as an attempt to create a sense of orthodoxy around the eclectic set of ideas broadly comprising "Nkrumahism" in the postcolonial state.

Meanwhile, on the ground, party and governmental institutions such as the Ghana Young Pioneers, the Ghana Builders Brigade (later renamed as the Ghana Workers Brigade), the Trades Union Congress, the National Council of Ghana Women (NCGW), the Young Farmers' League, and others set out to embed within the citizenry an emergent Nkrumahist way of life. Both the party and state were central to this envisioned way of life and to how interpretations of it were disseminated throughout the populace. Together, these institutions were thus to provide the discipline, regimentation, and foresight needed to embark upon not only the complicated infrastructural task of nation-building, but, more foundationally, the much deeper, ontological burden of creating new, de-colonized citizens. As a result, those involved in institutions such as the Ghana Young Pioneers and the Builders Brigade engaged in a range of activities including drill instruction, athletic competitions and displays, marching in public parades and rallies, self-help projects, and citizenship classes and lectures. From the late 1950s on, nearly all of these activities — either overtly or covertly — aimed to position the individual, through his or her performance of Nkrumahism's pan-African and socialist anti-imperial ideal, as the embodiment of the new Ghana and Africa. Moreover, to-gether with the time investments required of their members and the re-lationships forged through participation, the practices and programs put forward by the Young Pioneers, Builders Brigade, and similar organiza-tions pressured, if not challenged, longstanding notions of belonging in midcentury Ghana — including family, chieftaincy, community, gender, and generation — as the CPP sought to reorient the populace's worldview toward the mission of the state.

Through the enactments of the Nkrumahist way of life exhibited in the formal and informal rituals of the CPP's various wings and institu-tions, the Nkrumahist state therefore emerged as much as a performative enterprise as a conventional instrument of governance. Moreover, the Nkrumahist state was not alone in such a construction, for the rituals and expectations of what postcolonial life should be in Ghana shared many similarities with several other midcentury socialist and postcolonial states, including those of the Guinean state as studied by Mike McGovern and Jay Straker. Examining the Guinean Demystification Program, McGov-ern describes a political and cultural initiative specifically and necessarily designed to reach into the most intimate aspects of Guinean *forestières'* lives, including family relations, spirituality, and ethnic belonging.[45] At least in terms of intention and philosophy, the program would not have looked unfamiliar in Ghana, as Guineans — willingly and semi-willingly — incorporated aspects of Guinean revolutionary ideology into their lives in both the public and private performance of what McGovern describes as a state-sponsored cosmopolitanism. Here, an uncomfortable merging of a pan-African gesture toward Africa's precolonial past with scientific social-ism's anticapitalist modernism culminated in an iconoclastic program that at once positioned the country's *forestières* as "negative examples, stereo-types of savagery" and emergent "modernist national citizens."[46] Straker, also writing on the Guinean *forestières*, similarly relates that it is impossible to understand "the complexities of life histories, political sentiments, and cultural imaginings" in postcolonial Guinea without centering "the workings of state power in the cultural realm."[47]

In Ghana, for the thousands formally integrated into the party apparatus and the many more who had little choice but to live alongside it, party activities and pressures became a key component of their daily lives and relationships. As we will see in the third chapter in the case of the Ghana Young Pioneers, the national organization for school-age children, its time commitments, teaching, and leadership structure severely strained relationships within families and communities. As a result, in certain instances, parents, elders, and other community members came under the suspicion of some of the Young Pioneers in their lives, while many Young Pioneers themselves were similarly held in suspicion by the adults around them. At the same time, the movement also—both in reality and perception—held the potential for opening new pathways to political and social mobility for both its members and possibly their families. The Builders Brigade, with its built-in public employment program, offered even greater potential for mobility for its membership. However, in many cases, it also catalyzed increasingly caustic relationships with the communities that lived alongside the Brigade's many camps. In such communities, the granting of local lands for Brigade use, the supposed unruliness of brigaders, and the Brigade's (real and perceived) influence in local and national politics roused significant tensions. Yet, as we will also see, for many of the brigaders and their family members with whom I spoke, their experiences in the Brigade were defining moments in their lives, opening up new avenues for their transition into a socially recognized adulthood.

Similar stories played out in other CPP organizations as well. In the Trades Union Congress (TUC), for instance, workers encountered an institution that, over the course of the 1950s and 1960s, would transform its mission from worker advocacy to the state organization of labor. Guiding the TUC and the CPP's labor politics more broadly was a calcifying socialist ideology of work that sought to decenter the individual's personal ambitions in favor of the assumed shared goals of the nation. As a result, ideologically, productivity reigned supreme. This not only alienated many workers from an institution ostensibly established to serve their interests, but also distanced them from the fruits of their labor as they were increasingly asked to do more for less. Likewise, in the Bureau of African Affairs (BAA)—the most important of the CPP government's pan-African institutions—the party's expanding ideology of work, with its celebration of productivity and sacrifice, was embedded in the daily work lives of the Bureau's employees. Among those most affected were the many young female employees who made up the Bureau's typing, bookbinding, tele-phony, and clerical staff. The result was the emergence of an often turbu-lent workspace in which the party's modernist celebrations of women in the workplace collided with the gendered and generational prejudices of the government officials and high-ranking administrators put in place to run the Bureau's operations at home and abroad.

For scholars, the question of how Ghanaians themselves engaged with and understood the mushrooming Nkrumahist state and Nkrumahism more broadly has proved difficult to answer. Scholars in the late 1960s and 1970s in particular—representing the last significant wave of schol-arship devoted to the CPP—have largely assumed that most Ghana-ians simply ignored the party's rhetoric and endured its policies.[48] The bottom-up ethos of the social-historical tradition—which has fruitfully guided African historical and social scientific scholarship for at least two generations—has likely contributed to such conclusions regarding the state-citizenry relationship. Additionally, the very real disappointments of decolonization—culminating, in Ghana, with the economic hardships of the 1960s and the CPP's establishment of a quasi-police state—further justified a way of viewing the African postcolonial experience as an experi-ence mired in what Mahmood Mamdani has described as "decentralized despotism."[49] Through such a perspective, however, the state and its dis-course often emerge as alien forces acting upon the people, thus position-ing the populace as subjects of the new state. The result in such readings of the African postcolonial state, to invoke Jean-François Bayart's powerful idiom of the "politics of the belly," is a vision of the state that largely exists for the sole purpose of feeding itself.[50]

Historian Frederick Cooper has pointed to the dehistoricized, if not ahistorical, nature of many of these arguments. In the case of Mamdani specifically, Cooper has accused the political scientist of "leapfrogging" Africa's history of decolonization and early postcolonial encounters with self-rule in an attempt to show an artificial continuity from the violence and exploitation of the colonial past to the corruption and iniquities of the postcolonial present.[51] However, even Cooper's reflections on decolo-nization—with their tendency to deemphasize the importance of various forms of African nationalism in people's lives—often overshadow a signifi-cant reality: the fact that, at least in the case of Ghana, Ghanaians who lived through Nkrumah have a lot to say about both African nationalism and living with Nkrumahism. Few may have become the ardent anticolonial socialists—literate in the theoretical and practical intricacies of Marxist anti-imperialism—that Nkrumah and many of the CPP's most virulent ideologues imagined. Regardless, many welcomed and even sought the opportunity to discuss their experiences with the CPP and its ideology, reflecting on its hopes, disappointments, and, for some, oddities. Marxism, communism, and, as one man put it, the "Eastern forms of psychology" that in his opinion afflicted the CPP were prominent subjects of debate among those I interviewed.[52] So, too, were Nkrumah and the CPP's pan-Africanism, development projects, and extension of social services. The Nkrumahist state may not have been the defining feature of their lives, but it was one that made significant and often unanticipated incursions into those lives. Remembrances of opportunities created by the party's and government's various institutions and policies intersected with ones of deep-seated anxieties manifested through persistent fears of local spies, political and social backstabbing, and, most ominously, preventative detention. In this regard, Nkrumahism was something more than the systematized political and social program articulated by the Nkrumahist state apparatus: it was something that had to be lived through, negotiated, and constantly reinterpreted.

Living with Nkrumahism argues that such a framing of Nkrumahism helps reorient how we understand Ghanaians' relationships not only to the postcolonial state, but also to the expectations and ambiguities that characterized Ghana's transition to self-rule. Indeed, we can begin to think of multiple "Nkrumahisms" in Nkrumah-era Ghana. Some (but only some) of these clearly had direct connections to the rhetoric and worldview put forward by the institutions—governmental, party and party-affiliated, press, and others—of the Nkrumahist state. Other individuals, meanwhile, invoked the language of Nkrumahism as a means through which to articulate their personal aspirations or frustrations with their current political, social, or economic status, often as a mechanism through which to make claims on the new state. For others, this language served as a way of connecting oneself directly to Nkrumah himself, even if only in rhetoric or performance. Still others manipulated the language of Nkrumahism, and particularly a refashioning of its symbols—the red cockerel, Young Pioneers and Builders Brigade uniforms, and CPP songs—to distance themselves from a party and government from which they felt alienated, a party and government which, to some, was actively seeking to break down the family, community, ethnic, gender, and generational relationships they so prized.

What the archival, social-scientific, and journalistic record of the CPP era does, though, is seemingly ossify a very specific and orthodoxical interpretation of Nkrumahism that purports to explain the presumed successes, failures, and realities of the Nkrumahist project. Among the social scientists of the mid- to late 1960s and 1970s—who, in many ways, have had the last word on the CPP, at least among academics—such a perspective served to highlight both the deficiencies of the CPP government itself and the ruptures between theory and praxis. However, such a framework privileges state orthodoxy, even as it seeks to refute it, in that a state-centered image of the state-citizenry relationship emerges as the primary or even single reference point for understanding the Ghanaian postcolonial experience. This mode of analysis is not unlike the one that guided the CPP's own quest to systematize Nkrumahist thought and politics in the 1960s. With its centralization of political and ideological power, embodied first in the republican constitution and later in the one-party state, the CPP sought to set the terms of debate, nationally and internationally, on how best to understand the process of decolonization. This included how to interpret what the party characterized as the antiquated, "tribalist" oppositions that, in the 1950s, persistently vexed the CPP, along with the potentialities and shortfalls of the decolonizing citizenry and the power of the state itself. In other words, a relatively static interpretation of the CPP's own ambitions, aspirations, and deficiencies has often become the guiding construct through which Ghanaians' postcolonial imaginings are not just engaged with, but understood. *Living with Nkrumahism* aims to contextualize and historicize the process by which this orthodoxy came together and in turn increasingly came to represent the political, social, economic, and cultural terrain of the early Ghanaian postcolonial experience.

SOURCES AND METHODOLOGY

The study of Nkrumah's Ghana rests at the interstices of the colonial and postcolonial archive. In doing so, it forces the historian to confront the pronounced shift from the relative wealth of the colonial archive to, as one proceeds through the years after independence, the increasing paucity of the postcolonial archive. In the Public Records and Archives Administration Department (PRAAD) office in Accra, for instance, the pre-1957 archival record provides a relatively ordered and somewhat detailed accounting of the political actions and decision-making processes undertaken in the lead-up to independence, particularly in the form of cabinet minutes and memoranda. As with much of colonial African history, an even more robust archival record detailing the Gold Coast's transition to self-rule exists in the colonial metropole, most notably in the British National Archives.[53] For researchers interested in the 1950s, the late-colonial archive thus provides insight into debates over subjects including the priorities of the CPP government (and particularly its cabinet) as the colony sought to become a country, British perspectives on Gold Coast decolonization, the changes in administrative infrastructure necessary for the soon-to-be independent state, and, to a lesser extent, the operation of several of the colony's ministries. In some cases, these records continue into the early postcolonial period. However, increasingly as one advances through the 1960s, any semblance of a stable documentary record begins to evaporate. Files and narratives often lack context. Some are missing. Others may be dispersed or intermingled with unrelated material. Still others have found their way into catch-all collections, two of which dominate PRAAD-Accra's material on Nkrumah-era postcolonial Ghana: the Files on Ex-Presidential Affairs (RG 17/2/-) and those of the Bureau of African Affairs Papers (RG 17/1/-, formerly SC/BAA/-).[54]

The state of the Ghanaian postcolonial archive may in part be the result of the nature and decisions of the CPP government at the time, possibly reflecting the changing priorities of the government as it confronted the prospects of self-rule in the age of Cold War. It is also a consequence of the 1966 coup, when the new military government destroyed or confiscated many of the country's CPP-era files, particularly in Accra.[55] The result is a postcolonial archive in Ghana that is fragmentary and dispersed. However, it is also one that, despite the best efforts of the highly skilled and dedicated archivists who oversee its various sites throughout the country, regularly offers occasion to reflect upon the realities of postcolonial governance and the near-continuous budget shortfalls that have plagued this and other Ghanaian governmental institutions over much of the last half century.

At the heart of this book, then, is a struggle to make sense of this fragmentary archival record and put it into conversation with the changing political and ideological framework of Nkrumahist thought, the mechanisms of CPP governance, and the lived experiences of Ghanaians during the period. State- and party-run newspapers and magazines—most notably including the *Evening News*, the *Ghanaian Times*, and the *Ghanaian*—serve as another key resource in this endeavor, augmenting the formal archive with other, public expressions of the institutionalized worldview of the Nkrumah-led government. Moreover, the party- and state-run press was not static. It also was not necessarily Gramscian in its quest for discursive hegemony, but it did continually seek to set the terms of political and social debate in the country through a consistently shifting discursive practice operating under the rubric of Nkrumahism. In contrast to a scholarship that has limited the prominence of Nkrumah-era ideology in mid-century Ghanaian life, I argue that an evolving Nkrumahism served as the backdrop to many Ghanaians' experiences, as they had little choice but to operate in a political and social sphere in which the CPP increasingly sought to intrude into their political, social, cultural, and economic lives.[56] On a day-to-day level, the result was an environment in which many had to gain familiarity not only with the language and vocabulary of Ghanaian pan-Africanism and socialism, but also with its hidden assumptions, values, and norms. In many ways, it was in the press that these assumptions and values were most clearly articulated. In fact, it could be argued that the press—via most newspapers' daily coverage and editorials—often better exemplifies the moving target that was Nkrumahism during the decade and a half of CPP rule than do the speeches and writings of Nkrumah and other prominent CPP figures themselves. In these party and government publications we find the CPP's in-the-moment readings of and adaptations to a changing array of local, continental, and international phenomena, including strikes, attempts on Nkrumah's life, and Cold War intervention in Ghana and elsewhere on the continent.

Juxtaposed with my analysis of the Ghanaian state- and party-run press are a collection of forty-four oral interviews with Ghanaians who were both inside and outside the CPP's formal party apparatus. Among the most prominent figures interviewed were J. K. Tettegah (d. 2009), who for much of the Nkrumah years served as the general secretary of the TUC, K. B. Asante, K. S. P. (formerly J. E.) Jantuah (d. 2011), Kofi Duku, and Dr. M. N. Tetteh. Among these figures, only K. B. Asante remained an active and prominent presence in Ghanaian public life throughout the duration of this book's research and writing, while most others had retired and/or were still sidelined from any serious political work in the country. The majority of the book's interviews, however, are with an array of nonelite Ghanaian men and women who participated in either the CPP or opposition politics of the first decade of self-rule. Most notably, these interviews include oral narratives from and focused life histories of individuals associated with such Nkrumah-era organizations as the Ghana Young Pioneers, the Builders Brigade, and other political and social appendages of the CPP and its opposition. Most of these interviews took place in the particular individual's home or workplace and were conducted in English, Twi, or a mixture thereof. In some cases, interviewees generously took the time to sit for more than one interview. Meanwhile, a research assistant, who had been integral in locating potential interviewees, was present for most interviews and another aided in the translation and transcription of many of the non-English interviews.

Lower-profile regional archives and those of institutions like the George Padmore Research Library on African Affairs in Accra further reinforced the project's emphasis on the interactive relationship between the ideological and lived experiences of African decolonization and Ghanaian postcoloniality. The Padmore Library's Bureau of African Affairs collection (GPRL, BAA/RLAA/-), for instance, not only helped outline the Nkrumah government's pan-African agenda inside and outside the country, but also—through the personnel files it contained—provided a view into the day-to-day work life of those employed in the institution.

PRAAD's regional archives in Sekondi, Kumasi, Sunyani, and Cape Coast—all of which contain a rich array of material on Nkrumah-era Ghana—offered similar snapshots of life under Nkrumah and the CPP. For, in these often overlooked archives, at least in terms of understanding the national political scene, we find much more than the correspondence of a set of sycophantic bureaucrats attempting to carry out the orders of the central government in Accra. Rather, the records, correspondence, and minutes of the party's district and regional branches provide the intellectual and bureaucratic artifacts for understanding how the Accra government's policies, orders, and ideology were both interpreted at the local level and, in many cases, haphazardly implemented. They thus offer a complicated view of both local governments' and the populace's day-to-day engagement with the often-changing face of Nkrumahism, as each tried to make sense of local issues, including chieftaincy, labor, land ownership, development, political representation, and state loyalty, in the context of the emergent Nkrumahist state. As a result, in combination with the amorphous set of transnational "shadow archives," as Jean Allman refers to them—in the United States, Great Britain, and elsewhere—these regional archives represent some of the most valuable repositories for understanding the contradictions and complexities of Ghanaian political life in the 1950s and 1960s, particularly outside of Accra.[57] Even with these institutions, however, the types of questions one can usefully answer necessarily face a range of constraints connected to the contemporary realities and current state of a postcolonial archive that was originally constructed within the increasingly tightening political and social arena of the Nkrumahist state, and that subsequently, over nearly sixty years, has suffered periods of governmental and structural neglect.

ORGANIZATION

The methodological challenges faced in engaging the postcolonial archive inform the organization of this book, for each of its chapters engages both the possibilities and the frustrations elicited by the archive. As a result, the book's first two chapters reconstruct the mutually interacting local and global contexts framing both Nkrumah's political and intellectual development and the Gold Coast's transition to self-rule. In doing so, they place the anticolonial politics of Nkrumah and the CPP at the center of a growing set of transnational debates at the time over the structure and meaning of African self-rule. Central to this discussion is a rereading of the narratives and debates surrounding postwar pan-African anticolonial politics in relation to both the rise of the CPP and the resistance to it. These debates, however, were not just about institutional formations or territorial control. Rather, they were part of a process of contestation that integrated questions concerning everything from the ideological, civic, and moral makeup of the new Ghana to its physical and infrastructural landscape. Chapter 2, in particular, provides a framework for understanding the political, social, and institutional changes to an emergent Nkrumahism in relation to the wide array of expectations and allegiances that comprised the midcentury Gold Coast/Ghanaian political, social, and cultural scene. In doing so, it details the process by which Nkrumah and a range of other local and transnational actors set out to sketch a path for Ghana's future and its role in an anticipated soon-to-be liberated Africa alongside a competing set of alternative visions for the new country—local, regional, and national— that challenged the young but maturing CPP.

The following four chapters detail the process by which the evolving CPP-led state aimed to instill into the Ghanaian populace the pan-African and socialist consciousness that it saw as at the heart of a truly independent Ghana and Africa. Each in turn examines aspects of the variety of paths differing groups of Ghanaians took as they navigated this emerging political and social reality. Chapter 3, for instance, with its focus on Ghanaian youth, especially those involved in state- and party-run organizations like the Builders Brigade (later, Workers Brigade) and the Ghana Young Pioneers, emphasizes the immediate postcolonial period as one of internal political construction and international redefinition and experimentation.

Symbolizing the blank slate of decolonization's "new men," the country's young men, women, and children embodied the hope, aspirations, and presumed malleability of the nation. As a result, the chapter shows how organizations like the Brigade and the Young Pioneers placed youth at the center of a CPP-led process of national inculcation in the values and ideals of an envisioned pan-African and socialist citizenry constructed around an ethics of discipline, order, and civic activism. The chapter also reveals the tensions and arenas of contestation that surrounded these organizations as they set off waves of popular unease—some of which became subjects of public debate, while others (out of individuals' fears of detention) did not—over the state's role in everything from the attempt to alter Ghanaian familial and generational relations to the regimentation and perceived militarization of Ghanaian youth.

Chapters 4 and 5 focus on themes of work, productivity, and service to the nation, each key to the Nkrumahist worldview. Chapter 4 builds upon the previous chapter's discussion of an idealized pan-African and socialist citizenry through a social and cultural dissection of the politics of "work" in Nkrumah-era Ghana. Linked to issues of discipline, order, and productivity was to be a national conception of work tied to the collective good. In contrast to being a mechanism for personal economic gain and accumulation, work emerged as a nexus point of moral and civic discourse defined through obligations of sacrifice to the nation and the concomitant process of consciousness-building that was to follow these sacrifices. As presented within the context of party ideology, socialist work and production were thus to be a liberating experience, freeing the Ghanaian (and African) worker from real and imagined subjugation to the global capitalist system, even as the CPP used the idiom of socialist work to weaken and ultimately co-opt the country's previously vibrant labor movement. The result was a political and social environment surrounding work, production, and development that not only increasingly demanded more from the country's workforce, but which eventually, through many Ghanaian workers' reactions to it, forced the CPP into reframing its relationship with the broader populace in the early 1960s.

Similar themes of sacrifice and devotion to the nation, along with those of secrecy and subversion, intersect in chapter 5. Specifically, this chapter presents an international history of Ghanaian readings of the prospects of African decolonization during and after the so-called "Year of Africa," alongside an analysis of the institutional labor and gender politics of a specific Nkrumah-era state institution: the Bureau of African

Affairs. No Ghanaian institution had a greater role in the pursuit of African liberation than the Bureau, as it bore the responsibility of collecting, interpreting, and disseminating to audiences at home and abroad news and intelligence on the advancement of the Nkrumahist revolution. As a workplace, though, the Bureau was also the locus for an evolving set of institutional norms, assumptions, and, not surprisingly, gender politics. The chapter thus interrogates the interactions between the exceptional and the banal in the day-to-day work lives of the Bureau's employees, and particularly its female employees—highlighting the ways in which they sought to navigate their positions and interests as employees in relation to the changing institutional and political realities of employment in one of the most highly politicized institutions of the Nkrumahist state. The chapter in turn brings to the fore the growing gender, generational, and class anxieties that, by the early and mid-1960s, were often associated with the perceived stalling of the Nkrumahist revolution at home and abroad.

Issues of belonging, uncertainty, and attempted political and community self-redefinition frame chapter 6 as it unpacks the political and institutional construction of the one-party state. At the heart of the chapter are the ways in which Ghanaians sought to renegotiate their relationships with this emergent one-party state. Intellectually and structurally, the one-party state was a multifaceted and often volatile entity demarcating political, social, and economic life in the country. For Ghanaians, the political and institutional volatility that surrounded the country's one-party politics, and, more importantly, the mechanisms for policing the country's revolutionary purity and stability (e.g., political detention), led to the rise of an eclectic array of tools for popular self-redefinition and self-preservation. These included activities ranging from petitioning for pay raises and promotions in the language of Nkrumahism, to disengagement from politics, to even supposed displays of state and party loyalty that included reporting on one's neighbors and others. Foremost, the chapter argues that these activities were relationship-building exercises. As such, they were methods of self-preservation and promotion through which certain Ghanaians sought out—often with very troubling effects—new ways to connect to (or, for others, disentangle themselves from) a postcolonial state and ideology that, by the eve of the 1966 coup overthrowing Nkrumah and the CPP, had, for many, become distant and alien shadows of the populist, mass movement they claimed to embody.

1 ꙮ The World of Kwame Nkrumah

Pan-Africanism, Empire, and the Gold Coast
in Global Perspective

Many of us fail to understand that a war cannot be waged for democracy
which has as its goal a return to imperialism. It is our warning, that
if after victory, imperialism and colonialism should be restored, we
will be sowing the seed not only for another war, but for the greatest
revolution the world has ever seen.

— Kwame Nkrumah, "Education and Nationalism in Africa," 1943[1]

Brother, if any people need peace, it is Asians and Africans, as only a
peaceful world will enable them to develop their countries and taste
some of the good things of life which the West have long enjoyed.

— George Padmore to Kwame Nkrumah, 1957[2]

AT MIDNIGHT on 6 March 1957, Kwame Nkrumah stood on a stage in
Accra's Old Polo Grounds to usher in the birth of the new, independent
Ghana and to announce his vision for the new nation. "Today, from now
on," he proclaimed, "there is a new African in the world and that new
African is ready to fight his own battle and show that after all the black
man is capable of managing his own affairs. We are going to demonstrate
to the world, to the other nations, young as we are, that we are prepared to
lay our own foundation." He then continued his short celebratory speech
with an all-encompassing call to action in the struggle for African self-
determination: "We have done with the battle and we again re-dedicate
ourselves in the struggle to emancipate other countries in Africa, for," he
emphasized, "our independence is meaningless unless it is linked up with
the total liberation of the African continent."[3]

Nkrumah's independence-day pronouncement connecting Ghana's
liberation to that of the rest of the continent remains one of the most
famous declarations of Africa's decolonization-era history. It ought to be
read, though, on multiple levels—each of which reflects the intersecting

array of audiences, networks, and histories of African and international anticolonialism into which the Ghanaian prime minister aimed to embed the young West African state. At one level, Nkrumah was returning to the roots of his own pan-African activism, cultivated under the tutelage of the Trinidadian pan-Africanist George Padmore in London and Manchester. In doing so, he aimed to adapt this largely diasporic tradition to the challenges facing what he and others predicted would become a rapidly decolonizing continent. At another, Nkrumah was also harkening back to the Gold Coast's own political and intellectual tradition of anticolonial agitation. Rarely confining itself to the territorial boundaries of the colony, the political vision of the Gold Coast intellectuals and activists of the early twentieth century had taken shape as everything from nationalist to pan-West African to pan-African to even diasporic. As a result, during this period, figures including J. E. Casely Hayford, Kobina Sekyi, and J. B. Danquah, among others, positioned the Gold Coast at the political and intellectual center of early twentieth-century West African thought and activism. On yet another level, Nkrumah, with his pronouncement, sought to link Ghana's postcolonial ambitions with a broader, indeed global history of anticolonialism extending back to at least the end of the First World War. For Nkrumah, this international anticolonialism provided a model for understanding the world and, in particular, a global political economy constructed out of the violence, iniquities, and relentless resource extraction of European capitalist imperialism.

This chapter surveys the political and intellectual world that marked Nkrumah's growth as an anticolonial thinker and activist. It, however, does not seek to offer a biography of the future politician's early life but, rather, aims to present a transnational narrative that encircles Nkrumah as he came of age politically. More important than Nkrumah himself in the chapter are the multiple contexts—political and social, local and international— that surrounded the Gold Coaster during the first decades of the twentieth century, along with the various political and social networks that emerged out of them. These networks were colonial and extracolonial. They were also continental and transcontinental. Moreover, they were forged through the intersecting experiences of colonial subjecthood and racial exclusion already shaped by the global reach and impact of Euro-American ideologies of race, of colonial practices in labor and resource extraction, of social and political segregation, and even of, as Tony Ballantyne and Antoinette Burton have argued, the shifting spatial dimensions of the emergent nineteenth- and twentieth-century imperial world order.[4] For those living within the empires of the late nineteenth and early twentieth centuries, the empires themselves were not always, or at least not entirely, mere spaces for passive exploitation. Rather, they also provided new arenas for political, social, and cultural connections, bringing together colonized peoples across seemingly disconnected spaces, as both peoples and ideas spread within and beyond the formal and informal confines of a given empire.[5]

This chapter interrogates the processes by which competing yet intersecting political, social, cultural, and intellectual worlds came together to form the lively anticolonial politics of the first half of the twentieth century. In Africa and beyond, the interwar period in particular was a heyday of African and diasporic extraterritorial imaginaries. The result was a vibrant political and intellectual environment that included, among other things, a burgeoning pan-Africanism on the continent and abroad, a push and pull of competing notions of national and colonial self-determination, and a rising critique of the liberal underpinnings of the imperial system. Together, the formal and informal movements and ideas that arose out of these contexts comprised the political and intellectual backdrop that helped mold the worldview of the future Nkrumahist state. They also provided the roots to much of the radical anticolonial politics that would come of age in the 1940s, ultimately finding, at least in the African context, their most forceful expression in the organization and demands of the 1945 Manchester Pan-African Congress. As a result, this chapter aims to contextualize the "world of Kwame Nkrumah" and what would eventually emerge as the politics of the Convention People's Party as part of a broader, global trend in early twentieth-century anticolonial politics. Meanwhile, within the Gold Coast itself, the colony's own political traditions had roots of their own. As subsequent chapters will show, past and contemporary protests over land, colonial policies, the operation of the local and international cocoa market, and access to resources and services would, in many cases, come to underpin future Ghanaians' political imaginings well into the 1950s and beyond—albeit in ways that often did not fit neatly into the CPP's worldview.

EMPIRE, LIBERALISM, AND ITS CRITICS

Nkrumah came of age in the Gold Coast at a time in which, in both the West African colony and internationally, European imperial powers were expanding their political and ideological reach. It was also a time when, throughout the colonial world and beyond, an increasingly sophisticated array of critics of empire were coming into their own. Key, then, to understanding the imperial world order into which Nkrumah was born is a recognition of the extent to which such a world order was at once a relatively new development on the international stage and one with deep historical roots. In real terms, the continent's colonization was a haphazard and uneven process. Moreover, at the time of Nkrumah's 1909 birth, in nearly all of Africa, with the exception of parts of southern Africa and certain coastal enclaves, the events that marked the onset of the continent's formal colonization were less than a century old. In the region that would become the Gold Coast Colony, which had a long and intricate history with an array of European powers dating back to the fifteenth century, the attempted extension of formal European colonial authority into African affairs was highly incremental and even then it would not begin until at least the mid-nineteenth century. Moreover, it would take several more decades before British rule could be institutionalized along most of the southern Gold Coast.[6] Even more troublesome for British ambitions were the Asante in the territory's central forest region, where the British would spend much of the nineteenth century in a shifting pattern of war and uneasy peace with the Asante state.[7] Meanwhile, in the Northern Territories, it would not be until the early twentieth century that the British would be able to bring all the region's peoples under their administrative control.[8] As a result, even at its most rhetorical level, the notion of an aspiring European imperial world order that would encompass the continent cannot be said to have emerged until at least the aftermath of the Berlin Conference of 1884–85. Furthermore, as in the Gold Coast, the attempted real-world, wide-scale implementation and administration of this burgeoning imperial order would not occur for another two to three decades—a time nearly coinciding with Nkrumah's birth.[9]

Yet, the perceived European imperial world order of the early twentieth century also possessed the aura of a deeper, more overarching history in Africa and globally. Cultivated in part via the intersections between the rise of nineteenth-century liberalism and the real and perceived changes in the global political economy, notions of an age of empire would become naturalized in the global political imagination within one to two generations following the onset of colonial conquest. In Africa, the long history of the slave trade on the continent featured prominently in the political and cultural imaginations of both supporters and critics of the emergent imperial world order. For some of the most forceful early twentieth-century critics of the colonial project, Europe's late nineteenth-century colonization of Africa had clear echoes of the violence, indignities, and exploitation of the slave trade.[10] Others, however, often offered more measured analyses of Europe's imperial ambitions in Africa, at times not only crediting the Europeans for trying to abolish the last vestiges of the slave trade on the continent, but also tying this assumed eradication of slavery to the continent's and its peoples' modernization. Even those who at times expressed skepticism of and disappointment with certain European imperial intentions and actions in Africa often celebrated many of the presumed values of the colonial mission, including its promised expansion of social benefits (most notably, Western education and medicine), Christianity, infrastructural development, constitutionalism, and free trade. "We are head and ears in love with the British Constitution," the African editors of the Cape Coast–based *Gold Coast Methodist Times* declared in 1897. "The national greatness of the English people has been determined by their national laws and institutions," the newspaper's increasingly nationalist editors argued; "they have prospered, because of the humanitarian principles of their laws; because those laws are always in harmony with the genius of the christian [*sic*] religion. We too are anxious to march *en masse* after the great English nation; We [*sic*] want to do so willingly, voluntarily, intelligently, and gradually."[11]

Within Europe, questions over the purpose of and responsibilities embedded in the colonial project featured prominently in the continent's political debates. Among British intellectuals, for instance, as political theorist Uday Mehta details, nearly every major thinker from the late eighteenth through the nineteenth centuries sought to address the colonial question in their writings at some point in their career.[12] However, in a British political and intellectual context increasingly receptive to the language of individual freedom and choice as advanced by liberal thinkers like John Stuart Mill, the realities of colonial rule—particularly what it meant for Britain to rule over other territories and peoples—challenged the worldview of many inside these political and intellectual circles. Mill, for his part, offered perhaps the most famous attempt to resolve this apparent contradiction in the mid-nineteenth century, as he proposed a tiered view of the world that positioned colonialism as a process leading to social uplift, where, through colonial rule, so-called civilized and modern Europeans were to guide the colonized—"barbarians" in Mill's language—toward the light of civilization. Mill's writings, among others, would in turn help lay the intellectual groundwork for a perceived progressive colonialism that, in the liberal worldview, positioned the colonized along a paternalist path leading toward a modern society.[13]

As Mill and others debated colonialism, they also began the process of reimagining their philosophical ideals in relation to world history. In doing so, they drew clear lines connecting liberal values of individual freedom, equality before the law, and utilitarian governance to the philosophical and political traditions of antiquity.[14] Both politically and intellectually, the result was a naturalization of European liberal ideas within not only a particular school of European imperial thought, but also in key aspects of the global political imagination. As a result, by the late nineteenth and early twentieth centuries, prominent social commentators in both the colonial and metropolitan worlds turned to liberal thought and values in their political discourse. In doing so, they often projected onto colonial peoples their own assumptions concerning the enlightened human condition even as the ideal of a liberal imperialism began to fade from most colonial policy discussions in the second half of the nineteenth century.[15] In 1897 Nigeria, for instance, the African editors of the *Lagos Standard* heralded both the uniqueness and the universality of Britain's liberal traditions in their accounting of the promise of British colonial rule specifically. "The Natives of Africa—we venture to say *all* Africa, love the Queen not only for what she is," the newspaper proclaimed, "but for what she represents—the freest and best system of Government the world has ever known."[16] Others, likewise, turned to liberal notions of free trade and commerce, as they linked (albeit not uncritically) aspects of the colonial mission to the continent's future development.[17] By the early twentieth century, the political, economic, and social relationships of colonial rule had thus become intertwined, in both the colonial and the metropolitan political imaginary, with the idealized progressivism implicit in the liberal worldview.

For many living both inside and outside Europe's colonial territories, rhetorical gestures toward liberal ideals offered them new pathways to political and social claim-making during the first decades of colonial rule. At the 1900 London Pan-African Conference, for instance, organizers and delegates combined a language of racial self-help and uplift with a set of claims on the British colonial administration in which they demanded the free and fair treatment of Britain's colonial subject populations. Delegates at the conference also called for the creation of a range of protections for colonial peoples in areas including labor, politics, and property. In doing so, they charged the colonial government with an obligation for ensuring Africans gain the political, social, and economic means necessary for the continent's fruition in the modern world.[18] Likewise, in 1919, W. E. B. Du Bois, who had been present in London, sought to rejuvenate that conference's spirit as he organized in Paris the first of four Pan-African Congresses he would plan in the early interwar period. Set to coincide with the end of the

First World War and the opening of the Paris Peace Conference, the 1919 Pan-African Congress—like its 1900 predecessor—integrated a liberal narrative of racial uplift and self-help into its demands on Europe's colonial governments.[19] In doing so, representatives to the congress insisted upon a colonial system absent the exploitation, violence, and alienation that had characterized the first decades of colonial rule in Africa. This realignment of colonial rule, they argued, would ultimately require a commitment to such practices as holding African land and imperial capital investments in trust for the continent's peoples, the regulation and taxation of extractive industries for the public good, and the abolition of forced labor in all its iterations. Even more importantly for the congress-goers, they also called for the granting of African peoples "the right to participate in the government as fast as their development permits," and insisted "that, in time, Africa be ruled by consent of the Africans."[20]

Such pan-African demands for imperial reform coincided with a range of emerging international critiques of European imperialism during the first decades of the twentieth century. In Europe, debates over the wisdom, ethics, costs, and consequences of empire had long dotted the metropolitan political scene, with many worrying about the range of effects imperialism could have, and had had, on life in the metropole.[21] Just after the turn of the century, J. A. Hobson would extend aspects of these arguments further as he sought to dissect the operation of the imperial system as a whole.[22] A London-born economist who three years earlier had reported on the Boer War for the *Manchester Guardian*, Hobson presented a model for understanding imperialism that extended beyond the rhetoric of progress and civilization employed by colonialism's most fervent proponents as well as by those seeking reform. Instead, he tied the imperial project to capitalism's continuous need for expansion. Published in 1902, his *Imperialism: A Study* in turn detailed a political and economic process by which Europe's colonial ambitions in Africa and elsewhere aimed to extract new wealth from colonies abroad and create new markets within these colonies for the goods it produced at home.[23]

In a 1915 essay in the *Atlantic Monthly*, W. E. B. Du Bois published a similar critique of imperialism.[24] Emphasizing the colonialist roots of the First World War, Du Bois moved the economics of empire to the center of a quasi-Marxist analysis of the conflict. In doing so, he presented a picture of the nineteenth and early twentieth centuries as a period marked by the increasing racialization of global extractive labor and of growing European consumerist demand. For him, the nationalisms that many saw as one of the war's main causes, if not its primary cause, were in fact the direct result of a broader merging of interests between European capital and white labor over the last half of the nineteenth century. As a result, Du Bois argued that, through a period of labor reform in the late nineteenth and early twentieth century, white labor had become increasingly expensive, as workers demanded higher wages and better working conditions. For many white workers, the result was the creation of new avenues through which to accumulate wealth. However, the African American intellectual also insisted that it was only through the emerging colonial system that European capital was able to fund the mounting cost of labor at home, while also meeting the rising expectations of what was becoming a bourgeois working class. To this end, the forced labor campaigns made infamous by Leopold's Congo, but practiced to some degree in all the major powers' African holdings, provided European capital with a markedly cheaper and almost invariably nonwhite labor force. Echoing Hobson, Du Bois contended that the emerging colonial project introduced new sites into a global economy through which European capital could extend its extractive reach for the benefit of European personal and industrial consumption.[25]

Thus, for Du Bois, the First World War had its origins in the fragile but colonially buttressed and racialized alliance between European capital and labor. Key to the survival of this alliance was each side's ability to cater to the other's impulse to consume, an arrangement requiring ever more resources to sustain itself. As a result, in the decades leading up to the war, Europe's major powers competed with one another for greater control of the world's labor and natural resources. The Berlin Conference and the imperial pie-slicing that came out of it were but one mechanism to help temporarily regulate these impulses. For Du Bois, the war represented the inevitable breakdown of these agreements and their attempts to contain the expanding needs of imperial capitalism. To those in African and other colonies, the results were social conditions in which Africans and other colonial subjects had little choice but to serve as pawns in the fight for global control over labor and resources. Moreover, Du Bois averred that, absent the implementation of a postwar agreement rooted in a notion of democracy that could "extend . . . to the yellow, brown, and black peoples," any postwar peace had little chance of breaking free from the rapacious nature of European capitalism. He also predicted that, in time, "the colored peoples [would] not always submit passively to foreign domination" and would eventually push back against the exploitative nature of capitalist imperialism and the world system built around it.[26]

Two years later, in 1917, V. I. Lenin would offer an even more famous exegesis of imperialism in *Imperialism: The Highest Stage of Capitalism*, which would influence anticolonial thought across the world well into the twentieth century. In significant part an addendum to Hobson, Lenin's text centered on the growth and development of global finance capital and its role in the creation of the early twentieth-century world order.[27] Like Du Bois, Lenin rejected the predominant interpretations of the First World War as arising from nationalism—or what Du Bois called "sentimental patriotism."[28] Lenin viewed such narratives as political distractions emerging out of a broader process by which global capital had begun to consolidate itself through the monopolization not only of markets, but also of industries and institutions. The goals of expanding finance capital went beyond merely exporting goods to new markets, according to Lenin. They included controlling "spheres of influence" whereby global markets could become key drivers of the systematic redistribution of wealth to the imperial metropole. As outlined by Lenin, banking institutions in particular were leading global capitalism beyond the struggle for resource control to an increasing reliance on the mechanisms of finance. As such, Lenin outlined an early twentieth-century world system founded upon the accumulation, control over, and continuous reproduction of profit.[29]

What Lenin sought to detail in *Imperialism* was a historical and theoretical model of an imperialism that had loosened the imperial powers of Europe from many of their liberal moorings. In doing so, he—like Du Bois—situated the violence of the First World War as the natural outgrowth of the global rise of European finance capitalism. Imperialism, as understood by Lenin and later returned to by many subsequent anticolonial intellectuals, thus served little purpose but to divide the world among its various capitalist powers. Europe's African and Asian colonies were thus not only constructed to provide the labor, resources, and markets necessary for capitalist expansion. They also represented a new territorialized framework through which to manage each colonial power's expansion in relation to the others. The stakes of this arrangement for the various powers, Lenin argued, were immense, in that they sought to control that which, much as Du Bois had noted two years earlier, was uncontrollable. "The more capitalism develops," Lenin explained, "the more the need for raw materials arises, the more bitter competition becomes, and the more feverishly the hunt for raw materials proceeds throughout the whole world, the more desperate becomes the struggle for the acquisition of colonies."[30] As with his American contemporary, Lenin insisted that herein lay the roots of the instability of the twentieth-century world order, as global capital continued to mature out of its nineteenth-century adolescence and needed new spaces to grow on a map in which nearly all of the world's land had already been partitioned.[31]

For colonized intellectuals and others, Lenin thus provided a model by which to both analyze and critique the liberal and capitalist underpinnings of the early twentieth-century international system. He also offered them a mechanism through which to internationalize Marxism, taking it beyond the confines of societies with already established industrial proletariats. In Central Asia, for instance, Mirsaid Sultan-Galiev turned to aspects of Lenin's theoretical model in an attempt to extend the idea of the proletariat beyond social classes to entire dispossessed "nationalities," arguing that all Muslim peoples should be regarded as part of the proletariat.[32] For Sultan-Galiev, a Tatar who until his 1923 arrest was the most influential Muslim within the Soviet Union, such a framework allowed for the integration of Islam into the Marxist worldview on its own terms.[33] Moreover, it also offered a model in which, on the international scale, "nations" themselves had characteristics of social classes as described in Marxist theory. In this light, he insisted in 1918 that there were different types of proletariats based upon the relative wealth of the nations they inhabited, and that certain national proletariats would be more revolutionary than others based upon the level of oppression they had historically faced.[34]

Likewise, in Europe's colonies, figures like Jawaharlal Nehru broadened their intellectual framework in the 1920s as they too looked to Lenin and the Soviet Union for alternative models for interpreting the colonial system and the imperial world order. Nehru, who toured the Soviet Union with his father in 1927, used his reflections on his experience to compare and contrast the rapidly industrializing revolutionary society he witnessed there with an India that he viewed as comparatively much more conservative and set in its ways. Writing in 1928, Nehru stressed that, "for us in India the fascination [with Soviet Russia] is even greater [than elsewhere in the world], and even our self-interest compels us to understand the vast forces which have upset the old order of things and brought a new world into existence, where values have changed utterly and old standards have given place to new."[35] A little more than a decade later, in his 1941 autobiography, Nehru again returned to the subject of the Soviet experiment as he recalled with wonder how the interwar Soviet Union, during a moment in which much of "the rest of the world was in the grip of the depression and going backward in some ways," was able to overcome these trends as it redefined the Soviet place within the international community. Shifting to the subject of Marxism itself, the future Indian prime minister ultimately presented the "theory and philosophy" as a vehicle for providing new pathways to a "future . . . bright with hope," regardless of the bleakness of the past or present.[36]

In 1947, Nkrumah would publish his own Lenin-inspired treatise, *Towards Colonial Freedom*. In this relatively short pamphlet, Nkrumah detailed what he saw as the systematized ways in which imperialism created and maintained an imbalance of trade between Europe and its African colonies. For Nkrumah, as with both Lenin and Du Bois, capitalism could not function without imperialism. Instead, capital could only fleetingly sustain the pressure from its own persistent need for growth before it had to look elsewhere, or cannibalize the most profit-sucking element in the production process, namely labor. As with Lenin and Du Bois, Nkrumah maintained that the colonial system provided European capital an alternative by opening up a new set of unfettered arenas for labor and resource extraction, while at the same time guaranteeing markets for the sale of the colonizers' goods. The future Ghanaian president thus opened his 1947 text with a forceful declaration: "The aim of all colonial governments in Africa and elsewhere has been the struggle for raw materials; and not only this, but the colonies have become the dumping ground, and colonial peoples the false recipients, of manufactured goods of the industrialists and capitalists of Great Britain, France, Belgium and other colonial powers who turn to the dependent territories which feed their industrial plants. This is colonialism in a nutshell."[37]

MANCHESTER AND THE AFRICAN ANTICOLONIAL IMAGINATION

In terms of Nkrumah's intellectual development, *Towards Colonial Freedom* did not have its direct origins in the political and intellectual traditions of the Gold Coast. Instead, the pamphlet represented a coming together of a broader set of transnational anticolonial traditions and experiences in the future Ghanaian politician's thinking. In fact, what makes the text significant is not particularly its originality, but rather the diversity of political and intellectual influences—pan-African, Marxist-Leninist, and anticolonial revolutionist, among others— embedded within it. Nearly all of these influences found their most prominent expression in the diasporic radicalism of the 1930s and 1940s, culminating in the 1945 Manchester Pan-African Congress. In the United States, for instance, where he spent the decade between 1935 and 1945, Nkrumah lived, worked, studied, and organized in locations ranging from rural Oxford, Pennsylvania, to major American cities and black internationalist hubs like New York City and Philadelphia. As a result, at the center of Nkrumah's American experiences were the political and economic realities of being black in the Depression-era and wartime United States as he embarked upon a number of economic endeavors outside of his schooling, including hawking fish, laboring in a shipyard near Philadelphia, and working in a soap factory, before waiting tables on a shipping line running between New York and Vera Cruz, Mexico. Even more importantly, for Nkrumah, this was also a period of political experimentation in which he sought to embed himself into an eclectic array of pan-African political and social networks, including black churches, the Garvey movement, Paul Robeson's Council on African Affairs, and others.[38]

Aided by a letter of introduction from Trinidadian pan-Africanist C. L. R. James addressed to George Padmore, Nkrumah continued his political maturation after leaving the United States for Great Britain in early 1945. His only previous experience in the imperial metropole was a short layover in 1935 while waiting for his visa to the United States. As detailed in his autobiography, though, that moment had served as a political awakening. Arriving in London and learning of the invasion of Ethiopia by Benito Mussolini's Italy, Nkrumah reported how he had stood in shock at the British passivity to the news of this blatant transgression of African independence and international law.[39] Implied in the narrative Nkrumah presented in his autobiography was an understanding that the mission underpinning his return to London was an upending of the colonialist status quo, which had seemingly made the Italian invasion possible a decade earlier. Upon arrival, Nkrumah quickly joined Padmore in helping organize a new pan-African congress in the English industrial city of Manchester. Convened in October 1945, the Manchester Pan-African Congress brought together pan-African and labor activists to debate Africa's place in the postwar international community. In contrast to the Pan-African Congresses organized by Du Bois in the 1920s or the 1900 London Pan-African Conference, the Manchester congress offered a clear rebuttal to the rhetorical progressivism of the liberal imperial order, arguing for the first time for an immediate end to colonial rule in Africa and elsewhere. As stated in the congress's "Declaration to the Colonial Workers, Farmers, and Intellectuals," its delegates insisted upon "the right of all peoples to govern themselves" and "control their own destiny."[40] Furthermore, the declaration presented the struggle for self-determination as a mass project of "complete social, economic, and political emancipation" from the exploitation of capitalist imperialism.[41]

The Manchester congress thus provided its participants with a collective outlet for expressing their discontent not only with colonial rule, but, more significantly, with even the prospects for colonial reform. Reminiscent of both Lenin's and Du Bois's early twentieth-century interrogations of the colonial project, the congress's speakers and delegates focused their attention on the uniquely exclusionary and extractive nature of colonial rule, highlighting such issues as land alienation, forced labor, and inequalities in pay. In one of his addresses, for instance, Jomo Kenyatta, who nearly twenty years later would become Kenya's first president, contrasted a rapidly growing Ugandan colonial economy based upon cotton production with a colonial social reality in which "there [was] not a single African doctor."[42] Similarly, G. Ashie Nikoi, chairman of the West African Cocoa Farmers' Delegation (Gold Coast), painted a picture of British colonial rule in West Africa founded upon "broken . . . homes" and "natural leaders" alienated from "their rights."[43] Meanwhile, fellow Gold Coaster J. S. Annan—a trade unionist whose talk was covered by the Lagos-based *West African Pilot*—challenged the congress to address not only the problems of imperialism, but also the need to "set up administrative machinery to cope with the difficulties which lie ahead of us."[44]

Nkrumah, who accepted credit for writing some of the congress's most powerful declarations, adopted a similar reading of the event's current and future objectives. Even more importantly, he also viewed it as part of a broader radicalization of anticolonial politics globally and of a transnational rethinking of the role of empire in the postwar world. For instance, just weeks before arriving in London he had taken part in a similar conference in New York featuring approximately sixty representatives from locations including Uganda, India, Burma, Indonesia, the United States, and the West Indies.[45] As in Manchester later in the year, the Colonial Conference challenged colonial rule in Africa and elsewhere as the delegates connected imperial failures to extend to colonial peoples the right of self-determination to the perpetuation of the poverty, illiteracy, famine, and disease which characterized the social and economic conditions of the vast majority of those living under colonial rule. Furthermore, just as Du Bois and Lenin had done with the First World War, the delegates in New York insisted that European imperialism lay at the heart of the twentieth century's global wars, and, should it continue, only promised more violence to come.[46]

In his Manchester address on West and North Africa, Nkrumah would again pick up on many of these themes. According to the congress's minutes, Nkrumah reminded the delegates that "six years of slaughter and devastation had ended, and peoples everywhere were celebrating the end of the struggle not so much with joy as with a sense of relief." He, then, went on to warn that, given the inherently violent and rapacious nature of capitalist imperialism, this relief was sure to be short-lived "as long as Imperialism assaults the world."[47] The longtime Sierra Leonean trade unionist and activist I. T. A. Wallace-Johnson, who earlier in his career had written regularly for Gold Coast newspapers, echoed his younger Gold Coast colleague. In his speech, he rejected the arguments of those within Europe's empires who suggested that colonial rule served as a protection against "the tribal wars which took place in bygone years, and which might break out again if they [the Europeans] left West Africa." Perhaps waxing a bit too romantically about Africa's precolonial past, Wallace-Johnson, then, insisted that "Africans had been living in peace until the Europeans taught them to fight."[48] Others, likewise, returned to the necessarily undemocratic nature of the colonial system. In doing so, they presented a call to action in Africa, with the Gambian newspaper editor J. Downes-Thomas—whose address also gained the attention of the *West African Pilot*—asserting that "history shows that independence always has to be fought for."[49]

The Manchester Pan-African Congress culminated with a direct assault on the fundamental ethos underpinning the European imperial system, particularly in its African and West Indian manifestations. The congress's cadre of diverse delegations, with origins ranging from the continent itself to the West Indies to Europe and to North America, undertook a systematic dissection of nearly every official and popular justification of colonial rule—both contemporary and historical. Questions of African and other colonial peoples' suitability or preparation for self-government or self-determination were met with comparisons to the global violence Europe had just inflicted upon the world.[50] Meanwhile, promises of political reforms and technical and infrastructural development at best faced skepticism in light of the colonial powers' past record on the continent and elsewhere.[51] At worst, delegates depicted them as new examples and tools for the colonial powers' future exploitations.[52] Others took direct aim at the relationship between the European liberal ideals of individual freedom and democratic governance and the necessarily undemocratic and racially exclusionary nature of colonial rule.[53] Pointing to a problem that had long vexed European thinkers dating back to at least the nineteenth century, the Manchester delegates thus presented the political and philosophical gymnastics undertaken to justify the colonial project as more than mere hypocrisy. Instead, they viewed the contradictions embedded in European justifications of colonial rule as mechanisms designed for the colonized's continued subjugation.[54]

The world powers' own wartime rhetoric only provided further ammunition for the congress's critiques of the imperial system, most notably in regard to Winston Churchill and Franklin Roosevelt's 1941 signing of the Atlantic Charter. For Manchester's delegates, the charter's proclamation of the universality of a people's right to self-determination supplied a language with which to challenge Europe's imperial powers on their own terms. Even more significantly, with Churchill's clear refusal to acknowledge the possibility that such a universal right could extend to colonial peoples, the charter created a vehicle for the Manchester delegates and others to make clear the contradictions and double standards embedded within the imperial system.[55] As the Nigerian F. O. B. Blaize, representing the London-based West African Student Union (WASU) at the congress, is reported to have argued in his address before the congress, "British democracy seemed designed only for home consumption. Nigeria has been given a new Constitution, but her people cannot accept it because it is undemocratic. They demand that if the Atlantic Charter is good for certain people, it is good for all."[56] Speaking on the West Indies, J. A. Linton — reading a memorandum from a group of workers' organizations from St. Kitts and Nevis — also turned to the charter. In doing so, he noted how Great Britain's failure to recognize the rights of all of those living on the islands had led to a range of political and economic policies — such as a forced mono-crop economy and a property-based suffrage system — that had been detrimental to the islands' peoples. In response, the St. Kitts and Nevis workers' memo explained that what the Atlantic Charter provided them was the inspiration to begin exploring "greater unity, which can be attained only by a federation of the islands."[57]

At the heart of the Manchester congress was a sense of a world in transition and a belief that Africans and other colonial peoples had an important role to play in that transition. In preparation for a volume celebrating the fiftieth anniversary of the congress, F. R. Kankam-Boadu, who in 1945 was a Gold Coast delegate representing the WASU and who later in his career would direct the Ghana Cocoa Marketing Board, recounted how "without doubt all who accepted to attend the Conference must have had their minds geared to finding a new way for humanity." As Kankam-Boadu reminded his audience in his reminiscences, the congress occurred just as the Second World War had concluded, and that this was a war that had "been fought to save the world from the ravages of racial oppression, dictatorship and all manner of inhumanities."[58] In that light, the congress provided an opening for explorations into an alternative, and many delegates expressed a sense of personal and collective obligation in bringing forth this alternative. Writing in his 1990 autobiography, another Gold Coast WASU delegate and close Nkrumah friend—later turned bitter opponent—Joe Appiah, reflected on how "the journey to Manchester as a delegate . . . evoked in me all the emotion and sentiments of a Moslem pilgrim to Mecca." For Appiah, as with many of the congress's other delegates, the only answer to colonial rule had to be "force."[59]

AFTER MANCHESTER

The close of the Manchester congress left questions as to the exact actions to be taken in the months that followed. In London and Manchester, Padmore, along with the Guyanese pan-Africanist T. Ras Makonnen, undertook the task of publicizing the congress's resolutions and declarations via Padmore's Pan-African Federation (PAF). "After this publicity campaign has been crystallised," Padmore explained in a 1946 letter to Du Bois, "we intend to consolidate the organisational structure of the Federation by drawing in all Colonial organisations of a progressive character as affiliated bodies." As Padmore continued, he insisted that "objectively the task we set ourselves is fairly easy." The real obstacle for the PAF, he anticipated, would be the unfortunate lack of "cadres in England" willing to engage in the work of the struggle.[60] Yet, as Padmore's most recent biographer, Leslie James, has noted, more fundamental challenges afflicted Padmore's PAF in the late 1940s, particularly relating to the organization's funding structure.[61] As James explains, the organization's failure to secure a stable funding source not only required that Padmore write and publish the congress's report himself, but it also forced him to establish the PAF's headquarters in the cheaper city of Manchester as opposed to his own London base. As a result, Padmore became distanced from the day-to-day operations of the PAF as much of the organization's work fell upon the Manchester-based Makonnen—who, like Padmore, would later become an influential advisor to Nkrumah following Makonnen's 1957 arrival in the Gold Coast.[62]

As Padmore and Makonnen worked to establish the administrative infrastructure of the PAF, many of the congress's West African delegates turned their attention to the continent. For them, including a number from the Gold Coast, the congress was a moment of radicalization which they now sought to turn into a pathway toward political mobilization, a pathway that became embodied in the late-1945 formation of the West African

National Secretariat (WANS). Founded by I. T. A. Wallace-Johnson, Kojo Botsio, Bankole Awooner-Renner, Ashie Nikoi, and Bankole Akpata, the organization nominated the elder Wallace-Johnson as its chairman and invited Nkrumah to serve as its general secretary.[63] In name and membership, the organization was foremost a West African organization. However, it was also one largely formed out of the political context and networks manifested in the colonial metropole. Yet, for the activists who formed the secretariat, the organization harkened back to an array of late nineteenth- and early twentieth-century pan–West African political organizations, including the Gold Coast Aborigines' Rights Protection Society (ARPS) and the West African Youth League (WAYL), as they channeled their critiques of European imperialism through a language of West African political and economic unity.[64] For, as Wallace-Johnson and Nkrumah explained in the secretariat's "Aims and Objects," the WANS envisioned the "dawn of a new era" in West Africa. West Africans, they insisted, were now ready and committed to "combat all forms of imperialism and colonial exploitation" and, in doing so, to turn their attention to the broader "task of achieving national unity and absolute independence for all West Africa." The success of such a project, they continued, depended upon the organization and coordination of the "economic and political ideas and aspirations scattered among West African peoples but lacking in co-ordination."[65] In the case of the WANS, these "economic and political ideas" were necessarily to be expressed in explicitly socialist terms. Bankole Awooner-Renner—who, by the mid-1950s, would become a vocal critic of Nkrumah—even went so far as to propose within the secretariat's publications the idea of a "West African Soviet Union."[66]

The WANS, however, did not limit its political program to anticolonial and pan-West African abstractions. Instead, by taking on issues such as the buying and selling of cocoa in West Africa, the secretariat also sought to integrate key local concerns affecting the region's people into their broader critiques of the colonial system. In March 1946, for instance, an article in the organization's flagship journal, the *New African*, on a proposed colonial cocoa monopoly accompanied others containing the WANS's resolutions decrying the forced labor and land theft, among other forms of exploitation, that they associated with the colonial system.[67] Wallace-Johnson and Nkrumah further reinforced these sentiments in the organization's "Aims and Objects" as they—reproducing the Manchester resolutions on West Africa—held up the structure of the colonial cocoa market as evidence of the "incompetent" nature of colonial economic policy in the region.[68] Such arguments echoed interwar critiques of the monopolistic underpinnings of the early twentieth-century cocoa industry, which had dominated the West African press in the 1920s and 1930s. During this period, radical newspapers like Nnamdi Azikiwe's Accra-based *African Morning Post* not only detailed the effects of the government's cocoa policies on West African and specifically Gold Coast farmers, they also positioned these farmers on the frontlines of the colony's battle with "white capitalists."[69] Just under a decade later, the *New African* reiterated this belief, advocating for West Africa's cocoa producers to embark on a "total boycott" in response to any attempt by the government to limit the autonomy of the region's farmers.[70]

As the secretariat worked to develop its own press and publications from its British base, a set of reciprocal relationships also grew between the WANS activists in the United Kingdom and West African newspapers throughout the region. In Lagos, Nigeria, for instance, the *West African Pilot*—another of Azikiwe's newspapers—regularly covered the actions and pronouncements of the organization and its members, while in Freetown, Sierra Leone, the *African Standard* similarly reported on the organization's activities. Meanwhile, in the Gold Coast, the *Gold Coast Observer* and *Ashanti Pioneer* covered the secretariat and its members.[71] Furthermore, Nkrumah himself found a periodic voice within these Gold Coast newspapers, advocating, for instance, in a series of 1947 articles in the *Ashanti Pioneer,* for an "All–West African National Congress." In doing so, he directly referred to the pan–West Africanism of the 1920s and specifically the National Congress of British West Africa made famous by Gold Coasters like J. E. Casely Hayford and Kobina Sekyi.[72] Likewise, many of the secretariat's diasporic allies, most notably Padmore, also maintained an active presence in the region's newspapers over the period. In the case of Padmore specifically, Leslie James has calculated that, between 1937 and 1950, the Trinidadian pan-Africanist would contribute 508 articles to the *West African Pilot* and, between 1947 and 1950, another 182 to the *Ashanti Pioneer.*[73]

As a result, by early 1947 anticolonial pan-Africanists and activists from both inside and outside the continent had begun to advance a radicalizing discourse aimed at transforming a state of dependency into one of political and economic emancipation. Meanwhile, politically, Nkrumah used the two years between the end of the 1945 Manchester congress and his December 1947 return to the Gold Coast as a period of consolidation, building and solidifying his inner circle. Some members of this group—most notably Kojo Botsio, who would later serve as general secretary of the CPP and, over the course of the 1950s and 1960s, hold a number of different ministerial posts in Nkrumah's cabinet—would remain aligned with the Ghanaian president until the 1966 coup.[74] Nkrumah also spent much of his last two years abroad establishing connections with a range of leftist and West African groups in the United Kingdom, among them the WASU, the League of Coloured Peoples, and individuals associated with the Communist Party of Great Britain.[75] Meanwhile, Padmore, representing the PAF, sought to reinforce the Britain-based pan-Africanists' connections to an array of Indian and other non-African anticolonial movements and organizations.[76] At the same time, Nkrumah and the WANS also coordinated events in protest of colonial policies in territories like Nigeria, British Cameroons, and South African–controlled South West Africa (Namibia).[77]

From the perspective of the new Labour Government in London, the demands for self-determination and self-government emanating from the Manchester Pan-African Congress and beyond mirrored many of those that had long characterized the Indian political scene. India's 1947 independence and its violent aftermath further intensified British (and other colonialist) concerns about the African political situation both on the continent and within its metropolitan expatriate communities.[78] Among the British, fears of external communist subversion, potential ethnic violence, and instability catalyzed by the actions and rhetoric of a set of assumed Westernized rabble-rousers typified much of the colonial response to Africans' postwar demands for self-government even as a reform ethos was on the rise within the Colonial Office.[79] It was only after events such as the 1948 Accra riots that colonial officials inside and outside the colonies more openly began to heed prominent wartime warnings that only via significant political, institutional, and constitutional reforms could Britain avoid the prospect of both local and international opposition to its rule in Africa.[80] Yet, as historian Hakim Adi has argued, Britain's desire to reassert itself as a world power, along with the challenges of the growing Cold War, thwarted its commitment to reform—at least to the levels demanded in Africa and elsewhere—and forced it to look even more to its colonies as it sought to rebuild itself both politically and economically.[81]

However, for many of the anticolonial activists who came out of the Manchester congress, any talk of reform simply did not go far enough. To them, it was the colonial system itself that was the problem, and it had to be abolished. It was this perspective that Nkrumah would seek to cultivate in the Gold Coast following his return, the same perspective that would color his own and his government's reading of Ghana's and Africa's place within the international community throughout the 1950s and 1960s. By 1951, as the CPP came to power in the Gold Coast's first popular elections, the open, strategically attention-seeking activism of the CPP's infancy appeared to give way to more deliberate and localized interventions and, increasingly, negotiations for self-government and industrial and infrastructural development, as will be examined in the following chapter. However, the sense of immediacy expressed in the postwar demands for self-government in Manchester, parts of the West African press, and the CPP's founding mission statement continued to make itself felt in discussions of the broader questions concerning the reach and structure of what was assumed to be the necessarily transformative processes of decolonization and nation-building. If, as Richard Wright argued in 1956, decolonization offered the world's newly independent states an opportunity to reflect on how best to reorganize the "HUMAN RACE," it was believed in the Gold Coast that soon-to-be Ghanaians had to enter into their own debates over the goals and values engrained in the personal, societal, and international transformations forged through those processes.[82] To this end, what the Manchester-inspired anticolonialism provided Nkrumah and the CPP with was a shared transnational language through which to challenge a world order founded upon the intersections of European liberalism and capitalist imperialism, and with which to also begin the process of imagining an alternative to that world order.

⎯

The world Kwame Nkrumah came of age in during the first decades of the twentieth century was ultimately one in which the colonial project of the nineteenth and early twentieth centuries was maturing into the international political system that would mark the world order of the first half of the twentieth century. However, from its earliest days, this was a world order that would be contested on multiple fronts within Africa and elsewhere. The wide variety of political and intellectual networks—colonial, metropolitan, and diasporic—that came to shape this opposition to colonial rule emerged as the political and intellectual training ground for the young Nkrumah. Through his readings, interactions, and at times direct participation in the interwar period's anticolonial circles, Nkrumah came to adapt the anticolonial worldview into the vision for what would become the ethos of Ghanaian nation-building that he would cultivate in the Gold Coast after his return. Moreover, many of the ideas and assumptions of the anticapitalist critiques of the colonial system in particular and its liberal ideological moorings more broadly would continue to buttress the future Ghanaian leader's and state's worldview and policies for much of the following two decades.

2 ～ From the Gold Coast to Ghana

Modernization and the Politics of Pan-African Nation-Building

> The peoples of the colonies know precisely what they want. They wish to be free and independent, to be able to feel themselves on an equal [footing?] with all other peoples and to work out their own destiny without outside interference and to be unrestricted to attain an advancement that will put them on a par with other technically advanced nations of the world.
>
> —Kwame Nkrumah, *Towards Colonial Freedom,* 1947[1]

IN DECEMBER 1947, Kwame Nkrumah returned to the Gold Coast at the invitation of the prominent Gold Coast barrister and nationalist J. B. Danquah. At Danquah's behest, Nkrumah was to serve as general secretary of the recently formed United Gold Coast Convention. However, even before Nkrumah's arrival, the Gold Coast press had already begun preaching the Nkroful-born politician's virtues, with the *Gold Coast Independent* advising its readers in October that "in him one finds all the qualities that make for greatness." The newspaper further predicted that in the coming years Nkrumah would "play a great role in the future of West Africa, there can be no doubt."[2] The buzz around Nkrumah only intensified following his return. As M. N. Tetteh—who more than a decade later would hold a variety of positions in the Nkrumah government, including in the Ghana Young Pioneers—recalled, few things had a greater influence on his life than the enthusiasm with which people spoke of this man who had come from abroad to bring "freedom" to the Gold Coast. Tetteh explained that, for him and his colleagues, all of whom were just schoolboys at the time, "You may not know the details of it [i.e., what freedom meant], but you were happy," for the word alone promised a better future. As a result, when Nkrumah came to Tetteh's hometown of Dodowa shortly after his arrival in the colony, Tetteh was among the students who snuck out of school to see the new general secretary of the United Gold Coast Convention (UGCC). Following Nkrumah's speech, Tetteh claims to have declared

49

his allegiance to the Gold Coast politician and, along with many of his fellow young people, undertook the mission of "spreading the gospel of Nkrumah's message" to anyone who would listen. "[We were] very young," Tetteh recounted, "without knowing much about, without understanding much about politics, but with enthusiasm, we were following him."[3]

Tetteh was far from alone in offering such a reflection on Nkrumah's impact on the Gold Coast political scene. Ben Nikoi-Oltai, who would join the CPP shortly after its July 1949 formation, presented a similar personal and national narrative. For him, the defining events of the CPP's early years were the party's February 1951 electoral victory and, even more importantly, Nkrumah's subsequent release from prison. As remembered by the long-time Accra resident, the CPP victory drew a crowd of Gold Coasters to James Fort Prison, where the government was holding Nkrumah on charges of sedition and inciting an illegal strike.[4] Nikoi-Oltai recalled how, after Nkrumah's release, the crowd shepherded Nkrumah across the colonial capital to the seat of government at Christiansborg Castle, where Nkrumah assumed the newly created position of leader of government business. For Nikoi-Oltai, who would maintain a place in the CPP rank and file until the 1966 coup, this procession across Accra was a defining moment both in his life and for the nation. "That day," the Accra shopkeeper proclaimed, "I saw whites running away for the first time."[5] Another longtime party member, Kofi Duku, echoed Nikoi-Oltai in a 2008 interview as he recounted how within "less than. . . an hour, [the courtyard in front of] James Fort Prison . . . a big space, was filled to capacity." Upon Nkrumah's release, Duku continued, "Men and women, children and children yet to be born, that means women carrying babies with cloth tied around their waists, [were] singing various songs [of] joy and happiness."[6]

The victory that swept Nkrumah and the CPP to power was nothing short of profound. In the Legislative Assembly, the CPP won thirty-four of the body's thirty-eight contested seats, while the imprisoned CPP leader officially received more than fourteen times as many votes as his nearest rival in his Accra electoral district.[7] Following the election, control over the Gold Coast would officially remain in British hands for the next six years. However, as the leader of government business and, from 1952 on, prime minister, Nkrumah, along with the young CPP, gained wide-reaching powers over the colony's internal affairs. This included the establishment of their own cabinet and the relative freedom to pursue a legislative agenda seen as ushering in a broader program of political, social, economic, and infrastructural modernization. At its most foundational, this program aimed to incorporate key aspects of the Manchester radicalism Nkrumah and others brought from abroad in an attempted re-envisioning of the social, cultural, and even physical makeup of the Gold Coast itself. Governmental and constitutional affairs, the CPP argued, even including self-government, could only go so far. The real issue now was how to transform the colonial Gold Coast and the people who populated it into a modern nation.

This chapter details the construction of the burgeoning Nkrumahist vision for an emergent postcolonial Ghana in the context of the 1950s independence negotiations. This was a period in which, for many Gold Coasters and especially those aligned with the CPP, eventual independence appeared a foregone conclusion. At the same time, the actual path to it remained unclear, and, by the mid-1950s, looked increasingly messy as a number of formal and informal resistance movements emerged within the colony. Key to this period, then, was a complex set of local and national negotiations in which Nkrumah, the CPP, and the British each sought to balance their own interests and ambitions for the future Ghana with those of the many competing constituencies that composed the Gold Coast more broadly. For the CPP itself, the liminal nature of this period of shared governance offered an opportunity for the new government as it sought to securely begin building its future Ghana along the lines of the modern, ordered, urban, industrial, and cosmopolitan society that would serve as the idealized hallmark of official Nkrumahism for much of the next decade and a half. As a result, on the governmental level, the early and mid-1950s were a period of near-unprecedented investment and experimentation in fields ranging from education and healthcare to architecture and urban planning as the CPP set out to define the social and infrastructural parameters of modern African life.

As this chapter also shows, the responses to the CPP's actions were far from uniform. Rather, the CPP's efforts ushered in a variety of complicated local and regional reactions as diverse groups of soon-to-be Ghanaians negotiated their own desires and expectations for decolonization-era modernization in relation to all that was lost in the often all-encompassing nature of the CPP's plans and paths toward implementation. More than the remnants of an antiquated politics that most in the CPP and many outside observers presented them as, the localized and regional opposition movements (formal and informal) that arose against the CPP during the 1950s often countered the CPP's modernist imagination with their own alternative visions for the Gold Coast's/Ghana's future. In doing so, they frequently drew upon a range of historical, intellectual, and cultural traditions with much deeper roots than anything the CPP could provide. Writing on the Asante-led National Liberation Movement, for instance, historian Jean Allman has argued that many of these movements could even be read as nationalisms unto themselves.[8] However, even more may be seen as going on within these movements when they are juxtaposed with the CPP's developing Nkrumahist worldview. Not only did they compete with the dominant visions for the future put forward by the CPP, but they also often embedded within their own historically and culturally specific visions divergent strands of nationalism, internationalism, and modernization that at times resembled Nkrumahism, yet adapted to local realities. In this respect, the debates and often bitter and violent conflicts that emerged in the Gold Coast politics of the 1950s both challenged the CPP's increasingly centralized vision of Ghana's postcolonial future and represented a political eclecticism that, during the first decade of self-rule, an ever more orthodox Nkrumahism would long struggle to weed out.

MODERNIZATION AND PRE-INDEPENDENCE NKRUMAHIST COSMOPOLITANISM

From its founding, the CPP's agenda for the Gold Coast/Ghana was by definition ambitious. As Nkrumah detailed in his 1947 pamphlet *Towards Colonial Freedom,* he believed that, for any colonial territory, self-government was only part of the equation. At most, it opened the path for the more fundamental emancipation that would come with economic liberation and the quest for a form of self-determination that freed the colonized from the grips of capitalist imperialism. At an even more foundational level for a party still in formation, the emotion embedded within the call for self-government offered an unprecedented tool for mobilization. For the more measured politicians of the UGCC and its successor parties in the early 1950s, the CPP's appeals to emotion regularly proved a source of substantial frustration.[9] Nkrumah and the CPP, however, saw strength in their ability to envelop themselves in the anger, enthusiasm, and anticipation of the populace as they employed the message of self-government in the task of political organization. For them, the language of self-government became a mechanism through which to channel the party's ambitions through an array of popular aspirations and frustrations connected to Gold Coasters' everyday struggles. In the party press as well as in rallies, meetings, and other political and social events, the CPP in turn peppered its abstract anticolonial rhetoric with reflections on the daily plights of Gold Coasters seeking such forms of relief as access to schooling, employment, and pathways out of an economic reality defined by stagnating wages and hyperinflation.[10]

Not dissimilar to the model employed by the Rassemblement Démocratique Africain (RDA) in Guinea, the CPP of the late 1940s and early 1950s sought to create an overarching multiethnic and socially diverse umbrella under which to organize the populace.[11] Again, as with the Guinean RDA and, in East Africa, the Tanganyika African National Union (TANU), women and especially market women stood at the heart of the CPP's mass support, transmitting the party's message via song, dance, dress, and other popular and socially democratic means of communication.[12] The party, for its part, responded in kind with regular coverage in its rallies and press of issues it deemed of particular concern to women. In doing so, its women writers, especially, used the party press to gin up enthusiasm for the party around issues including market struggles, education and employment for women, and the state and quality of women's activism within the party infrastructure.[13] Meanwhile, female-centered spaces like the markets allowed for the further rapid spread of the party's message. Reflecting back on the early years of the CPP in his *Nkrumah and the Ghana Revolution* (1977), C. L. R. James thus recalled not simply the centrality of women in the CPP's mobilizing efforts, but, more importantly, the power they held. "The market," the Trinidadian recounted, "was a great centre of gossip, of news and of discussion. Where in many undeveloped communities the women are a drag upon their menfolk, these women, although to a large extent illiterate, were a dynamic element in the population, active, well-informed, acute, and always at the very centre of events." To the Marxist James, they, not the educated of the party, drove the CPP's agenda. As a result, he matter-of-factly asserted, "In the struggle for independence one market-woman in Accra, and there were fifteen thousand of them, was worth any dozen Achimota graduates"—of which Nkrumah was one.[14]

Joining the colony's women in the CPP were similarly significant groups of youth, farmers, and workers. As with M. N. Tetteh, who joined the Nkrumahist wing of the UGCC in 1948 and later the CPP, the Gold Coast's young people tended to be attracted to the excitement surrounding the new party. In time, they began their own deliberations on what the CPP and its message meant and promised in terms of the prospects for their own futures. As with other constituencies, this included schooling and employment following their education as well as personal and social independence from their elders. Others like Kofi Duku—who, after leaving school in the late 1940s, had bounced from one location to another in the western and central Gold Coast before settling in Accra—spoke in an interview of the sense of community and belonging that the party provided him amidst the din of the postwar colony.[15] Meanwhile, farmers turned to the CPP out of opposition to many of the colonial government's agricultural policies. For cocoa farmers specifically, the onslaught of swollen shoot disease—a fatal virus infecting cocoa trees—in the colony's oldest cocoa-growing regions, followed by the government's decision to cut down blighted trees, threatened the livelihood of thousands.[16] The CPP, for its part, with its vocal opposition to the government's forced eradication campaign, appeared to be a means by which the affected farmers as well as those who feared the disease's spread could gain a voice on the national stage. As a result, historian Francis Danquah notes, farmers' groups had by late 1950 begun sponsoring CPP candidates in preparation for the 1951 election.[17]

In seeking to address the concerns of nearly all of its major constituencies, the CPP positioned the colonial government as unable and unwilling to meet its obligations to its subject population. Indirect rule and similar methods of governance, the party contended, were specifically designed to leave Gold Coasters, as with other colonial peoples, in a state of dependence and unprepared for the modern world.[18] The day-to-day mission of the CPP, then, at least from the perspective of the party's local emissaries, was to establish the social and institutional framework necessary to both meet the needs and expectations of its varying constituencies and prepare these constituencies with the tools required of a modern society. When, for instance, a group of secondary school students in Cape Coast were expelled for striking in opposition to the 1948 arrest of Nkrumah and other UGCC leaders, the Nkrumahist wing of the UGCC began establishing a set of schools of its own, catering to the colony's politically active youth. The first of these schools opened in Cape Coast in July 1948. Over the next several years, the Nkrumahist wing—over the objections of the UGCC's broader leadership—and later the CPP would found one to two dozen similar institutions throughout the southern Gold Coast.[19]

For the CPP, education served both an ideological and a practical purpose. No other issue more fundamentally represented the hopes and ambitions of both the individual and the nation as a whole than education. To the CPP, though, colonial education was a sphere deeply fraught with contradiction. As articulated in 1949 by the Nkrumah-founded *Accra Evening News*, it was where "you see Imperialism almost at its worst." Hailing access to schools as "the greatest liberating force," the newspaper chastised the colonial government for what it considered to be the rationing of education. The most notable method by which this was done was through the imposition of an array of school fees on students and their families so that only a limited number of students could afford to attend. Relatedly, the *Evening News* also questioned the government's decision not to make schooling compulsory for all of the Gold Coast's children, especially at the primary level. It was these types of decisions, the newspaper insisted, that explained a literacy rate in the colony of only ten percent, and a situation where both parents and children were desperate for greater access to schooling at all levels. "Parents want to send their children to school," the *Evening News* argued, "but cannot get admission for them. Children cry to go to school but cry in vain, for there is no accommodation for them. In the face of this the Education Department is absolutely helpless and hopeless in trying to cope with the position. It draws up a Ten Year Educational Development Plan and the whole thing is a complete washout."[20]

Following the CPP's initial electoral victory, the new government thus catapulted education to the top of its legislative agenda, announcing in early 1951 its plans for the implementation of fee-free primary education in the colony beginning in January 1952.[21] As detailed in the government's report on educational development, "The aim of the course [primary school education] will be to provide a sound foundation for citizenship with permanent literacy in both English and the vernacular. On completion of such a primary course," the report continued, "children will be ready to proceed to one of varying types of course in the next stage of their education, according to their aptitudes and abilities."[22] Over the next several years, the CPP's waiving of (most) school fees led to a rapid increase in enrollments in the colony's primary schools. In the six years between 1951 and Ghana's 1957 independence, for instance, enrollments at the primary and middle school levels soared in the colony from approximately 220,000 students to more than 570,000. The number of primary schools also grew, rising from approximately 1,000 in 1951 to over 3,400 in 1957, while the number of middle schools (senior-primary schools pre-1952) went from 600 to 900.[23] Additionally, increases at the primary and middle school levels spilled over to secondary school enrollments, which more than tripled, rising from a modest 2,937 students in 1951 to just under 10,000 in 1957.[24]

Increased enrollments, however, were not enough for the CPP in the advancement of its educational program. As elsewhere, education carried with it a range of intersecting political and social agendas. Among some in the colony's local and expatriate anticolonial circles, a two-dimensional picture of the colonial educational system emerged. Writing, for instance, in his 1954 account of his previous year's travels in the Gold Coast, Richard Wright flattened the complexities of Gold Coast colonial education and the histories of its alumni into little more than a prescribed set of programs designed to "guarantee that the educated young African would side with the British."[25] As exhibited in aspects of the *Evening News*'s coverage of the colony's educational system, the party press at times appeared to sympathize with such portrayals of Gold Coast colonial education, praising instead the new opportunities opened by the Nkrumah-linked schools for both social mobility and for the cultivation of new political loyalties.[26] Many Ghanaians themselves evoked not entirely dissimilar critiques of the colonial-era educational system during the period and beyond, arguing that it was clear that a change to the colony's educational system was needed at the time. During a 2008 interview, for instance, longtime Accra resident N. Sifah, who was generally ambivalent about Nkrumah and the CPP's legacy in Ghana, praised Nkrumah specifically for recognizing the deficiencies of colonial education and seeing that the "traditional schools—Achimota, Mfantsipim, and so on—were not enough."[27]

Technological and scientific education was of particular importance to the educational revolution the CPP envisioned for the aspiring country. As the government would argue well into the 1960s, it was only via the attainment of the skills and knowledge embedded within a technically and scientifically oriented curriculum that the decolonizing Gold Coast could produce a citizenry equipped to meet the demands of nation-building.[28] As a result, as outlined in its 1951 development plan, the new government emphasized the need for the extension of technical and trade education in the colony, focusing on subjects including "technology, agricultural science, commerce and industry." Furthermore, opportunities to study in these new programs were to be open to students of both sexes.[29] Even in the comparatively resource-poor Northern Territories, the plan also touted a commitment to scientific education in the region, emphasizing the recent installation of "science laboratories" in a new secondary school in Tamale. At the same time, the plan promised the construction of additional secondary schools in the region once more students became available.[30] Meanwhile, on the national stage, an emphasis on student scholarships in fields including engineering and medicine would accompany the country's enrollment numbers in the CPP's 1957 presentation of its educational achievements.[31] Four years later, the CPP would further commit to the centrality of technological and scientific learning in Ghanaian schools as the postcolonial government sought (ultimately unsuccessfully) to turn the country's educational system on its head by attempting to transform the classroom into a site of experiential, hands-on learning.[32]

The CPP's attention to the Gold Coast's/Ghana's educational system had direct links to its broader and much more visible plan for the colony's/country's architectural and infrastructural landscape, especially in its urban centers. In many of the colony's cities and towns, the urban population boom of the early and mid-twentieth century had accentuated existing social and economic tensions, particularly over issues of land. In Accra, which witnessed its population triple in the first third of the twentieth century and then double again by 1949, the effects of nineteenth-century land reforms designed to commoditize land collided with the rapid migration of the interwar and postwar periods.[33] As a result, land values in the city ballooned in the decade following the war. By 1955, for instance, some areas of the city were seeing a more than 350 percent increase in land values over their 1947 levels. The commercial sector endured even more drastic increases as land values nearly quintupled over the eight-year period.[34] For the city's traditional Ga residents, often priced out of this new land market, frustrations with the city's changing urban landscape mounted throughout much of the 1940s and early 1950s as migration to the urban center intensified.[35]

The CPP aimed to transcend the local concerns driving Accra's urban politics with a vision of a new, international Accra replete with modern infrastructure, architecture, housing, offices, and industry. By the time of the country's independence celebrations, new venues such as the famed Ambassador Hotel, the Accra Library, and the State House dotted the city's modernizing landscape.[36] Also, as architectural historian Mark Crinson has detailed, during the buildup to independence, the Gold Coast Public Works Department commissioned the British architectural firm Fry, Drew, Drake & Lasdun for the planning of a national museum, which opened in 1957. Moreover, the museum itself was part of a broader planned cultural district outside the city's established commercial and residential neighborhoods that included the newly developed Accra Technical Institute, the YWCA, and the National Archives as well as an anticipated science museum.[37] Meanwhile, planning for the architecturally modernist Accra Community Centre, which in 1958 would house the first All-African Peoples' Conference, and, in later years, the administrative offices of the Ghana Young Pioneers, also began in the mid-1950s.[38]

Similar, but often smaller-scale projects were undertaken in other major cities as well, including Kumasi, which saw the construction and expansion of a new bank, a post office, and a hospital during the period.[39]

Likewise, east of Accra in the small fishing town of Tema and just north of the Volta River town of Atimpoku, the promise of planned cities complemented the modernist re-envisioning of the Gold Coast's more established urban centers. Tema, for its part, largely represented a blank slate for the CPP and its allies. Constructed to house the country's planned industrial harbor and serve as the burgeoning country's industrial center, it was to be the city of the future. Housing and commerce were to develop in carefully defined neighborhood units with envisioned populations of between three and five thousand people. According to Keith Jopp, writing in a 1961 pamphlet promoting the government's plans for the city, the size and structure of these neighborhood units were to be a reflection of "a typical Ghanaian village." Groups of four neighborhood units were in turn to make up individual "communities"—each with a population of twelve to fifteen thousand residents—within the larger city. Each community was to have its own banks, schools, churches, shops, and services, including clinics, nurseries, and entertainment.[40] Through its structure and layout, Tema was thus to be the living embodiment of the emerging Nkrumahist worldview, as it provided the new Ghana an ordered, disciplined, and methodically planned urban center through which not only the nation's industrial development could flow, but also its civic productivity. Even more importantly, the city's new industrial harbor, which began operations in 1962, was to be Ghana's and, more broadly, West Africa's connection to the broader global economy via a newly established, African-controlled production and export network.[41]

At least in terms of its growth rate, Tema did not disappoint in the 1950s and 1960s. Transforming from a small fishing town of approximately two thousand residents in 1948, the city and surrounding area had a population of more than twenty-five thousand by the country's 1960 census and just under one hundred thousand by 1970.[42] Jopp even went so far as to predict a potential population of more than two hundred thousand for the new city.[43] Catalyzing Tema's growth, geographer David Hilling notes, was the establishment of the city as "Ghana's foremost industrial region, with an aluminium smelter, steel works, shipyard, oil refinery and a wide range of consumer goods industries (cigarettes, textiles, radios, soap, paints, footwear, motor vehicles, [and] foodstuffs)."[44] Meanwhile, in Akosombo Township—Ghana's other major planned city—the growth rate never rivaled that of its coastal and industrial neighbor, yet the ambitions for the township were no less lofty. The CPP envisioned a city with a population of between thirty and fifty thousand residents replete with such urban conveniences as a cinema, a hospital, an international hotel, and a community center.[45] By 1963, though, the township had only one school, which, as historian Stephan Miescher relates, was primarily open only to the administering Volta River Authority's expatriate staff and senior Ghanaian officials.[46] Additional concerns over sanitation, unemployment, stray animals, squatting, and the growth of neighboring slums came to plague not just Akosombo but also Tema in the second half of the twentieth century.[47] Regardless, together with Accra, both Tema and Akosombo were to help form what the CPP envisioned as Ghana's "new Industrial Triangle."[48]

With their focus on clean lines and utilitarian spaces, these new and renewed cities were to provide the physical manifestation of the Nkrumahist worldview in the construction of the new Ghana, blending what architect Jane Drew described as "a loose westernized pattern, perhaps more like that of California than Europe," with the organic and localized ambitions of a burgeoning independent Africa.[49] As art historian Janet Hess has argued, for the CPP, the Gold Coast's urban transformation was to serve as a visible, permanent showcase of the broader social and cultural revolution of the CPP-led nation-building project.[50] Ghanaian urban spaces— through their modern amenities, the designs of their buildings, their grids in the case of the planned cities, and their inclusiveness—were thus to emerge not only as icons of an emerging African modernity, but also as the transnational hubs of a burgeoning postcolonial African cosmopolitanism. These cities were very much ideological projects. As such, they were

FIGURE 2.1. Marching with the times. *Source: Evening News,* 6 March 1957.

to be the sites of Ghanaian pan-Africanism, welcoming and catering to everyone from ethnically and religiously diverse groups of Ghanaians and other Africans to international dignitaries, tourists, activists, and expatriates. It was in these settings that Ghanaians and others were to create, as described by Nate Plageman, the "new shared experiences of belonging" required for independence.[51]

NKRUMAHIST MODERNIZATION AND ITS DISCONTENTS

The rising economic fortunes of the colony during the 1950s helped drive the CPP's massive investment in educational and infrastructural development. What in the 1940s had been an economy constrained by stagnating wages and runaway inflation had, by the mid-1950s, become one reinvigorated by skyrocketing cocoa prices, which in turn injected unprecedented levels of new revenue into the late-colonial economy. By the 1954–55 fiscal year, for instance, the government-run Cocoa Marketing Board, which oversaw the colony's cocoa sales, enjoyed export proceeds that had nearly doubled their 1947–48 levels, topping out at £G77.5 million.[52] Additional contributions to the Gold Coast coffers came from the colony's mining industry. From the 1950–51 to the 1951–52 fiscal year alone, the colony's mining exports increased by nearly £6.5 million to a total value of £23 million.[53] Moreover, as historian Robert Tignor points out, Gold Coasters themselves—who enjoyed a per capita income double that of their Nigerian counterparts—were among the wealthiest Africans on the continent.[54] As a result, by the early 1950s many inside and outside of Africa had begun to argue that nowhere on the continent was there a better testing ground for the prospects of African modernization than in the Gold Coast. More importantly, such arguments, as part of the flourishing anticolonial politics of the period, not only had a receptive audience among the various stakeholders on the colony's political scene, they also directly connected a still nascent Nkrumahist worldview to a broader transnational discourse of large-scale development, with strands connecting Afro-Asian anticolonialism, American and Soviet Cold War interests, United Nations planning schemes, and imperial decolonization politics.[55] As such, for Nkrumah and many within the CPP, large-scale industrial development stood at the core of the postcolonial society they envisioned, providing the bedrock upon which all else was to be built.

However, even as the CPP-led government enjoyed this period of economic growth, concerns over the increasingly central role of foreign capital and technical expertise in the Gold Coast's modernization agenda increasingly worked their way into segments of the party infrastructure and especially Nkrumah's cadre of expatriate advisors. In the case of Tema, for instance, George Padmore, who had recently completed a short trip to the Gold Coast, wrote to Nkrumah in November 1951 in order to strongly caution him against putting too much faith in the British firm—Halcrow and Partners—commissioned to advance the harbor project. In doing so, Padmore resurrected the specters of the multilayered states of political and economic dependency that had marked the Gold Coast's colonial history and, just as importantly, of the postwar economic struggles and imperial neglect for their basic needs (namely in terms of housing and water) that many Gold Coasters believed had caused them hardship. Padmore thus counseled the CPP leader that his immediate attention foremost should be in resolving these issues before embarking upon the potentially fool-hardy plan to construct—via British (imperialist) assistance—something as ambitious as an industrial harbor.[56] In another instance, Padmore em-phasized the need for an indigenous Gold Coast production source of its own for the colony's urban development, namely in terms of the construc-tion and maintenance of the colony's many new schools, dispensaries, post offices, community centers, and housing options. The "real opposition" to the CPP, Padmore advised a Nkrumah still recovering from the colony's recent electoral battles was "not the Danquahs, who are helpless." Rather, he proclaimed, it was "the white officials," who he believed were con-stantly devising new ways to continue to exert their will on the decoloniz-ing colony.[57]

The political realities that Nkrumah and the CPP government faced in the late-colonial Gold Coast were, however, much more complicated than the abstractions outlined by Padmore suggested. In practical terms, the Gold Coast simply did not have the economic and technical resources necessary to independently pursue the government's grandiose develop-ment agenda. Just in terms of labor, the government's development plans required a complicated mix of skilled and unskilled labor to undertake the construction phase of any particular project. Even before construction began, though, the government also required the labor, know-how, and resources of specialized architectural and engineering firms to research and design the project. No such firms with the capabilities of working at the scale demanded by the CPP's development projects existed in the Gold Coast.[58] Additionally, the CPP had to negotiate its own tenuous posi-tion within the context of the late-colonial political system. As a radical,

African-led government ultimately operating within the British-run colonial state, both Nkrumah and the CPP had to balance their own anti-colonial desires with their need to be seen as legitimate and responsible political actors by a colonial apparatus that, prior to the CPP's electoral victory, had—among other things—portrayed the Nkrumah-led party as an "extreme Nationalist group" engaged in acts of "lawlessness."[59] Even more significantly, the CPP had to face a populace with often widely divergent ideas of what Nkrumahist modernization could and should mean for them, especially when its transformations encroached upon their daily lives and belief systems.

It was in Tema where the CPP faced its first major challenge to its modernization agenda following the CPP government's proposal to relocate the current fishing town to make way for the new harbor and industrial city. As noted earlier, the Tema project was intended to be a cornerstone of the CPP's developmentalist agenda, only rivalled by the nearly contemporaneous Volta River Project. From the perspective of the CPP, the result of the project was not simply to be the material construction of a harbor and city. It was also to embody the procedural nature of the decolonization process itself for the emergent country. At one level, it was to represent one of the colony's pathways toward the economic self-determination demanded by Nkrumahist conceptions of national and continental independence, as it promised a future driven by economic self-sufficiency and national and international interconnection. Moreover, in its order, newness, and grandiosity, the Tema project also represented for many in the CPP a Ghanaian future liberated from the baggage of history that many saw as afflicting other parts of the colony. Through Tema, the government thus envisioned the creation of a living embodiment of the new Ghana, forged out of what many viewed as relative nothingness. For, as one group of social surveyors explained in 1966, prior to the government's 1952 announcement of its plans to build in Tema, the ethnically Ga town was for all intents and purposes "an almost forgotten and insignificant fishing village."[60]

As a community, however, Tema's residents understood the town as having a deep and important history, one that dated back to the sixteenth century. As with the communities that came to comprise Accra and other nearby towns like Teshie and Nungua, Tema represented one of the original seven Ga coastal communities, which oral tradition held were established after a Ga migration from the east.[61] In the centuries that followed, Tema and its fellow Ga towns periodically served as coastal trading ports for nearby Akwamu before their nineteenth-century integration into the British colonial state.[62] By the twentieth century, most of Tema's residents were engaged in the fishing industry in some fashion. In most cases, men took their chances in the canoes, while women generally smoked the fish and sold it in the markets or inland.[63] Small-scale farming supplemented the livelihoods of many of the town's residents. However, in contrast to those working the agriculturally richer land further inland, the Tema Ga never directly reaped the benefits of the Gold Coast cocoa revolution of the late nineteenth and early twentieth centuries. Instead, the area became known foremost for the production of local crops, initially calabash. By the early 1950s, tomatoes would bring the greatest profits into the area aside from fishing.[64] Meanwhile, in terms of population, the interwar and postwar years proved to be periods of growth in the town, with the population nearly doubling between 1937 and 1948 and doubling again over the next four years. As a result, by 1952 the town had grown to nearly four thousand residents.[65]

As the CPP proceeded with the planned Tema project in the early 1950s, the government entered into a complicated political and cultural environment, particularly as it related to questions of land and land ownership. Not unlike elsewhere in the Gold Coast, individuals rarely had direct rights of ownership over Ga lands. Instead, they usually only possessed a range of usufructuary rights over the lands to which they gained access. Even then, the types of social and productive activities in which they could engage on the land were also often circumscribed.[66] However, what tended to distinguish Ga notions of land ownership from those of many of their Akan neighbors inland were the limitations placed upon even a chieftaincy's, or stool's, authority over the land. In contrast with many Akan, Tema stool holders' authority over the land was largely indirect, with much of it being filtered through the broader local Ga power structure. Most importantly, this included the town's priests, who in many ways served as custodians of the land for the gods.[67] As a result, at least at the abstract level, it was the community's gods who maintained direct ownership rights over the land. As delineated by colonial anthropologist Margaret Field, these gods foundationally inhabited the land and the various topographical features that dotted it. The gods in turn could not be dislocated or alienated from the land, therefore making it impossible to permanently and irrevocably transfer ownership to another entity, as would be required by the Tema project. As such, the use and maintenance of the land carried with it a meaning that transcended the economic or even the social. Instead, it reflected a necessary negotiation, the purposes of which included the preservation of an equilibrium in the community's relationships with both the physical and spiritual worlds.[68]

Thus, Tema itself was traditionally defined through its connection to the spiritual beings inhabiting the land in and around the town. Moreover, as with the region's other Ga communities, the lagoons surrounding the area further provided the town its cultural and spiritual meaning.[69] Two lagoons—Sakumo to the west and Chemu to the east—bookended the town. As outlined by Field, it was in Sakumo Lagoon that the town's most influential god (Sakumɔ) resided. As Tema's "senior god," Sakumɔ presided over the village's annual feast (Kpledzo) in which the community celebrated that it had "lived through another year."[70] Through Kpledzo, the intimacy of the bond between the spiritual world and the land further comes to the fore. At its most foundational level, Sakumɔ's ushering in of Kpledzo marked the arrival of the April and May rains and the beginning of the agricultural season. Just as importantly, though, it also initiated the first of a series of festivities, continuing through August, that would pay tribute to the coming "transfig[uration]," as Field has it, of the earth brought by the rains. This included the new fertility bestowed upon the land by the rains as well as the new resources provided by rising water levels in the lagoons.[71] As a result, for the community's Ga residents, to be Tema-born meant to be from this specific place between these two lagoons and to be in observance of this cyclical process connecting the land to the town's spiritual roots and fortunes going forward. As such, the community's relationship to this particular place was said to be so powerful, one of the government's social surveyors noted, that Tema-born Ga faced an interdiction against residing outside of the town's traditional and spiritual lands between the lagoons.[72]

At its foundation, therefore, the CPP's planned development of the area surrounding Tema threatened the Tema Ga's connection to their historical and spiritual roots. In order to make room for the planned harbor and particularly the new industrial city, the government announced a resettlement scheme that would move the town approximately two miles to the east, just beyond the confines of Chemu Lagoon. In Tema, debates immediately began over whether it was even possible for the community to move, as certain residents argued that many deities—especially those tied to specific sites, like Sakumɔ to his lagoon—could not be dislocated from their homes.[73] Others, as detailed by government welfare officer G. W. Amarteifio and anthropologist David Butcher, argued that, even if it were possible to move the gods (those Field calls "place-god[s]"), no one had the ritual knowledge necessary for doing so.[74] The sheer number of gods in the area further complicated the discussions, with Amarteifio and Butcher estimating that as many as 220 gods were recognized in Tema at the time. Furthermore, the social surveyors reported that, in the eyes of many in the community, all of these deities would have to be relocated from the land as part of the town's proposed resettlement.[75]

Regardless, the CPP quickly moved to acquire the land. For the government, the project required its full ownership of the Tema land as well as significant parts of the surrounding area. As one February 1952 cabinet memorandum explained, the government sought to obtain "not only the area of the port and the site of the actual township [i.e., the industrial city], but also a surrounding agricultural belt or open space which would be used for market gardening, firewood plantations and the like." From the perspective of the government, such a move—indicative of the search for order and clearly demarcated spaces pursued in other midcentury planned cities—was central to its vision of an emerging postcolonial society, as the CPP aimed to thwart later, likely inevitable attempts at "uncoordinated development [i.e., slums] immediately adjoining the town."[76] As a result, by the middle of the year the CPP would bring before the Legislative Assembly a bill allowing the government to take possession of approximately sixty-three square miles of land in and around Tema, while proposing compensation of £10,000 or 3 percent of the land's value for the people of Tema.[77] On 1 July, the bill passed the Legislative Assembly.[78] Shortly thereafter, the government undertook the first of what would be several social surveys of Tema and the surrounding area, the result of which was a proposed resettlement scheme in which the government would provide twenty new housing units of ninety-five rooms each at the relocation site.[79] After this scheme proved unworkable, the government altered its plan, proposing instead a new resettlement community (Tema Manhean, or Tema New Town) comprised of large circular and semicircular compounds, with individual housing units. As detailed by architect David Whitham, each compound was to "contain a total of forty to fifty rooms."[80]

Despite the series of concessions that the Gold Coast government attempted to make in the relocation scheme, persistent protests would plague the government's actions in Tema. Even as early as the government's initial land acquisition efforts in 1952, key figures in the Legislative Assembly disputed the fairness of requiring the people of Tema to give up their lands to the Gold Coast government in perpetuity. As William Ofori Atta of the Ghana Congress Party (GCP) maintained, the requirement that any stool cede its lands "absolutely and permanently" did not appear to be "in accordance with Gold Coast customary law."[81] Ofori Atta, J. B. Danquah's nephew and the son of the former king of Akyem Abuakwa, did not stop there. Rather, he further suggested that, when considering all of the constituencies with claims on Tema's lands, Tema's chiefs and even the people of Tema did not have the authority to sell the land to the government. Instead, he argued that they were simply holding it "in trust" for not only the village's present residents and future generations but also "their ancestors who are dead."[82] Nii Kwabena Bonne II, the Accra chief and businessman who had orchestrated the famed 1948 Accra boycott, echoed Ofori Atta in his own remarks in the Legislative Assembly. For Nii Bonne, though, the key concern was what he interpreted as the shortsightedness of contemporary agreements ceding stool lands to a government that "has been in power only 18 months." As he pointed out, "generations unborn will depend upon the land," and such a hasty decision to force a sale of the land had the potential of mistaking and/or neglecting their future needs.[83] Still others portrayed the entire Tema project as an elaborate waste of money.[84]

In Tema itself, initial opposition to the CPP government's plans centered on accusations that the government had defrauded the community. Approximately a week after the Legislative Assembly passed the land acquisition bill, the chiefs of Tema and neighboring Nungua and Kpone complained that the government had not consulted them prior to bringing the bill before the assembly. The Tema mantse (paramount chief) went so far as to accuse the CPP's minister of housing, A. Ansah Koi, of attempting to "prejudice the Tema Stool and people in their fight to maintain their right to live on their God-given land." He also rejected claims by certain government ministers that the area's chiefs had paid off opposition figures like Ofori Atta "in order to champion their cause in the Assembly."[85] By early August, though, the Tema mantse would soften his position as he offered his consent to the sale of the harbor land and the leasing of the land necessary for the industrial city.[86] However, in doing so, he unleashed a wave of popular protests in the town against both the government and the chief, as priests, youth, and market women challenged the authority of the chief to transfer ownership of the land—with all that it entailed culturally, economically, and spiritually—to "strangers." The protests culminated in an attempted populist destoolment of the chief and assertions from many members of the community that under no circumstances would they leave their homes and traditional lands.[87] As one longtime Tema resident, Samuel Kofi Kotey, recalled, the Tema mantse had lost his legitimacy among many in the community, as the protesters accused him of "collect[ing] some money from the government" and forsaking his responsibilities to Tema.[88]

The protests in Tema would go on for much of the next seven years. In order to try and assuage the community, the government regularly sought to amend its compensation packages with promises of a new fishing beach, rent-free farm lands with seventy-five-year leases, and, for some, cash payments.[89] As Peter Du Sautoy—who for much of the period headed the Gold Coast's Department of Social Welfare—argued, the government believed it was doing everything it could to ensure an orderly, respectful, and mutually beneficial resettlement.[90] Regardless, suspicions abounded. Meanwhile, over the course of the 1950s new groups continuously arrived in the area in anticipation of the job opportunities associated with the construction of the new harbor and industrial city. The result was a ballooning population that reached approximately ten thousand by the end of the decade, further exacerbating tensions within Tema itself and between the Tema-born Ga and the government.[91] As Du Sautoy contends, these "newcomers" established illegal housing units and shacks that would ultimately have to be removed. Moreover, they also constituted a new population, which did not have clear rights to the compensation programs offered by the government and would thus eventually have to be relocated.[92]

It was not until 1959 that the CPP completed the resettlement of Tema, much later than anticipated and, finally, only largely via the threat of force. In the end, even the most adamant resisters of relocation took up homes in Tema Manhean. As Kotey (who was born in the old town but grew up in Tema Manhean) recounted, the government's decision to resort to force offered even the most virulent protesters little choice but to retreat. According to him, "they planned to stay, but when the Caterpillar [bulldozers] came, the machine began breaking the houses before they [the protesters] could run to the town here" and attempt to claim one of the new homes.[93] Another longtime Tema resident, Seth Laryea Tettey, recalled the emotions of the move. "So 1952, they prepared to settle the indigenes, our fathers and mothers, from that side [between the lagoons] to this side [Tema Manhean], and so finally in 1959, we were relocated here." For a people who in his estimation had lived in the area for "four or five hundred years," such a move was not an easy one. "When you go," he exclaimed, "you want to come back."[94] Meanwhile, priests and families undertook the complicated work of extricating the community from the land. This included attempts to identify graves, the undertaking of an elaborate ceremony presided over by the high priest of Sakumɔ to dissolve the community's "great oath not to move," and the unveiling of additional ceremonies aimed at appeasing the gods of the lagoons as well as the ancestors and other spirits.[95]

NEGOTIATING MODERNIZATION

Due in part to the ambition of the planned development and in part to the protests that accompanied it, Tema—both the relocated old town and the new industrial city—became a high-profile symbol of Nkrumahist modernization and, in turn, a subject of keen interest for observers both inside and outside the Gold Coast throughout the 1950s and well into the 1960s. During this same period it also emerged as a site for numerous academic and government-sponsored social surveys.[96] In the eyes of those looking at Tema in the 1950s and 1960s, the conflicts surrounding the resettlement involved issues not unfamiliar to other localities and even world regions caught in the midst of mid-twentieth-century modernization. For such observers, the community's strong and persistent affinity to its traditional lands and all that they contained and involved represented a clash between the interests of that community and the pressures of an encroaching modernity. Many in turn proposed that the overarching question in Tema—as elsewhere—was that of how to negotiate the human dimensions of these transitions in the face of the development needs of the country. Writing, for instance, in the foreword to government welfare officer G. W. Amarteifio and his colleagues' 1966 study of the Tema resettlement experience, the German architect Otto Koenigsberger described the problems afflicting Tema as indicative of those vexing modernizing projects worldwide, with their technocratic blind spot for human concerns. "The nations of Africa and Asia refer with justifiable pride to the many large water-storage projects and artificial lakes created since the war. Much publicity has been given to the resettlement of animals from these areas, yet how small," he reflected, "is the number of publications on the human resettlement problems that must have arisen as a direct consequence of these projects."[97]

Such an emphasis on the human concerns of resettlement guided Amarteifio's and his coauthors' social survey—still the most important of those produced in the period—and their keen interest in the religious and spiritual dimensions of the opposition to the resettlement scheme. As

Amarteifio's contribution to the study details, opposition to resettlement largely arose out of a group of youth, market women, and, of particular importance to Amarteifio's team, priests. As with the arguments put forward by some in the Legislative Assembly, most notably Ofori Atta, the protesters insisted on a delineation of the discrete types of rights to the land possessed by different groups within the community: the living, the ancestral, and the divine. In many ways aligned with the account offered by Field, a narrative of the conflict emerged in the Amarteifio social survey centered on popular attempts to restore the sovereignty of the divine over the land and thus in opposition to illegitimate chiefly and governmental infiltration. As outlined in the survey, the challenge for the government, of which Amarteifio had been a representative since 1949, was how to balance the interests and perspectives of the local community with the realities of midcentury nation-building. As with many of the social surveys conducted during the period, the result was a political and intellectual framework that bound off the Tema-born Ga's concerns and interests from the broader debates surrounding them, locally and nationally, particularly as they related to the conflicting hopes, expectations, and anxieties embedded within the politics of Nkrumahist modernization.

Similar narratives emerged among certain anticolonial pan-Africanists observing the Gold Coast's transition to self-rule. Touring Tema near the height of the turmoil over resettlement during his 1953 visit to the Gold Coast, the African American author and journalist Richard Wright noted with admiration the construction taking place in the town and surrounding area. Wright, though, also waxed poetic in his travel journal about the conflict enveloping the town. Tema, he argued, was at a crossroads defined by the promises of a "great habor [sic]," the world's attention, and "new ideas." With this modernization, however, Wright also recognized that something would be lost. "The past will die," he asserted, "and the new and strange future will come upon them [Tema's residents]. And the men who will bring this about will call it success. . . . The means will become the end and the human heart is lost, human passion will rot . . . [and] will become the enemy."[98] For the ever-philosophical Wright, Tema embodied a broader dialectical struggle enveloping not only the Gold Coast but the decolonizing world as a whole. In this world, past and present collided, and the challenge of the decolonization moment was finding how to guide this necessary transition in the most humane and efficient way possible.[99]

The CPP itself adhered to a variation of such a view of the struggles it faced in Tema and elsewhere. Modernization in the form of industrial development was at once a necessary disruption and a global wonder, with its promises of national self-sufficiency, growing productive capacity, towering infrastructure, and centralized administration. Lost in the modernizing process, though, many outside the CPP would complain, was any sense of the uniqueness of the Gold Coast's and its diverse peoples' cultures. For instance, Danquah lamented in a 1955 interview with the African American sociologist St. Clair Drake (who would later head the Sociology Department at the University of Ghana, Legon) that, under the CPP, "Nationalism in the Gold Coast is political nationalism[,] not cultural nationalism."[100] The longtime nationalist politician would further insist that even those efforts made by CPP leaders to celebrate the Gold Coast's cultural heritage (e.g., the wearing of cloth or northern smocks) were largely superficial. The result, according to Danquah, was not only an erasure of the Gold Coast's vibrant history of cultural production from the contemporary political terrain, but, more tragically, its actual degradation in the face of momentum for a generic, ideologically driven alternative.[101] The CPP, however, countered such portrayals by arguing that the political and historical moment ushered in by decolonization demanded nothing less than a full commitment to urban and industrial modernization, with the party and government, to use the language of the *Evening News*, "heralding the birth of the new era of freedom."[102]

The residents of Tema were neither ignorant of nor deaf to these national and even international debates surrounding modernization. Even more significantly, many also viewed the resettlement controversies as a way to engage in those debates and reframe them in accordance with their individual and community interests and ambitions. Key among the frustrations expressed by many of the community's residents was the government's inability to live up to its promises of modernization, particularly in regard to housing. In accordance with the CPP's own visions of midcentury modern living and fascination with industrial production, Tema Manhean's housing compounds were to be built of cement-rendered sandcrete blocks with asbestos-cement tile roofs.[103] Residents, however, complained of water leakages in their homes, space shortages, and a lack of plumbing and electricity in the houses. Meanwhile, others, to better meet their space and other living requirements, transformed kitchen spaces into additional living quarters, maintaining the common and socially significant practice of doing most of their cooking outdoors.[104] Still others protested that "the houses were not built in consonance with our traditional set up," meaning that the planners, government officials, and social welfare officers who put together the plan envisioned the housing structures as largely designed to meet the needs of only one's immediate and thus nuclear family. As a result, when more senior relatives came to visit an occupant, the occupant was, at least according to one man, rendered temporarily homeless as he gave up his room to those in his extended family.[105]

In their descriptions of the residents' housing frustrations, longtime Tema residents Seth Laryea Tettey and Samuel Kofi Kotey—both born in the old town—reiterated the everyday complaints about the housing found in the various social surveys conducted during the 1950s and 1960s. However, Kotey quickly shifted his analysis of the resettlement conflicts away from the houses themselves. Instead, he emphasized what was both lost and gained through the Tema development project. As Kotey explained when asked about the quality of the new houses compared to those of the old town, he noted that the "old houses were mud houses, but these were block houses. Yes, so people were happy with the [quality of the] houses." The nature of his response, however, hinted at what one might consider a sense of generosity on his part toward what he appeared to deem an odd question with an obvious answer. At best, the issue of the quality of the housing seemed peripheral to him; the housing was the minimum expected of the government. More significantly, he used the opportunity of the question to then recount a story of a tree currently standing in his compound in Tema Manhean that had been given to him by an aunt during the turmoil of resettlement. In contrast to the new houses, which were literally and symbolically rootless, the tree, which was planted from a cutting from one bulldozed during the government's clearing of the old town, now—at least in one reading of Kotey's story— maintained roots and a lineage in Tema's past and present as well as his own. "I planted it, '59," he emphasized. "It has grown big. When we came to the new town here, I planted this tree here. The people there they cut a branch of this and planted it there. So this is how everything came about."[106]

Born in the original town in the 1930s before moving to Tema Manhean in 1959 and spending much of his career working in the new city, Tettey echoed many of Kotey's sentiments. Unlike the younger Kotey, whose childhood was marked by the resettlement protests, the elder Tettey would have been among the generation of young men who were among the most active in the resettlement protests, albeit Tettey himself was vague about any potential personal role in the activism and even of the nature of the protests themselves. For Tettey, who decades later would briefly enter the National Assembly as part of Hilla Limann's short-lived self-proclaimed Nkrumahist government, the resettlement disputes were the dual result of aborted promises and misunderstandings in which the seemingly logical principle that if "there is a change, it should be a change for the better" got obscured. This had to do with everything from the housing options provided in Tema Manhean to the social and civic amenities promised to the town's residents: new markets and shops, bars, football pitches, and a community center. In other words, Tettey emphasized that Tema's residents were not only aware of the rhetoric and promises of modernization promulgated by the CPP, but were also combining their historical and cultural objections to resettlement with demands that they be given the resources required so that they could fully reap the benefits of CPP-led modernization and the postcolonial reality the Nkrumah-era promised. To this end, Tettey asserted that, given the government's inability—under the CPP and its successors—to meet these expectations, Ghana's government should give the land back to its "rightful owners . . . so that, from our end out of our own volition, if any developer comes, we could sit down and then talk everything over with you so we have direct benefits, instead of going to court."[107]

The tragedy of resettlement for Tettey, at least as it played out in the 1950s, was thus what it meant to the future of Tema's Ga community. Resettlement, he lamented, had scattered the community, bringing with it the loss not only of the community's ancestral and religious lands, most fertile farm lands, and fishing grounds, but also of its community and family cohesion. As a result, in the decades following resettlement, Tettey explained:

> We have part of our people living beyond the motorway [north of the industrial city]. They are farming. They have been farming, but subsistence farming. But we here formerly, we fished and we farmed, but subsistence. Some pepper, some tomato, because it wouldn't augur well if you have some fresh fish, and you have to walk to the bush to get some pepper. All our farm lands here have been taken over. I am telling you, Community Three [in the industrial city], that was the most fertile land for tomato, that red soil there, when you come from inside the Community and you get to the crossroad, the key road over there where you have the harbor, that land we farmed there with our grandfathers, lorries would come there and we would load them seasonally. But all have been taken over. There is no land.[108]

Furthermore, he recounted how, during the construction, new people came into Tema from throughout the country and abroad. Themselves attracted by the promises and expectations of Nkrumah-era modernization, these individuals were brought in by the new road and rail networks connecting Tema to Accra and further afield in search of work in the harbor and industrial city. In doing so, Tettey recalled, they further crowded out the Tema-born Ga's connection to Tema.[109]

In regard to both Kotey and Tettey, their experiences of resettlement and the legacies of their relocation should not be primarily understood as a matter of a simplistic conflict between tradition and modernity, or simple opposition of the local versus the national or of locals versus incoming waves of "strangers." Rather, they rest in broader concerns over the complicated relationships between the past and the present forged out of the expectations, demands, and contradictions of decolonization-era nation-building, particularly as framed by the nascent Nkrumahism of the 1950s. Individuals interviewed by social surveyors in the late 1950s and early and mid-1960s relayed similar perspectives. Some, for instance, spoke with enthusiasm of what they viewed as Tema's envisioned transformation into a cultural and industrial hub in the new urban Ghana. "At first Tema is [sic] a village," a student from Tema New Town (Tema Manhean) wrote in 1959, "but now it has becoming [sic] a city" with promises of a future that will include a "secondary school," "big stores," a "community center," and a "proper market."[110] Likewise, another individual who had arrived in Tema in the mid-1950s celebrated the new leisure opportunities offered by Tema's development as he reflected with the surveyors about how he would regularly go to the cinema with his family in "New Tema Village" (Tema Manhean) as well as attend football matches in the city.[111] Meanwhile, others complained that this new urban way of life also held the potential for troubling social consequences. As suggested by one local Methodist minister whose church was razed in the demolition, all the opportunities that this modernization had brought had—at least in terms of his congregation—made the community "weak in spirit" and "materially minded."[112]

NATIONS, NATIONALISMS, AND ALTERNATIVES TO THE CPP

As the residents of Tema began to challenge the CPP's plan for their resettlement, other groups also were offering visions for the Gold Coast's future that often conflicted with, if not outright contradicted, those of the

CPP. As early as 1953, Muslim day laborers in Kumasi and Accra turned to the intersecting issues of religion and class in the Gold Coast's urban "stranger" communities (zongos) in protesting what they viewed as an increasingly corrupt and unrepresentative government in Accra. In doing so, they formed the first major Gold Coast political party—the Muslim Association Party—with a lineage independent of both the CPP and UGCC.[113] Moreover, similar complaints also arose in the colony's southeastern region, where, as Kate Skinner has shown, Ewe intellectuals and nationalists cultivated an Ewe politics, along with a print and oral literary tradition, that challenged the CPP with demands for a reunified Togoland.[114] Likewise, in the colony's Northern Territories, where the CPP's reach was likely the most superficial through much of the early and mid-1950s, groups of northern chiefs and elders organized around the idea of a shared northern identity that, according to them, had to be protected from undue southern, primarily Akan, interference.[115] As in Tema, there was more than a return to a quasi-traditionalist identity politics at the heart of these movements' and parties' opposition to the CPP. Rather, they reflected a broader reframing of the colony's political, social, and cultural diversity in relation to both a wide range of Gold Coast communities' individual histories and aspirations and the promises of midcentury decolonization, modernization, and nation-building.

In September 1954, the founding of the Asante-led National Liberation Movement (NLM) raised the stakes of Gold Coast opposition politics. As detailed in Jean Allman's history of the movement, the politics and economics of cocoa dominated the NLM's complaints against the CPP government. By the mid-1950s, as international cocoa prices reached all-time highs of 131 to 149 shillings per sixty-pound load, the CPP government aimed to fix the prices paid to farmers at 72 shillings per load.[116] From the perspective of the young men who founded the NLM, frustrated by what they viewed as the government's unnecessarily low prices, the CPP's pricing structure did little more than replicate the extractive and exploitative cocoa policies of the British colonial government.[117] In justifying its policies, the CPP argued that the surplus garnered through the government's fixed-pricing scheme offered the most efficient mechanism for bringing forth the national benefits of its aggressive development agenda. It further maintained that the pricing scheme would also allow the government to prepare for a time when international cocoa prices dropped.[118] As the colony's foremost cocoa-growing region, though, the income generated from cocoa rested at the heart of Asante life. Not only did it fund the day-to-day life of farmers and their families, but, as one popular song recounted, it allowed the region's young men to marry, build houses, send their children to school, and buy lorries.[119] As Allman argues in her analysis of the NLM, "The freezing of cocoa pricing was thus perceived as a direct attack on the social and intellectual fabric of Asante."[120]

As in Tema, Asante opposition to the CPP quickly turned to the living relationship between the past and the present. Asante, it was argued, had a proud and distinguished history of independence, resistance, and autonomy associated with that of the rest of the Gold Coast, yet also unique to itself. Asante's uniqueness was even reflected in the political structure of the Gold Coast, where not until 1944 was Asante fully integrated into the colony's legislative apparatus.[121] Even more importantly, though, as T. C. McCaskie has shown, European travelers had for more than a century been constructing a historical and cultural genealogy for the Akan state that, in their minds, potentially extended back to ancient Egypt and Ethiopia.[122] In his analysis of these European narratives, McCaskie turns to Philip Curtin's classic study of eighteenth- and nineteenth-century European images of Africa as he notes that, for the classically trained travelers at the time, it seemed natural to connect what they saw in Asante and elsewhere to that with which they were already intellectually familiar.[123] By the late 1930s, the Asantehene himself had in turn begun to integrate key aspects of these narratives of Semitic roots into the official record of the empire's origins. In doing so, he embedded within the Asante ruling elite, specifically, a lineage that not only reached far beyond West Africa, but one that was also distinct from those of the commoners he governed.[124]

As they rose on the Gold Coast political stage, Asante politicians in the 1950s—some with current and past connections to the CPP—were loath to cede such narratives of Asante exceptionalism. Even prior to the cocoa pricing disputes that catalyzed the birth of the NLM, Asante politicians rejected what they deemed as the constitutional snub that categorized Asante as a mere region within the larger confines of the Gold Coast. As B. F. Kusi, an Asante politician previously affiliated with the CPP, declared in 1953, "All Ashantis express the sentiment that Ashanti is a nation." Doubling down on this assertion, he further proclaimed, "We are not a region at all; we should be considered a nation and that should be accepted by everybody."[125] Of even greater interest than Kusi's declaration of Asante nationhood, though, is the historical narrative he set forth in his speech. Founding his historical perspective on a belief in Asante's exceptional place within the Gold Coast, Kusi aimed to decenter the CPP's stranglehold on the Gold Coast's anticolonial narrative. In doing so, he traced a historical line that directly connected Asante's nineteenth-century wars against the British to the Gold Coast's present situation. "We saw the danger ahead," he informed his colleagues in the Legislative Assembly, and recognized that "if we put our heads under the British people they would turn this country into a sort of South Africa. Therefore though they [the British] were staying on the shores along the coast [not coincidentally also areas of significant CPP support], we in Ashanti determined to prove to them that we were self-governing before they came."[126]

On the ground, the NLM's rise was nearly as dramatic as that of the CPP itself four years earlier. As Allman highlights, "youngmen" (*nkwankwaa*), cocoa farmers, and market women, among others, drove the movement during its first months of existence.[127] In doing so, they recruited many who had previously been drawn to the CPP's populism with a message that combined demands for an end to the government's proposed cocoa pricing scheme with accusations directed at the CPP of governmental corruption, exploitation, and mismanagement. Shortly thereafter, the NLM proposed the establishment of a federalized political structure for the new Ghana. As articulated by those within the NLM, the proposed federal structure foremost sought to protect the emergent country's regional diversity by allowing each region key avenues of subnational self-determination and self-government. As such, for many in the NLM, it was also designed as a mechanism for the political, cultural, and social expression of Asante exceptionalism. By late October 1954, the Asante chiefs and, most importantly, the Asantehene threw their support behind the NLM, leading some within the party to portray support for the NLM and opposition to the CPP as evidence that one was "a true and loyal subject of the Golden Stool."[128]

By mid-1955, NLM-influenced resistance to the CPP had taken hold in Asante, escalating beyond the government's and possibly even the colonial administration's control. Looking worriedly at the situation evolving in the colony's wealthiest region, colonial officials reported an influx of rifles, machine guns, and other weapons being smuggled into Asante. Likewise, they noted that "small bands of people" were being trained to "attack, and possibly murder, Gold Coast ministers."[129] Reports of murders, assassination attempts, intimidation, and the dynamiting of the homes and offices of both CPP and NLM supporters thus feature prominently in the late-colonial record.[130] Furthermore, alliances emerged between Asante youth and the groups who supported the Muslim Association Party in the

Kumasi zongo.[131] Meanwhile, for those living on the wrong side of the political divide in 1955 and 1956, the situation in significant areas of the Gold Coast was deteriorating so rapidly that they found little choice but to move to politically safer ground. For supporters of the CPP, this meant migrating south to Accra, while NLM supporters in Accra and other areas of widespread CPP loyalty moved north to Kumasi.[132] Even prominent Asante CPP politicians found it difficult, if not impossible, to return to their home districts out of fear for their safety during the mid-1950s, as the Gold Coast, to borrow from Allman, "teeter[ed] on the brink of civil war."[133]

Even more disconcerting for the CPP was the extent to which the NLM's vision of a political alternative to the CPP appeared to be reaching outside the confines of its base of support within Asante. In October 1955, for instance, a pro-CPP chief from the western coastal town of Busua wrote to Nkrumah in order to advise him that an "Elderly man" had approached him "seeking assistance of the whole chiefs in [the] Ahanta area . . . to assist him in bringing [the] N.L.M. into Ahanta District."[134] In another instance, a report from the Wassaw South and Central constituencies, also in the west, noted how the "Wassaw Fiasi Area . . . is now tending to go the NLM way." The area, the party observer asserted, had succumbed to the "tribalist" influence and "political trickery and obstinacy" of the NLM as the Wasa youth advocated for what the party perceived as a narrowly defined nativist approach to future local and national elections.[135] Meanwhile, in the Central Region town of Swedru (Agona), political anthropologist Maxwell Owusu reports, the CPP's failure to adhere to its earlier campaign promises to stop the forced cutting of cocoa trees infected with swollen shoot disease opened the town's residents to the NLM's message in the mid-1950s. As a result, by 1955, the non-Asante town would inaugurate its own branch of the Asante-based political party.[136]

In other locales, Asante politicians and activists sought to rally support for the NLM and the parties allied to it by turning to local concerns over the rootlessness of the CPP, its agenda for the Gold Coast/Ghana, and especially Nkrumah. "You [women]," NLM activist Nancy Tsiboe exclaimed to a predominately Ewe audience during a 1956 rally in the coastal town of Anloga, "will all agree with me that only a married man with a family knows how to manage a home. And you will agree with me that he alone can manage a country." Family, ancestry, marriage, and reproduction stood at the heart of the African way of life, Tsiboe intimated—yet, as portrayed by the former Ghana Congress Party candidate for the Legislative Assembly, Nkrumah came to power unmarried and without any legitimate children. Additionally, he came from an area (Nzema) far from the region's historical centers of political and economic power, from an undistinguished and purportedly untraceable family, and, as rumor had it, had been born to a goldsmith father with supposed Liberian origins. As Tsiboe maintained, Nkrumah's lack of connection to the past—both his personal past and that of the nation—thus made it impossible for Gold Coasters to "know where he really comes from." Moreover, she further insisted that it was this lack of respect for what came before him and before the CPP that distorted the CPP's vision of what a Gold Coaster or Ghanaian was and what he or she could be, and led to the party's promotion of an agenda that she portrayed as vulgar, corrupt, mismanaged, and un-African. It was also an agenda that, via its anti-chief politics, had inculcated "disrespect into our children." "If Mr. Nkrumah truly wants self-gov. [sic]," Tsiboe concluded, "he would go to the <u>Ashantehene</u> [sic] to discuss it with him," for it was through figures like the Asantehene that the Gold Coast's past, present, and future came together.[137]

THE MAKING OF NKRUMAHISM AND THE 1956 GENERAL ELECTION

The CPP responded to its various opponents' historicizations of the Gold Coast with its own return to history. In doing so, party surrogates positioned the NLM and its vision for the Gold Coast inside the broader context of Asante's history in the precolonial and colonial Gold Coast. Here, the CPP looked to gain support from groups such as the Ga and Fante along the Atlantic coast, non-Asante Akan inland, and parts of British Togoland as they resurrected narratives of a Gold Coast past dominated by—as described by the CPP—the exploitation, tribalism, and legacies of slavery and the slave trade of the former Asante Empire. Writing to the secretary of state for the colonies, for instance, one Kumasi-based CPP supporter claimed in 1955 that, like the Asante Empire of the eighteenth and nineteenth centuries, the NLM's opposition to the CPP signaled little more than Asante's propensity for "stubbornness, violence, bloodshed, etc." As a result, he narrated a version of the Asante past dating to "the ancient days [of] the Ashanti Kings" that he connected to the NLM and the present Asantehene in which he argued that history had clearly shown that, when left to their own devices, the Asante operated in the Gold Coast "with the ultimate aim to dominate and subjugate the people of this country."[138] Others, likewise, highlighted the contemporary and historical divisions among the groups that comprised Greater Asante, while also pointing to the economic and social infeasibility of the NLM's demands for a federal constitution and, from some, threats of secession. To this end, groups from what in 1958 would become Ghana's Brong Ahafo Region tacitly deconstructed the historical and ideological framework of a unified, prestigious Asante with allusions to the many victims of Asante's imperial reach.[139]

The CPP in turn claimed to be speaking for all those disenfranchised and violated by the "traditional" order epitomized by Asante and its allies' complicated precolonial history in the Gold Coast as the Nkrumah-led government planned for an alternative future. In doing so, the party devised an array of often competing narratives, with certain ones framed for discrete local settings and others for the national and international stages. Here, seemingly paradoxically, the CPP sought to centralize its message and the loyalties it was to generate, while, at the same time, strategically cultivating in many communities vernacular readings of the party's message. As Paul André Ladouceur writes in reference to the Kusasi-Mamprusi conflict in the Gold Coast's far northeast, by the 1950s Kusasi supporters of the CPP—along with those from several other historically "stateless" groups in the region—had begun to apply the CPP's anticolonial rhetoric and specifically the vocabulary of "colonialism" and "imperialism" to their own opposition to what they viewed as their "subjugation to an alien African ruler [the Mamprusi nayiri] . . . and his representatives."[140] Similarly, in Kumasi's zongo, where the NLM-allied Muslim Association Party offered a strong repudiation of the CPP, the CPP sought to make inroads by inserting itself into the community's existing conflicts, particularly around the office of headman. In doing so, the party actively sought to create cleavages within the zongo's political environment by attempting to prop up potential headmen who had already offered their support to the party. As Enid Schildkrout has shown, the result was a political environment in this highly localized space where loyalties were only "sometimes related to interethnic rivalries." More importantly, according to Schildkrout, such political loyalties more often reflected deeper histories of local alliances and disputes that both the CPP and those opposed to it sought to exploit.[141]

At the national level, however, the CPP sought to consolidate its message into a singular narrative of unification and nation-building. Over the course of the 1950s, the CPP would relentlessly unleash charges of tribalism on nearly every opposition movement or party that arose. As presented by the CPP, though, these charges were not only intended to surround the Gold Coast's various anti-CPP movements and parties with an aura of anachronism. More importantly, they also aimed to siphon the colony's local and regional variation out of the emergent country's political scene. This attempt extended beyond politics per se to include the colony's many localities' unique histories, needs, ambitions, and struggles. If the goal was independence, the CPP insisted, and, more than that, a place as a modern nation within the growing midcentury international community, then the populace had to be united in mission and in self-identification, subsuming individual and local interests for the greater good. "In the Convention People's Party," Nkrumah thus argued in 1955, "no individual is greater than the Party and the principle of democratic centralism, that is, the subordinating of individual opinion to the decision of the majority has always been the guiding principle in the formation of the plans and policies of the Party."[142] Moreover, the party, along with many others inside and outside the Gold Coast, insisted that this sense of a shared path forward had continental implications if the Gold Coast was to serve—in Padmore's words—as "the beacon light" for Africa's transition to self-rule.[143]

The CPP's approach to the NLM and its allied parties was thus intended to quell a number of competing constituencies in the Gold Coast and abroad, while expatriate figures like George Padmore unfailingly presented the rising opposition to the CPP in the 1950s as little more than an imperialist ploy designed "to demoralise [a] sympathetic public among anti-colonialists" that therefore had to be demolished.[144] However, in communities where the CPP sought to elicit support, the party recognized that it had to create and foster a narrative—or multiple narratives—that not only spoke to a broad audience, but made members of the community comfortable with what truly was a radical message coming out of the CPP, locally and nationally. Furthermore, the CPP also had to speak to the changing political and economic realities of the mid-1950s as it sought to protect its highly aggressive development agenda. For, by the mid-1950s, as local protests against the CPP gained momentum, questions over the efficacy and wisdom of its modernization efforts increasingly took on a new level of urgency in both local and international circles. The 1953 release of the University of Manchester economist W. Arthur Lewis's report on the Gold Coast's industrial potential only fueled such concerns, as the future Nobel Prize recipient argued for the tabling of many of the Gold Coast's industrial plans.[145] More troublingly for the CPP, by April 1956, Lewis had also begun to withdraw his support for the centerpiece of the CPP's modernization agenda—the Volta River Project—as he insinuated, among other things, the potential for continued unrest in the soon-to-be independent country.[146] Others with stakes in West Africa—the Colonial Office, the Commonwealth, and private industry—had also grown increasingly wary of the political situation in the Gold Coast, with British officials arguing in September 1955 that the uncertainty in the Gold Coast was giving credence to the dystopian worldview articulated in the Commonwealth by what they described as the South African "prophets of doom."[147]

As a result, with tempers flaring in the West African colony and the CPP holding an increasingly weakened hand both in its negotiations for formal decolonization and in the pursuit of its modernization agenda, officials in London resolved in May 1956 that the only way to avoid a looming crisis was to hold a new general election. Strategically slated to occur in mid-July, after the meeting of the Commonwealth prime ministers, the election was largely viewed as the final major hurdle before independence. For their part, the CPP and its various news outlets portrayed the choice for voters as one between a modern, unified future and a tribal, imperialist past. The *Evening News* in particular described the NLM as "treacherous Black imperialists, detractors and nincompoops who have plotted to delay your [the citizenry's] freedom."[148] The NLM countered the CPP's indictments with a narrative of its own focused on the celebration and resurrection of the greatness of the Asante past in the face of the CPP's "foreign" threat and what it saw as the emerging dictatorship of Nkrumah and the CPP. "Unlike the CPP manifesto," the *Ashanti Pioneer* argued in the lead-up to the July vote, "that of the NLM and its allies does not ask the electorate to return them to power to 'continue the work,' that is, the work of studied corruption, nepotism, inefficiency and attempted dictatorship." Instead, a vote for the NLM and those aligned with it was a vote for the belief that "the highest justification for the achievement of independence is to project the best in our own cultural heritage, the pivot of which is the time-honoured institution of chieftaincy."[149] To this end, another *Ashanti Pioneer* author added in a poem that "We do not have to change ourselves," while demanding that the newspaper's readers "Vote to save your ancient soil, / Vote for your dignity. / Vote to redeem what the stranger stole, / Vote for the Cocoa Tree."[150] In effect, the election was to serve as a referendum on the CPP and its vision for the new Ghana.

As the day of the election approached, the colony was on edge about what the vote would bring, with many fearing a return of the violence of the previous year. However, the violence never surfaced and, as the polls closed, attention turned to those commissioned to count the votes.[151] For the NLM and its allies, the results were nothing short of disappointing, as the vote returned the CPP to the Legislative Assembly with another comfortable majority (71 of the assembly's 104 seats). Even in Asante, the opposition did not fare as well as anticipated, with the NLM capturing—in conjunction with its allied parties—just 13 of the region's 21 seats.[152] Even defeated Asante CPP candidates claimed victory, as they pointed to the relatively narrow margins by which they had lost their districts.[153] Similar stories played out in other opposition strongholds. In the north, where the Northern People's Party had hoped for a clear victory, the party secured only 15 of the region's 26 seats. In Trans-Volta Togoland, two candidates from the Togoland Congress Party, two independents, and another from the Federated Youth Organisations formed the opposition's five-seat delegation from the region.[154] Meanwhile, inside the CPP, the vote appeared to validate what Nkrumah and party officials believed to be a mass of support behind its vision for an independent Ghana. Riding this momentum, as the new legislative session opened in August 1956, Nkrumah joined the assembly to introduce the CPP's official motion for independence. A little over a month later, he returned to the Legislative Assembly to announce that the British House of Commons had officially established 6 March 1957 as the date for Ghanaian independence.[155]

～

After the general election, the depth of the popular support for the CPP and its vision for the new Ghana remained a matter of contention. The NLM sought to raise doubts in the immediate aftermath of the vote by arguing that, if one examined the results regionally as opposed to nationally (i.e., in accordance with the party's federalist principles), the anti-CPP parties had won the majority of regions. However, such arguments held little sway outside the political circles of the various parties' own sympathizers.[156] Beyond the NLM's and its various allied parties' interpretations of the meaning of the vote, several scholars have pointed out the markedly low voter turnout during the election, even compared to the low turnouts in the Gold Coast's two previous general elections in 1951 and 1954. Allman hypothesizes that the low turnout may have been the result of the transformation of the NLM from a broad-based popular movement to a political party that to many, by mid-1956, had proven itself to be indistinguishable—in leadership style and structure—from the CPP.[157] Likewise, Richard Rathbone, considering Gold Coast nationalist politics more broadly, proposes that the low turnout may have indicated the shallowness of popular support for party politics in the Gold Coast in general.[158] Both Rathbone and Allman in turn encourage scholars to take seriously the alternative and multivalent forms of politics and pathways of political belonging, identification, and action that comprised the political scene of the Gold Coast's transition to self-rule, for the six years between the CPP's rise to power and Ghana's 1957 independence foremost marked a period of rich political diversity in the Gold Coast. As such, it was a period where a vast array of new movements, parties, and popular protests arose to challenge the CPP with competing visions of their own and of the emergent country's futures, at times even adopting and adapting aspects of the CPP's message and vision for their own purposes. However, this was also a time when the CPP itself began the sustained process of formally defining and centralizing its particular vision for the country (for all intents and purposes, "Nkrumahism") via its political and developmental agenda—and, in turn, quashing not only opposition to it, but also strategic and organic attempts to instill internal variation within it.[159]

3 ⤳ A New Type of Citizen
Youth and the Making of Pan-African Citizenship

You know that the circumstances of our Party in the early days did not warrant an organisation of any consistent ideological studies for our Youth. The Party was in death grip with imperialism and colonialism and it was a grim fight every inch of the way. The struggle for freedom was so vital that everything; including the Party's ideology was put aside for the interim. Now that the battle is won and we are free, we must put into our youth the ideology upon which our Party stands and operates, so that long after we are gone the ideal for which we fought will stand for ever [sic].

—Mary Osei, Young Pioneers District Commissioner,
Kumasi North, 1963[1]

FOR THE Convention People's Party, independence ushered in a new set of opportunities and challenges as the party sought to govern unburdened by the authority of the Colonial Office in London. Internationally, an anxious enthusiasm surrounded the country's independence as officials, journalists, activists, and others looked to the Accra government for guidance on Africa's future. Nkrumah, for his part, embraced the new country's position on the African and international political scenes, announcing just weeks after independence his intention to host the continent's first Conference of Independent African States (CIAS).[2] By the end of 1957, plans for the conference were well under way. In mid-April 1958, representatives from the continent's eight independent states met in Accra to discuss and affirm the shared nature of their countries' and the broader continent's past and future struggles against colonial rule.[3] In December, the CPP convened another, much larger pan-African affair in Accra—the All-African People's Conference (AAPC), which featured approximately two hundred and fifty delegates and observers from at least sixty-two of the continent's political parties and liberation movements.[4] Continuing upon the path paved by the April conference, the AAPC reaffirmed the pan-African and anticolonial vision of the new Nkrumah government by echoing the 1945

Manchester Pan-African Congress's call for African self-determination, while also incorporating new debates on such subjects as the legitimacy of violence in African liberation struggles, questions regarding postcolonial governance, and the promise of Afro-Asian solidarity and nonalignment into the conference's anticolonial program.[5] Meanwhile, the formation in November 1958 of the Ghana-Guinea Union, which allowed for limited shared sovereignty between the two young states, reframed local questions regarding the rights, responsibilities, and even structure of the new Ghanaian nation-state in a necessarily transnational and pan-African context.[6]

The international acclaim that accompanied Ghana's independence, however, collided with a struggle within the country to construct and define the institutions and political and social values of the new state. The six years of shared governance that preceded Ghana's 1957 independence had been characterized by increasing African influence and control over the Gold Coast government's internal affairs. Independence, however, did not just extend the government's control to the arenas of foreign affairs, security, and oversight. More fundamentally, it also forced the CPP and the country as a whole deeper into intricate debates over what and who constituted the new nation, the rights and obligations of the Ghanaian citizen, and the concept of postcolonial citizenship itself. The CPP's and specifically Nkrumah's pan-African proclivities further complicated the country's nation- and state-building initiatives, with policies and rhetoric that stretched what some saw as an already shallow self-identification with the party and nation as the CPP imagined them. To those breathing the increasingly rarified air of the CPP's internal hierarchy, the government's political and social ambitions promised for some a path to an envisioned deepening of the country's connections to a transnational socialist nation-building project. However, on the ground, these ambitions also represented an often unpredictable set of opening and closing doors of opportunity, at times contributing to a general atmosphere of confusion and stress that had to be negotiated.

This chapter interrogates the intersections and tensions between citizenship, youth, and nation in the Nkrumahist politics of the late 1950s and early 1960s. In doing so, it builds upon the previous chapter's analysis of the transition to self-rule as a period of political constriction by juxtaposing this pre-independence reality with that of early-postcolonial Ghana as a site of international and pan-African experimentation. The torrent of local and international optimism that accompanied Ghana's independence was not artificial. Rather, as seen in the previous chapter, it was a reflection of an increasingly demanding set of expectations of rapid infrastructural modernization, job creation, wealth redistribution, and elevated standards of living. In the press and in its rallies, the CPP fueled these expectations with images of a Ghanaian future marked by modern cities, growing educational systems, new industries, and rapid scientific and technological development. At the same time, the CPP government and party apparatus also sought to temper these expectations with a discourse of civic responsibility constructed around a language of shared sacrifice, collective well-being, and party-defined political and social activism that centered on the nation's youth. The Eden of the fully realized Nkrumahist nation, the CPP argued, could thus only be achieved through a countrywide commitment to and engagement with the CPP- and specifically Nkrumah-defined nation-building project in each of its national and transnational iterations. For the country's young people, the result was a civic ideal in which they became the targets of and models for a concept of postcolonial citizenship rooted in discipline, order, and state-guided activism. Not only did this place them at the center of the postcolonial political stage, it also opened their broader relationships—familial, community, and peer—to intense state pressure.

DISCIPLINE, ORDER, AND CITIZENSHIP

The first months of Ghanaian self-rule were characterized by a process of self-definition. Ideas of nation, state, and citizenship framed this definitional process as the CPP government and others strove to balance desires for pan-African and anticolonial inclusivity with the state's need to set limits and maintain order. The question of who was and who was not to be considered "Ghanaian" was among the first issues addressed. The artificiality of colonial boundaries, along with West Africans' long tradition of regional mobility and intermarriage, complicated initial attempts to construct a definitive conception of Ghanaian nationality and, in turn, of the citizen. In the National Assembly, for instance, debates quickly arose as to the status of long-term residents in the country who happened to lack clear Ghanaian lineage. This included British and other citizens of the Commonwealth, who previously could expect a certain set of rights and protections within the colony connected to their and the former Gold Coast's shared position as members of the British Empire. Now, the government proposed that additional requirements for citizenship be placed upon such long-term residents, including being of "good character" and possessing "sufficient knowledge of a language indigenous to and in current use in

Ghana."[7] Other concerns over the roles of language and chieftaincy in delineating "Ghanaian-ness" further obscured the attempted clear distinction between who did and who did not qualify as Ghanaian. This inevitably also raised questions as to the efficiency and fairness of the country's proposed naturalization process.[8] Complementing these considerations were concerns over the process through which an individual could secure entrance into the country and, perhaps more important for the CPP, the circumstances under which the government could remove someone.[9]

Underlying the National Assembly debates over citizenship, immigration, and deportation was a desire within the CPP to at once define the mechanisms of the modern nation-state and legitimize the government's usage of these administrative tools in managing the state. Complicating the CPP's ambitions on both the local and national levels were continued protests over the legitimacy of the CPP and of Nkrumah himself. In the country's interior, Asante opposition to the party persisted into the early 1960s. As late as 1962, for instance, a secret group of Asante dissidents calling itself the "Ashanti Command" was openly advising Nkrumah to "beware and watch your steps" before crossing into Asante.[10] The group also cautioned the police and military against blindly following the "orders" and "commands" of a government it deemed illegitimate, warning the two security forces that each "drop of Ghanaian blood that you may inadvertently shed will be avenged seven-fold."[11] Likewise, a similarly strident Ewe opposition in Trans-Volta Togoland also refused to subside quietly after the transition to self-rule. By May, the situation there was being discussed on the floor of the National Assembly as the government solicited debate on what it deemed as the region's "lawlessness." The situation on the ground in Trans-Volta Togoland, CPP minister of the interior Ako Adjei argued, had proven itself to be rife with the potential for violence. As a result, he insisted that the government would be well within its rights to confront the dissidents' violence with the pacifying violence of the state.[12]

Even in Accra, the most reliably pro-CPP city in the country, the first months of self-rule forced the Nkrumah government into addressing a rising tide of political and social discontent, particularly among the city's indigenous Ga residents. Emerging in the neighborhoods surrounding Bukom Square, part of Nkrumah's own electoral district, Ga frustrations with their employment prospects and urban overcrowding revealed a broader disenchantment with the cosmopolitan visions of the city presented by the CPP. The government, for its part, had long promised that the benefits of modernization—most importantly, jobs—would trickle down to the city's residents. Yet, from the perspective of many within the city's Ga quarters, by mid-1957 these promises were proving illusory. Tied to these frustrations was a more localized dissatisfaction with the perceived underrepresentation of Ga officials in government and party offices and—echoing the complaints of their neighbors in nearby Tema—the sale of Ga lands to groups primarily comprised of Akan "strangers."[13] As such, Accra Ga took to the streets in mid-1957 with demands that "Ga lands are for Ga people" ("*Ga shikpon, Ga mei Anoni*") and calls of "People of Ga descent, arise" ("*Ga mei abii, nye teashi*").[14] Moreover, as the Ga movement transformed itself from an inchoate group largely composed of unemployed school-leavers into a formal opposition party, other Accra-based constituencies with histories of supporting the CPP—including drivers and ex-servicemen—began to openly question the party's commitment to meeting their needs. The drivers, angered by the CPP government's efforts to regulate the transportation sector, went even further in expressing their frustrations with the postcolonial social and economic situation in the city with promises of a strike.[15] As the strike began on 23 July, the day after Nkrumah's return from the Commonwealth Prime Ministers' Conference in London, food shortages and rapid inflation only added to the unrest in central Accra.[16]

Not unlike the colonial administrators before them, CPP officials attempted to rationalize, if not dismiss, the protests. To them, the opposition the government was encountering in Accra as well as elsewhere in the country was a reflection of the broader structural changes accompanying the country's social adaptation to postwar modernization. Urban modernization—fundamental to the Nkrumahist vision for any former colony's economic independence from capitalist imperialism—carried with it an acute need for significant and relatively rapid job growth. In the late 1940s and early 1950s, the CPP had fully capitalized on popular frustration with the gap between the social and economic allure of the colony's cities and the real opportunities for employment and social mobility within them. Independence had now brought with it the expectation that the CPP live up to its pre-independence promises of full employment. As a result, at issue in the months following independence was a debate among the public and within the CPP itself over the social contract of self-rule. In the eyes of the CPP, that contract, forged out of the promises and sacrifices of the anticolonial struggle and six years of British-CPP shared governance, was based on an envisioned state-citizen relationship in which each party member and, later, Ghanaian citizen was to commit her- or himself entirely both to the collective struggle against colonialism and to the Nkrumahist nation-building project. In turn, the citizenry was to come to enjoy the social and material benefits national reconstruction had to offer. These included—again, as already articulated by the CPP— full employment, material advancement, economic security, greater access to education at a variety of levels, modern cities and their amenities, and sustained personal and professional growth.

The CPP thus took a dual approach to the unrest of the first months of self-rule. At their most blunt, the party and government exercised their newly acquired powers by threatening certain opposition groups and their leaders with police action and deportation, including in Trans-Volta Togoland. The result for some was dislocation from communities that their families had lived in for generations.[17] As Kate Skinner notes, between 1958 and 1961 an estimated 5,700 refugees left eastern Ghana for French Togoland.[18] In French Togoland and, after the country's 1960 independence, Togo, some retreated from politics to engage in farming and other economic activities.[19] Others, however, continued to mobilize politically from outside Ghana against the CPP government as they refused to forgo their ambitions for a reunified Togoland. Among those interviewed by Skinner, nearly all claimed to have remained active in politics after their dislocation, constructing an opposition in exile that would long exasperate the CPP government in Accra.[20] Meanwhile, in Accra, the CPP mobilized against what it viewed as the rising "tribalist" opposition within the Ga community. Most visibly, on the streets, the CPP organized its own Ga supporters (as members of the Ga Ekomefeemo Kpee, or Ga Unity Party) to serve as a counterweight to the protest movement (embodied in the Ga Shifimo Kpee, or Ga Standfast Association), leading to violent clashes between the two groups. According to Dennis Austin, one particular incident on 21 August resulted in fifty-three arrests. However, the episode did not end there. As Austin reports, the next day a group of CPP supporters, including the party's national propaganda secretary, Kwatelai Quartey, attacked several of the Ga Shifimo Kpee's leaders with knives and bottles.[21]

The CPP's response to the unrest at the governmental level was more nuanced. The government ostensibly attempted to renew the social contract it had sought to forge with the populace over the previous six-plus years as it pursued a new set of civic and economic programs aimed at curbing underemployment and unemployment, most notably with the proposed establishment of a National Workers Brigade.[22] At the heart of the envisioned Brigade was to be a political and ideological program designed to create and model for the populace the values and behaviors of the government's ideal postcolonial citizen. Moreover, the Brigade was also to help solve what the CPP viewed as its youth problem. The country's youth, ranging from schoolchildren to unmarried young men and women, at once represented the future of the nation and one of the greatest challenges to it. Supposedly unencumbered by the burdens of the colonial and—in the CPP's terms—"tribal" past of their parents and elders, the country's young people were imagined to be open to the political, social, and economic transformations demanded in the postcolonial world.[23] However, they also comprised one of the most vulnerable groups in the country. Not only were they subject to the social authority of their families, communities, and elders, they had also—as the colonial cash economy took root and the colony urbanized in the twentieth century— become increasingly economically dependent on an employment market ill-prepared for their rapidly growing numbers.[24] Furthermore, both colonial and CPP governmental reports in the years leading up to the country's independence echoed broader continent- and empire-wide themes of delinquency, idleness, promiscuity, and vagrancy in their discussions of the country's youth.[25]

The proposed National Workers Brigade was thus to be a substantial and multifaceted undertaking. Renamed the Builders Brigade by the end of May, it was to provide the country's young women and men a means by which to serve the new nation through the creation of a nationwide network of uniformed work camps. In these camps, eligible young men and women—initially meaning any unemployed individual between the ages of fifteen and forty-five—would receive training in modern agricultural practices, road and housing construction, and sewing and other craftwork.[26] In the eyes of the CPP, the Brigade's focus on mechanized agricultural and infrastructural development was to offer the citizenry and the country's young men and women in particular a celebration of "the dignity of manual labour and national service."[27] Moreover, the camp environment was designed to bring the country's youth together in order to cultivate a sense of camaraderie and unity amongst brigaders as they collectively went about the day-to-day labor required of them—labor deemed by the government as essential to the construction of the new nation. Furthermore, the government proposed that, over time, the mission and structure of the camps would change from that of individual, discrete work camps into cooperative settlements. In these settlements, residents were to be employed and involved in a range of personal and state-sponsored productive enterprises all designed for the technical, agricultural, and industrial betterment of the nation.[28]

Nearly all of the early plans for the Brigade called for brigaders to be hired for a period of two years. Furthermore, an initial plan for the organization recommended providing most brigaders a salary on a sliding scale of one to two shillings a day, dependent upon years of service, while also supplying them food, uniforms, and medical services.[29] A slightly later variation promised brigaders a small allowance tied to the type of work they performed, minus deductions to cover meals and incidentals.[30] By the time the Brigade celebrated the induction of its first recruits in November 1957, the plan had undergone considerable revision, as the cabinet debated several competing and often very different formulations of the program. In these debates, the primary areas of contention were those of pay, costs (e.g., of meals and uniforms), and qualifications for eligibility, with the issue of age restrictions emerging as a continuing point of contestation between the cabinet, the expatriate advisors hired to study the various proposals, and members of the National Assembly. This ultimately resulted in the eventual lowering of the forty-five-year age cap to twenty-four.[31] As a result, those who joined the Brigade's first camps in Accra and in the Northern Region village of Damongo earned three to four shillings a day, with some artisans collecting an additional allowance for the purchase and maintenance of equipment. Further supplementing their pay, Damongo brigaders also received free food, housing, and uniforms, while their counterparts in Accra's nonresidential camp received two meals a day, free transport to and from work, and a set of dress and work uniforms. Furthermore, as the face of the Brigade in the country's capital, Accra brigaders also attended citizenship lectures and literacy classes supported by the government.[32]

Inspiring the CPP's vision for the Brigade was the Israeli experience with youth mobilization. To many in both the Ghanaian and Israeli governments, including the two states' prime ministers (Nkrumah and David Ben-Gurion), the countries faced similar challenges as they each confronted their post-independence futures.[33] Both of the states, it was argued, were relatively small, young countries formed out of struggle, which positioned them as vulnerable both locally and internationally. As suggested by the two prime ministers, among the greatest challenges for each state was the monumental task of translating the excitement and emotion of their respective struggles into enthusiasm for the essential but tedious task of national reconstruction. Writing in an August 1957 letter to Nkrumah, for instance, Ben-Gurion emphasized to his Ghanaian counterpart the difficulty of such a task. "From such experience as we have had in the nine years of our independence," the Israeli prime minister advised Nkrumah, "I know that it is comparatively easy to arouse the people to fight for their independence, but much more difficult to persuade them to devote themselves to the everyday unromantic work of construction and development."[34]

Ghanaian officials, for their part, praised Israel as a model of a thriving, disciplined, and unified new nation. It was also a nation, the West Africans pointed out in contrast, that was forged out of the harshest of political and environmental realities. The situation in Ghana, CPP Northern Region secretary Adjingboru A. Syme argued in 1957, was much more conducive to success, given the country's "green and fertile" land and absence of "enemies threatening us."[35] As part of a mid-1957 delegation of Brigade officials to the Middle Eastern state, Syme celebrated the communal ethic of the Israeli kibbutz. Moreover, as detailed in a 1958 pamphlet recounting his travels, Syme noted with interest a daily routine in kibbutz life that included "picking peaches and grapes, laying irrigation pipes, irrigating the fields, assisting in machine cultivation in the fields, and helping on the poultry farms and in the cattle sheds." This labor, he further highlighted, was followed by "theoretical studies of the work of the Kibbutz" in which Israelis inquired into a range of subjects, including the "Organizational Structure of the Kibbutz," "Management and Administration of the Kibbutz," "The Places of Women and Children in the Kibbutz," and "Peculiar Problems of the Kibbutz."[36]

The Ghanaians were particularly drawn to the regimented nature of the programs preparing Israeli youth for the Middle Eastern state's youth paramilitary wings, the Gadna and Nahal/Zahal. In Syme's pamphlet he described training, beginning in preadolescence and continuing until age eighteen, in which Israeli boys and girls engaged in physical activities ranging from hiking and camping to sport. Through this training they were to learn the values, rights, and responsibilities of the Israeli citizen. "The whole idea of the Youth movement," Syme argued, "is to instil the spirit of living together, working together and playing together in them [the youth] and this is done between the ages of 10 and 18." In discussing the Gadna specifically, Syme further emphasized the paramilitary nature of youth life, explaining that young Israeli men and women studied everything from Morse code to electronics and engineering to military field training. As a result, as each member of the Nahal or Gadna reached the age of majority at eighteen, he or she was prepared to begin his or her requisite term of military service, as well as to transition into life as a productive member of a kibbutz.[37]

Documents circulating in the Ghanaian prime minister's office further detailed and celebrated the political, social, and cultural aspects of the Israeli youth programs for study by CPP and incoming Brigade officials.[38] As a result, the Israeli programs provided a model for what would become a large part of the first cohorts of brigaders' day-to-day life. As in Israel, Ghana's Brigade camps integrated a regimented program of patriotic ritual into a labor system structured around vocational training and agricultural work. Brigaders opened their days with marching and drill instruction, flag-raising ceremonies, the recitation and singing of Brigade pledges and songs, and physical training exercises followed by labor in their camp's fields or on its various construction projects. In Accra, brigaders punctuated their work of constructing the Brigade's base camp in the city's Kanda section with breaks for songs, games, athletic competitions, and coursework. In contrast, more than six hundred kilometers north in Damongo, yam production and other agricultural work dominated the brigaders' daily activities.[39] As new camps were established throughout the country, brigaders gained the opportunity to specialize in their work, focusing on everything from fishing and farming to carpentry, sewing, auto mechanics, and musical performance.[40]

Meanwhile, former brigaders spoke of their involvement in the organization's activities in terms of their ambitions to attain the skills and values necessary to be respected and admired citizens in their communities. In many cases adopting the modernist and politically disciplined notion of citizenship advocated by the CPP, several of the brigaders and family members I interviewed in 2007 and 2008 celebrated the personal and professional opportunities the organization had to offer. Speaking, for instance, of his brother's experience in the Brigade, Accra resident E. B. Mensah emphasized the possibilities for social mobility provided by the Brigade: "Somebody will come from a poor family, their father cannot even afford to give a *kyale wɔtee* [a set of rubber sandals], but if he go[es] there [to the Brigade camp] and the father see[s] how they are dressed, people like[d] the way they are dressed." To Mensah, however, the issue of dress was about more than simple fashion. It was about a transformation—for, on the personal level, the dress of the brigader designated the wearer as an individual committed to the dual tasks of bettering himself or herself and, in so doing, serving the nation. Moreover, he continued,

"If you [are] with them [the Brigade], and you are semi-educated or you have not got any education at all, they [the Brigade] will send them [the brigaders] to school to learn how to read and write." The result, in Mensah's opinion, was a social situation wherein, following their contracted two-year employment with the Brigade, young brigaders were to be able to take their acquired skills and translate them into full-time blue-collar and even white-collar employment.[41]

Others expanded upon Mensah's portrayal of Brigade life. As one former brigader, Yaa Fosuawaa—who worked in Brigade camps in the Eastern, Brong Ahafo, and what is now Upper West Regions—explained in 2008, when Nkrumah "started the Brigade, he employed all of us. He gave us all jobs, both men and women."[42] Organizationally, these jobs tended to adhere to a clearly gendered but at times fluid division of labor. Women, for their part, generally advanced the Brigade's mission through cooking, sewing, planting, selling Brigade-made goods, and craftwork. As Fosuawaa explained, "We [the Brigade women] were planting cassava. We were also cooking for the men. Sometimes we cooked *gyigyi* [a local food made of dried cassava similar to *fufu*] and sometimes we cooked *yakayake* [buns made of *gari*]. Sometimes we cooked yams or cocoyam. We cooked it with whole boxes of tinned pilchards. We planted sugarcane, yam, cassava. Sometimes, the women also planted."[43] Female brigaders would sell these crops, along with craftwork and other goods produced within the camps, in the neighboring towns, while some were also shipped to the country's urban centers.[44]

For Fosuawaa, the Brigade proved to be a personal and professional boon. Having not attended school prior to her employment with the Brigade, she—like most Ghanaian women—made her living through cooking food for sale, other trade, and some small-scale farming. After entering the Brigade, though, Fosuawaa and a select few other women gained often unanticipated responsibilities. As a result, in her conversations about her Brigade experience, she highlighted the sense of social mobility she had gained through the organization, particularly in terms of her ability to transcend the gendered power dynamics within the camp. It was through the Brigade, she emphasized, that she and others gained both the privilege and the responsibility of "watching over men."[45] Meanwhile, the Brigade, as a paying employer, also allowed her to meet the more mundane necessities of her life. Most importantly, this included providing her with the income necessary to pay her wards' school fees. Furthermore, she recalled that the situation was not much different for men, for she insisted that the Brigade had provided many of its male members with the opportunity to better position themselves for securing regular, long-term employment in the coming years, which they could later leverage in their marriage pursuits.[46]

For other Brigade women, their participation in certain seemingly masculine tasks—most notably, driving tractors—situated them within a political and social discourse designed to promote the modernist and progressive dimensions of Nkrumahist development. As in Ghana's Eastern Bloc counterparts, such defeminized female labor was meant to illustrate a social and cultural revolution in which women were to have the same rights, responsibilities, and opportunities to contribute to the nation-building project as their male colleagues.[47] Moreover, over the fifty years since the CPP's overthrow, these women have emerged as one of the most durable symbols of the social innovations associated with the Nkrumahist revolution, as numerous interview participants emphasized, at least to some extent, the masculinization of women's work in the organization as a central feature of Brigade life. Furthermore, they did this despite the relatively small number of women who likely engaged in such work. As historian Owusu Brempong noted, reflecting on his cousin's experience in the Brigade's Techiman camp, "She was a girl . . . [and] she came there and was a truck driver for tractors." According to Brempong, "in those days, women driving tractors was wonderful. People were flabbergasted to see women trained and driving tractors, and the women who did it were highly respected to do a man's job."[48] E. B. Mensah echoed Brempong's sentiments, saying, "The most hardest thing they [the brigaders] do is tractor driving . . . [and] they train the women, because if you hear [of] a woman driving you would be surprised . . . [and] you would be very happy."[49]

For a government concerned about unemployment, the Brigade's work regimes were intended to help diversify the employment opportunities and expectations of Ghanaian youth. Key to the Brigade's agenda, then, was preparing the country's urbanizing young men and women for a return to the land, but on a different set of terms.[50] These young brigaders were not to engage in just any form of agricultural labor. They were to learn to cultivate the land in a way that accentuated the newly independent government's vision of a distinctly modern and industrializing Ghana. In the Brigade's camps, mechanized production, especially in farming, was to reign supreme. At its most basic level, mechanization promised greater yields, efficiency, and ease in cultivating more land for a range of crops.[51] At the same time, it was also to signify the country's shift in agriculture to a modern industrial ideal, analogous to that taking place in or imagined for cities like Tema, Accra, and elsewhere. To this end, images of brigaders driving tractors, plows, bulldozers, and other heavy machinery regularly dotted the Ghanaian political as well as agricultural landscape in the first decade of self-rule. Not dissimilar to the iconography of the hammer and sickle in the Eastern Bloc, in Ghana such imagery was to bring to the fore for the country's young people specifically and the populace more broadly their role and responsibility in building the new nation.[52]

On its face, in the late 1950s, the Brigade was an unqualified success. From its earliest days it was extremely popular among the country's unemployed. In preparation for the organization's 1957 opening, initial applications for the Brigade's Accra and Damongo camps exceeded 21,000.[53] By June 1959, the Brigade had expanded from its two inaugural camps to twenty and was employing approximately 8,500 brigaders.[54] By mid-1959, the government connected the Brigade to an approximately 28 percent drop in the country's registered unemployed over the course of the organization's eighteen-month existence. At the same time, it also forecasted an even greater fall, as the organization intended to expand its membership to more than 25,000 Ghanaians over the coming years.[55] By the time of the 1966 coup—according to reports issued both under the CPP and after the coup—the Brigade, which over the preceding years had undergone several structural reorganizations, had reached 25,000 brigaders in up to fifty-two camps.[56]

CHILDHOOD AND DISCIPLINE

As the Brigade expanded in the late 1950s and early 1960s, the CPP increasingly turned its attention to another segment of the Ghanaian youth: schoolchildren. In the press, discussions of the nation's schoolchildren often featured (highly gendered) lamentations over their laziness, sexual impropriety, and rudeness along with calls for both national service and social support. Central to much of this discussion was a discourse centered upon the perceived moral failings of the upcoming generation and the need for reforms—both government-sponsored and coming from families and schools.[57] Inside the government itself, debates over the nation's schoolchildren tended to emphasize their role in the broader nation-building project. In doing so, CPP and other officials often highlighted what they characterized as a troubling "lack of patriotism" among the country's youngest citizens.[58] Attempts to rectify the situation included the creation of a special cabinet committee commissioned with studying the problem. In August 1958, the committee returned with a set of recommendations for several curricular reforms, including such measures as the institution of recited pledges of loyalty during the school day.[59] Meanwhile, by the third year of self-rule, the government's focus had turned to the establishment of a formal youth organization of its own for the country's schoolchildren.

The actual debates over what such an organization should look like, however, had begun several years earlier. As early 1955, for instance, George Padmore had counseled Nkrumah on the need to begin planning for a formal Ghanaian postcolonial youth movement. He drew comparisons to the mobilizing success of both Maoist China and the exiled Chinese nationalists connected to Chiang Kai-Shek. Padmore also advised Nkrumah that popular international, colonial-era youth organizations such as the Boy Scouts could serve as models for the future of Ghana's own youth movement. However, according to the Trinidadian, it was essential that Ghana, as a newly independent state, forge its own, independent movement.[60] M. N. Tetteh, who in the late 1950s and early 1960s was one of the CPP's key youth organizers, took an even stronger tone in his own insistence on the importance of Ghana having its own youth movement. As viewed by Tetteh, a newly independent country's unquestioning reliance on such colonial-era institutions—most notably the highly popular Boy Scout movement—only served to weaken the nationalist consciousness of the country's youth through the promotion of what Tetteh described as an imperial conception of citizenship and civic duty.[61] By definition, such notions of citizenship were not connected to Africa, but instead to Europe and the Commonwealth; independence, he asserted, thus demanded that "we . . . train our own children where they should go, because African culture is not European culture."[62]

The Ghana Young Pioneers promised to fill this void. The government first introduced the Young Pioneers into the cabinet debates in late 1959. As with the Builders Brigade, the organizational model for the Young Pioneers had its origins outside of Africa. In part, the government again turned to the organizational models of the Israeli youth movements in its vision for the Young Pioneers and the regimentation of the country's schoolchildren. More importantly, the Ghanaians also looked to the Soviet Union, even naming its own youth movement after the Soviet Young Pioneers. In both the Israeli and Soviet settings, young boys and girls ranging in age from early childhood to adolescence engaged in a set of essentially state-centered political and social programs designed to deepen their attachment to the state project. At their core, these programs aimed to blend political and cultural education with a collection of discipline- and character-building exercises framed around the cooperative nature of their nation-building endeavors.[63] Among the most popular activities in both countries' youth movements were hiking, camping, and gymnastics, which the organizations combined with the public performance of songs, recitations, and drill. Furthermore, in both the Israeli and Soviet contexts, the schoolchildren participating in their respective movements were uni- formed, with the Soviet Young Pioneer uniform—including buttoned shirts, skirts or trousers, hats, and a neckerchief—serving as the primary model for its emerging Ghanaian counterpart.[64]

In the CPP, debates around the structure and mission of the Young Pioneer movement centered on the political and social potential of the country's youngest citizens. Themes of politics, culture, and patriotism in turn drove the discourse surrounding the movement's planning. In many ways echoing the advice he had received from Padmore four years earlier, Nkrumah insisted in a 1959 cabinet memorandum that the mission of any new youth movement had to be "in consonance with the Ghanaian en- vironment and social conditions, and the peculiar Ghanaian approach to the role of the youth in the community." What exactly a "Ghanaian ap- proach" to youth organization was, however, was largely left unspecified by the prime minister. Instead, Nkrumah emphasized the broader social benefits of a movement "engaged in healthy activities such as sports, calis- thenics, voluntary social service, work camps, etc."[65]

By June of the following year, Nkrumah returned to the cabinet with a formal plan for the Young Pioneers. "The immediate object of the move- ment," he explained, "is to inculcate in these children a feeling of pride for the country. As such, the Young Pioneer [sic] will fashion the outlook of the youth towards this ideal. It will seek to foster physical fitness, re- spect for manual work, self-discipline, sense of duty and responsibility, and, above all, a love for and a strong desire to serve, the fatherland." In practice, the prime minister continued, late-afternoon and weekend events and meetings were to provide the country's schoolchildren with this nationalist worldview through civic instruction and exams, manual skills training, nature study, and an introduction into the health sciences. Older children would likewise engage in community-wide self-help and develop- ment projects, while at the same time participating in "pre-military train- ing" as a way to "inculcate patriotism and loyalty for the country which is so lamentably absent from the outlook of the present day youth of Ghana."

Moreover, Nkrumah expressed the hope that at least part of the Young Pioneer program could eventually be integrated into the regular school curriculum, and he encouraged the country's teachers to offer "their full support and inspiration" to the movement.[66]

Other prominent government officials outlined additional potential Young Pioneer activities. Similar to the youth cultural spectacles in Guinea analyzed by Mike McGovern and Jay Straker, in Ghana these included the organization of youth forums and festivals celebrating the uniqueness of Ghana and Africa, broader public education campaigns, and domestic and international programs of political and cultural exchange.[67] Meanwhile, initial plans for the movement envisioned dividing the country's schoolchildren into three age groups: the African Personality children (4–7 years), the Young Pioneers (8–16 years), and the Kwame Nkrumah Youth (17–20 years). Likewise, attempts to better integrate the country's young men and women into the party apparatus further resulted in the 1962 creation of the Young Party League (21–25 years) under the Young Pioneer administrative umbrella.[68] Charles Ballard, one of the first scholars to study the Young Pioneers, has reported that, by the eve of the 1966 coup, additional plans were under way for further expansion of the movement through the inclusion of three-year-olds.[69] As a result, over the nearly six years in which the Young Pioneers were in existence, the youth organization grew exponentially, with the movement beginning in 1960 with a nucleus of approximately three hundred Accra-based schoolchildren. By late 1965, it claimed a membership roll of just under 570,000 members.[70]

Meanwhile, inside the Young Pioneers' daily operations, its organizers sought to create a curriculum that was at once modern, explorative, disciplined, and ideologically sound. Meeting up to three times a week after school, Young Pioneers would engage in song, recitation, and drill instruction, along with physical fitness routines, sporting events, camping and hiking trips, and wilderness training programs.[71] At party rallies and other events, Young Pioneers serenaded audiences that included everyone from their parents and neighbors to (at times) very prominent officials, with eulogies to the party and particularly to Nkrumah.[72] Other musical and stage productions aimed to educate broader audiences with tales of Nkrumah's role in resurrecting the glory of the African past, through performances that often blended songs in both English and vernacular languages with a call-and-response history of the CPP and the African liberation movement. As one Ashanti Region example demonstrates, after opening their performance with the still-popular nationalist anthem "Yen Ara Asase [This Is Our Land]," a group of Ashanti Region Young Pioneers recited a play that connected the CPP's struggle for self-government to the majestic legacies of "the great walled cities and towers of Zimbabwe," the medieval empires of Ghana, Mali, and Songhai, and "the art of Ife and Benin."[73]

In other instances, Young Pioneer songs and activities highlighted the intersections between the CPP's planned modernization of the country and the increasingly socialist message promoted by the postcolonial government in the early 1960s. In one popular Young Pioneer song, for instance, students sang about their commitment to the socialist nation-building project, reciting lines including:

> I'm a socialist student.
> Building the Road.
> Building Socialism Road.
> We're apostles of the new Ghana.
> We're building the socialist road.[74]

Here, the Young Pioneers embedded within the imagery of the country's late-colonial and early postcolonial infrastructural development a key component of the Nkrumahist ideological message of collective national self-help and individual responsibility. Similar songs and recitations further emphasized how even the youngest Ghanaians had a role in the Nkrumahist project. "A little man I am," another popular recitation asserted,

> Ghana's reconstruction rests on me.
> My love of work and Field Craft,
> Shall be put in Work and Happiness.
> Comradeship and Forebearance [sic],
> This is to be revived at all cost.
> We have to revive once and for all,
> To build a virile nation.[75]

According to former Ashanti Region Young Pioneer Kwasi Assiore, the goal of such songs and recitations was to serve as a constant reminder that the youth's work was "for the country, not for the individual."[76]

Not unlike youth movements elsewhere in Africa and in the socialist bloc, other Young Pioneer activities promoted this message. Lectures, for instance, emphasized the distinction between capitalist and socialist modes of production, highlighting what one regional organizer described as the security of a socialist "planned economy" over capitalism's "anarchy of economy."[77] Students in the Young Pioneers responded to such lectures with essays replicating the messages of their leaders in both the party and the Young Pioneers. For instance, in a 1962 essay, thirteen-year-old Kumasi Young Pioneer Charlotte Mensah came out in vehement support of the government's 1961 budget. In doing so, she argued—very much in line with the arguments put forward by the government—that the budget's controversial compulsory savings plan foremost served as a safety net for the country's workers against the potential threat of unemployment.[78] In another essay, Young Pioneer Opoku Afiriyie described with pride his and his colleagues' role in Kumasi's 1962 Positive Action Day festivities. As Afiriyie detailed, his day began with the Young Pioneers marching from the Young Pioneer Centre in Kumasi to the center in Asawase. He recounted how, after arriving at the Asawase center, he had sought to obey the Young Pioneer code of "Love of Work" by undertaking the task of selling copies of *The Nkrumah Youth* before heading back for the CPP's Positive Action Day rally in Kumasi.[79]

Politically, the government thus sought to present the Young Pioneers as part of an increasingly all-encompassing process of ideological socialization. The goal was similar to that described by Thomas Burgess in Zanzibar, where the post-1964 revolutionary government embarked upon its own Young Pioneer movement. In both countries, the governments sought to use their respective Young Pioneer programs to construct, borrowing from Burgess, "a fairly neat, one-dimensional, top-down assertion of state power, free of visual hints of irrepressible individualism, resistance, or negotiation."[80] In Ghana, for many Young Pioneers themselves, the movement and its ideological mission became central features of their childhood identities. Kwasi Assiore, for instance, recalled, "They teach [*sic*] us marching, how to dress, how to learn, how to do other things."[81] Similarly, E. B. Mensah remembered a movement centered upon the cultivation of leadership skills in the country's young people. "At times, they [the Young Pioneers] go to camp," he explained, "and they [the organization's leaders and officials] train[ed] them how to govern the country and all these things." As in his portrayal of the Builders Brigade, Mensah stressed that the goal of the movement was to ensure that the country's young people knew how to "act in the future when they come to that side," meaning positions of leadership and adulthood.[82] Here, the disciplinary and ideological training of the Young Pioneers formed part of a broader program of character-building framed around the assumed needs and ambitions of the emergent nation.

Former Shama Young Pioneer Joseph Yawson, while speaking with several members of his former Young Pioneer cohort, echoed Mensah's sentiments. Together, Yawson and his colleagues suggested that, on its face, the movement provided the state an opportunity to foster what they described as a "sense of patriotism to learn about the ideologies and principles [of the state], what Nkrumah speaks for." However, in their broader discussion of the movement, these former Young Pioneers insisted that the movement also carried with it a deeper mission connected to the character of the youth. In doing so, they emphasized its role in helping to develop a sense of self-reliance and personal and collective responsibility among the youth. In particular, Yawson and his Shama colleagues emphasized the inextricability of these character traits from the development of the new nation, arguing that the building of a young girl's or boy's character was as much a civic initiative as a personal one. For them, the youth—through the guidance of the Young Pioneers—came to model for all Ghanaians the requisite respect for work, commitment to timeliness, patriotism, and obedience necessary in a modern, postcolonial socialist state.[83]

SPIES, "SMALL SOLDIERS," AND GENERATIONAL CONFLICT

The CPP's not-so-subtle mission with both the Brigade and, after its 1961 formal launch, the Young Pioneers was the reorganization of the political and social hierarchies of Ghanaian society around the new country's youngest and most malleable members. As Kumasi North District commissioner Mary Osei stressed at a 1963 ideological seminar, "The socialist generations have to be moulded from Childhood" and "cared for and steeled from their youth." Such a commitment, she insisted, would ensure "that there should be no moral cripples in our country, no victims of incorrect education and pernicious example."[84] The organization of the youth not only promised to advance and sustain the Nkrumahist nation-building project, but, perhaps even more importantly, to protect it from foreign and international subversion. Furthermore, embedded in the mission of both the Brigade and the Young Pioneers were the intersecting realities of the changing face of local party politics, Ghanaian familial relations, and Nkrumahist pan-Africanism and socialism. On the ground, party and governmental officials sought to supplant the gerontocratic authority of the country's traditional elders by presenting the party, the state, and their various institutions and wings—the Brigade and Young Pioneers among them—as not simply a political party and government designed to bring public goods to the people. They were also to be the diviners of generational mobility and social and cultural growth in the emergent nation.[85]

The result within the CPP was a growing vision of a cosmopolitan, youth-centered nation that would challenge conventional gender and generational expectations in the emerging Nkrumahist state. In turn, many Young Pioneers and especially brigaders looked to the CPP's youth organizations to fulfill these aims. Social expectations regarding marriage and parenthood featured prominently in the lives of all young Ghanaian men and women. However, the twentieth-century rise of the cash economy and the urbanizing trends that followed situated early and midcentury youth, especially young men, in a position wherein proof that they could sustain a family derived from their ability to secure stable, long-term employment.[86] Both Yaa Fosuawaa and E. B. Mensah, as discussed earlier, emphasized the ways in which many young male brigaders turned to the organization in order to ensure access to the wage economy and thus translate their income into improved marriage prospects.[87] Meanwhile, like most of their counterparts outside of the Brigade and the CPP's other civic initiatives, young women held the expectations of a womanhood necessarily defined by marriage and motherhood. For many, though, the Brigade—due to the nature of its various forms of labor, the structure of camp life, and the payment system—offered them a means to challenge and expand such conventionally gendered expectations. Largely entering the Brigade during the beginning of their marriageable years, in their late teens and early twenties, many female brigaders found it possible to use the organization in order to (at least temporarily) put off marriage and childbearing as they pursued the present and anticipated benefits of membership in it.[88] As Fosuawaa—who emphasized how the Brigade had provided women the opportunity to gain supervisory positions in its camps—noted, the Brigade allowed female brigaders to skirt gender expectations of male leadership while also providing an income that allowed them to prepare—professionally, economically, and socially—for the future.[89] In sum, Brigade life came to represent a link between new and existing pathways to a socially recognized adulthood.

The CPP, for its part, did not fail to recognize the importance of this transition to a socially recognized adulthood to the Ghanaian youth and particularly to the country's brigaders. Rather, the party and government actively integrated the concept and imagery of this transition into the public rhetoric and performance of the Nkrumahist state. In so doing, the CPP contrasted the order, discipline, and social and cultural mobility offered by the Brigade with the divisions and inequities that had defined colonial life. For, as explained by Kojo Botsio, then minister of commerce and industry, Brigade activities and labor were to cultivate a new national work ethic among Ghanaian youth.[90] Likewise, J. E. Ababio—the Brigade's national organizer—proclaimed that the Brigade's foremost aim was to imbue in its male and female members the skills, confidence, productivity, and technical discipline necessary to guide the country's future agricultural and infrastructural development. Moreover, each brigader had the responsibility of embracing the challenges and responsibilities that came with this training. "You," Ababio argued, "are incontestably the future back-bone of this Country and even more, a source of emulation to the whole African continent."[91] As such, the Brigade's top official was directly connecting the transformative nature of the Brigade—that is, both the personal and national growth that was to come through Brigade life—to the future of the nation and continent.[92]

Thus, from the perspective of the government, the social regimentation embedded within Brigade life, along with that of the Young Pioneers, was as much about social renewal as it was about bringing social order. Just as importantly, among those interviewed, many involved in the organizations still held similar perspectives on what their and their family members' participation in the organizations meant to them. For instance, former Young Pioneer E. B. Mensah, reflecting on his brother's Brigade experience, explained that brigaders "started like as small soldiers. They [the Brigade] uniformed them, and then, if there is some activity, they [the Brigade] used to take them there and watch how things are going." In his description of the Brigade, Mensah echoed the narrative he had given of his own experience in the Young Pioneers: "They [the brigaders] are [sic] being trained to respect and see how best in the future they can handle the country. In the nutshell, they are [sic] being trained as young men for the future."[93] Taken together, Mensah and others suggested that the two organizations promised to clear the cobwebs of the past and contribute to the productivity and development of the future.

From the perspective of the CPP, this process had implications that extended beyond the localized sphere of Ghanaian decolonization and nation-building. The ramifications of such a transformation of Ghanaian youth reached outward into the broader Cold War and the struggle for African liberation and unity as together Ghana and Africa sought to break the bonds of foreign control. Moreover, specifically in regard to the Young Pioneers, youth in the movement were to serve as clear symbols of the new

African modernity. In the movement's gliding school, for instance, those admitted to the program were depicted as pushing the boundaries of the possible, transcending the everydayness of the land.[94] On other occasions, select groups of Young Pioneers, among others, were to represent the cosmopolitan nature of the new nation as they traveled to the Soviet Union, East and West Germany, and the United Arab Republic, in addition to other locales, where they engaged in specialized technical, scientific, and ideological training. As one Young Pioneer official reported after leading a youth delegation to the United Arab Republic in 1962, such experiences not only fostered a sense of international camaraderie, but also allowed Ghanaian youth to witness and reflect upon the rapid development and modernization efforts taking place outside of Ghana.[95] According to former Shama Young Pioneer Lawrence Bessah, who traveled to the Eastern Bloc in the mid-1960s, such trips were both personally edifying and politically formative, as, in his case, he gained the opportunity to experience the cultural melting pots that were the Soviet Union's international youth festivals.[96]

At their most ideological level, the rituals, symbols, and activities that comprised life in the Young Pioneers and Builders Brigade were at the same time designed to single out the two organizations' members for distinction in Nkrumah-era Ghana and to reposition them at the political and social center of the Nkrumahist revolution. However, the meanings of these symbols and rituals were by no means universally agreed upon. Moreover, both for their members and for the public at large, no symbol of either the Brigade or the Young Pioneers proved to be as potent and contested in the popular imagination as their respective uniforms. As Ben Nikoi-Oltai—a former CPP stalwart, albeit, by at least 2007 and 2008, turned harsh critic of the CPP's youth programs—explained in a 2008 interview, for many at the time seeking to understand these movements from the outside, the transformation embodied in the simple donning of a uniform was a dramatic and potentially dangerous one. "Why, immediately you [are] in uniform, they put you in a different category," the Accra shopkeeper insisted. "You put on [a] uniform and you know you are a special person." In his view, the Young Pioneers in particular had a role in "brainwash[ing] the youth" so that they would "feel that they are [sic] the power behind the government." To Nikoi-Oltai, this was part of an attempted reorganization of the Ghanaian social and familial environment, whereby organizations like the Brigade and the Young Pioneers became conduits through which children could circumvent their parents and elders in forging imagined relationships to the state. Moreover, he hinted that, in some cases, the power of the uniform led some to believe that they might even have the power to subvert the hierarchies of the state itself. As such, at least for Nikoi-Oltai, who had joined the CPP at its founding, the uniforms of these movements came to represent an emerging set of generationally defined social ills in the early 1960s—ills he specifically connected to the at times troubling reach of the CPP's "Eastern [i.e., communist] forms of psychology" into the fabric of Ghanaian life.[97]

Tied to popular questions surrounding the Brigade and Young Pioneer uniforms were others regarding the regimented pattern of each movement's daily activities. The proposed regimentation of Brigade life elicited an immediate response from the country's (largely) politically neutered formal opposition. For instance, speaking to the National Assembly in August 1957, Dagomba South MP Alhaji Yakubu Tali insisted that a uniformed youth movement was "Hitler's own idea." According to Tali, Hitler had "hardened his young men" with a system of uniformed forced labor specifically designed for his own self-aggrandizement as opposed to the benefit of the nation.[98] Two years later, Tali's Wala North colleague, Jatoe Kaleo, sardonically commented on what he viewed as the superficiality of the Brigade's regimented and potentially militarized lifestyle following a visit to its Damongo camp. According to Kaleo, the "activities there are marching, singing songs of praise to our dear Kwame Nkrumah, [and] waving [of] Ghana flags," while, in his opinion, brigaders did "practically nothing as far as trade is concerned."[99] Other opposition MPs recounted incidents in which uniformed male brigaders converged upon polling stations and opposition rallies, threatening and attacking opposition supporters.[100] The result, insisted the leader of the Ashanti Region's United Party Youth League, was an atmosphere of intimidation, cultivated by the Brigade, in which "villagers cannot, because of fear, go to their farms, their only gainful employment."[101]

At the popular level, Ghanaians had a variety of reactions and apprehensions connected to the regimentation and performed discipline in the Young Pioneers and Builders Brigade. Key to these reactions were concerns over the organizations' real and perceived efforts to militarize the youth, with many fearing that the government would arm and mobilize them. Rumors to this effect ran rampant in mid-century Ghana. "They [the Brigade]," Nikoi-Oltai noted, "train you as a soldier. Their dresses, their caps and shoes, green like the army. . . . They march around. They march as soldiers march. They do parade. . . . They have weapons, [the]

Workers Brigade. They've got everything, guns, everything." When asked why the government would give its brigaders weapons, Nikoi-Oltai explained, "Politics is [a] very subtle organization. It's [a] very bad thing, very subtle. They [the politicians?] have something at the back of their minds." In his conversations about the Brigade and Young Pioneers, Nikoi-Oltai thus constructed a narrative of the two organizations and their activities that juxtaposed an at times laudatory reflection on the various nation-building activities they undertook with rumored accounts of the arming of Ghanaian youth. Still, from the perspective of this Accra shopkeeper, such measures—rumored or real—ultimately were shown to be necessary for Nkrumah and the CPP, particularly as the Ghanaian leader navigated an array of threats on his life in the early and mid-1960s.[102]

Others also commented on the Brigade's and Young Pioneers' perceived militaristic atmosphere, often with much less sympathy for the CPP's initiatives and the threats the government faced than that expressed by Nikoi-Oltai. Explaining, for instance, in 2008 that the brigaders "were trained like soldiers," Koforidua farmer and former Kwahu Praso Young Pioneer Kofi Ampadu connected the Brigade to Nkrumah's need for a reliable voting base. He claimed with a certain amount of cynicism that "every governor wants crowds of supporters and would do anything to attract people."[103] Another former Young Pioneer and Accra resident, Nicholas Budu, further related, "Once you do anything [against the party] and they [the brigaders] catch you, they will beat you like soldiers [beat people]."[104] Eden Bentum Takyi-Micah—a former Central Region pupil-teacher—similarly presented the brigaders as regular transgressors of the social and ethical norms of Ghanaian society and the generational hierarchies implicit in these norms. In doing so, he recounted an anecdote in which a brigader, purportedly caught up in the authority he saw as bestowed upon him by his position, negligently destroyed the garden of one of his senior neighbors. According to Takyi-Micah, after the old man protested to the brigader, the brigader responded with threats that he would beat the elderly man should he continue with his complaints. For the former pupil-teacher, such incidents highlighted the contradictions inherent in Brigade life. For, even as Nkrumah and the CPP promoted the organization as a disciplined and productive labor force, Takyi-Micah insisted, "they were always misbehaving. They had no respect for anybody, except the party CPP."[105]

As for the Young Pioneers, individuals both with and without past links to the organization offered similar opinions of the effects its regimentation had on the country's schoolchildren. Koforidua resident Lawrence Asamoah, reflecting on his childhood friends' experiences in the movement, described the role of the movement's members as that of "a small police."[106] Former Nkawkaw resident and Young Pioneer Jacob Sesu Yeboah expressed a similar belief. Belying Yeboah's interpretation of the Young Pioneers, though, was his own frustration with an organization that had failed to live up to expectations he had at the time for a movement that he believed would prepare him for a future career in the military. As a result, he unfavorably compared the level of regimentation in the Young Pioneers with what he remembered of his time in the Boy Scouts. Leaving the Boy Scouts to join the Young Pioneers after the Ghanaian organization's inauguration in Nkawkaw, Yeboah spoke of how, when he joined the movement, he initially expected the Young Pioneer program to be a continuation of that of the Boy Scouts, which he emphasized was characterized by discipline and physicality. The reality of the Young Pioneers, though, disappointed him, as he lamented the general laxity of commitment that surrounded the organization's day-to-day activities. "They don't [sic] train as a soldier," he argued, as he contrasted the physical fitness training and survival skills he learned in the Boy Scouts with the after-school, largely ideological program of the Young Pioneers.[107]

Others focused on the persistent accusations of spying that followed the Young Pioneers. Commenting on perhaps the most common rumor circulating around the organization, many of the individuals I spoke with presented the Young Pioneers as a movement specifically designed to train schoolchildren to spy on their parents, family members, and other elders. As former Shama Young Pioneer S. Atta-P. Anamon explained, spying "was the perception." However, he insisted, "it was not so."[108] Yeboah concurred. According to him, "the question is the time" put into the movement, not spying. Young Pioneers, he recounted, would attend school until midafternoon and then, after school let out, would participate in disciplinary and citizenship-training exercises until—by his calculation—around six o'clock. As a result, he suggested, "You have to come home, but the time is late. So that thing, it troubled parents," who had their own expectations of their children.[109] Anamon agreed, noting that the time commitment involved in being a Young Pioneer "was a problem for some parents. Over here within our setup as Africans, children have to go home and help their parents. I'm using myself as an example. My father was a farmer, so when school closed I have to burn some charcoals in the farm and carry them back home. And it is the same time that we attended meetings instead of going to the farm, so naturally my father will not be happy. There were others who have to sell *kenkey* and other things to support the family. So that is why parents were protesting." The result, according to Anamon and his Shama colleagues, was a context in which stories of spying and other forms of social and cultural subversion emerged from a popular misreading of the movement and its activities. More importantly, they argued, in discussing questions of spying in the Young Pioneers one should also consider an individual's sense of personal and societal obligation. While Young Pioneers were not explicitly trained to be spies, they contended, these schoolchildren "were being trained to protect the state, and so if you go contrary to the state interest, then they will go directly to report you." This reporting, however, was not a matter of deceit or betrayal for Anamon or his compatriots. Rather, it was part of a broader moral shift in a child's political and social development around the transformative pan-African and socialist politics of the Nkrumahist state.[110]

Many others, however, were not convinced by such a reading of the Young Pioneers, particularly in light of their understanding of their own time in the movement. For former Ashanti Region Young Pioneer Kwasi Assiore, his participation in the movement was not necessarily coerced, but it also was not a free choice. He presented the Young Pioneers as a CPP-led attempt not only to take over from parents and elders the process of socializing children, but to infiltrate families themselves. As a result, he viewed the question of spying as central to the movement's legacy: "So our work [as Young Pioneers] is, we make ourselves like the CIA, so anything we hear, we go and tell our comrade. The leaders, we call them comrade. And here is so-and-so, and the comrade will take a step and report it to the DC, this is [the] district commissioner, [who] will take it to the regional commissioner. From there, it comes to the party's office. You will be there and one day they will arrest you."[111] Former Accra-area Young Pioneer Nicholas Budu echoed his Ashanti Region contemporary. According to him, in the Young Pioneers schoolchildren were taught that "when you see or hear somebody criticize the government, when you inform the police, they would arrest the person and send him to prison." As a result, the program had far-reaching social and cultural implications for both the children involved in the organization (including himself) and the families and communities of these children. "Life," he recalled, "became unbearable for Ghanaians, because if you are in the house and your mother and father talk against the government, if you are a Young Pioneer, you go and report them."[112]

SOCIAL DISRUPTION, INDISCIPLINE, AND ADMINISTRATIVE INEFFICIENCIES

For the CPP, the many divergent popular reactions to the Builders Brigade and Young Pioneers collided with its idealized picture of a burgeoning, revolutionary Ghanaian youth in the first decade of self-rule. In both the party and government, the stakes involved in transforming this ideal into a reality could not have been higher. As one Ashanti Region Young Pioneer official avowed in 1962, "If we are able to inculcate into the youth Nkrumaism, Ghana will be a country of paradise."[113] To this end, the disciplinary and ideological training in the two organizations were to lay the groundwork for a deeper process of revolutionary acculturation and socialization among both the Ghanaian youth and, by extension, the populace at large. In both organizations, this process was at its heart envisioned as a citizenship-building exercise in which the question of citizenship itself became much more than one of simple nationality. Rather, ideal citizenship emerged out of the public exhibition of one's unbreakable bond to the state, and, thereby, the modeling of this bond for others. In the eyes of the CPP, this was a political as well as a social and cultural process, linked to a CPP-defined and increasingly CPP-controlled modern, socialist, and pan-African postcolonial ideal. As a result, as both organizations sought to achieve their respective aims, conflicting ideologies of generation, gender, and community marked the popular and, in some cases, official narratives surrounding them, as the party and government together sought to take control of the social and civic acculturation of the country's youth — often at the expense of their families and communities.

Few of the individuals I interviewed spoke more emphatically about the sense of loss and social disruption fostered by the CPP's vision for Ghanaian youth than Eden Bentum Takyi-Micah. A longtime opponent of the CPP, Takyi-Micah tied the Brigade specifically to the breakup of established Ghanaian communities. To his eye, the institution decimated the country's villages and towns, as it enticed young men and women away from their communities and families with shallow, materialist promises of "smart uniforms," free housing, and electricity, in turn leaving their elders to fend for themselves and their communities.[114] Moreover, he and others lamented that the Brigade did so while the realities of camp life cultivated in the towns and villages surrounding Brigade camps an atmosphere of violence, corruption, promiscuity, absentee parenting, and drunkenness.[115] Meanwhile, a long list of disputes over the acquisition of Brigade lands and the rights of local farmers created the impression of an organization set on disrupting the social and economic fabric of Ghanaian rural communities. As a result, farmers and others wishing to assert rights to lands acquired by the Brigade regularly petitioned it and the government for compensation and other forms of relief in exchange for lands lost to the growing number of Brigade camps.[116] Furthermore, inside the Brigade itself, some brigaders complained of the unevenness with which Brigade policies, promotions, and assignments were handled, as they depicted in petitions to the government an organization struggling with problems of patronage, favoritism, petty rivalries, intimidation, and punitive disciplinary actions.[117]

Such organizational and management concerns also arose regarding the Young Pioneers. Despite being the most important symbol of the organization, uniforms were constantly in short supply. Likewise, Young Pioneer administrators expressed regular frustration with a lack of discipline among the institution's staff, absenteeism among the organization's members, and disappointment with the speed of the movement's social, cultural, and political progress.[118] The difficulty of motivating students—especially, as one 1965 education official put it, the "brilliant" ones—to eagerly engage in organizations and movements like the Young Pioneers proved particularly irritating for the CPP and Young Pioneer administration.[119] In Tema, an unnamed middle-school-aged Young Pioneer interviewed by St. Clair Drake in 1965 highlighted why the government would have such concerns. According to her, participation in the Young Pioneers had its benefits. At times, the activities they engaged in were fun and possibly educational. However, she explained that, "frankly . . . many of these activities are not taken seriously so as a result the children loose [sic] interest in them and so normally [at best?] a handful of people do turn up for them." She further noted that the one activity that really drew the children's attention was marching, but even that was not enough to sustain interest in the program as a whole, for she insisted that "many of the children who have had some training in the other activities before find it boring to go and be taught the same thing."[120]

Meanwhile, Young Pioneer officials also looked with frustration at the interference of parents, elders, and other family members with their ability to advance the mission of the movement. In efforts intellectually similar to—albeit less dramatic than—the "demystification campaigns" undertaken by Sékou Touré's government in Guinea, Young Pioneer officials turned their attention to an array of cultural practices that they deemed as unmodern.[121] These included scarification and female circumcision. As one of the movement's first organizers, M. N. Tetteh, explained, he took it upon himself to have the organization identify these practices as antithetical to the values of a modern nation and the social and cultural unity on which the Nkrumahist state was to be founded. The result was a purported ban on any child with facial markings or any circumcised girl from taking part in some of the most prestigious Young Pioneer activities, including meeting foreign dignitaries and all travel out of the country. In this way, the Young Pioneers—albeit likely unsuccessfully—sought to create an incentive by which to entice parents and elders into compliance through the public shaming of those who engaged in such practices. Similar acts of shaming, which often included the loss of one's uniform, also occurred for those who failed to live up to the Young Pioneers' code in other ways, such as through tardiness, absenteeism, and other undisciplined habits.[122]

Moreover, other Ghanaian young people tested the CPP and Young Pioneer leaders' ambitions for the country's youth with their own, personal exercises in self-fashioning and social exploration. Much of this simply did not fit within the disciplined, socialist, pan-African model provided by the CPP. For instance, as Nate Plageman has shown in his study of highlife music, young Gold Coasters/Ghanaians had long used social clubs and dance halls as venues for often rebellious self-expression.[123] By the early 1960s, though, the CPP was seeking to clamp down on such spaces with attempts to create a national highlife culture that fit within the CPP's collective ambitions for the country by controlling the messages expressed in the music and people's relationships to it. Much to the government's chagrin, newly independent Ghanaians continued to use the music, and nightlife more broadly, as means for "individual rather than collective" expression.[124] Likewise, Ghanaian young people often rejected newly constructed urban community centers, where presumably they might have encountered more supervision from officials and others, preferring other venues in their pursuit of leisure and recreation.[125] Still others—many of whom were unable to find a place within either the Young Pioneers or the Builders Brigade—sought out alternative forms of work (legal and illegal) as they tried to make their way through the realities of the new state.[126]

However, the most pressing and longest-lasting issue facing the Young Pioneers and the CPP youth agenda more broadly was funding and access to supplies. As one Ashanti Region Young Pioneer official reminded his superiors in 1962,

> It is [an] undisputed fact that youth work needs both [to be] practical and [founded in] theory. We have, on paper, an elaborate

programme of activities such as Radio Mechanics, Telegraphy, Sewing and Knitting, Crochetting [sic], Flying and Gliding, etc. We need materials before these activities could be properly run to cater for the interests of the children. But these materials are not forthcoming. That is, we are producing nothing, no results. The children expect these materials; they have been long expecting them and that is why most of them seem to lose interest in the Organisation when these things are not forthcoming. The reason for non-supply of these materials and equipment is usually said to be lack of funds. This may be correct on [the] one hand and equally wrong on the other hand.[127]

Such concerns afflicted nearly all of the CPP's nation-building initiatives in the 1960s. Meanwhile, for the country's young people, these shortages created a sense of competition within the Young Pioneers in particular, as entrepreneurial members took it upon themselves to obtain or self-manufacture their own Young Pioneer uniforms or at least parts of them. With the uniform came prestige, and as a result, Kwasi Assiore recalled, physical brawls between children would often break out over access to uniforms.[128]

Yet, despite the troubles facing both the Young Pioneers and the Builders Brigade, by the mid-1960s they had become the face of the Nkrumahist social and cultural revolution on both the Ghanaian domestic and international stages. Together and separately, members of the Brigade and Young Pioneers were highly visible at party rallies, marched in parades, recruited tirelessly for the party, and greeted and performed for the country's numerous African and non-African visitors. During his 1965 visit to Accra, Che Guevara celebrated the Brigade specifically, noting that "the standard of discipline and respect for authority" embodied by the young men and women who composed the Brigade "had resulted in a natural progressive outlook on all its actions."[129] Similarly, in regards to the Young Pioneers, Bechem Training College principal V. Ayivor reminded a group of Young Pioneers in 1963 of their unique role, as citizens, in building the nation. "A good citizen," he argued, "is one who owes a duty to the Nation he belongs [to] and obey [sic] the laws of the Nation." The purpose of organizations like the Young Pioneers, he advised his audience, was to inculcate this sense of duty and responsibility into the country's young people and "train the Youth of Ghana to be good citizens of tomorrow."[130] Moreover, as the emergence of the one-party state increasingly closed off non-CPP options for political engagement in the early and mid-1960s (as will be seen in subsequent chapters), the Brigade and the Young Pioneer movement emerged as key conduits through which members could perform their generationally defined roles as revolutionary nation-builders. As young, radical, disciplined socialists, these nation-builders—through their labor and commitment to the party—were, in the eyes of the CPP, to lead the new Ghana and Africa more broadly to their rightful places alongside the world's developed nations in the postcolonial international community.

⌒

As the CPP unveiled the Builders Brigade in 1957, Nkrumah and Ghana still basked in the glow of the country's recent independence. Tied to this was the broader sense of hope and anticipation that many held for the continent's postcolonial future. Much, however, had changed by the 1960 unveiling and 1961 launch of the Young Pioneers. The so-called 1960 "Year of Africa" culminated with the decolonization of nearly all of West and Central Africa, even as, as the following chapters will show, events in Ghana weakened Western confidence in the country's prospects for a liberal democracy.[131] For Ghanaians, the rules of citizenship in turn shifted with these changes, augmenting the political, societal, and generational frictions that accompanied the formation and expansion of both the Builders Brigade and Young Pioneers. Through the public performance and promotion of a specific forward-looking, socialist, and cosmopolitan citizenship rooted in the tightly defined activism of the country's young men, women, and schoolchildren, each organization sought to emblazon in the national and international imagination a portrait of a generation of revolutionary nation-builders. At the heart of their cultivation was to be a process of socialization designed to eclipse the past and mobilize for the future. This preparation was in turn to be part of a broader international socialist youth movement, with a nexus of international exchange connecting Africa and beyond, as they all confronted an international environment perceived to be increasingly plagued by threats of capitalist imperialism, neocolonialism, and—perhaps most troubling—political and social apathy.[132] For, as Brong Ahafo regional secretary Nicholas Anane-Agyei reminded an Odumase Young Pioneer audience in late 1962, "the task of building Ghana into a socialist State and maintaining it as a show-piece on the African continent was not the responsibility of one man, but a collective responsibility."[133]

4 ⤳ "Work and Happiness for All"

Productivity and the Political Economy
of Pan-African Revolution

> The direct social character of labour in a socialist society, where the
> possibilities and needs of society are taken into account in advance,
> helps the workers to develop new interests. Moral inducements to
> work arise in addition to material incentives. Owing to this, labour
> is becoming ever more meaningful, gradually turning from a mere
> means of existence into a matter of honour.
>
> —Anoma Okore, "Labour in a Socialist Society," 1963[1]

IN A January 1965 article for the state-run magazine the *Ghanaian*, journalist E. B. Mac-Hardjor outlined for his readers the centrality of work
and productivity to the postcolonial nation. "A visit to the agricultural and
industrial establishments in Ghana today leaves a clear impression that
farmers and working people have caught the spirit of socialist construction and are steadily working forward to fulfil the targets of the Seven-Year
Plan," Mac-Hardjor noted with satisfaction. In the Ghana of Nkrumah,
the journalist explained, much had already been accomplished, with Ghanaians witnessing the construction of new roads, hospitals, schools, and
other institutions over the previous decade. Much more, however, was
needed for the country to achieve its aims, and everyone had a role and
responsibility in contributing to this mission. Work thus stood at the center
of every Ghanaian's civic duty. Moreover, Mac-Hardjor asserted, it was
specifically to be work characterized foremost by a commitment to ever-
greater results, accountability, and personal sacrifice. "The good worker,"
he declared, "knows no time limits. A day's work which is better than that
of yesterday, which is useful and leaves the worker satisfied with his output, is all the time demands. For now in Ghana," he further emphasized,
"working for the state is working for ourselves."[2]

   This chapter interrogates the politics of work and the conceptualization of "work" and the "worker" in postcolonial Ghana. If the youth were
to represent the ideal citizens of the future, the country's workers were

to be the architects of this future. At times replicating the rhetoric of the Builders Brigade and Young Pioneers, themes of productivity, discipline, and self-sacrifice pervaded CPP discussions of work and workers. These qualities, party and government officials insisted, were not just foundational to the construction of the modern, industrial, pan-African society promised by the CPP. More importantly, they were central to the national and eventually continental collectivization of the benefits and opportunities of such a society. As such, work as envisioned by the CPP was not to be about personal gain or accumulation. Rather, it was to unite Ghanaians of all walks of life in the party-led and party-defined nation-building project. Speaking to such a theme in a 1964 *Evening News* article, for instance, one party writer explained, "If you are a factory worker, making soap, canning fruits, sewing clothes, producing nails or footwear in the state enterprise, what this means is that you must aim at PRODUCING MORE EACH DAY. This in effect is the key to the prosperity of some advanced socialist states as compared to their capitalist and semi-colonial epochs." In Ghana, he continued, socialist productivity would necessarily lead to the distribution of the goods and services found in a modern, independent state: infrastructure, a secure food supply, and a reliable healthcare system, among other public goods.[3]

For workers, particularly those in well-organized professions and labor unions, this emphasis on productivity demanded a refocusing of their energy and allegiances away from their personal ambitions and toward those of the state. It also meant the imposition on their daily and work lives of an often alien, inconsistently applied, and in real terms ill-defined burden, not only on workers personally, but also on the country's producers as a whole, as they were continuously pressured into doing more with increasingly less. In this context, the chapter traces the CPP's attempted reorganization of the country's workforce and the competing moral economies of work it generated during the first decade of self-rule as the state sought to assert its control over the meaning of "work" in the country. This entailed a blending of pre-independence concerns about productivity and efficiency with a larger moral and civic discourse that centered on an imagined socialist collectivity. On the ground, however, the CPP's attempts to impose its ambitions took a darker turn as the government persistently sought to chip away at worker autonomy, self-expression, and, for some, opportunity. Workers themselves responded to the CPP's initiatives in a myriad of ways. For some, as chapters 5 and 6 will examine in greater depth, the CPP's varying degrees of co-option of the country's labor and trade union movements provided them, as both skilled and unskilled workers, opportunities to connect with the government and party in the pursuit of their individually defined personal and professional ambitions, often at the expense of their fellow workers. Others, meanwhile, emerged disillusioned, while still others openly challenged what they interpreted as the party and state's further intrusion into their daily lives. The result, as this chapter will show, was not necessarily the politics and ethics of work the CPP envisioned for the postcolonial state, but what, for many, evolved into a political economy of alienation.

"WORK" AND THE "WORKER" IN THE GOLD COAST

The struggle over the meaning of work in Nkrumah-era Ghana was deeply embedded in the broader politics of labor in Africa. As several scholars have shown, conflicts over what constituted work, how long one should work, and when workers should be paid had driven both African and other colonial debates over the labor process since at least the second half of the nineteenth century.[4] In South Africa, for instance, William Worger has detailed the nearly two-decade process by which the colony's new diamond industry sought to create and bring under its control a productive and reliable African workforce. For much of the 1870s and 1880s, Worger argues, mineworkers successfully pushed back against the mining industry's pressures as they sought to assert their independence via such acts of personal and collective autonomy as the breaking of contracts, protests against wage cuts, desertion from the mines, and the theft of diamonds.[5] While seen by the workers as assertions of their individual and collective will in this new labor environment, for mine operators and colonial officials, such actions reinforced their stereotypical view of Africans as lazy and unreliable workers—or as "fitful and capricious as children," in the words of one settler quoted by historian Keletso Atkins in another South African context.[6] As Worger shows, mine operators and colonial officials in turn responded to this perceived worker intransigence with the broad criminalization of the African working population, subjecting South Africa's black mine workers to an array of new policies designed to limit their mobility and place them under surveillance.[7]

Approximately half a century later and four thousand kilometers north of the South African diamond mines, a similar discourse developed in the Kenyan port city of Mombasa. At issue there, as historian Frederick Cooper highlights, was a labor regime largely consisting of temporary, migratory work. Placing colonial attacks on African casual labor within the context of late nineteenth- and early twentieth-century metropolitan labor concerns, Cooper emphasized colonial officials' attempts to forge a "respectable working class" out of what they perceived as an unruly and undependable African workforce.[8] As seen through the eyes of colonial officials, the casual labor of the coastal city's docks presented a number of problems for employers and for colonial productivity, the most notable of which was the creation of a work environment wherein employers had little room for disciplining and controlling their employees. The result, many colonial labor experts insisted, was a stunting of African working peoples' personal and social evolution into a respectable, modern working class.[9] More broadly, anthropologist John Noon argued in 1944, the implications of this social and cultural "retard[ation]" of worker growth reverberated throughout the colonial African sphere as productivity diminished while the social costs of production (e.g., in the form of detriments to education, health, and nutrition, among others) increased.[10]

For workers, however, decisions not to work or to show up late and irregularly had few consequences, at least at the level of casual labor, as many operated in a colonial labor market often characterized by worker shortages. As a result, should things fall through with a certain employer, workers generally had the option of securing another short-term employer. Cooper thus notes that, with "little fear of the 'sanction of the sack'" in colonial Africa, most workers often had "nothing to lose but a day's work."[11] What was needed, colonial officials believed, was a new type of professional worker, one rooted in and disciplined by the institutionalization of more structured conceptions of productivity, management, and efficiency. The model African worker was therefore to be a man who was wholly committed to his job, in great part because his short- and long-term livelihood was bound to it. The result was to be a tying of the worker not simply to his work or even his profession, but to a specific job. As envisioned by the colonial government, this newly created sense of dependency was key to its interwar modernization agenda, as the lack of worker mobility promised to provide the colonial government the political, economic, and social stability necessary for the agenda's success.[12]

In a colony where much of the wealth lay in the hands of rural small-scale producers, the realities of the late-colonial Gold Coast labor market differed significantly from those of South Africa and coastal East Africa. However, the official representations of African work in the Gold Coast still largely followed the model outlined by Cooper in Mombasa and Worger in Kimberley, with issues of productivity and efficiency dominating the colonial rhetoric of the period. As elsewhere, central to these debates in the Gold Coast was the question of control over workers' time both on and off the job. By selling their labor, if one were to follow Marx, workers were also selling their time, thus shifting control over the physical and emotional exertion inherent in the labor process. Meanwhile, from the perspective of management, control over a worker's time ensured his or her—but mostly his—dependency on the employer.[13] As such, the struggle over time in the labor process not only became a continual point of conflict in the relationship between the worker, his work, and his employers. It also became one of the key mechanisms through which management and the colonial state sought to contest the independence of the colonial subject.

Among the first sites of labor conflict in the colonial Gold Coast were the colony's gold mines. Largely situated in the western and central forests, the mining industry demanded a stable and relatively large workforce. As historian Jeff Crisp demonstrates, as early as the late nineteenth century, colonial and mining officials focused their attention on the mobilization and control of the region's prospective workers. Labor shortages and a largely unskilled workforce untethered to specific mines thus represented the most immediate threats to the industry's productivity and profitability. Both colonial and mining officials responded to the colony's uncertain labor situation with a set of policies and practices that included everything from the physical abuse of the colony's miners and the monopsonization of the labor market to modest improvements to working and living conditions.[14] As a result, late nineteenth- and early twentieth-century miners faced a labor market and working conditions not only designed to limit their choices and mobility on the job, but also tailored to the regulation and management of their time on and off the metaphorical shop floor. Mining communities themselves were in turn reshaped as sites of intense security and policing, replete with boundary fencing and surveillance systems. Furthermore, Crisp notes, even those not directly engaged in mining felt the effects of the mining labor regime, as those involved in ancillary industries—most notably goldsmiths—endured increased levels of scrutiny and government harassment in the colony's mining centers.[15]

Mining officials' attempts to control workers' day-to-day activities both on and off the job rarely went uncontested, with miner-organized work stoppages, slow-downs, and strike actions occurring as early as the 1880s and 1890s. Complaining in an 1885 issue of the Mining Journal, one late nineteenth-century official quoted by Crisp grumbled about an "unsteadiness and indifference as to whether or not they [the miners] continued to improve in learning how to work as miners." The official explained that "when railed for their faults the reply would invariably be 'we get no pay.' I countered this with the only means at my disposal i.e. persuasion and starvation, but this could not prevent many pieces of work being done in a slovenly, indifferent fashion."[16] By the early twentieth century, mine employees had thus emerged as one of the most militant and politically aggressive groups of workers in the Gold Coast. Not only did they challenge their working conditions and pay, but, just as importantly, they also protested the limits placed on both their leisure and work lives. Moreover, at times they even confronted the government and mine officials with demands for increasingly inclusive definitions of who qualified as a mine employee in negotiations over pay scales.[17] Furthermore, between 1930 and 1937, the colony's miners embarked upon at least a dozen significant strike actions. The 1941 passage of the Trades Union Ordinance, which legalized African unionization, further paved the way for the more formal organization of the colony's mine employees in the first half of the twentieth century.[18]

For the Nkrumah-aligned nationalists of the late 1940s and early 1950s, the labor activism of the Gold Coast miners, along with that of the colony's railway and harbor workers, gave the appearance of a ready-made anticolonial force. As Nkrumah suggested in his foreword to a 1950 history of Gold Coast miner activism written by future CPP member of parliament J. Benibengor Blay, "The heroic struggle of the Gold Coast Mines Employees' Union is an integral part of the whole struggle for the liberation of Ghana. . . . The struggle in either case is not a small one," he continued, for it pitted "a small but well-organized, wealthy and powerful group with a lot of experience in the disposal of human affairs" against "a mass of people poor [and] inexperienced in industrial relations." Just as "in the Colonial Liberation Movement," Nkrumah affirmed, in trade unionism "'organization decides everything.'"[19] Nkrumah, among others in the CPP, thus put forward a reading of the Gold Coast's labor history that subsumed the activism and particular interests and ambitions of the colony's workers into a broader narrative of a nascent nationalism that only needed to be refocused. The goal, if not the obligation, for the CPP was in no uncertain terms to be that of further cultivating an already burgeoning anticolonial, nationalist ethos among the colony's working population and aligning it with that of the CPP.

By 1952, though, the tone with which the CPP approached the colony's workers had started to shift, as the party began to challenge ideas of work that viewed labor as an individualized economic activity. Work, party and government officials increasingly insisted, had to be understood within the context of broader ideas of nation-building and national economic emancipation. The labor movement in turn was increasingly envisioned to be the productive force behind this shared project. As such, publicity campaigns directly connected labor activism to the pursuit of national self-government and to the party's broader promises of infrastructural development, healthcare, employment, and educational expansion. "We have by our united efforts achieved political freedom," Nkrumah advised a group of trade unionists in 1956. "Our next united task," he declared, "is the achievement of economic justice: freedom from want, & freedom from disease, filth, and squalor." The success of such a project depended on not only unparalleled "industrial and agricultural developments," but also a productive, efficient, and organized labor force. "We, as Government," the prime minister claimed, "are firmly resolved to build an economically strong nation that will improve the standard of living of its people." However, he averred, the government could not do this alone: it needed workers loyal to the party and committed to working together and with the CPP for the common good.[20]

On the ground, the CPP moved quickly to bring the colony's labor movement into its fold. In doing so, it launched a formal assault on the independence of Gold Coast labor. This process began with what labor scholar Richard Jeffries outlines as the promotion of several minor, but Nkrumah-backed, trade unionists to leadership positions in key unions.[21] The 1954 appointment of Nkrumah ally J. K. Tettegah as secretary-general of the Gold Coast (later, Ghana) Trades Union Congress (TUC) further formalized the CPP's attempted co-option of the Gold Coast labor movement. As head of the TUC and the national and international face of Gold Coast/Ghanaian labor for much of the next decade, Tettegah set out to politically, if not institutionally, bind the TUC to the CPP. By at least 1958, Tettegah and other prominent TUC and CPP officials had begun to insist that, while existentially separate, the TUC and CPP were foundationally one and the same ("Siamese Twins"). As Tettegah exclaimed at the time, "there is only a division of labour between us."[22]

The loss of labor's independence under the pre-independence CPP came to haunt both the workers' movement and the party.[23] As early as 1953 and 1954, the prominent railway and harbor union leader Pobee Biney—then a CPP MP—had begun to complain about what he deemed the "strange discipline and policies" of the party he represented.[24] Biney's

fellow railway and harbor union activist Anthony Woode suffered a similar frustration with the party. Initially a CPP backbencher, Woode would
ultimately be expelled from the CPP for purportedly holding communist
sympathies. Woode in turn took to the Legislative Assembly floor in 1953
to openly chastise Nkrumah and the CPP for favoring political expedience
over the needs and interests of the colony's workers. He then went on to
advise his colleagues to "rebel strongly against how these things are going
now."[25] Other workers, trade unionists, and those sympathetic to their
cause, meanwhile, complained about the narrowness of the CPP's definition of who qualified as a worker, and the supposed delusions of grandeur
displayed by many of those who claimed that mantle. "When poor cattle-
driven workers are made to think that because they are members of the
TUC and the CPP, therefore they are the only people who labour, and
that those who do not belong to the CPP do no work," a columnist for the
opposition-affiliated *Ashanti Pioneer* asked in early 1957, "what else can
they [the CPP-affiliated workers] do but believe strongly that they are the
only workers in this country?"[26]

FIGURE 4.1. The worker's shelter on a rainy day. *Source: Evening News,* 29
June 1956.

WORKING FOR SOCIALISM

As the CPP's relationship to labor shifted in the 1950s, so did the party's understandings of socialism's relationship to work. In his earliest writings, Nkrumah had positioned the alienation of the worker and the extraction of African labor at the center of both the colonial project and the anti-colonial uprisings he envisioned coming in the postwar years.[27] As illustrated in chapter 1, much of this work sought to reanimate a set of early twentieth-century socialist critiques of colonial capitalism and liberalism that dated to the thinking of such figures as Vladimir Lenin, W. E. B. Du Bois, and, among nonsocialists, J. A. Hobson. Writing in his 1953 analysis of Gold Coast nationalism, Nkrumah confidant and advisor George Padmore similarly pointed to an African-imperial binary structured to manipulate both the African producer and the African consumer in favor of the interests of large-scale European trading companies and global capital. Taking the imperial behemoth the United Africa Company (UAC) as his primary target, Padmore warned of the "octopus-like" reach of such colonial companies into African economic life. As portrayed by Padmore, over the previous several decades the UAC had constructed an economic system capable of "meet[ing] . . . African producers and consumers at every level" of the market's production and consumption cycles. For Padmore, such an economic system was necessarily exploitative, as it provided these companies seemingly unfettered control over vast swaths of the colonial economy. As a result, Padmore insisted, it was the unevenness of this relationship that lay at the heart of the widespread resentment Gold Coasters felt toward the colonial government.[28]

As the CPP embarked upon its period of shared governance in the early and mid-1950s, the perceived inseparability of the anticolonial critique of capitalism and the demand for Ghanaian self-government was rarely questioned. The same held for the ideological and analytical connection of the Gold Coast colonial experience with that of the rest of the continent. For the CPP, the centralization and subsumption of labor within the nationalist movement was a direct response to the party's readings of the nature of the colonial system. At its root, colonialism, for the CPP, was a network of contradictions. On the one hand, colonial rule had brought key features of modern investment and infrastructure to a continent largely seen as politically and economically backwards. The most notable of these investments included the construction of railway lines, Takoradi harbor, hospitals, and schools—all of which the CPP viewed as essential to any modern nation. However, carrying on from the anticolonial intellectual tradition that had matured at the Manchester Pan-African Congress, extraction and exploitation still stood at the heart of the CPP's and its allies' understanding of this investment and its effects on both individual and collective labor. For the most ideological elements of the CPP, although not necessarily from the perspective of workers themselves, the alienation of the worker—in the Marxist sense—thus played out through the dislocation of the worker from the social and economic benefits of his or her labor.

From the perspective of many in the CPP, then, Ghanaians' relationships to work had fundamentally been subverted by the colonial system. As such, Ghanaians who had bought into the colonial mode of production were seen as having been conditioned in a way that led them to adopt their perceived individualistic conceptions of work, according to which they unquestioningly went about their daily work for their personal benefit and not the collective good of the nation. Their ambitions, prominent CPP activist Cecil Forde suggested to a group of student activists in 1960, were thus indicative of a people "born in a society with all [the] trappings of a bourgeois mentality," built around the principles, ethics, and mores of personal accumulation. Taking on the subjects of charity and philanthropy specifically—exactly the kind of activities that, in the eyes of many, would seem to showcase capitalism's concern for the common good—Forde explicitly challenged what he subtly characterized as a social practice and politics of personal aggrandizement and pridefulness associated with an accumulationist mindset. Such practices could "exist only in capitalist societies," for, "in a real socialist [society], [there is] no need for charity. The wealth of the nation belongs to the people—all of them without exception."[29] Others, meanwhile, focused directly on the mechanics of work. In doing so, they emphasized the challenges faced by the party and government in their attempts to mobilize a workforce that, in their eyes, was molded out of the colonial experience and in consequence plagued by an "'I-don't-care-what-may-happen' attitude."[30]

As a result, it was argued that self-rule not only demanded an attitudinal shift among the country's workers, but, more importantly, it required an organizational shift in both the workforce and the economy. As Kofi Baako, one of the party's chief ideologues, reminded an audience in a 1961 speech at the United States embassy in Accra, foreign firms had manipulated and utilized the political and economic environment of colonial rule so as to profit from the colonies' subject populations. Emerging out of the colonial investment, though, Baako further explained, was a tax base that, for much of the colonial period, funded many of the infrastructural projects that had made the postwar prospects for independence in Ghana and elsewhere viable in the 1950s. However, he asserted, this investment had also come at a significant cost. Self-rule, by contrast, was thus to be a process constructed around the decentering of private capital—foreign and, in many cases, also domestic—on the national economic stage. This in turn was to occur through a marrying of capital's interests and potential contributions to the nation with those of the public sector in the creation of a production-oriented, socialist economy. As Baako explained, "I have often said that both capitalism and socialism need capital for development but whereas under the former capital is largely in the hands of private men and women who determine how and where it should be used, under the latter system, it is in the hands of the State which is in better position to use it for profitable and beneficial purposes."[31]

For Baako, the socialism that he presented to his largely American audience necessarily distinguished itself from "the type we see in other places" (read: the Eastern Bloc).[32] It was to be a socialism adapted to the specific historical and contemporary experiences and character of an emergent Ghana and Africa—both of which were trying to make their way in the international context of the Cold War. Providing his version of what would eventually become perhaps the foundational tenet of mid-century African socialism, Baako, then, explained that, "In an ex-colonial territory which has emerged successfully into independence and which is anxious to repair a hundred years of damage done to its social, political, and economic systems we can find no better solution to our problems—than adopting socialism which in fact is our own traditional way of life." Through such a statement, Baako thus aimed to present Ghana's socialist vision as, to adapt Amilcar Cabral's famous phrase, a "return to the source."[33] Furthermore, Baako built upon this historicized narrative as he reminded his American audience of its own history and the world in which it had emerged: "You, as Americans, were born into a society quite different from ours. Your great nation was born under entirely different circumstances and was allowed to grow in an entirely different world."[34]

The envisioned bond created between the worker and the state through the labor process in turn framed the CPP's relationship to work. Work under socialism was to be more than an act of material self-interest and self-presentation. Rather, in line with Michael Burawoy's characterization of the politics of labor in other socialist states, work was to become "the arena for emancipation to the exclusion of all else."[35] To this end, the act of laboring was understood to be central to the broader ontological transformation incumbent upon the Nkrumahist revolution. The worker was to shed the alienation necessarily engendered by working under the capitalist mode of production and reunite with his or her craft.[36] This process of reunion was to be a rejuvenating experience, and one in which all individuals were to partake. Decisions not to work or ambitions of embarking upon individual profit-making enterprises were a threat to the Nkrumahist revolution at home and other socialist endeavors abroad, creating what party ideology and rhetoric presented as a key roadblock in the state's efforts to tackle the foremost political, social, and economic challenges of the day. As Nkrumah himself articulated on the eve of independence in 1957, "The emphasis of the struggle has now shifted from the anti-imperialist phase to the internal one of the struggle against the enemies of social progress, that is against poverty, hunger, illiteracy, disease, ignorance, squalor, and low productivity." Progress on all these fronts, he insisted, required no less than a "new order of harder work and complete dedication to the service of the nation to be born on March 6."[37] The call to self-rule, he added three years later, was thus to be one of "Work, Work, Work."[38]

"THE NEW STRUCTURE" AND THE SECOND DEVELOPMENT PLAN

From the perspective of the CPP, the transition to a production-centered economy demanded even greater government control over the labor process. The result was a further extension of the CPP's influence over the country's labor movement during the first decade of self-rule. Inside both the CPP and the Trades Union Congress, concerns over the TUC's lack of statutory authority led to the introduction of the 1958 Industrial Relations Act. Purportedly driven by the wishes and efforts of "the organised working people of this country," the act took direct aim at the remaining independence of significant portions of the Ghanaian trade union movement. At its most basic level, it sought to consolidate the movement with the intended creation of twenty-four—later, sixteen—state-sanctioned national unions operating under the auspices of the TUC.[39] Even more importantly, the act made union membership compulsory for nearly all workers within the country's industrial and commercial sectors, catapulting the number of unionized Ghanaian workers from approximately 38,000 in 1949 to over 320,000 in 1961.[40] By the 1960 release of the TUC's outline of the rights and duties of its members, party support by the country's trade unionists was no longer simply promoted; the TUC now mandated it.[41]

Inside both the CPP and TUC, officials were adamant about the unqualified benefits of the Industrial Relations Act and what the TUC's so-called "New Structure" had in store to workers. For his part, A. J. Dowuona-Hammond, parliamentary secretary to the Ministry of Labour and Co-operatives, presented the statutory changes under the act as a cure to the scourge of unscrupulous trade union leaders robbing the country's workers of their "hard-earned money."[42] Tettegah, meanwhile, promoted the new centralized national unions of the TUC as "the army of Ghana Labour."[43] Further explications of the New Structure and Industrial Relations Act tied the centralization of labor to the introduction of a guaranteed "living wage" (six shillings and six pence per day) and a system of incentive bonuses, "decorations," and "promotions for exemplary work done" to "increase productivity and enhance the economy of the State."[44] Additionally, the TUC emphasized plans for increased access to vocational training, paid leave after twelve months of continuous employment, paid maternity leave, and, for a "majority of workers," free "medical attention."[45] Moreover, as P. B. Arthiabah suggests, the Industrial Relations Act's collective bargaining provisions were envisioned as providing for a greater union voice in management as well as in "the appointment of union leaders on public boards and corporations."[46]

Many of these promises, however, did not pan out, at least not at the scope pledged by the CPP government. Workers, though, still found it necessary to regularly engage with the TUC's New Structure, often through attending formal and informal classes featuring themes of productivity and suitable workplace behavior. In a similar vein, the TUC organized worker emulation contests aimed at presenting the working rank and file with idealized models of the moral and social benefits of their work and of the labor process more broadly.[47] The 1962 inauguration of the Kwame Nkrumah Ideological Institute (KNII) in the coastal Central Region town of Winneba further institutionalized ideological education in the CPP's and TUC's worker-education programs. At the KNII, agricultural and labor officials with positions in key party institutions gained access to weekend and day classes, along with degree programs, wherein they studied the principles of African socialism, capitalist and colonial praxis, and methods of political mobilization through lessons in labor organization, scientific means of production, and Marxist theory.[48] For those left out of such classes, party officials and KNII students and staff traveled the country in an effort to engage both skilled and unskilled workers, farmers, trade unionists, and others in public forums educating the populace on everything from labor productivity and citizenship to comparative analyses of socialist development and politics.[49]

At the heart of the changing relationship between workers, the trade union movement, and the state was the impending release of the CPP's Second Development Plan (1959–64). Intended to be funded by a governmental surplus generated through nearly a decade of elevated international cocoa prices and international borrowing, the new plan envisioned a rapid stimulation of the country's industrial, agricultural, and commercial sectors.[50] Pitching the plan to the National Assembly in March 1959, Nkrumah connected its "implementation and fulfillment" to the foundation of the CPP's promised "welfare state." He explained, "It is the aim of my Government to create the means for the good life, and create a society in which everybody in Ghana can enjoy the fruits of his labour and raise the economic and social standards of the people."[51] Reiterating the social ambitions of the Nkrumahist revolution—namely, "abolish[ing] disease, poverty, and illiteracy"—Nkrumah in turn promised the establishment of more secure food supplies and greater access to potable water, the widespread electrification of the country, and better housing options. In doing so, the Ghanaian prime minister tied the realization of these ambitions directly to the plan's emphasis on industrial development and agricultural expansion and diversification.[52]

Upon its release, the development plan appeared nothing short of revolutionary. Not counting the Volta River Project, which would be paid for through the general development fund, the plan called for an investment of £G250 million in the country. Agricultural investment was to emphasize the extension of educational services to rural villages and towns, while also working to reduce the country's dependence on cocoa and, at the same time, increase the cash crop's production yield. Rubber, bananas, cattle, cereals, and fisheries all received special attention in the government's plan. Likewise, in the industrial sector, the government projected the "establishment of not less than 600 factories" during the plan's five-year span. These factories were to engage in the production of "over 100 different products," although, in order to ensure a quick transition from conception to production, initial priority was to be given to goods seen as having low start-up expenses relative to their import costs.[53] Specifically, these industries and goods were anticipated to include tanning, the bleaching and dyeing of textiles, flour milling, radio assembly, motorcar assembly, and the production of fertilizers and cosmetics.[54]

In their vision for Ghanaian industry, the plan's authors did not skirt the realities facing the country. Among the most pressing challenges facing the program's success, they predicted, would be the relative lack of local technical know-how in given industries, along with the variable quality of worker discipline in a routinized factory environment. They also noted a likely imbalance in domestic and foreign investment in the new industries proposed by the plan. Furthermore, the plan's authors pointed to tariff protections and methods for controlling cost-of-living increases as additional areas for research and possible action as the industrial development scheme unfolded. Despite these potential challenges, though, the plan's authors insisted on the centrality of the expansion of industry and manufacturing to the country's further economic development. Not only did the growth of domestic industries promise to counteract an increasing imbalance in the country and diversify the economy. It also held the potential of rapidly increasing employment opportunities for the country's educated young men and women and of building upon the public services (electrical, water, transport, etc.) constructed under the 1951 Development Plan.[55]

Infrastructural developments in the areas of education, healthcare, communications and broadcasting, electrical and hydrologic utilities, and housing were further to help raise Ghana's working people's quality of life at home. Just as significantly, they were also to ease the burdens of their work lives, specifically through the introduction of new forms of technological and infrastructural innovation. The net result was to be an increase in the productivity of each individual worker, the working population as a whole, and the nation. By 1960, the CPP press would thus begin to describe the shifts in labor and industrial policy, ideology, and practices that accompanied the Second Development Plan and the TUC's New Structure in the language of a "Fair Deal" for workers. As Nkrumah explained at the 1959 groundbreaking ceremony for the new TUC Hall of Trade Unions, "If we must give increased wages to our workers, if we must ask them to increase productivity, and if we must expect them to work hard to build our nation, then we must recognize their rights as human beings; give them dignity; raise their status and their standard of living. If we can do all these things, then we are really on the march towards our economic and industrial emancipation."[56] Only through economic and industrial emancipation, defined largely as ending the country's dependency on foreign capital and international commodity markets, Nkrumah and the CPP argued, could Ghana truly fulfill its political liberation at home and abroad.

AUSTERITY, AGITATION, AND REVOLT

The New Structure and the Second Development Plan, however, met with a harsh set of domestic and international economic realities. Concerns over an emerging global recession pulled back the unusually high international prices that for the previous several years had characterized the global market for many prominent commodities. As late as 1958, cocoa prices had largely been spared from this decline.[57] The situation would change drastically by mid-1960, when cocoa prices plummeted from highs of £G304 per ton in 1957–58 to a low of £G140 in March 1961.[58] Moreover, this occurred at a time when cocoa accounted for 60 percent of the country's total exports.[59] However, even as global cocoa prices declined, the country's cocoa producers and the government-controlled Cocoa Marketing Board (CMB) faced further pressures to prop up the country's economy as they each sought to profitably unload their produce. Meanwhile, even before the government's release of the Second Development Plan, the future Nobel Prize–winning economist and government economic advisor W. Arthur Lewis had already started cautioning the CPP about the plan's size and structure. Similarly, Lewis also chided key government agencies and planners—especially the CMB—for unrestrained spending and excessive ambition. The result of their irresponsibility, the West Indian economist asserted, was an atmosphere characterized by a "kind of megalomania," wherein planners seemed to be outlining policies for a country of "50 million people with £400 a year," not one of "4.5 million people whose average income per head is only £55 a year."[60]

Drops in cocoa and other commodity prices coincided with even more stringent demands on the nation's producers and limitations on worker autonomy. In 1959 and 1960, for instance, the CPP returned to the Industrial Relations Act, amending it twice. In doing so, the government, for all intents and purposes, moved to further nationalize the trade union movement, increase surveillance on worker activities, and make it extremely difficult (if not functionally impossible) for workers not to join state-sanctioned unions.[61] These reforms thus added to a rising sense of disaffection among many of the country's workers, encouraging the circulation of a growing set of stories of corruption and mismanagement within both the CPP and the TUC. As one leading member of the Sekondi railway workers' union, A. Y. Ankomah, explained to Richard Jeffries in 1971, "We heard they [CPP officials] were buying Borgward cars with our money. They tried to persuade us the TUC was doing a good thing by establishing these shops for the workers, but the leaders took things on credit and never paid, so the shops had to close down. And they went with other people's wives. Really, there was so much corruption and wife-stealing."[62] A. B. Essuman, another of Jeffries's informants, echoed Ankomah as he described the disconnect between how the CPP and TUC saw the world in which the workers lived and how the workers themselves experienced it. According to him, party and TUC officials would come to town and blindly herald the accomplishments of the socialist state, telling people that no Ghanaian would ever "have any difficulty getting milk and margarine," even as local markets were experiencing severe shortages.[63] Even when items were available, former Young Pioneer E. B. Mensah added, people with party connections would often hoard goods, only to resell them at exorbitant prices during times of scarcity.[64]

The effects of Ghana's economic decline were thus real and profound for vast segments of the population. Furthermore, many of the government's actions at the time only exacerbated the hardships felt throughout the country. These actions included a 1961 government-mandated wage freeze for the country's workers just as the country was beginning to face a period of severe inflationary pressures. Even before the wage freeze, economist Ann Seidman notes, many Ghanaians—especially those earning the state minimum wage of six shillings and six pence a day—often found it difficult to make ends meet, with many spending as much as 60 percent of their income on food alone. Even more fundamentally, significant portions of the population could not find any work at all. As detailed in the previous chapter, institutions such as the Builders Brigade promised to alleviate the pressures of unemployment for some and, by 1960, a reported 12,000 Ghanaians had found employment in the organization. Yet, as reported in the 1960 census, another 163,810 remained formally unemployed, compared to just under 350,000 who were employed in wage-earning or salaried positions. Furthermore, even in the much smaller pool of "registered" unemployed, nearly every region in the country, with the exception of Accra and the Volta Region, witnessed a notable increase in the number of unemployed between 1961 and 1962.[65]

As workers and others dealt with the employment and wage uncertainty of the early 1960s, the market shortages recalled by E. B. Mensah and Richard Jeffries's interview participants began to foment increased discontent of their own in many of the country's cities and towns—with many individuals focusing their frustrations with these shortages on Nkrumah's pan-African ambitions. In a 2007 interview, for instance, Accra resident Thomas Daniel Laryea contrasted the Nkrumah government's substantial investment in African liberation—which, according to Laryea's analysis, the Ghanaian head of state was using to influence people like Robert Mugabe, Julius Nyerere, and Jomo Kenyatta—with a definition of Nkrumahism centered on the well-being and progress of his native Ghana. In the markets, Laryea recalled, "milk, sugar, sardines, and all these things Nkrumah said he thought were there weren't necessarily. . . . So people were angry." Laryea continued by denouncing Nkrumah's ambitions abroad: "Why," he asked, "should you give it [money] to African people [outside of Ghana]? They should take care of themselves. We should also take care of ourselves."[66] Former Central Region pupil-teacher Eden Bentum Takyi-Micah similarly complained about the CPP's supposed robbing of the nation's previously abundant coffers for what he considered the fool's errand of "liberat[ing] the whole of Africa." "You know," he emphasized, with likely intended hyperbole, that at the time of independence "our population here was very little," and the coffers were so full that "I will sometimes say that amount [the cash reserve] which the British [left us], if they [the CPP] had shared it among us, everybody would have been a millionaire. But all the same," he continued, "as I have already told you, Kwame Nkrumah was aiming to liberate the whole Africa, as it's said . . . [and thus] started throwing our money out."[67]

In rural areas, the costs of the decline were even more dramatic. Key to the Nkrumahist vision for Ghana was the prioritizing of urban development over the needs of the country's rural population. However, more than three-fourths of the country's population lived in towns and villages classified by the government as rural (below five thousand people).[68] Additionally, they comprised approximately two-thirds of the country's labor force through nonindustrial and small-scale labor, including in the fields of "agriculture, forestry, hunting, and fishing."[69] Furthermore, through its dependence on cocoa and other commodity production, the government relied on the productive capabilities of the country's rural population to fund much of its urban development.[70] The result was a widening gap in living standards between the country's rural and urban populations, in many cases further boosting rural migration to the country's urban centers.[71] Meanwhile, those who stayed in rural areas often encountered the persistent stress caused by the loss of farming lands to state-run institutions like the Builders Brigade and the government's growing number of state farms. Not only did these new organizations and institutions have their own ideologies of collective labor, which often conflicted with those of local communities, they also forced many within these communities into relationships with the state for which they were unprepared as individuals and communities dealt with the alienation of their lands and governmental efforts to influence the types of crops they were to produce.[72]

Just as it did with the trade-union and industrial-worker population, the CPP in turn sought to challenge the social and economic autonomy of the country's rural producers. The mid-1950s attempts to cap the prices paid to cocoa producers (see chapter 2) represented just one aspect of this process. With the country's farmers, however, the CPP faced a constituency with a long history of activism and independence that dated back to at least the cocoa revolution of the early twentieth century. Most famously, in the colonial era, this activism took shape in an array of cocoa "hold-ups," in which producers refused to sell their goods in protest over everything from low prices to what they viewed as unfair purchasing protocols.[73] Moreover, as Marvin Miracle and Ann Seidman have shown, Gold Coast agricultural producers also turned to a system of cooperative organizations in their attempts to protect their interests and take on the colonial government's agricultural policies.[74] However, in the first years of self-rule, the CPP embarked on an initiative to strip these cooperatives of their autonomy in favor of what Kojo Botsio—then the governmental minister overseeing cooperatives—described as "one supreme organization." According to Botsio, the new cooperative movement was to be organized "on strictly democratic terms."[75] Yet, as with the TUC's New Structure, the result of this consolidation—in addition to the establishment of the government's emerging state farms system—was an attempt to subsume agricultural autonomy under the party and governmental infrastructure.[76]

Meanwhile, in an attempt to reassert its relevance, the country's formal opposition sought to trade on the resulting discontent among the country's industrial and agricultural producers. In the *Ashanti Pioneer*, for instance, the newspaper's editors regularly devoted space to workers' and farmers' grievances. As one worker complained in a mid-1960 letter to the paper, the CPP seemed to be working with an unorthodox definition of socialism, one in which the government benefited at the expense of the poor. "If," the letter writer argued, "we must work towards Social Freedom [read: socialism] then something must be done for the poor worker and farmer through whose toil and sweat the country derives her huge revenue." According to the letter writer, the lack of visible results from its development plans represented the ultimate failure of the young government. For, he exclaimed, "We hear of developments taking place here and there, but," he asked, "where are they in reality?"[77] Opposition member of parliament Joe Appiah echoed these sentiments approximately two months later in August 1960 as he warned his CPP colleagues in the National Assembly of the growing alienation of the country's working people. "We all know that the workers have the patience of an ass," the Atwima-Amansie MP explained, but "their specific moral gravity is an unknown quantum and when they kick, they kick most effectively and without serving notice."[78]

By early 1961, the economic realities facing the country and the uncertain prospects for the Second Development Plan demanded a response from the government. However, the CPP's initial reaction to the realities it faced did not include drawing back on its development ambitions. Rather, the Nkrumah government stubbornly advocated for an even greater commitment to the plan's agenda and goals. In February 1961, for instance, this included planning within the CPP cabinet for a government takeover of several gold mining companies and their mines.[79] Three months later, Nkrumah expanded upon this theme of nationalization as he informed the cabinet of his desire for all new industrial projects to be "fully State-owned."[80] Meanwhile, the government further extended its call for sacrifice from the country's industrial and agricultural producers and the populace at large. Workers needed to work harder and longer, while farmers needed to grow more and expect less in return. "Try, try, and do double work," one popular CPP song proclaimed. "The work is great, but the time is short."[81] As Thomas Daniel Laryea succinctly noted, "It was a very difficult time."[82]

Sacrifice and the 1961 Budget

In July 1961, the CPP, facing a deficit of more than £G36 million, offered its formal response to Ghana's weakening economic position by releasing what others have widely described as the postcolonial government's first "austerity budget."[83] At the heart of the budget was a new set of tax policies. As a revenue-generating device, direct taxation—especially at the individual level—had long proved an unreliable instrument for solidifying state accounts. As one United Nations official reported in 1959, only 11,000 of Ghana's 4.5 million residents paid the country's income tax annually, netting between £600,000 and £700,000 in revenue.[84] Focusing on the country's workers and cocoa farmers, the proposed budget aimed to streamline the government's income tax structure through the creation of a national compulsory savings scheme and the establishment of additional import taxes on a range of so-called "luxury" goods. Under the budget's savings plan, those earning more than £120 per year were to dedicate five percent of their wages to the purchase of National Investment Bonds—the face value of which, plus interest, they could redeem in ten years.[85] Cocoa farmers—the only group of farmers required to participate in the scheme—were to contribute ten percent of their sales, measured per load, to the savings plan.[86] As Cambridge economist Nicholas Kaldor, one of the foremost proponents of national saving schemes, advocated in reference to plans like those proposed in Ghana, such a scheme allowed for a shift in domestic spending away from individual consumption toward economic and infrastructural development and "building up capital assets." Meanwhile, on the popular level, Kaldor reasoned, "The advantage of the [savings] scheme, as against straightforward taxation, is that people are merely asked to postpone their consumption and not forgo it altogether."[87]

As expected, opposition officials railed against the proposed budget. In doing so, they met its call for what they presented as an unwarranted and unprecedented set of personal sacrifices imposed upon Ghanaian working people with dramatic denunciations of CPP corruption and waste. Appiah, for his part, spoke in the National Assembly of farmers, traders, workers, and businessmen already struggling to make their way. The budget only promised to burden them further, he argued, raising the prices of everyday goods in order to pay for such grandiose projects as new embassies, the TUC's new Hall of Trade Unions, government ministries, and international conferences.[88] Agona Kwabre MP Victor Owusu, meanwhile, concentrated on the budgetary follies being proposed in the name of African unity. In doing so, he questioned the logic governing decisions to give nearly £G10 million in aid to Mali, Guinea, and Upper Volta, while also raising additional questions about the government's increased investment in the country's military, police, Builders Brigade, and Young Pioneers. "In a year of fallen cocoa price, acute food shortage, rising prices of consumer goods and general impoverishment of the people," he challenged the CPP, "to call for more sacrifice from the people is fool-hardiness on the part of the authorities and an obstinate refusal to face facts."[89]

The United Party opposition was not alone in expressing discontent with the proposed budget. As St. Clair Drake and Leslie Lacy have shown, concerns about the efficacy of the budget's tax plan were expressed by even some members of the CPP itself.[90] Representing the Dagomba North district, for instance, Sulemana Ibun Iddrissu emphasized the disproportionate effect the proposed budget would have on those living in rural areas. Price hikes on supposed luxury goods—which included sugar, flour, and kerosene—contradicted the socialist ethos of Nkrumahism, Iddrissu argued, as the government proposed to raise the prices not on goods that "will beat the conscience of the colonialists, imperialists, and the capitalists," but on goods central to most Ghanaians' daily lives. Even the proposed increase in taxation on automobiles was unjust and misguided, he added, as it would require transport drivers to increase their fares, burdening both drivers and passengers, while having little effect on the day-to-day lives of the most well-to-do Ghanaians.[91] "I have been in this house for seven to eight years," Iddrissu thus declared, "and I know from my own experience that the people in the rural areas are going to be victims of these tax proposals. I do not feel that we who are the students of Nkrumaism based on Marxist Socialism should stand here and introduce these tax proposals which will only benefit the few and impose hardship on the majority."[92]

Despite fervent opposition, the Nkrumah-led government continued pushing for the budget with unabated energy. Throughout the debates surrounding the measure, prominent CPP MPs and ministers characterized the budget as everything from a tool for combating inequality to a test of "loyalty and true citizenship."[93] Furthermore, in his 10 July address to the National Assembly, the ministerial secretary to the Economic and Planning Secretariat, Kwaku Amoa-Awuah, emphasized that the budget was an additional and essential step in the struggle for "the independence and unity of the whole of the continent of Africa against foreign domination, both political and economic."[94] Volta Region MP Regina Asamany, likewise, reminded her colleagues that the sacrifices of the present would foretell the prosperity of the future by ensuring the continued construction of new schools and hospitals, the acquisition of modern farming equipment, greater access to pipe-borne water, and the expanded electrification of the country, among other public goods and services. None of these services came without real monetary costs, Asamany reminded her fellow MPs. For her, the question was ultimately one of defining the goal of Ghana's postcolonial revolution. If, as Nkrumah himself envisioned and as most of the CPP's members in the National Assembly at least tacitly signed on to, it was to be one of truly transforming the country into a "show-piece for others to emulate," then her colleagues must honestly ask themselves, "Where is the money [to pay for these services] to come from?"[95]

Following two days of debate in July 1961, the budget passed through the National Assembly with little real threat of rejection. As the Ho East CPP MP, H. K. Boni, advised his colleagues, "Everyone agrees that this Budget has broken tradition." However, while rephrasing the lyrics of a popular Akan song, he justified this break by asserting

> This sacrifice has got to be made;
> Who will make it?
> We must make it.[96]

The Government and the Strike

Among the first and most fervent popular rumblings over the budget came from the railway and harbor workers in the Western Region cities of Sekondi and Takoradi. As Richard Jeffries shows, shortly after the budget's passage, the cities' railway and harbor workers had begun writing to the TUC requesting a suspension of the mandated payroll deductions associated with the government's savings plan.[97] The TUC's failure to respond to their demands led the workers to redirect their appeals, this time directly to the government via the CPP's minister of transport and communications, Krobo Edusei. Again to no avail.[98] As a result, on 4 September 1961, just days after the first deductions went into effect, railway and harbor workers in Sekondi and Takoradi walked off the job.[99] Their colleagues in the anti-CPP hotbed of Kumasi followed shortly thereafter, with those in Accra joining them within a day. By midweek, the country's railway and harbor workers had effectively plummeted the country into a nationwide strike, paralyzing its key transportation and export sectors.[100] Moreover, workers in a range of other sectors—including portions of the civil service—also followed suit, further expanding the strike's reach. As Jeffries has persuasively argued, though, the workers' grievances were only partly related to the budget. Rather, the strike was part of a more widespread worker disaffection with the government, the country's current economic climate, and especially the CPP's and the TUC's role in the transformation of the country's formal labor movement into a movement that many saw as corrupt and unresponsive to the needs and interests of the country's workers.[101]

Inside the government, the strike took both the CPP and the TUC by surprise. Further complicating the situation, in July, Nkrumah had left the country for a two-month tour of the Eastern Bloc, which took him to the Soviet Union, several of its satellites, and Maoist China. In his stead, he left behind a "presidential commission" headed by longtime CPP stalwarts K. A. Gbedemah, Kojo Botsio, and Chief Justice Arku Korsah. As the strike hit, the commission found itself unable to act in Nkrumah's absence. Initial pleas from it and the TUC for the striking workers to return to work and await Nkrumah's return went unrequited. By the end of the week, as the strike spread, the government had effectively lost control of labor in the country's major cities, particularly in Sekondi and Takoradi. Not only were the railways and the country's lone major harbor not operating, but nearly all public services—including sanitation, water, and transportation—had also been halted.[102] As a result, by 14 September, health concerns grew within the cities, as the cabinet raised worries about the potential for "an epidemic

breaking out in the municipality." The cabinet also cited what it characterized as the troublingly "hostile" nature of the strikers and their harassment of
"a large number of the people who were willing to return to work," leading
to the declaration of a state of emergency and curfew in Sekondi and Takoradi beginning on the evening of the fourteenth.[103]

Underpinning many of the local and international debates surrounding
the strike was a critique of the CPP's conception of socialist work. Long heralded by the party press as the nation's most dedicated worker, Nkrumah was
often portrayed as the ideal against which all of the country's workers were to
measure themselves. However, as the strike unfolded, the opposition press,
led by the *Ashanti Pioneer*, juxtaposed stories of the strike and the struggles
of the country's workers with others framed around themes of presidential
leisure and unfocused labor.[104] Others addressed the contradictions between
the party's calls for socialist sacrifice and the alleged misbehavior and exploitation by groups of CPP members of parliament and party officials.[105]
American Peace Corps worker and committed socialist Al Lee built upon
these themes a few years later as he reflected on his term in Ghana in the
early 1960s. In doing so, he presented the country as one where key ministers, MPs, and other government officials ran amok, drinking and dancing
the night away in the country's most expensive bars and hotels. For Lee, the
contradictions between the rhetoric and the reality he witnessed appeared
so ridiculous that he asked his American readers to "imagine Robert McNa-
mara as the drunk at the next table" and to "imagine the Federal bureaucracy as tangible as the dew on a 22-ounce bottle of Star Beer."[106]

On the ground, the situation remained tense, even as it began to show
signs of easing in some parts of the country. By the end of the second
week of September, railway workers in Accra would return to work. Yet,
at the same time, employees of several of Accra's major private firms, including UTC Limited and SCOA Motors, were now threatening to strike
in protest against possible layoffs. "If they [the private firms' workers] did
not come out [on strike]," the commissioner of police advised the cabinet on 12 September, "they feared that they would run the risk of being
laid off." Meanwhile, in Kumasi, the trains had begun to operate again by
12 September and employees of the Division of Public Construction and
the Water Works Department had ended their strikes, signaling a potential easing of the political situation in the country's second-largest city.[107]
In the west, however, the strike continued unabated, as the government
called in the army to aid the local police forces. The Builders Brigade was
also brought in to restore key public services and return the region's harbor
and railways to operation.[108] Meanwhile, civil service officials undertook

a forceful campaign set on persuading those who had walked off the job to return to work and dissuading others from leaving. In doing so, they emphasized to their employees the illegality of the strike and threatened to withhold pay from those who absented themselves from work in order to attend strike-related events and protests.[109]

Even after Nkrumah returned to the country on 16 September, tensions in the west persisted. Seeking to quell the unrest, Nkrumah initially took what Drake and Lacy describe as a "conciliatory" tone by lifting the state of emergency in Sekondi and Takoradi and ordering the release of those arrested.[110] However, as they had done with the presidential commission, the Western Region workers balked at the president's call for them to end the strike. Taking to the nation's airwaves again on Wednesday, 20 September, the eve of the country's Founder's Day holiday, Nkrumah took a much harsher tone as he reiterated the strike's illegality under the country's Industrial Relations Act. He also undertook an extensive explanation of the political and economic conditions requiring the sacrifices associated with the July budget. "This is not an ordinary industrial strike arising from a dispute between employers and their workers [based] on conditions of work," Nkrumah insisted to his national audience. "Its ostensible object is to force Government and Parliament to withdraw legislation initiated by the Government and approved by Parliament concerning the entire economic and financial policy and programme of work of the Government." He then demanded that all striking workers return to work by 7:30 a.m. on Friday, 22 September. "Those who do not do so," he warned, "will have given clear indication that they and the instigators behind them are determined to bring about the overthrow of the Constitution by illegal means."[111] By the beginning of the next week, the strike had been effectively broken.

The CPP and the Redefining of State Power

The ramifications of the strike for the CPP and the country at large should not be minimized. Inside the party, the 1961 strike was seen as a populist rebuke of the CPP that could only be quelled through the threat of force. Most contemporary observers in turn viewed the event as a turning point in Ghana, with some even suggesting that, by the middle of September, Nkrumah's regime was near collapse.[112] At the time, the opposition also clearly believed the CPP's end was in sight, as it funneled money to the strikers and to the market women who supported them throughout the nearly three-week disturbance.[113] Likewise, K. A. Gbedemah—an icon of CPP politics since the party's inception and member of the presidential commission charged with managing the country's affairs during Nkrumah's absence—also appeared to use the strike as an opportunity to begin discussions with the American embassy about a future for Ghana without Nkrumah. "I would be sorry to have to do it [overthrow Nkrumah]," Gbedemah told embassy officials during the strike's first days, "but [the] country has had enough of Nkrumah's arrogance, whims, and madness."[114] However, as Dennis Austin suggests, in practical terms, reports of Nkrumah's imminent demise at the time of the strike were premature. Few, if anyone (even Gbedemah), in Ghana had the political influence and popular support necessary to remove Nkrumah from power and establish a new government.[115]

Regardless, the implications of the strike reverberated throughout the Ghanaian political atmosphere of late 1961. As the CPP sought to restore order to the country, the government widened its utilization of the 1958 Preventative Detention Act (PDA), which provided it with the legal authority to detain Ghanaian citizens without trial for up to five years.[116] In its post-strike crackdown, the government turned its attention not only to the strike leaders and workers who walked off the job, but also to the opposition and even some of the CPP's own officials. By early October 1961, at least fifty opposition officials had been detained.[117] In the CPP's highest echelons, Nkrumah also demánded the resignation of six of his ministers, including both Botsio and Gbedemah.[118] In an attempt to counter charges of party corruption, the Ghanaian president also required several other ministers to forfeit much of their property to the state if they wished to retain their positions in the government and—perhaps more importantly—stay in Nkrumah's good graces.[119] As understood by officials in the American embassy, the message underlying this ministerial reorganization was one of growing instability and even "reckless[ness]" in the country, as, in the words of one official, Ghana continued its "trend away from [an] atmosphere congenial to private enterprise and toward an exclusively socialist economy." The reorganization, he suggested, while quoting Nkrumah's statement on Gbedemah's dismissal, had proven that it was "'undesirable that men with varied business interests be members of [a] government which must be increasingly animated by socialist ideals.'"[120]

Beyond the cabinet, nearly all Ghanaians felt the tightening grip of the state after 1961. As subsequent chapters will show, fears of arrest and detention effectively ended open dissent. Likewise, members of a wide array of CPP governmental and party institutions—none more important than the Young Pioneers and Builders Brigade (rechristened the Workers Brigade in October 1961)—were popularly labeled as some of the most dangerous agents of a hardening and unpredictable government. As one longtime Accra resident summarized the mood of the country in the early

1960s, "It wasn't safe to talk. I didn't know whether you were an agent or a spy."[121] The result for workers, and particularly for the CPP's ideology of work, was a deepening focus on the discipline, order, and revolutionary vigilance of the workforce as well as what the party presented as the increasing problem of class among the country's citizenry. As a result, for the CPP's most ideological elements, the real affliction among Ghanaian workers and the populace as a whole was not discontent with government and TUC policies in the aftermath of the strike, but rather the fact that socialist consciousness had yet to take root among the Ghanaian populace. In short, the CPP and TUC would argue, the Ghanaian worker had still to shed the materialist ambitions that had defined his or her commitment to the capitalist, bourgeois colonial mentality.

WORK, SOCIALISM, AND CLASS IN THE AFTERMATH OF THE STRIKE

Few concepts remain closer to the heart of Marxist ideology, politics, and theory than class. At the root of Marx's definition of class was the worker's relationship to his labor and more broadly the process of production. It was through their control of production, the German philosopher argued, that the capitalist classes gained the power to alienate the laborer from his

FIGURE 4.2. Forward to a socialist Ghana. *Source: Evening News*, 1 May 1963.

or her labor, stripping him of the meaningful link between what he did and who he was.[122] For Marx, however, class was not a static or stationary status, but a positionality that itself had to be unpacked, differentiating the sociological from the political and ontological. The result in aspects of Marxist theory was the emergence of a way of thinking about class that distinguished emphases on specific social groups from the emergence of a class consciousness, which was to signal a rising awareness of one's shared plight and a collective organization against it.[123]

The historical sociology of class in Africa differed substantially from that of Europe, Nkrumah would argue in his theoretical writings. Precolonial African social systems, he insisted, rested on the institution of the clan and its assumed ethos of "the initial equality of all and the responsibility of many for one."[124] The horizontal system of social stratification associated with this form of African communalism fundamentally distinguished itself from the vertically oriented hierarchies of Marxist conceptions of class in Nkrumah's mind. The colonial introduction of classes—in the Marxian sense—was therefore part and parcel of a broader sociological and industrial revolution on the continent. In many ways following Marx, Nkrumah presented this revolution as necessary for Africa, as it forced the continent to enter into the modern industrial world.[125] Yet it also irrevocably disrupted the precolonial social order and instilled in the populace a sense of individualism and materialist self-interest that threatened the collective goals of the CPP-defined projects of nation-building and continental solidarity. Thus, the role of the party was to be that of curing the nation and particularly its workforce of the presumed "false consciousness" of this bourgeois colonial mentality. As one CPP journalist put it in 1961, the CPP's most important mission in the early 1960s was to be that of reasserting itself in the country by unabashedly guiding the Ghanaian worker and others away from an "individualism which seeks happiness and wellbeing at the expense of his fellow men." This, he continued, could only be done through the transfer of the "means of production" to "public ownership" through a process whereby "the claims of private individuals to live on returns from capital ownership would be swept away."[126]

Among the CPP's ideologues and in the party press, the true challenge for the party and government was thus to be that of eradicating Ghana's and, by extension, Africa's "antisocialists." Emerging in 1960 and 1961, dramatic critiques of the "pot-bellied bourgeoisie" soon accompanied a growing emphasis on Marxian class struggle in the party press.[127] "Capitalism was not the creator of classes and class differences," the *Evening News* advised its readers in early 1961. "Classes existed before capitalism, under the feudal system and even earlier. But capitalism substituted new classes for the old. Capitalism created new methods of class oppression and class struggle."[128] Community education programs, meanwhile, carried this language to the broader populace as the CPP sought to inform the nation's workers, farmers, brigaders, and others as to "why a lazy and malingering worker is an anti-socialist in Ghana today."[129] In other instances, the party extended its focus on Ghanaian class issues to denunciations of such common practices as gender discrimination in employment, declaring, for instance, in one internal party newsletter that such practices were antisocialist, un-African, and "a crime against our womanhood."[130]

For many workers, however, the result was a situation of increasing isolation and growing demands on their labor. The 1962 release of the CPP's *Programme for Work and Happiness* and, shortly afterwards, the unveiling of the government's Seven-Year Development Plan (1964–71) only intensified these demands as the government called for even greater attention to the nation's productivity. Even more ambitious than the 1959 development scheme, the Seven-Year Development Plan promised an estimated investment of more than £G1 billion and in turn demanded even more from the nation's producers. This included nearly £G100 million from the populace in the form of "direct labour investment" (i.e., local self-help projects) and another £G340 million from "Residents' net private savings."[131] In response to these demands, one *Evening News* labor correspondent, writing in April 1963, called on his colleagues in the labor movement to refocus their attention to "Marxism-Leninism"—the "real philosophy of the working class and proletariat of the world"—and work together to increase production, overcome self-interest, and educate themselves in the needs of the nation as they strove to unleash the promise of Nkrumahist development.[132] Former militant trade unionist now turned TUC official D. K. Foevie further confirmed the new purpose of work, labor organization, and class consciousness in post-strike Ghana when speaking to a group of mineworkers, also in 1963. In his speech, Foevie confirmed to them that they should no longer look to the union as a means for the expression of their independence as workers. Instead, he argued, "The union now has a new task. They [the unions] have to teach the workers that they belong to the industry—it is the duty of the union to assist management in improving skills and to make every worker share the responsibility of getting work done, rather than always being critical of management."[133] Fundamentally, this new reality demanded that workers rethink who they were as workers (individually and collectively) and in turn the nature of their relationship to their work, one another, and the nation.

On the ground, some discontented individuals protested the CPP's new development program, particularly when it came to the plan's direct labor investment. In the Western Region villages of Armahkrom and Etsease, for instance, several men raised the ire of the local Village Development Committee in 1964 through their refusal to take part in the villages' communal labor projects. In an outright rebuke of the CPP's development agenda and its call to national service, one of the men, a Mr. Nkesa, defiantly told the committee that he "oppose[d] the idea of communal labour in this village" and promised to "poison the minds of the others who have already taken part." Another man, a Mr. Toku, went even further with a proclamation of his personal independence from the state by declaring that "I am neither under any <u>Osagyefo</u> [Nkrumah] nor Govt. [sic] in this Ghana." As he continued, he directly challenged the government's interpretation of the realities of life under Nkrumah-era development policies. "In the colonial days," he argued, "all roads were constructed through funds supplied by the-then Colonial Govt. [sic] and I actually can't understand why a 'Free Ghana' keeps all funds of the country and forces poor people to construct roads through communal labor."[134] Meanwhile, in Asante, the anonymous "Unknown Warriors" of the "Ashanti Command" attacked the CPP's *Programme for Work and Happiness*—the ideological treatise underpinning the Seven-Year Development Plan—by chastising the CPP for its proposed austerity measures. "You ask us to tighten our belts," they argued, "whilst you yourself [Nkrumah] wear no belt at all and are lavishly living in ostentation, squandering the Nation's Revenue on useless pursuits, buying cars for frivolous girls and wasting heavily on unprofitable international conferences."[135]

The more common response to the CPP's actions and rhetoric, however, was one of malaise. The party's and government's efforts to increasingly narrow the definition and purpose of work in the country came at the expense of not only the formal, wage-earning working population, but nearly all involved in the country's labor force—trade unionists, farmers, civil servants, and others. The result was the introduction of a wide range of fissures into a complicated existing array of moral economies of work, productivity, accumulation, and consumption held to by diverse groups of Ghanaians. For instance, as Jennifer Hart has detailed in relation to the country's self-employed drivers, governmental attempts to regulate the country's taxis and *trotros* (privately owned minibuses) threatened a vibrant work culture that had developed as far back as the 1920s. As Hart articulates, Ghana's drivers prized their independence, viewing any interference in their affairs as a threat to their business and their opportunities for social mobility.[136] Similarly, numerous scholars have outlined the longstanding cultural politics of production, accumulation, and social mobility connected to the Gold Coast's and Ghana's cocoa industry. As noted in chapter 2, for many in prominent cocoa-growing regions like Asante, access to and control over the wealth brought in by cocoa had deepseated ramifications for both producers' individual identities and those of the community and the social groups of which they were a part.[137] Others, meanwhile, rejected altogether the premise that the government should be involved in various development schemes, with one man in Tema insisting in 1960 that no government could "care about the success of the enterprise [in this case, a groundnut scheme] as much as they would have if the project were being financed by private individuals."[138]

Thus, the CPP's efforts to control the narrative of work, and, after the 1961 strike, its willingness to exercise the power of the state, threatened the autonomy of the country's varied work cultures. As a result, few perhaps better illustrate the effects on the mood of the country's workers and producers than the unnamed protagonist in Ayi Kwei Armah's *The Beautyful Ones Are Not Yet Born*. As Armah illustrated with his protagonist, the Ghanaian worker of the mid-1960s—seemingly defeated by the country's political and economic situation—had abandoned his hope for the future and in turn went about his daily work in a stupor, simply waiting out the clock so that he could return home and then repeat the process the following day. With rents rising, wages stagnant, and businessmen, policemen, and party officials all dedicated to "cutting corners, eating the fruits of fraud," the party's call for "Hard Work" and the promises of what that work could hold in store for the future had lost all meaning to him. As party officials dined on imported foods, drank the finest alcohol, and drove big cars through the aptly named streets of the Esikafo Aba Estates ("The Rich People Have Come Estates"), Armah's dejected subject quipped that not "any amount of hard work could ever at this rate bring the self and the loved ones closer to the gleam."[139] The result in Nkrumah's Ghana, if one were to follow Armah, was an environment of ambivalence, apathy, frustration, and cynicism, particularly among its working population.

Historian Emmanuel Akyeampong, in his cultural history of alcohol in Ghana, recounts similar sentiments of disillusionment and alienation. "Drinking," Akyeampong argues, "numbed the pain and gave solace" to the late CPP-era worker.[140] Labor scholars—primarily writing in the 1970s and early 1980s—similarly document an "uncharacteristically passive" period in the working population's history. According to Jeff Crisp, in the country's gold mines, growing unemployment, combined with a memory of the government's "coercive" response to the 1961 strike, made the working rank and file wary about the potential benefits of formal, collective resistance.[141] Instead, he notes, mineworkers approached their work with what the State Gold Mining Corporation complained of as "laziness, apathy, carelessness and lack of interest."[142] In a similar vein, Richard Jeffries, writing on the Sekondi and Takoradi railway and harbor workers, highlights popular anxieties associated with reports of spying by others, as well as over one's own participation in such activities. As one trade unionist recounted to him in 1971, "Oh, there was a great deal of bitterness, but we were too afraid to oppose the party line. After some of our officials were dismissed from their jobs and one was detained, we realised that certain people were acting as spies. But later it was not so much that they had special spies, we all became spies. Even I was prepared to be a stooge, I must admit it. What else could one do to look after oneself?"[143]

As disillusioned workers retreated into silence, the CPP refused to yield in its advocacy for socialist work and, above all, productivity. Lazy, undedicated workers, officials argued, had to be weeded out and reeducated in the political and moral benefits of their labor. Relatedly, the elite, the bourgeoisie, and the antisocialists had to be suppressed, their wealth redistributed, and their consciousness realigned to the socialist mode of production. "The die is cast," a 1964 *Evening News* editorial declared. "It is now total discipline and unconditional surrender to the expressed REVOLUTIONARY STRENGTH OF THE PEOPLE. All forms of bourgeois survivals . . . and cunning neo-colonialist devices to corrupt the people and sabotage the construction of Socialism in Africa's Ghana will be wiped out together with the very basis of capitalist-imperialist culture itself which is laziness, selfish individualism, social isolation, and a sense of overweening egotism."[144]

꒰

By 1965, when journalist E. B. Mac-Hardjor declared that "working for the state is working for ourselves," the question of work had thoroughly embedded itself in the ethos of the Nkrumahist project.[145] To those in the CPP, work was more than a physical or even mental activity; it was a moral act, one that was to link all Ghanaians together in a program of cooperative development. Moreover, the worker was to be the engineer of the nation, as he or she overcame the individualism, personal avarice, and mentality of the colonial economy to labor for the collective good. It was workers' productivity, discipline, and self-sacrifice that would bring about the benefits of Ghana's envisioned modern, industrial society. Yet, workers' individual and collective independence also threatened that vision. The government insisted that workers and the labor movement had to be meticulously governed and regulated, lest they succumb to the wills of those the CPP deemed to be the country's "antisocialists." As the CPP's investigation into the 1961 strike suggested, "The present plot was the result of the coming together of the 'elite' and of some of the more unprincipled of the 'self-seekers.'" The result, the government's report on the incident further proposed, was a disturbance in which the country's workers had been deceived into support not for better working conditions, pay, or representation, but for an opposition-led unconstitutional takeover of the government.[146] The path forward was thus to be one of unadulterated state control not only of labor, but of all aspects of Ghanaian productivity and society under the mantle of "Work and Happiness for All."

5 ⤳ Working for the Revolution

Gender, Secrecy, and Security in the Pan-African State

> The year 1960 is the most challenging and significant year in the
> history of Africa. It is the climax of the African revolution.
>
> —Gloria Lamptey, "Women, Help Build African Personality," 1960[1]

THE POLITICAL and social ramifications of the CPP's response to the 1961
strike and of the political environment the party and government sought
to create in the post-strike years unnerved even some of the most ardent
supporters of the Nkrumahist mission. The detentions that began in the
weeks after the September disturbance continued until well after the work
stoppage, leading to a rapid proliferation of fears of arrest, party informants,
and spies. As one longtime Koforidua resident explained in 2008, "Here in
Koforidua near the Methodist [Church], the elderly men used to meet and
talk there, so they [the informants] also went there and arrested anyone who
spoke ill of Nkrumah."[2] By 1964, the situation in Ghana had so deteriorated
according to one American Peace Corps worker in Togo that, upon hearing
accounts of life in Ghana, she presented the country's political and social
environment as "chillingly similar to the one in [George Orwell's] 1984."[3]
Even some of Nkrumah's longest-standing and closest allies in the international socialist and pan-African movements had begun to publicly question
the policies of the Ghanaian leader in the early and mid-1960s. Writing in
the *Trinidad Evening News*, for instance, the prominent Trinidadian Marxist and pan-Africanist C. L. R. James—who in the 1940s had helped pave
the way for Nkrumah's move to Great Britain—called for an accounting of
the political situation in Ghana, absent ideology. To James, Nkrumah had
oscillated from one Western political and economic model to another and
in turn failed to ground his revolutionary program in African historical and
cultural realities. The result, for the Trinidadian, was corruption, disunity,

and authoritarianism. The path Nkrumah had taken was harmful not only for Ghana itself, James argued, but for Africa as a whole.[4]

Inside the CPP and its various party and government institutions, however, the aftermath of the September 1961 disturbance ushered in a new era as party and governmental officials constructed a narrative around the strike that directly connected it to the perceived declining fortunes of African decolonization in the early 1960s. Here, fears of neocolonial subversion were supreme, and, officials argued, it was imperative that the party and government adapt. In November 1961, for instance, two months after Nkrumah's ultimatum ending the strike, A. K. Barden—the director of the Ghanaian Bureau of African Affairs—took this message to his senior staff as he cautioned them toward vigilance in the new Ghana. The direct impetus for Barden's admonition rested in the recent sacking of an employee of the bureau's Linguistics Section for what Barden described as a lack of verbal discipline during a recent event at the American embassy in Accra. Barden, then, expanded upon his cautionary note with the announcement of a structural reorganization of the bureau's security apparatus.[5] Among the bureau's new security initiatives was the limiting of the public's access to what, by 1961, had emerged as the institutional face of Nkrumahist pan-Africanism on the continent.[6] This included a cordoning off of the bureau from unauthorized personnel and severe restrictions on photographing the institution's headquarters. Barden, then, went on to complain about what he felt was the widespread indiscipline of the bureau's workforce, citing tendencies among employees and even members of the senior staff to arrive late for work and leave early.[7] As a result, by early 1962, the bureau had not just become a much more closed-off institution than it had been just a year earlier. More importantly, its changing structure and culture signaled a broader shift toward an increasing sense of conspiracy and paranoia within the government and party.

The intersecting themes of state and institutional security and individual productivity expressed in Barden's comments to his senior staff reflected two countervailing political forces following the 1961 strike. At the heart of Barden's statements was a cautionary tale regarding the changing institutional apparatus of the Nkrumahist state in the aftermath of the strike. The political environment, Barden tacitly advised his staff, had shifted, and all members of the bureau were now responsible for adjusting to this new order. At the same time, Barden's pronouncements exemplified Nkrumah and the CPP government's attempts to rejuvenate, if not double down on, the political and social revolution they envisioned for both Ghana and the continent. For Nkrumah and others in the CPP trying to make sense of the popular revolt that began in the industrial cities of Sekondi and Takoradi but quickly spread elsewhere, corruption, bribery, and internal and external subversion had stalled the revolution both at home and abroad. In Ghana, the arrests and purges that followed the strike promised for the CPP a resurrection of the purity and populist enthusiasm of the nationalist struggle. Meanwhile, inside the party itself, the party's leadership aimed to return to the CPP the clarity of its anticolonial essence as it recommitted itself and the Ghanaian populace to the country's accelerated socialist reconstruction and the achievement of complete African liberation and unity.

This chapter and the following one thus interrogate the wide variety of experiences Ghanaians had as they negotiated the increasingly authoritarian environment of the Nkrumahist state in the early and mid-1960s. Key to this analysis is the shifting and unstable nature of Nkrumahist ideology itself during the period as events inside and outside of Ghana forced Nkrumah, the CPP, and others to reassess not necessarily their visions for the country and continent, but more aptly the methods by which they hoped to turn them into a reality. Thus, this chapter juxtaposes the international history of Ghanaian readings of neocolonial and Cold War intrusions in African decolonization movements with an analysis of the daily work lives of those employed in the Bureau of African Affairs. Here, the bureau is both mundane and exceptional. At once, it was perhaps the most ideologically driven and orthodox political institution in the Nkrumahist state, and, on the other hand, a site whose employees' daily affairs were often characterized by the most routine of labor concerns. For, at its foundation, the bureau was a workplace, one defined by an evolving set of often-contested institutional norms and assumptions. Through the use of the bureau's personnel files, this chapter explores the intersecting worlds of the transnational and the intimate in the day-to-day work lives of the bureau's employees, and its female employees in particular. In doing so, it emphasizes the ways in which the bureau's employees were forced to balance increasingly rigid and gendered regimes of institutional and state security with, as seen in the previous chapter, a driving set of political and social pressures all Ghanaian workers faced: an ever-intensifying state emphasis on individual and national productivity. Such an analysis of the bureau not only outlines a set of gender, generational, and class anxieties associated with the changing nature of political and work life in 1960s Ghana, but also points to a broader emerging state discourse constructed around the assumed antisocialist dangers of a perceived feminizing revolution.

BETWEEN LIBERATION AND COLD WAR
IN THE "YEAR OF AFRICA"

In the period between Ghana's 1957 independence and the 1961 strike, most of the continent outside of the southern African settler states had made or was in the process of making its transition to self-rule. However, the example of Guinea's 1958 independence, where French authorities sought to systematically destroy the emergent country's infrastructure following its famed "*non*" vote, proved to the continent's anticolonial activists that the inevitability of Africa's successful decolonization could not be taken for granted, even beyond the continent's settler states.[8] The year 1960, the so-called Year of Africa, further tested the narrative of inevitability surrounding African decolonization. The year opened with the independence of Cameroon under a leadership that many radical anticolonialists saw as little more than an appendage of France.[9] Addressing the Cameroonian situation in January 1960, for instance, the *Evening News* highlighted what it saw as the distinctly neocolonial nature of Cameroonian decolonization, as the newspaper opened its coverage of the occasion with the perhaps overly provocative question, "Independence of Cameroons: Is It Genuine?"[10] In June, the Congo would also gain its independence, followed by Nigeria in October. By the end of the year, more than a dozen other mostly francophone former colonies would emerge as independent states. From the perspective of Accra, however, most were under the still-heavy influence of their former colonial governments. Even more troubling for Accra's anticolonialists, many of these new postcolonial governments continued to express faith in their previous and current relationships to their former colonial powers, particularly in the francophone sphere.[11]

Events in South Africa and the Maghreb further clouded the enthusiasm in many anticolonial circles surrounding decolonization during the "Year of Africa." In North Africa, the Algerian war of independence continued to rage unabated, further drawing the continent's and international community's attention to the widespread violence and upheaval caused by the conflict.[12] Furthermore, the French decision to utilize the Algerian Sahara as a nuclear testing ground led to widespread protests across Africa and elsewhere, culminating, in Accra, with what historian Jean Allman has detailed as the mobilization of a spirited, albeit ill-fated, anti-imperial and antinuclear expedition to the bomb site.[13] In South Africa, the March 1960 massacre of sixty-nine unarmed protesters at an anti-pass rally in Sharpeville revealed additional fissures in the hopeful narratives surrounding decolonization and the Year of Africa. Coming just weeks after British prime minister Harold Macmillan famously declared to the South African parliament that a "wind of change" was sweeping through the continent, the events in Sharpeville were such a transgression of international norms that even some of the apartheid government's most reliable allies, including the United States, felt it necessary to condemn the attack.[14] Meanwhile, in Ghana, the attack occurred as the CPP was preparing to host what it billed as its largest and most important anticolonial and pan-African conference since the 1958 All-African People's Conference: the 1960 Positive Action Conference for Peace and Security in Africa. As a result, together with the French actions in North Africa, Sharpeville helped set the increasingly radical tone of the 1960 conference and its aftermath.[15]

No event, though, further complicated the narrative of the Year of Africa more than the local and international chaos surrounding the decolonization of the Congo. As the Congo made its transition to self-rule in 1960, instability quickly struck the emergent country as political rivals and western Cold War actors sought to destabilize the democratically elected government of Patrice Lumumba's Mouvement National Congolais (MNC). Inside Ghana, the situation in the massive Central African country drew an inordinate amount of attention from the CPP government and the Ghanaian press. As early as January 1960, for instance, the CPP had begun to signal its willingness to offer substantial economic, technical, and administrative assistance to the Congolese government upon the country's independence, much as it had done with Guinea a little over a year earlier. The Congolese themselves appeared highly receptive to the potential Ghanaian aid package, as the MNC reportedly advised the CPP in early January that, "without such an assistance," the MNC government "would undoubtedly be compelled to still depend at [sic] the mercy of the imperialists."[16] With tensions rising in Central Africa as the Belgians hurriedly moved toward the Congo's decolonization in early and mid-1960, events escalated rapidly, severely weakening the authority of the nascent Lumumba government and casting the soon-to-be country's political situation into a state of disarray.

However, in Ghana, the instability that accompanied Congolese independence only reinforced the CPP's commitment to the Lumumba government. By late July, as preparations for a United Nations peacekeeping mission in the Central African country were under way, prominent officials in the Ghanaian army began prepping the CPP cabinet on a potential Ghanaian role in the UN initiative.[17] By the end of August, more than eleven thousand international troops had made their way to the Congo, approximately a fifth of them Ghanaian.[18] In the same month, Nkrumah also purportedly signed an agreement with Lumumba for the formation of a supraterritorial union between the Ghanaian and Congolese states modeled on the existing Ghana-Guinea union.[19] By late 1960, though, Nkrumah had grown increasingly frustrated with the events on the ground in the Congo and particularly with the nature of the UN peacekeeping expedition. As a result, on 10 October, he went on national radio to announce his six-point plan for resolving the Congolese conflict. This included (1) an end to any impositions placed on Ghanaian soldiers' attempts to carry out their duties in the Congo; (2) international backing of the MNC-led Congolese parliament; (3) the withdrawal of Belgian troops from the Congo and an end to Belgium's "surreptitiously re-arming" of the infamous Force Publique; (4) the shuttering of the "imperialist"-run private radio stations operating across the Congo River in Brazzaville; (5) the extension of financial assistance to the duly elected Lumumba government; and (6) the installment and recognition of the Lumumba government's representatives in the United Nations.[20] Internationally, though, Nkrumah's proposals received little attention. Instead, Belgian, American, and Soviet interests drove the international debate surrounding the Congo. Meanwhile, the situation on the ground in the Congo continued to deteriorate in late 1960 as Lumumba and several of his most prominent MNC officials were detained and put under house arrest. Approximately three months after Nkrumah's October speech, Lumumba, along with three other high-ranking MNC officials, would be kidnapped, severely beaten, and assassinated. Over the days following his assassination, Lumumba's murderers would proceed to mutilate the Congolese prime minister's body, dissolve it in sulfuric acid, and grind down his skull and teeth.[21]

Ghana's Year of Africa

In July 1960, the Bureau of African Affairs' director A. K. Barden was urging Nkrumah not to let "the more dramatic events" in the Congo "overshadow and obscure" other developments, both positive and negative, transforming the continent. For Barden, the tensions that characterized Ghana's relationship with the decolonizing West African states of the French community were at their foundation the result of a lack of communication between Ghana and its francophone neighbors. Barden similarly posited hope for reform in the Cameroons: the Republic of Cameroon and the Anglophone Southern Cameroons. In doing so, Barden reminded Nkrumah of the impending unification plebiscite scheduled for February of the following year.

Barden also explained that, although still facing uphill battles, proposals for an African common market and the establishment of a continental trade union federation provided even further hope for the future of African unity through the institutionalization of continental economic unity.[22]

Lumumba's assassination, however, coupled with the events of the previous year, sent shock waves throughout Ghana and the CPP government. For Nkrumah himself, serious questions arose about the viability of what he and the CPP increasingly portrayed as the bourgeois nature of the early African anticolonial struggle in the Cold War context. According to Nkrumah, no group or organization held as much blame for Lumumba's death as the United Nations and its perceived American backers. Announcing the assassination to the Ghanaian public, Nkrumah told his national audience that "history records many occasions when the rulers of states have been assassinated." But, he insisted, "The murder of Patrice Lumumba and of two of his colleagues . . . is unique in that this is the first time in history that the legal ruler of a country has been done to death with the open connivance of a world organization in whom that ruler put his trust."[23] Shortly thereafter, mass demonstrations broke out in the streets of Accra, with protesters stopping in front of the American, French, British, and West German embassies. At the American embassy, the protesters—including market women, Young Pioneers, brigaders, and university students—tried to make their way into the building and "fired musketry" before being dissuaded by their leaders.[24] Some of the most extreme supporters of Nkrumah's pan-African cause even went so far as to call for the United Nations' secretary-general Dag Hammarskjöld's head. As one Bureau of African Affairs agent insisted, "This is not the time [in world history where] an imperialist agent like Hammarskjöld could kill an African king and be allowed to escape with his own life."[25]

In Ghana, the continental events of 1960 and early 1961 coincided with the country's transition to the First Republic in July 1960. Further consolidating administrative power in the hands of the CPP and Nkrumah himself (now retitled as Ghana's first president), the republican transition both formally and symbolically extricated the young state from Great Britain and its colonial and potentially neocolonial legacy with the removal of the British queen as the official Ghanaian head of state. The 1962 release of the CPP's *Programme for Work and Happiness* following the 1961 strike further continued the process of political centralization accompanying the transition to the First Republic as the CPP formally outlined a path to an eventual, formal one-party state in the country.[26] As the document suggested, the one-party state was to be an exercise in an organically derived African democracy. The *Programme* argued:

> Independent African States are faced with urgent and pressing problems of reconstruction, for the solution of which all the available resources both human and otherwise must be mobilized. This situation is almost analogous to a state of war and national emergency which is always met in the older established countries by the formation of coalition or national governments. Moreover, a multi-party system is entirely alien to the traditional concept of government in African Society.
>
> For these reasons, a one party system provides the best answer for the problem of government in Africa. However, a one party system can operate successfully and satisfactory only in a truly free and independent country. Otherwise, it becomes a dangerous weapon which can be used by the colonialists, neo-colonialists and their agents in puppet regimes and client States to oppress the masses and subdue the will of the people.[27]

Speaking to the National Assembly in 1962, Kpandu South MP Prince Yao Boateng historicized the rationale for the CPP's initiatives. The shift to a one-party state would "re-Africanize" Ghana, and the people would go on to "abolish the ballot box, and look to the *Asafo* to perform their ancient role of election." The move, the Volta Region MP insisted, was "neither evolutionary nor revolutionary." Rather, it was a chance for the people of Ghana to "come back to the past and to what our forefathers did."[28]

For their part, the CPP, by bringing an end to what some in the party portrayed as the "democratic shadow-boxing" and "parliamentary obstructionism" of the formal opposition, envisioned creating a political structure and environment where it could, for the first time, truly work toward cultivating a greater sense of "ideological purity" in the Ghanaian populace.[29] For Sulemana Ibun Iddrissu, the whole idea of a "democracy" versus "dictatorship" dichotomy was a falsehood since every government was a gradation of each. "In this world of ours," he argued in the National Assembly, "there are people who suffer under what we call dictatorship and there are others who also suffer under what we call democracy." Seemingly pushing aside traditional conceptions of democracy altogether, the Dagomba North MP, then, insisted that the real question all Ghanaians needed to ask themselves was what type of "dictatorship" they wanted. "Is it the dictatorship of the minority over the majority or the dictatorship of the majority over the minority?" According to him, "True democracy as we understand it is of course the dictatorship of the many, and that is the dictatorship of the proletariat over the bourgeoisie."[30] Thus, as theorized by the party, the transition to the one-party state was to bring the CPP's mission for Ghana and Africa full circle. For, with it, the political and developmental goals of the CPP's promised political, social, economic, and infrastructural modernization would intersect with an assumed acceleration of the mass ontological transformation of the Ghanaian citizenry demanded by the Nkrumahist revolution. The result was to be a metamorphosis within Ghana and even within the CPP itself, as the country and party transformed the narrow mission of the nationalist struggle for (nation-state) independence into a transnational, cosmopolitan movement rooted in the ethics of socialist collectivism, communalism, and self-sacrifice.

The threats of internal and external subversion exemplified by the continental events of 1960 and 1961 not only colored the CPP's official reading of the 1961 strike, but more importantly also guided the governmental and party reforms that followed. Multiparty governance, in particular, the *Evening News* argued in 1962, had created a political and social environment rife with internal and external subversion.[31] The August 1962 attempt on Nkrumah's life in the northern town of Kulungugu only further intensified such rhetoric. Writing in a 1964 article in the Bureau of African Affairs' flagship magazine, the *Voice of Africa*, bureau director A. K. Barden connected the attack—which injured Nkrumah and killed at least two others, including a child preparing to present the president with a bouquet of flowers (see chapter 6)—to counterrevolutionary forces. "Counter-revolution," Barden maintained, "was set in motion" by the reforms enacted by the CPP following the 1961 strike, namely the party and government's attempted crackdown on bribery and corruption. "And Kulungugu and the subsequent bombings in the country have been acts in furtherance of counter-revolution," the bureau's director insisted, "that is the determination to halt the people's march to socialism because socialism threatens the ill-gotten gains of a few."[32] The *Evening News* similarly connected the bombing to the interplay between domestic and international forces of counterrevolutionary subversion, arguing, in its 11 August 1962 edition, "Who can therefore deny the fact that the assassination attempt was planned and directed from Washington, London, Paris, or Brussels with local bastards and shameless stooges?"[33]

As a result, what emerged in the country in the aftermath of the 1961 strike and the local and continental events of the early 1960s was an increasingly closed-off security state. Citizens now regularly came under the suspicion of party and state authorities for a variety of real and perceived political and social crimes (see chapter 6). Abroad, even some of the country's most prominent expatriates and representatives came under the ever more watchful eye of the government. Furthermore, several highly prominent foreign-born officials, including Ghana's top military official, Major-General H. T. Alexander, were removed from their positions during this period—much to the chagrin of the British and American governments.[34] Others, even figures with longstanding pan-Africanist connections to Ghana, left the country to pursue their visions of the African revolution elsewhere. For African American expatriate Bill Sutherland, who had served as the personal secretary to K. A. Gbedemah since the early 1950s, this meant travel first to Israel and later to Tanzania followed by Zambia before continuing on to other anticolonial hotspots.[35] Even Erica Powell, Nkrumah's British private secretary and one of his closest confidants, acknowledged the harassment she faced in the early 1960s as, in her opinion, unscrupulous high-ranking party officials sought to shut her out of Nkrumah's inner circle.[36] As a result, as viewed by the CPP, the struggle of the day was thus to be one against what it saw as a rising tide of domestic neocolonialism and foreign subversion within the maturing country and decolonizing continent.

ON THE HOME FRONT:
NEOCOLONIALISM AND REVOLUTION

For those aligned with the party and its various wings, including those employed in prominent party- and state-run institutions, the realities of this battle, as the CPP aimed to advance its revolutionary project at home and abroad, had wide-ranging and often unexpected implications. To the post-1961 CPP, the opposition was both formal and informal, internal and international, public and private. This juxtaposition of the intimate and the alien in turn characterized the nefariousness and ambiguity of the neocolonial threat to the party, country, and continent. Anyone, it was believed, regardless of party affiliation, history, or relationships, had the potential to be working for the "imperialists" and thus against the interests and mission of the state. Any action or inaction, therefore, needed to be scrutinized in relation to the revolution and the question of revolutionary fidelity. As Nkrumah reminded attendees at a 1962 seminar at the Kwame Nkrumah Ideological Institute, neocolonialism, defined as "the granting of political independence minus economic independence," remained the greatest threat to the

"African Liberation Movement." Through it, he argued, the imperialist and capitalist powers aimed to embed in the continent's newly independent countries a local elite designed to serve above all the interests of the imperialists, albeit under the shallow guise and rhetoric of democracy.[37] The role of the revolutionary citizenry was thus that of securing and protecting the nation and party from this ethereal, ubiquitous threat, and the burden of upholding such vigilance was to be at once societal and personal.

As a result, the day-to-day maintenance of the African revolution in Ghana was a multifaceted affair. Institutions such as the Bureau of African Affairs and the Kwame Nkrumah Ideological Institute aimed to position Ghana on the literal and ideological front lines of the struggle as they sought to merge the pan-African revolution at home with the African liberationist politics of the continent. At the Ideological Institute, the institute's students combined their political and ideological studies—which, as chapter 4 noted, included subjects such as Nkrumahism, scientific socialism, and African politics—with additional courses in more traditional fields of study including statistics, nutrition, English, and French.[38] Training at the institute was to be theoretical, practical, and evaluative, with the theoretical components focusing on topics including the "Qualities of a Nationalist," the "Evils of Colonialism and Neo-colonialism," electioneering, and party organization. Meanwhile, a student's practicum was to be spent visiting major party organizations: the party headquarters, the TUC, the Young Pioneers, and the Builders Brigade, among others.[39] At the institute itself, Ghanaian students were also to be joined by anticolonial students from other parts of the continent.[40] As one former KNII student related, entrance into the institute was neither guaranteed nor easy. For him, at least, it was determined by an examination which many failed to pass. According to him, "We were lucky a few of us passed the examination. To our credit, we were admitted and we were learning fine." At the institute, he further recounted, things were "very nice, everything was going alright, [we were] thinking within the course of time—within three years—we would come out" with degrees in hand.[41]

As the KNII foremost focused on the political and ideological education of the select group of Ghanaian and African students it admitted, the Bureau of African Affairs, which predated the KNII, undertook the task of administering Ghana's role in the African revolution at home and abroad. Formed in late 1959, the bureau had its origins in the remnants of George Padmore's Office of the Adviser to the Prime Minister on African Affairs. Under Padmore, the Office of the Adviser augmented Ghana's foreign policy initiatives—particularly those of civil service institutions such as the Ministry of External Affairs (later, Foreign Affairs)—by, in the words of Padmore's biographer Leslie James, providing the "resources and expertise on Africa" necessary for Ghana to offer the continent's freedom fighters both "practical and ideological support."[42] As early as late 1957 and early 1958, Padmore and his office would play a leading role in the organization of the 1958 Conference of Independent African States and the 1958 All-African People's Conference. The AAPC, in particular, W. Scott Thompson argues, "was to be Padmore's conference," as he set out to establish a new pan-African tradition distinct from the Manchester Pan-African Congress and the Du Boisian conferences of the interwar period.[43] In addition, Padmore used his office as a mechanism for recruiting promising British-based African students to come to Accra, where they were to continue their studies with the support of the Ghanaian government. As one young Malawian student who left London for Accra explained in a 1961 letter to the minister of education, Padmore was able to draw him to the Ghanaian capital in 1959 "by his simplicity, by his sincerity, by his sympathy with my efforts to educate myself and, above all, by his very great interest in my country Nyasaland."[44]

Padmore's September 1959 death, however, initiated a reorganization of the Office of the Adviser, resulting in its formal integration into the CPP's foreign policy apparatus. Within days of Padmore's death, Nkrumah named Kofi Baako—one of the party's chief ideologues—as the director of the newly renamed Bureau of African Affairs.[45] By December 1959, the cabinet had begun debate on granting the new bureau statutory approval, and, by the end of the year, Thompson notes, the bureau would absorb into itself the operations of the Accra government's most prominent pan-African institutions, including the All-African People's Conference Secretariat.[46] Established out of the 1958 conference, the AAPC Secretariat was to provide a permanent institutional infrastructure for the organization of future conferences, while also serving as the conference's international and continental mouthpiece. By late 1959, the bureau had taken over the publication of the AAPC's *Bulletin on African Affairs*, and many notable officials now had positions in both institutions.[47] By 1960, the transformation of the Office of the Adviser and the broader integration of the Ghanaian pan-African apparatus into the Bureau of African Affairs was largely complete, with the bureau formally gaining statutory approval with A. K. Barden—reporting directly to Nkrumah—as its new director.[48]

Under Barden, the bureau rapidly expanded its official and unofficial mission. Similar to Padmore's Office of the Adviser, the bureau undertook the collection and dissemination of a wide range of information pertaining to the struggle for continental liberation and African unity, with researchers and journalists reporting for internal and external audiences on the changing situations in such anticolonial hotspots as South Africa, the Rhodesias, Ruanda-Urundi, and the continent's Portuguese colonies.[49] At their height, circulation for the institution's two most prominent publications—the *Voice of Africa* and the *Spark*—reached ten and fifteen thousand copies per issue respectively.[50] By way of comparison, in 1960 the *Evening News*—the official mouthpiece of the CPP—printed fifteen to twenty thousand copies per issue and the opposition *Ashanti Pioneer* seven to ten thousand, with the *Daily Graphic* maintaining the largest circulation at eighty thousand copies per issue.[51] In addition to the *Spark* and the *Voice of Africa*, the bureau press also offered such auxiliary publications as the *African Chronicler*, the *Freedom Fighter*, the *Pan-Africanist*, and a parallel French edition of the *Spark*, *L'Étincelle*. As a result, by as early as 1960 and 1961, the bureau had begun attracting the attention of anticolonial activists and freedom fighters from as far afield as southern and eastern Africa, Nigeria, Great Britain, the United States, and the Soviet Union.[52] Bureau-led education and reading campaigns further raised the institution's public profile in the early and mid-1960s as the institution provided free copies of Nkrumah's speeches and of several of its own publications to interested parties.[53] Similarly, the bureau continued the Padmorean policy of inviting students and freedom fighters to Ghana to attend government- and party-run institutions, including the country's secondary schools, the KNII, and, for some, secret guerilla training camps scattered throughout the country.[54]

WORK AND GENDER IN THE REVOLUTIONARY WORKPLACE

For those employed in party- and state-run institutions like the Bureau of African Affairs, such institutions were as much workplaces as they were conduits of the Nkrumahist revolution. Inside the BAA's offices specifically, the institution's distinctly pan-African mission framed how both the bureau's administration and its employees understood their work and their relationships with it and one another. The bureau, A. K. Barden noted in a 1964 meeting, required a special type of worker, who, reflecting the inherently political nature of the institution's mission at home and abroad, was to be an individual wholly dedicated to the security and prosperity of the state. Each employee, Barden and his fellow administrators stressed, had an obligation to his or her job that extended beyond his individual needs and desires and encompassed the fruition of the state and the continent at large.[55] The result was a work environment in which traditional labor concerns such as sick leave, pay scale, and productivity not only became imbued with the CPP's fetishization of work and productivity, but also, and just as significantly, with obligations to the security of the state and the pursuit of continent-wide liberation and unity. As the *Spark*'s founding editor Kofi Batsa argued in 1985, the bureau was to serve as "the factory of the ideas of Kwame Nkrumah. It was our job," he continued, "to take his ideas, turn them into actuality—and to create the Africa he imagined before it was too late."[56]

The advancement of the Nkrumahist model of African revolution thus became the defining feature of nearly all of the work of the bureau. This would come to include not only its formal anticolonial and political operations, but also its secretarial, cooking, and cleaning services. Given the scope of the duties involved, bureau employees therefore came from a variety of backgrounds. The institution's top officials tended to rise out of the party's political and ideological wings, most notably including the National Association of Socialist Students Organisations (NASSO). By the late 1950s, NASSO, which had its origins as a CPP study group largely based outside of the country in the early 1950s, grew over the subsequent years into the official "ideological wing of the Party."[57] Between 1959 and 1961, when the organization was folded into the KNII, its members and officials—the most notable of whom was the polarizing minister of presidential affairs, Tawia Adamafio—led the progressively leftist shift that defined much of the CPP politics of the early years of the First Republic. In doing so, they transformed the organization into a key agent in what journalist Colin Legum has described as a broader, party-wide "attack [on] the 'ideologically weak' older party leaders."[58] Among these party officials were many of those purged after the 1961 strike, including Kojo Botsio and K. A. Gbedemah.

An ex-serviceman, Barden, for his part, had his start in African affairs by working directly with Padmore in the Trinidadian's Office of the Adviser to the Prime Minister on African Affairs, first as his stenographer and later as his private secretary. During their time together, Padmore regularly expressed his great faith in Barden's skills and discretion. In one January 1959 memo, for instance, Padmore remarked that "A. K. Barden, my Stenographer Secretary has so efficiently handled in addition to his confidential duties the general administrative work of the office. Besides enjoying his confidence and loyalty," Padmore continued, "he is painstaking, courteous and one who can always be relied upon to shoulder responsibilities."[59]

For Barden's efforts, Padmore "strongly recommend[ed]" that Barden be promoted to be his private secretary. This move, Padmore argued, was to be part of a broader staff restructuring of the office, which would allow it to more effectively and efficiently adapt to the rapidly changing political environment on the continent.[60] In the following months, Padmore would continue to write to key officials in the CPP government seeking promotions, adjustments in pay scale, and increased responsibilities for Barden, citing his demonstrated skill and diligence in working with confidential and time-sensitive material.[61]

More broadly, in its daily operations, the bureau depended upon a relatively large group of men and women who served the institution as everything from drivers, custodians, and security guards to clerical assistants, bookbinders, and typists. Labor in the bureau was highly gendered, particularly at the trade, service, and clerical levels. Male laborers served the institution as drivers and security guards, among other trade- and service-related tasks. Most enjoyed a pay scale regulated by the government's broader civil service and day laborer protocol, which determined their pay based upon formulae connected to the tasks they completed, their lengths of service, and their skill grades. As a result, for watchmen and drivers at the soon-to-be bureau-affiliated African Affairs Centre (AAC)—an expatriate hostel for freedom fighters—wages ran up to £9 and £10 per month, respectively, in late 1959.[62] Meanwhile, on the job, the bureau's male employees were tasked with such assignments as keeping the institution's automobile fleet running, ensuring the mobility, safety, and efficiency of the bureau's leadership and its expatriate charges, maintaining its offices and keeping its infrastructure operational, and safeguarding the security and secrecy of its premises.

It was the BAA's female employees, however, who served as the administrative lifeblood of the bureau's institutional mission. Comprising the bulk of the bureau's clerical and secretarial staff, these women maintained and secured the institution's vast filing system, managed its telephone systems, served as bookbinders in its rapidly growing archive and library, and featured prominently in the institution's typing pool. For these women, bureau employment offered access to the formal economic sector and the regular paychecks it entailed. As with their female colleagues in other formal sector employment, at home, these paychecks likely supplemented the broader household income, along with what they accumulated through outside labor—cooking, sewing, and trading, among other forms of work—completed in the informal sector.[63] In other instances, single and married women may have held their earnings for personal use.[64] Bureau employment may have also served as a site of transition for the women employed. Furthermore, as in other areas of the formal sector, some of the bureau's female employees may have sought to take advantage of the benefits, security, structure, and prestige of formal employment—and specifically state employment—prior to moving on to other types of activities, including marriage, motherhood, and self-employment. As sociologist Margaret Peil notes in her 1972 study of Ghanaian factory workers, "women were twice as likely as men to plan self-employment in the future." At the root of many of these women's ambitions for self-employment, Peil adds, was a desire for the more flexible work environment it offered, thus providing them more leeway in dealing with the demands of marriage and motherhood, as well as with other gendered expectations of them as women.[65]

At the sociological level, the women of the Bureau of African Affairs were part of a global generation of women making their way into and redefining the world's offices. Looking at the Canadian and American contexts, for instance, geographers Kim England and Kate Boyer have recently shown that, in the decades between 1940 and 1970, the number of women in clerical positions in the two countries "rose a staggering 300 percent." By 1970, women would come to hold approximately three-quarters of all American and Canadian clerical jobs.[66] Such a shift was also exhibited in postwar Britain. As education historian Stephanie Spencer recounts, for a generation of young women, the educational reforms that followed in the wake of the British government's 1944 Education Act, and the personal and social upheaval of the war itself, had led many to marry and have children younger and in turn cultivated a vision of employment as a mere "stop gap before marriage." By the 1960s, however, Spencer suggests that formal employment had become a central objective of many British young women as they—like their American counterparts—had become dissatisfied with their domestic options. As Spencer reminds us, this generation "was also the generation which occasioned the reprinting of Simone de Beauvoir's The Second Sex fourteen times between 1961 and 1962 and read Betty Friedan's Feminine Mystique which identified the dissatisfaction with housework felt in middle-class America."[67]

The politics of 1960s Ghana's generation of young women may have differed from that of their American, British, and Canadian counterparts, but their growing presence in the workplace carried with it many of the same conflicting messages. Although demographically small in number (making up approximately 10 percent of all Ghanaians employed in the

nomy), politically, women in the formal sector—like their fe-
eagues in the Builders Brigade—came to represent the virtues
w, modern Ghana of which Nkrumah and the CPP preached.[68]
ımahist revolution, the CPP argued, was to be as much a gender
revolution—one challenging gender expectations and opportunities—as a
political one. The goal of the revolution in this regard, the *Programme for
Work and Happiness* insisted, was "complete equality between the sexes"—a
principle that theoretically was even supposed to extend to marriage.[69] Here,
the CPP followed other radical and revolutionary socialist states in the early
and mid-twentieth century as it framed its calls for gender equity as part of
the broader heroic and emancipatory quest of the nation.[70] As a result, newspapers and magazines, ranging from the state- and party-run *Evening News*
and *Ghanaian* to the largely independent *Daily Graphic* and opposition
Ashanti Pioneer, positioned formally employed women as the embodiment
of the social transformation presently under way in the young and modernizing country. In these reports, educational reforms, innovations in the home,
and changing societal expectations—all advanced by the CPP, at least from
the perspective of the party—liberated Ghanaian women from the tedium
and isolation of the home. Moreover, it was argued, these reforms and innovations provided women with the means and responsibility necessary for
actively advancing the country's socialist revolution in workplaces and in
fields ranging from the office to medicine and politics.[71]

As might be expected, the party's most prominent women's groups
were among the most active in promoting such a message. Speaking in 1962
before the National Council of Ghana Women (NCGW), for instance,
party activist and NCGW national secretary Margaret Martei proudly reminded her audience of not only the centrality of Ghana's women to the
country's nation-building project, but just as importantly of Nkrumah and
the CPP's role in creating such a space for them. As Martei explained, the
CPP, through the creation of the NCGW, had created a mandate whereby
"all Ghanaian women . . . should effectively organise themselves into an
active group in the reconstruction of Ghana." More to the point, she asserted, "This means that we as women of Ghana must work side by side
with our men to reconstruct Ghana."[72] Martei continued by highlighting
the uniqueness of the current generation of Ghanaian women, while also
calling them to arms. As "women of the modern atomic age," she insisted,
Ghana's women had both the right and the obligation to "claim equality with men and . . . prove this by being marchers to our men in all the
fields of [national] reconstruction."[73] For not only Martei, but the party as a

whole, the promotion of women into positions of responsibility signaled a particular type of social modernity in the country, as the country's women took on a central role in the advancement of the Nkrumahist revolution at home and abroad.[74]

Inside the bureau, however, the perceived modernity of women in the workplace competed with the bureau's almost exclusively male management's understanding of the institution's mission and role in the larger African revolution and the Nkrumahist revolution itself. At its foundation, the revolution appeared to be a distinctly masculine enterprise for the bureau's political leadership. In the bureau's major publications, for instance, the revolution was frequently celebrated in male-centric portrayals of individual anticolonial struggles. Women, if they were featured at all, were most often disembodied, faceless victims of capitalist imperialism or caricatured threats to the anticolonial cause. The true revolutionaries were therefore presumed to be the men engaged in the anticolonial struggle. It was they, the bureau's publications suggested, who were actively combating the imperialists on both the literal and figurative front lines of the struggle and the ideological battlefield of ideas. Even in Barden's own history of the Ghanaian nationalist struggle, which he published in a 1964 edition of the *Voice of Africa*, women were only mentioned once, and only in conjunction with men beholden to what Barden presented as the antisocialist ideals of capitalist individualism, corruption, and greed.[75] A further examination of existing copies of the *Voice of Africa* shows similar tendencies. During the magazine's five-year run, for instance, it published less than a dozen articles written by women or featuring women as major actors in the continental struggle.[76]

This near-absence of women from the bureau's publications was unique among CPP publications, obscuring a legacy of women's anticolonial activism in the Gold Coast that, as discussed in chapter 2, led figures like C. L. R. James to position them at the center of the nationalist struggle.[77] In his autobiography, Nkrumah himself had commented on the central role of women in the Gold Coast struggle, stating that, from the CPP's inception, "women have been the [party's] chief field organizers" and were responsible for "bringing about the solidarity and cohesion of the Party."[78] Moreover, the CPP press itself, from the earliest days of the *Accra Evening News* in the late 1940s, had long presented women in its publications as integral to the nationalist struggle and the party's anticolonial mission. As a result, party publications featured individual Ghanaian women and the country's women as a whole as historical and contemporary actors tasked with advancing the anticolonial struggle, cultivating the country's nationalist consciousness, and, as writers, constructing the party's own narrative of the struggle.[79]

However, as historian Jean Allman has shown, by the early 1960s, many of these women's contributions to the nationalist struggle had been erased from the CPP's public memory, at least in terms of their specificity.[80] Moreover, as represented in much of the party press, the threats of both internal and external subversion implicit in the Cold War and in the neocolonial challenges to African liberation were now almost invariably construed in masculine terms. Settler colonists, foreign agents, and European and American governments all carried with them a stated and unstated masculine aura within the CPP's publications.[81] Liberation in turn demanded that the most dedicated, diligent, and attentive individuals serve the cause. What this meant for the day-to-day operation of the Bureau of African Affairs was a work environment in which the bureau's top officials viewed its female labor force as ill equipped to handle the rigor and unique demands of working for the African revolution. As a result, bureau women endured a workplace stigma that classified them as everything from inefficient and unproductive workers to active threats to the institution's proper operation, security, and productivity.

FEMINIZING THE REVOLUTION

The foremost issues shaping the bureau administration's impression of its female workforce tended to be those of sick and maternal leave. Writing, for instance, in a 1962 report on a clerical assistant named Dinah Patterson, bureau assistant secretary D. B. Sam openly mocked Patterson for a recent illness and her subsequent absence from work. Sam emphatically noted that Patterson purportedly could not work because of "a boil attack on a vital part of her anatomy!" Further vexing Sam may have been the fact that it was Patterson's mother—not Patterson herself—who telephoned the bureau to advise her daughter's supervisors of her intended absence.[82] Three weeks later, after missing work once again, Miss Patterson received another reprimand from Sam. Here, the assistant secretary described his charge's "habit [of falling ill as] incompatible with the efficient running of the Bureau." For this reason, he informed the young clerical assistant that her "case [was] getting intolerable" and surmised that, as a result of her and what he anticipated to be others' absences from work, "our output [would] drop and the Bureau will not deserve its existence."[83]

Similarly, on another occasion in 1965, clerical assistant and telephone operator Mercy Odoom lost a day's pay and received a warning for attending to a sick child. Odoom, who does not appear to have had a history of frequent absences or other significant disciplinary issues, promised her bosses that this would be an isolated incident. However, an apparently frustrated D. A. Dzima—another of the Bureau of African Affairs' assistant secretaries—responded to Odoom's claims by dismissively noting in his report that "this is the usual lame excuse offered by our young mothers." Debates over Odoom's case went all the way up to the bureau's highest ranks, with E. Ofori-Bah—the bureau's new director and longtime executive secretary—responding in agreement to Dzima's assessment of Odoom's "excuse."[84] In other instances, like that of Victoria Menka, administrators openly defamed their female subordinates, with one bureau official labeling the clerical assistant in a 1964 report as "another lazy girl who goes out more than ten times a day." With such a character flaw, the report's author asserted, "It will take her a long time to become a Book Binder."[85] Still others, including school-age expatriates, apparently became objects of sexual intrigue among key bureau senior staff as well as that of the BAA-affiliated African Affairs Centre, as rumors circulated about prominent bureau officials—including Barden and AAC director T. Ras Makonnen—maintaining relationships with some of their young female employees and wards.[86] In one 1965 case, for instance, a young Kenyan student studying in the country accused a bureau official of unwanted sexual advances, as he purportedly sought "to play sex" with her.[87]

In all of these instances, issues of gender, generation, and class contextualized the bureau's treatment of its female staff. Rarely did even the most unproductive men ever suffer the same scrutiny and ridicule as these women, even when many of the bureau's most integral tasks—including the publication and circulation of its own news organs—went neglected.[88] This was also often ridicule that, especially in the case of Dinah Patterson, not so subtly connected imagery of the female body with threats to institutional productivity and state security. Moreover, bureau administrators appeared to reserve much of this ridicule and criticism for Ghana's so-called "modern women."[89] In some ways intersecting with the youth in the Young Pioneers and Builders Brigade, these women comprised the generation of women celebrated by the party press as the future of Ghana. Broadly speaking, they had benefited from the opportunities opened to them by the social and educational reforms initiated by the CPP in the early and mid-1950s. As outlined in chapter 2, the most important of these reforms, by far, was the 1952 introduction of fee-free primary education into the then colony. The 1961 institution of fee-free, compulsory primary and middle school education only added to the exponential growth in student enrollments during the Nkrumah era. As a result, if the aspirations of their compatriots in other segments of the formal sector give any indication, Ghana's female school leavers may have viewed these educational opportunities as opening another world to them, one that had the potential to offer an array of possibilities independent of the real and imagined constraints of marriage and childrearing (even if only temporarily).[90]

Inside and outside the bureau, however, late-colonial debates over the family and individual familial obligations underpinned, at least in part, the treatment of women on the job. As alluded to in chapter 3, the early twentieth century witnessed shifts in the financial expectations of men in regard to their families. Here, as Jean Allman, Lisa Lindsay, and others have shown, West African men and women alike increasingly invoked an ideal whereby a male wage-earning adult would support his wife and children by providing them regular access to the cash economy, even if only symbolically since most women themselves were already involved in an array of their own cash-generating endeavors.[91] In the Gold Coast and post-independence Ghana specifically, the societal obligations and expectations of the patrilineal and (most notably among the Akan) matrilineal familial structure collided with a rising modernist discourse centered on the monogamous nuclear family. As a result, notions of male respectability, at least in part, became bound to a man's ability and willingness to support and maintain his wife, children, and, in many cases, other family members.[92] Midcentury economic and social realities—including income shortfalls, housing shortages, religion, and distance from extended families—further reinforced such a conception of male respectability.[93] By the early 1960s, the CPP itself had begun to advance such an ideal in increasingly more prominent and influential venues, including the *Evening News*, the *Ghanaian*, its *Programme for Work and Happiness*, and inside the National Assembly with the introduction of the 1963 Maintenance of Children Bill, among others.[94]

As the image of the modern male breadwinner came to represent male respectability and, by the 1960s, a revolutionary ideal, the representation of women in Ghanaian workplaces oscillated between that of the realization of the radical social transformation envisioned by the CPP and that of the caricatured proxy for a lazy, undisciplined, and self-serving threat to the revolution. The result was a social environment wherein women who left the home for the workplace often endured acute forms of surveillance and skepticism from their male colleagues and bosses. In so doing, they faced regular questions about their abilities or willingness to balance their obligations in the home (productive and reproductive) with those on the job and for the nation. As one columnist writing in the state-run monthly the *Ghanaian* insisted in 1964, even women purportedly recognized that their responsibilities on the job and at home, as well as physical capabilities, differed from their male counterparts'. In his opinion, this made them the strongest opponents of the ideal of "equal pay for equal work" in the country since, he argued, women themselves simply accepted that they could not do equal work.[95] In another instance, a self-described "Nkrumahist citizen," in a letter to the *Evening News'* "What the People Say" column, decried the laziness, inefficiency, and unreliability of "a shapely,

FIGURE 5.1. Their interest in gossiping is above any business. *Source: The Ghanaian*, January 1962.

beautiful-faced and sweet-mouthed housewife" recently employed to serve as a typist in the registrar-general's office.[96] Even Nkrumah at times propagated such ideas, for instance, as he lamented in his 1963 May Day broadcast "how our telephone girls who are normally so friendly, polite, and well-behaved at home are rude and abrupt" in the workplace. "In the shops," he explained to the nation, "the assistants ignore the customers while they chat among themselves and treat them [the customers] with nonchalance and disrespect, forgetting that but for these same customers they would not be in employment."[97]

At issue for many male party leaders and journalists was a presumed disconnect between what they assumed to be the intrinsic traits of Ghanaian womanhood—talkativeness, materialism, and distraction—and the productive needs of the nation and continent. As a result, writers such as the popular columnist Kwesi Bonsu, writing in a 1963 edition of the *Ghanaian*, found it possible to openly question the wisdom of allowing too many women into the country's workplaces despite party interdictions against such gender discrimination.[98] On the job, Bonsu insisted, "Many of our girls . . . do only a few hours work for a whole week" and instead pass their time in "silly talk and sheer gossip."[99] For Bonsu and others, not only did this gossip and idle chatter take away from the productivity of a given workplace, it also challenged the progress of the country's socialist revolution, as it weakened the state by engulfing the social, economic, and moral transformations embedded in socialist work in an array of personal rivalries, conspiracy theories, and attempts at self-aggrandizement. To combat such scourges, even the leaders of the country's most prominent women's organizations made regular pleas to the country's women to "eschew laziness, rumour-mongering, and gossiping."[100]

In the day-to-day operations of the Bureau of African Affairs, where issues of institutional security and secrecy were paramount, concerns over loose lips, gossip, and talkativeness extended beyond questions of mere productivity. Rather, they carried continental implications embedded in fears of infiltration. As Barden relayed to his senior staff in 1961, the bureau—with its uniquely pan-Africanist mission—was particularly susceptible to such intrusion. He even claimed that, according to his sources, the bureau had in fact already been penetrated, with at least a few of the institution's employees possibly serving as spies for foreign governments.[101] He therefore advised the bureau's senior staff to always remain mindful of the threats the institution and they, as its administrators, faced. "Officers . . . could be invited to parties," he warned his staff, "to be lured into giving information and that they should be discretionary in their attendance at parties." The goal, he insisted, should not be to reject all such invitations, but rather to remain "vigilant at all times."[102] Three years later, many of these same themes reemerged as Barden and several of his subordinates accused an individual recently seconded to the bureau from the United Ghana Farmers' Cooperative Council of divulging bureau activities to nonprivileged personnel and spreading lies about his previous wages.[103]

Such institutional and state concerns over security and secrecy cultivated a culture in the bureau of surveillance and discipline on the job. Not only were bureau employees, like all employees of government and party institutions, required to take an oath of loyalty upon acceptance of employment, but, on the job, they were also to have their daily movements and activities monitored and recorded by their various supervisors.[104] In other instances, job descriptions and evaluations for particular positions in the institution subjected even employee moods and personal dispositions to notation, critique, and regulation.[105] Such a system, Barden implied in a 1961 outline of workers' responsibilities and duties, was foundational to efforts to refine the values and work ethic of the special type of worker demanded by an institution like the Bureau of African Affairs. This included a call on workers to approach their labor with, in Barden's words, "cheerfulness, hopefulness, honesty, sobriety, discipline, secrecy, and . . . knowledge." For workers themselves, however, the result was a workplace where employees often faced severe sanctions for seemingly normal worker coping mechanisms such as "clock watch[ing]," showing "a sign of laziness and lack of interest in your work," and leaving desks and designated workspaces without permission.[106]

As with the cases of Dinah Patterson, Mercy Odoom, and Victoria Menka in relation to leave time and job performance, the sanctioning and surveillance of employees for loose talk and other activities deemed threats to the bureau took on highly gendered undertones. This was particularly acute in a 1962 case involving a group of women caught, in the language of bureau assistant secretary D. B. Sam, "squatting" and eating outside of the bureau-sanctioned canteen. In his letter of reprimand, Sam chastised the women for displaying what he described as not only a general lack of regard for hygiene by eating outdoors, but also for "a considerable decline in your standard of discipline." As Sam reminded his chastened employees, Barden himself had advised them "on a number of occasions" of their need to take their meals in the bureau's canteen as opposed to in their offices or the agency's compound. Given that they had "repeatedly flouted the Director's warnings," Sam insisted that their actions "constitute[d] a serious offence." As a result, Sam informed the women that they were to serve a three-day suspension, which included a forfeiture of pay.[107] Moreover, after receiving an apology from the women, Sam argued that neither he nor the director could rescind the stated punishment, for such leniency would defeat the pedagogical purposes of the sanction. "It must . . . be brought home forcibly to you," he counseled them, "that should you in future be found guilty of breach of discipline more severe action will be taken against you."[108]

In the cases of these women, however, the severity of their punishment suggests a concern that extended beyond Sam's frustrations over hygiene and indiscipline to a broader institutional anxiety over the women's efforts to socialize outside of management's direct supervision. From management's perspective, such activities had both security and productivity implications for the institution, the state, and the continent. As discussed earlier, narratives of collusion, incompetence, and talkativeness drove Ghanaian accounts of the shortcomings of the Year of Africa, including in regard to the Congo crisis. As understood by the CPP, the decline of the MNC and especially Lumumba's assassination were as much the result of the actions of undisciplined, self-serving individuals working secretly with the Belgian and American governments as a product of a failed system for reining in potential neocolonial threats.[109] Similar narratives played out in Ghanaian accounts of what were perceived as stalled anticolonial struggles in southern and Portuguese-controlled Africa. Such perspectives buttressed fears of foreign infiltration not only into these regions' various liberation movements, but also within Ghana itself.[110] As Nkrumah conveyed to his audience at the 1961 laying of the KNII foundation stone, throughout the Gold Coast's nationalist struggle "the imperialists and the colonialists were not sleeping." Rather, he insisted, "They worked fast with our [the CPP's] opponents, and produced the National Liberation Movement, which exerted itself to wreck everything the nation had gained so far and bring back colonialism again upon the people . . . exactly what they are now enacting in the Congo, and very soon possibly in Angola."[111]

In the day-to-day life of the bureau, unsupervised social encounters thus carried with them in the eyes of the bureau's security-minded senior staff the potential for outside subversion and the dissemination—intentional or not—of sensitive information. In part due to their assumed chatty nature as women and in part due to the nature of their work, the bureau's female employees came to represent acute threats to the institution and the state. It is important to remember that the bureau's female employees—as clerical assistants, telephone operators, bookbinders, and typists—were not simply charged with mundane clerical and secretarial duties. Rather, they were on the front lines of the Nkrumahist revolutionary struggle, as they gained direct access to, filed, reproduced, and transmitted some of the most sensitive materials connected to the bureau's activities at home and abroad. It is also important to remember that they were not alone, for women in similar positions populated the offices of other party- and state-run institutions, as well as in the government's ministries and the broader civil service. As with the bureau telephone operators, telephonists in other institutions came to represent the day-to-day voice of the institutions for which they worked. As such, they maintained a direct connection between their respective worksites' bureaucracy and the outside world.[112] Likewise, in the bureau and elsewhere, receptionists served as the face of their particular institutions, screening and recording the activities of visitors, alerting the institutions' senior officers of surprise visits by the president and other top party officials, and, in the case of the BAA specifically, managing the public's access to the bureau's publications.[113]

What this reliance on female labor meant inside the bureau specifically and possibly within other party- and state-run institutions more broadly was a potential feminization of the revolution. Female labor, caught up in the supposedly beguiling and undisciplined ways of women themselves, thus had to be monitored with great care so as to ensure that the influence of an unsavory few did not pollute the productive, disciplined, and dedicated work of the institution. Idle chatter, gossip, and unsupervised socialization—largely seen as women's issues, at least in the day-to-day affairs of the bureau—thus had the potential of weakening the Nkrumahist project and in turn exposing Ghana and Africa as a whole to the sometimes real and sometimes imagined neocolonial threats posited by the CPP's vision of the ever-changing face of capitalist imperialism. However, in the case of the bureau specifically, as the institution's operations and bureaucracy rapidly expanded in the early and mid-1960s and as the party made increasingly prominent efforts to highlight its commitment to gender equity, the bureau's top officials had little recourse but to turn to the country's young, educated female workforce as they sought to advance the institution's mission at home and abroad. As a result, in nearly every facet of the bureau's day-to-day operations, the institution's female employees stood at the center of the struggle for continental liberation even as they—as women—in this specific workplace and in the party press more broadly, came to symbolize for the men around them antisocialist indiscipline, the perils of individualism, and potential neo-colonial subversion.

⤳

In the half century since the 1966 toppling of the Nkrumah regime, no institution, except perhaps the Ghana Young Pioneers, has remained as controversial as the bureau. Often seen as analogous to the American CIA or the Soviet KGB, reports from the 1960s connected the institution to such activities as the importation of Soviet arms into Ghana and espionage within independent African states, including Togo, Liberia, and Nigeria.[114] Even more disconcerting were accusations of a potential Ghanaian role in the 1963 assassination of Togolese president Sylvanus Olympio.[115] Among American officials, the bureau—with its direct connection to Nkrumah's office and "'affiliate' political parties outside of Ghana"—resembled the "Communist Politburo."[116] Other reports highlighted possible covert activities, including the embedding of freedom fighters involved in guerilla training programs in defunct Builders Brigade camps and—in the Ghanaian anticolonial apparatus more broadly—the purported establishment of a "West African High Command" for training foreign revolutionaries.[117] Moreover, the Americans viewed bureau publications such as the *Spark* as "nothing more than vehicles for Soviet propaganda that had [the] effect of embarrassing [the] USG [United States government] in Ghana, [the] rest of Africa and at home."[118]

In the day-to-day operations of the bureau itself, though, the institution's unique position within the Nkrumahist pan-African apparatus manifested itself in the banalities of its employees' daily work lives. However, these banalities reflected broader changes within the Ghanaian state as the CPP and its various leaders sought to make sense of the postcolonial world emerging out of first the hopes and later the disappointments of the Year of Africa and the aftermath of the 1961 strike in Sekondi and Takoradi. For bureau employees—just one group of Ghanaians forced to confront the changing political realities of the postcolonial state on a daily basis—their work demanded that they juggle tasks that at their most quotidian included the bureaucratic and secretarial administration of the revolution amidst the ever-present fears, subversion, and intrigue that necessarily followed in the bureau's wake. The ramifications of such a politicized work environment had perhaps the most dramatic effect on the institution's female employees. Here, seemingly conventional and politically inconsequential contestations involving these women over such issues as sick and maternal leave, pay scales, and space were transformed into wide-ranging debates over threats to national productivity, state and institutional security, and social and ideological discipline. Moreover, these debates tapped into broader discussions of the nature and expectations of women in the revolution as Ghanaians of all walks of life sought to adjust to the changing political and social realities of the ever-tightening arena of the Nkrumahist state.

6 ⤳ Negotiating Nkrumahism
Belonging, Uncertainty, and the Pan-African One-Party State

Nkrumaism and Party action is to be all-pervasive in society.

—American Embassy, Accra, to Department of State,
  Washington, "Ghana's Future Labor, Employment,
  and Trade Union Policies," 1962[1]

For our socialist aspirations to mature we need only first rate
adherents to our socialist ideals. I mean people who conform
because they conform and not because they think they must conform
somehow. You may want to know who a non-conformist is. To my
mind the non-conformist is not the person who does not know and so
does not conform: he is the one who knows but refuses to conform.

—Afari-Gyan, "The Task of Mental Decolonisation," n.d.[2]

IN LATE January 1964, Ghanaians went to the polls to vote on a referendum for the formal establishment of a one-party state in the country, bringing into constitutional alignment the ambitions outlined in the CPP's 1962 *Programme for Work and Happiness*. In everything but name, however, Ghana was already a one-party state—and, for all intents and purposes, had been one for some time—by the time of the vote. As Dennis Austin bluntly asserted, the results of the vote were "nonsensical." During the referendum, a purported 92.8 percent of Ghanaians voted in favor of the motion. In five of the country's nine regions, including the traditionally anti-CPP stronghold comprising the Ashanti Region, the government registered not a single vote against it. Even more bizarre, if one were to take the vote on face value, was the fact that more than 60 percent of the 2,452 "no" votes cast in the country came from Accra—the seat of government and the area of the country where the CPP has historically elicited the most support. The reports of irregularities during the vote were so widespread, according to Austin, that the referendum had little in common with a genuine "test of public opinion." Rather, he portrayed the vote as little more than "an administrative exercise by the party." More importantly, following the vote, Ghanaians further witnessed the symbolic eclipse of the nation that they had celebrated in 1957 as the CPP replaced the Ghanaian national flag with a version of the party flag. As a result, as Austin put it, through the referendum "Ghana became a Convention People's Republic." Serving as perhaps the most astute midcentury commentator on Ghanaian politics, the former extramural tutor ultimately presented the 1964 referendum as the "logical outcome of the nationalist demands put forward by Nkrumah and the CPP in 1949." To this end, he reflected, "In their [Nkrumah and the CPP's] beginning was their end. The Leader who was sentenced—in open court—in 1950 was now in control of the judiciary; the nationalist party which had led the attack on colonial rule had become the state."[3]

Likewise, in the non-Ghanaian press and elsewhere, scholars, journalists, and even some African politicians actively and consistently critiqued the evolving nature of the Nkrumahist state and its pan-African projects in the early and mid-1960s. In Liberia, for instance, President William Tubman insisted that, in Ghana, "it is Nkrumah first, Nkrumah last, and after that, if there is anything left, Ghana."[4] In South Africa, Nelson Mandela lamented the path Ghana had taken as he questioned a Ghanaian anticolonial apparatus that had "turned out to be something quite contrary to what it was meant to be." For Mandela, this breach of faith specifically included the Bureau of African Affairs.[5] Meanwhile, among most Western news outlets, stories of CPP corruption, violence, and arrests accompanied caricatures of presidential megalomania and the real and assumed paradoxes of a Ghanaian socialism that was often erratically enacted.[6] As one *New York Times* writer surmised in mid-1965, "Nkrumah's decisions today are based not so much on practical necessities as on ideological commitment; not on what actually *is* but on what ideologically *should be*." As a result, he claimed, "It is not too much to say that if Nkrumah were given the choice between ridding Ghana of all its ills on practical lines in a decade or on his own rigid ideological lines in three, he would unhesitatingly choose the latter. Such is the depth of his commitment."[7]

Issues of uncertainty, belonging, and attempts at personal and community self-redefinition in Ghanaians' relationships with the Nkrumahist one-party state frame this chapter. Intellectually and structurally, the one-party state was a multifaceted and often volatile entity born out of an overt rejection of Western liberal democracy and conceptualized in response to both real and imagined threats of internal and foreign subversion. By the mid-1960s, the policies emerging from this worldview would come to play a central role in demarcating Ghanaian political, economic, and social life. Even more importantly, the one-party state's implementation was procedural, dating back to at least 1961 and 1962 and involving a complex set of negotiations that often reframed Ghanaians' relationships with one another, the party, the government, and Nkrumah himself. For some, single-party rule and Nkrumahist politics more broadly had proven themselves to be deeply alien to their way of life and to how they envisioned their relationships with their communities and with the government. To borrow from the prominent Ghanaian political anthropologist Maxwell Owusu, for them, Nkrumahist politics—with its unprecedented demands for ever-increasing levels of work, service, and sacrifice to the state—was simply "too un-Ghanaian" to work in the country.[8] Others, in contrast, embraced the emerging political and social apparatuses of the one-party state as vehicles for personal and professional gain. In the midst of deeply felt political and social uncertainty, they learned the language and political choreography of the state and deployed them in ways that advanced a wide-ranging set of personal and social interests. Engagement with the party and state—rarely a secure bet, but one they saw as worth making—provided the means by which to cultivate new, politically advantageous relationships. It also allowed them to do so within a set of institutions and organizations that opened pathways to both political and social mobility as well as volatility.

This chapter in turn interrogates how Ghanaians understood the political and social uncertainty of the final years of Nkrumahist rule and how they made their ways, as individuals and citizens, through it. Accordingly, it returns to the closing arena for political engagement described in chapter 5 by tracing the politics and philosophy behind the construction of the one-party state. Multiparty democracy, the CPP declared, had not only proved a failure that slowed the country's revolutionary program, but, through an (at best) irresponsible and (at worst) treasonous opposition, opened up conduits for both internal and foreign attacks on the state and Nkrumah. One-party democracy was therefore to be formed out of the bond between the people and the state and maintained by the policing—by self and state—of that bond. As a result, for many in Ghana, the transition to the one-party state marked a moment of dramatic social and cultural violence, upheaval, and personal and collective danger. This chapter thus explores the diversity of ways in which Ghanaian men and women navigated the increasingly rigid political and social realities of their daily lives and—to an extent—political imaginations in the early and mid-1960s. In doing so, it presents Ghanaians' varying interactions with the state and party, along with the narratives Ghanaians themselves created around Nkrumah and the CPP, as tools of self-preservation framed as avenues of network building. These tools were employed in a set of activities, actions, and practices consciously and unconsciously designed to ensure one's place in what appeared to many, although not all, to be the political and social community of the future.

CHOREOGRAPHING THE ONE-PARTY STATE

Long before the 1962 announcements detailing the CPP's plans for a one-party state, accusations of an emergent Nkrumahist dictatorship had featured prominently in the opposition's and others' anti-CPP rhetoric. In early and mid-1950s Asante, for instance, such recriminations served as the bedrock of the Asante-led NLM's charges against Nkrumah and the CPP. In some cases, versions of these allegations followed Nkrumah as far back as his days in the United Gold Coast Convention and the West African National Secretariat.[9] As one early 1950s list of charges against Nkrumah asserted, the then Gold Coast prime minister "ha[d] attempted to create himself a dictator of the country . . . against the political and social traditions of the country." Tied to this claim of dictatorship were accusations of nepotism, empty development promises, theft of farmers' money, and "the practise of heathenism as against the principles of Christianity."[10] Allusions to an Nkrumahist dictatorship even made it into the first principles of the NLM, with the movement's "Aims and Objects" pledging that the nascent party would "banish [the] lawlessness [and] intimidation" it associated with the CPP. To achieve these aims, the NLM promised to "safeguard the interests of farmers and workers" and "build a prosperous, healthy, tolerant, democratic, and a God-fearing Gold Coast Nation."[11]

The CPP's early postcolonial legislative agenda, which included the 1957 dissolution of regionally and ethnically based political parties and, in 1958, the introduction of the highly controversial Preventative Detention Act, further encouraged opposition accusations of a rising Nkrumahist dictatorship. The PDA, as it came to be popularly known, was to offer the government the bureaucratic and judicial flexibility through which to deal with threats to the new nation. As Nkrumah told the National Assembly when introducing the bill in July 1958, "In less than two years of independence, Ghana has already achieved considerable world influence.

Ghana has achieved that influence primarily because we are regarded as a country in the forefront of the movement for the independence of the whole of the African continent." This mission, he in turn declared, had opened the country to the "many forces in the world today who would like to see us fail." The bill was therefore justified as a protective measure designed to ensure the security of not only the state, but the entire socialist project, both at home and abroad. Its measures—most notably the ability to detain those accused of being threats to the state for up to five years without trial—were to be the instruments for securing the achievement of the country's political and social goals. "Quite clearly . . . freedom cannot exist" in Ghana, the prime minister concluded, "nor can the Courts function, under a threat of violence and lawlessness or in a situation in which civil strife or war is threatened."[12]

The opposition responded to the 1958 bill with deep mistrust. Gonja East MP J. A. Braimah, for instance, insisted that "by introducing this Preventative Detention Bill into this House, the Government are behaving as if the British had not left behind in this country a deep respect for individual rights and an understanding of the practical mechanics of democratic law and government."[13] Sekyere West MP R. R. Amponsah added to those sentiments, protesting, "This Bill, if passed into law, will have dealt a death blow to the liberty of the individual in this country, and will have quenched the desire of people all over Africa to watch and to copy what happens in Ghana, because they expect—and they have the right to expect—true leadership from this country, since this country is the first African State to be independent." Amponsah, then, asked, "Is this the type of leadership that we claim to give our fellow Africans on this Continent?" As the United Party representative and former CPP official continued, he painted a picture of a government consumed by unwarranted fears of treason, subversion, and sabotage. The effect, he argued, was that the CPP was now authoring, with this bill, the slow destruction of democracy and civil liberties in the country, in favor of "one-party dictatorship."[14]

Opposition allusions to the threat of a CPP-led dictatorship were renewed *en force* in the buildup to the 1960 plebiscite on the republic. As one 1960 United Party (UP) pamphlet declared on the eve of the vote, "The country is once again at the cross-roads of its future. One road leads to republicanism and dictatorship, the other to elective monarchy and true democracy in conformity with our traditions." Returning to the chieftaincy claims of the since-banned NLM and its allied parties, the UP countered the centralizing ambitions of the CPP by proposing a system of diffused power in which a nonpolitical monarch—chosen on a rotating basis from a group of chiefs to be designated as "Head[s] of Region"— would carry out the functions of the head of state, while an elected prime minister maintained the political functions of the government. The CPP's republican option, the UP argued, would not only give the president too much power, it would also subject him to "divided loyalty," in that the new constitution would force him to weigh his allegiance to the party he represented against the interests of the nation he served.[15]

In 1962, following his recent dismissal from the party, the newly exiled K. A. Gbedemah also returned to the theme of a CPP dictatorship in an open letter to Nkrumah. Using the CPP's *Programme for Work and Happiness* and proposed Seven-Year Development Plan as his foils, Gbedemah detailed what he described as Ghana's descent into "jungle law." "Anyone who was present at the State House in Accra on that morning when the First Republic was inaugurated and heard you take your oath as President 'to preserve and defend the Constitution and to do right to all manner of people according to law without fear or favour, affection or ill will' must have had great hopes for the new republic," Gbedemah maintained. "In barely two years of Republican rule," though, the former minister of finance asserted, "if these persons have kept in touch with Ghana affairs, how sad and disillusioned they must be to contemplate what has happened, watching the gradual degeneration of the basic democracy we then had, into a totalitarian regime and a Police state." Gbedemah went on to level a range of accusations against the man he had helped elect in 1951, including the abuse of the PDA, the illegitimate and arbitrary deportation of non-Ghanaians from the country, the unlawful seizure of ministers' property, and the antisocialist nature of Nkrumah's putative palatial living and cult of personality.[16]

Prior to the early 1960s, the CPP, for its part, vehemently fought back against opposition allegations of an intended CPP dictatorship. In doing so, it relied on the political optics of the colony's and, later, country's electoral results as evidence of both a true Ghanaian democracy and popular support for CPP policies. What the young country needed, the CPP regularly argued, was what it described as a legitimate and responsible opposition. What the Gold Coast and Ghana got, with first the Danquah-led Ghana Congress Party and later the NLM and its allied parties, Nkrumah recounted in his autobiography, was an opposition dedicated to cultivating "discontent among the people and misunderstanding in the world press" by making unjustified accusations of nepotism and corruption within the

CPP and the government. Perhaps even more importantly in the context of the early 1950s, Nkrumah further criticized the early opposition for what he presented as its disingenuous condemnations of the party's supposed abandonment of its principle of "self-government now" during the period of British-CPP shared governance.[17] As shown in chapter 2, the violence following the 1954 formation of the NLM only further delegitimized the opposition in the eyes of Nkrumah and the CPP. From their perspective, the NLM and its allies sought little more than to thwart the popularly elected CPP with demands for federation (and, later, secession) and challenges to the centralized national framework put forward by the Nkrumah-led party.

If, as shown in chapter 5, by the early 1960s single-party rule was to represent to the CPP and its allies the regeneration of an organic African democracy on the continent, then the idea of a formal opposition was not only redundant, but explicitly neocolonial. Here, the very meaning of democracy was being reimagined outside the model of parliamentary governance and viewed through the lens of perceived direct threats to African independence. As the prominent Zimbabwean nationalist Ndabaningi Sithole explained in the September 1961 edition of the Bureau of African Affairs's *Voice of Africa*, both one-party and two-party states had the potential for providing democratic governance, at least in their structure. It was only an accident of history that distinguished the two systems of government in relation to Europe and Africa. For Sithole, two-party governance—as a legacy of colonial rule and potential tool of neocolonial influence—institutionalized fissures in African political systems for former colonial powers to manipulate. The former colonial powers' success in such an endeavor rested upon what Sithole portrayed as the true nature of an African opposition: "The Opposition, in the Western sense, to justify its existence," Sithole explained to the *Voice of Africa*'s Ghanaian and continental readership, "must continue to find loopholes in the Ruling Party, not for the purpose of keeping the Ruling Party in power, but for the sake of overthrowing it at one point or another." As such, he insisted, "To cause the downfall of the Ruling Party is the alpha and omega of opposition."[18] What the one-party state offered in contrast, Sithole argued, was a renewed relationship between the people and the state by blurring the distinctions between the two, making them one and the same through each's mutual identification with the other.[19]

At the center of Ghana's domestic troubles, the CPP concluded, was a gap in understanding between the party and the broader populace. According to the party, this was in part cultivated by the opposition and in part a product of the lack of shared experiences, ideas, and politics among disparate groups of Ghanaians. The result, the CPP Central Committee would suggest, was an entrenched and wide-ranging ideological indiscipline that plagued both the party and the country. It was this indiscipline that was stunting the Ghanaian and African revolutions as it opened the country and continent to the subversive effects of Cold War neocolonialism. "Inner-party reform" led by groups of "Vanguard Activists," an undated Central Committee memorandum insisted, was what was needed to close this gap.[20] These activists, Nkrumah outlined in 1961, while referencing a 1959 speech that could be considered one of the CPP's earliest public gestures toward what would become the ideology underpinning Ghanaian single-party rule, were to be "drawn from the most politically educated section of the Party . . . [and] trained at special courses to explain the aims and objects of the CPP to those who [do] not clearly understand them." To accomplish their tasks, he continued, these activists should "live and work among the common people," to bridge and begin to eliminate the gap.[21]

However, the party's vanguard activists also carried with them a mission that extended beyond inculcating into the populace the discipline and ideals of the socialist way of life. They were also to serve as the broader populace's voice to the party. In doing so, they were to be able to critique the CPP itself on issues of public concern, including potential corruption and bureaucratic overreach into Ghanaian daily life.[22] The party's ultimate goal with its Vanguard Activists was to create new mechanisms for relationship-building in the new Ghana. Through them, the party and the people would, in the CPP's view, again become one—united under the authentically democratic umbrella of the Nkrumahist state. In his 1959 speech, Nkrumah thus presented this relationship as the "truest form of *Democratic Centralism*," a governing framework founded upon an overarching, class-blind political system in which "decisions [were to be] freely arrived at and loyally executed."[23] The result, in subsequent years, however, was to be a political community that fluctuated between a vision of an idealized union of state and citizenry and the social and cultural turmoil that would come to accompany the policing of it.

Connecting to the State

The on-the-ground manifestations of the one-party state's relationships with the citizenry were diverse and, in most cases, highly choreographed. They often merged the public and the private, as many Ghanaians—along with many non-Ghanaians in the country—viewed the party and state reforms of the early 1960s as opportunities through which to reenvision their paths to political and social gain. Inside the Bureau of African Affairs, for instance, the institution's personnel files show a staff clearly cognizant of the party and the institutional administration's shared worldview, particularly as it pertained to ideals of productivity, security, and secrecy. As a result, requests for promotions, pay raises, and similar forms of employee recognition came to follow a highly regimented discourse of Nkrumahist self-presentation and rhetorical acquiescence. In a 1965 petition, for instance, a group of bureau typists—one man and five women—appealed to the new director, E. Ofori-Bah, for a reevaluation of their pay scale by speaking directly to the bureau's interests in security and party loyalty. "We feel that we are doing a very important job for the Bureau," typist Jonathan Tetteh Yumu explained on behalf of himself and his female colleagues, "since most of the things we type are strictly private and confidential."[24] Yumu then continued with a direct gesture toward the sense of socialist collectivity, discipline, and productivity the bureau's administration aimed to instill in its workforce: "We want to make it clear that we are not out to cause trouble but rather we are only asking that our position should be improved a bit in order to enable us to give more efficient and loyal service to the Bureau."[25]

Driving the petitioners' request was a dual concern over the inflationary tides of the Ghanaian economy in the mid-1960s and the failure of the bureau to respond to these economic challenges on behalf of at least some of its workers.[26] What is interesting here are the language employed and the mechanisms of redress sought by Yumu and his colleagues. Not only did they speak the language of the regime and emphasize their adherence to the values and mission of the institution and the CPP, but they also couched their argument in terms of a reciprocal relationship merging the bureau, the party, and the bureau's employees together under the Nkrumahist umbrella. All the typists were asking for, Yumu and his colleagues tacitly argued, was that one of the most prized and important institutions of the Nkrumahist revolution not fall behind other government departments and state organizations in its ability to take care of its workers. What with uniform costs, transport, and, according to the typists, their diligent commitment to the "National Pension Scheme," their pay, which began at £G10 per month (compared to the £G15 to £G18 per month made by typists in other government and private institutions), simply made it difficult for them to make "two ends meet" in the current economy. Higher pay, they implied, would make it easier for them to serve the party and the state to their utmost abilities.[27]

In another instance that predated this petition, another typist—this time a man named Bernard B. C. Akoi—wrote to A. K. Barden in December 1961 requesting that the bureau deduct ten shillings per month from his paycheck as a donation to the country's Second Development Plan. Akoi hoped that this contribution, coming just months after the 1961 strike, would help "foster the speedy reconstruction of Ghana by our ABLE LEADER OSAGYEFO DR. KWAME NKRUMAH, President of the Republic of Ghana, in his bid to build the country into a socialist state."[28] In return for his philanthropy, Akoi only asked that the bureau publicize his actions on the radio and in the print media—which it undertook to do by contacting the *Evening News*, the *Daily Graphic*, Radio Ghana, and the Ghana News Agency on Akoi's behalf.[29] In his response to Akoi, Barden praised Akoi's gesture as "proof of the quality of your patriotism," a sentiment he repeated in his comments to the press. However, the bureau's director challenged the typist to go even further, expressing his hope "that the same ideals which motivated your action will inspire you to dedicate your services to the good of the state."[30]

Akoi's actions do not appear to have led to any immediate monetary benefit. Rather, his reward was likely to have come in the form of new prestige in the bureau and his community. It was, at its foundation, an act of relationship building, one in which he sought to strengthen his connection to the party and bureau by inviting them to publicly transform him from a nameless civil servant into, at least for a brief period, a contributor to the Nkrumahist cause to be usefully celebrated at a moment of substantial political upheaval. The benefits for the CPP clearly extended well beyond the ten shillings a month Akoi promised the state, for it offered the party and government an opportunity to buttress their claims of a nationwide, popular buy-in and role in its revolutionary program. At few times in Nkrumah-era Ghana was such an image of ground-level support for the Nkrumahist cause so important to the CPP as in the months following the September 1961 mêlée, as the party press dedicated itself to publicizing anecdotes of Ghanaian men and women who eschewed the strike in favor of what one group of anti-strike railway workers described as the national interest. According to the state-run periodical the *Party*, men such as these railway workers, and presumably Akoi, were representative of "the new man our Osagyefo the President has said Africa needs."[31]

As for the typist Akoi, his offer of a donation to the cause was not his only petition to the bureau's administration, nor his only attempt to shape his rhetorical commitment to the bureau's and the CPP's Nkrumahist sensibilities.

Approximately a year and a half later, Akoi again wrote to his superiors asking for a further review of his pay scale following his successful examination and qualification for the post of Stenographer Grade II. Initially receiving a salary of £G185 per annum upon his promotion, Akoi hoped to see it raised to £G225—a level purportedly more in line with that of his coworkers. In his petition, Akoi explained that, after he had completed the stenography qualifications, the bureau transferred him to the Press Division, "where I have been the only typist responsible for typing all manuscripts for both *The Spark* and *Voice of Africa*, including all correspondence of that Section." As a result of this unshared workload, he reported that he was regularly forced to "stay in . . . during break and after closing to finish some outstanding work." As a good servant of Ghana, Akoi insisted that he was "happy to shoulder all these responsibilities, because I feel that is in conformity with the Party's Programme of 'Work and Happiness.'" As a result, what Akoi wished to suggest to his superiors was that his petition for an adjustment in pay was intended not necessarily for personal gain, but designed to bring about equity within the bureau's stenographer pool.[32]

In the political climate of 1960s Ghana, the rhetoric of Akoi and his fellow typists' petitions was not unique. Rather, it served as a vehicle through which individuals' relationships to the state could be expressed and, they hoped, recognized. Similarly, the Builders Brigade and Young Pioneers had their own rhetorical patterns to which their members gestured as they sought to interact with their respective organizations' various hierarchies. Specifically, Young Pioneers and brigaders often reinforced the two organizations' educational and socializing missions in order to showcase for themselves and the public their personal and collective progress toward the idealized image of a productive, revolutionary Nkrumahist youth. This was particularly true in the Brigade, where growing numbers of frequently nonliterate and semiliterate young men and women engaged in a daily regimen of Nkrumahist praise and performance—marching, songs, pledges, parades—in addition to their vocational education and public works projects. Success for the Brigade itself depended not just upon the personal and professional discipline of the brigaders themselves, but just as importantly on the visibility of their achievements. The result was an intricate system of political and social patronage within the institution, embodied in and expressed through a highly choreographed and often public repertoire of Nkrumahist loyalty, discipline, and dedication.[33] As such, those who failed to make the requisite adjustments in self-presentation often had their wants and needs ignored.[34]

In the eyes of the CPP, Ghanaians' everyday attempts to forge and publicly express their relationships to the party and the state were foundationally existential acts bound to the fate of the Nkrumahist revolution. The party—comprising both its members and institutional framework—was no longer just a political party. As Nkrumah would assert in 1960, "The Convention People's Party [was] Ghana and Ghana [was] the Convention People's Party."[35] The nascent one-party state of the 1960s thus comes into view, as an object of enquiry, not just in terms of the formal, constitutional institutionalization of single-party rule in and of itself, which only dates from the 1964 referendum, but in the transformative effects the logics of one-party governance—as part of a broader postcolonial and Cold War context—had on the Ghanaian habitus. At its heart, the transition to the one-party state was the culmination of an often alienating process of destruction and redefinition of political, social, and cultural capital under CPP rule. Beginning as early as its 1951 electoral victory, ideas of transformation had stood at the center of the CPP's vision of and for Ghana, and the destruction of the colonial edifice was but one part of this intended transformation. Tied to it was also to be the weakening and reconfiguring of such traditional institutions as chieftaincy, the *asafo*, and local governance.[36] Family, too, emerged as a locus of intentional and at least partially achieved rupture under the CPP as the party and government aimed to address issues ranging from family composition and structure (i.e., monogamous versus polygamous marriages) to the government's role in a child's social and cultural growth. This dialectic between old and new, colonized and decolonized, and socialist and capitalist shaped not just the political discourse of 1960s-era Ghana, but the implications of this discourse for the political, social, and cultural relationships that grew out of an ever-tightening political environment.

THE TYRANNIES OF REVOLUTIONARY BELONGING

Ambiguities in definitions of community stood at the center of popular, day-to-day responses to single-party rule. As defined by the CPP—possibly dating back as far as the late 1940s if we are to turn to the party's famed proclamation, "seek ye first the political kingdom and all else will be added to it"—the political community was to surpass and encompass all others. As such, the political upheavals of the 1950s buildup to independence should not simply be read as political struggles between those aligned with the CPP and those opposed to it. Rather, the conflicts of the 1950s unleashed a period of personal and professional self-definition and redefinition based upon an individual's allegiances and upon the past and future she or he imagined, personally and collectively. New relationships were thus built around this period of struggle, while others were weakened and, in some cases, broken. The NLM and its allied parties, in this moment, did not merely offer an electoral alternative to the CPP. As recounted in chapter 2, they promised a political alternative to the CPP deeply rooted in a complicated array of regional, ethnic, and religious identities, histories, and social relations. In doing so, they manifested their own cultures and politics of belonging—both new and old—that challenged the centralized vision of the CPP with the multiplicities inherent in late-colonial Gold Coast communities. Moreover, as former Ashanti Region Young Pioneer Kwasi Assiore recalled, the conflicts over the values and aims of these competing politics of belonging, with their disparate visions for a postcolonial Ghana, often reached down to the familial level, as families divided over the politics of the CPP and NLM. As Assiore explained, "If you are my brother and you're CPP and [I am] NLM . . . , we will be in the house and nobody will be talking, because we are enemies."[37]

As Ghana made its transition to the one-party state, legacies of community, family, and individual political alignments found their way into the political and social networks of the 1960s. Former supporters of the NLM and other opposition parties were often singled out for ridicule, questioning, or surveillance, while many former NLM and subsequently United Party officials had already served or were currently serving time in detention—some of whom would remain in prison until the 1966 coup.[38] Such threats to one's wellbeing broke down the open expression of the diverse political imaginings that marked the 1950s during the First Republic, thus fundamentally shaping the archival and, to an extent, even oral record of the period. For, by the early to mid-1960s, the public expression and exploration of this diversity in the political arena had been largely sent underground out of fear of often-severe political repercussions. It is also important to note that, both locally and nationally, the CPP had a long memory in dealing with the legacy of the 1950s conflicts. As a result, in some instances, well into the 1960s, whole communities would continue to endure CPP-defined categorizations and loyalty tests, based upon the government's perception of the communities' allegiances during the days of the CPP's struggle with the NLM. As one 1962 security file noted in regard to two individuals (Kwadwo Nyame and Kwaku Atuahene) accused of insulting party officials and holding secret meetings designed to "reviv[e] the U.P.," their hometown of Pramso itself—a purportedly "notorious U.P. town"—became part of the evidence against them. "We all know how this town looked like during those N.L.M. days," the report against them stated. "Any revival of the atrocities there will mean a big threat" to the party and government. For this reason, in what was probably a reference to at least the threat of Nyame and Atuahene's arrest, the report euphemistically contended that, in order to be sure such an anti-CPP spirit could not be resurrected, the accused must be made to "feel that the C.P.P. is the only Party in Ghana."[39]

In another incident involving a man, James Kofi Nkonwa (Nkowa), accused of defaming Nkrumah and questioning the government's arrest of three prominent CPP officials in the aftermath of the Kulungugu bombing, the report against him again turned to the history of the accused's community. His town of Jachie, the report indicated, was to be lauded for its "very progressive" nature. It was Nkonwa himself, "known . . . for a long time to be anti-C.P.P.," who imperiled the morale and wellbeing of the community as he sought to spread an antiparty and antigovernment message by slandering the president and the government. He was also accused of abusing his position as "a leading member" of the area's Seventh-Day Adventists to speak ill of the Young Pioneers, presumably invoking popular criticisms of the movement as an un-Christian organization. The result, the report suggested, was a situation in which a number of "boys and girls of this church refrained from joining the movement, even though the children like the movement." As a result of these actions, it was recommended that the accused "should be made to feel and realise that the C.P.P. Government is the government of the day and he must have respect for it." In another not so subtle reference to probable arrest, the report on Nkonwa proclaimed that "if he [Nkonwa] parts with his family for sometime [sic] he will have sense and others of his group will learn [a] lesson out of it."[40]

For the CPP, the active policing and coercing of both individual and community allegiance to the party was not only a matter of security (i.e., designed to protect state interests), but also of socialization (i.e., imagined as part of extinguishing the remnants of the country's colonial mentality). As one CPP author named Afari-Gyan explained in an undated essay that in many ways channeled the work of a range of anticolonial thinkers, the overriding challenge to the CPP in the mid-1960s was psychological.[41] In his analysis of the Ghanaian situation, Afari-Gyan argued that it was not until 1957 that the country's citizens had come to see "colonialism . . . as an evil." Prior to independence, he argued, Ghanaians "thought colonialism and talked colonialism," and, in the schools, "ate and drank colonialism." It was an inextricable part of their lives and their understanding of themselves and the world around them. "We sang the praises of British monarchs instead of our nationalist leaders. To the mass of people the mark of the educated man was how near English he was." Nkrumahism, in contrast, preached conformity, he argued, although not conformity in the sense that all Ghanaians were to be the same. Rather, Nkrumahist conformity entailed a revolutionary ethos driven by one's commitment to the collective awakening of the Ghanaian mind to the Nkrumahist project. As a result, the highest crime of the early postcolonial moment, according to Afari-Gyan and presumably the CPP at large, was not necessarily an ignorance of the revolution that might lead one to certain antisocialist or colonialist behaviors, but recognition of the revolution and its values and an attempt to actively subvert those values.[42]

For individual Ghanaians and their families, the personal, social, and economic consequences of dissent or nonconformance were far-reaching and, in many cases, devastating. Moreover, they often extended beyond the individual. As longtime Accra resident N. Sifah explained in 2008, "You see, we have extended family [here in Ghana]. When you say extended family, it is not myself and my wife, but my father is my responsibility. My mother is [my] responsibility. . . . And then your sister's children. . . . Then my mother's sister's children." Thus, Sifah noted, the question all Ghanaians had to ask themselves before undertaking any action was, "how many people are going to suffer as a result of anything?"[43] For Sifah, engagement with the state was therefore firmly embedded with a set of costs and benefits that extended not just to himself and his household, but to a wide array of familial and social networks. Another man, Kofi Ampadu, who was a Young Pioneer in the Eastern Region town of Kwahu Praso, recalled maintaining a similar sense of discretion and caution in dealing with or speaking of the party and state, even inside his family. In his case, he recounted how his parents expressed significant dismay at his schoolboy eagerness to join the Young Pioneers. Like many of his compatriots, Ampadu, who was previously a Boy Scout, coveted the uniform and cap of the Young Pioneers and joined the movement in anticipation of attaining the youth program's adornments. In the end, though, Ampadu was disappointed by the Young Pioneers, due to the organization's inability to live up to its promises. Ampadu also claimed that only upon reaching adulthood and coming to better understand the culture of fear that engulfed many in Ghana during the Nkrumah years did he come to fully appreciate his own family's response to his participation in the Ghanaian youth movement.[44]

The challenges and risks Ghanaians faced in engaging the party and the state in the early and mid-1960s evolved in part out of the seemingly tenuous progress of the Nkrumahist revolution itself, both at home and abroad. The regular allegations of corruption and mismanagement that plagued state and party institutions, including the Ghana Young Pioneers, the Builders Brigade, and the Bureau of African Affairs, were central to this perception of halting progress. Regarding the Brigade, for instance, accounts of low-level extortion for even the right to apply to join the organization had begun to make their way public as early as 1958.[45] In the aftermath of the 1966 coup, a commission of enquiry would be convened to investigate the Brigade: as the commission heard testimony detailing significant levels of malfeasance, waste, and abuse, newspapers such as the widely circulated *Daily Graphic*, likewise, highlighted purported incidents of violence and corporal punishment by Brigade officials against brigaders in its post-coup reporting on the organization.[46] In the meantime, by 1966, the Brigade's budget had ballooned to £G8.5 million, making it among the largest single institutional expenditures under the CPP.[47]

The rumors of familial espionage and child spies (see chapter 3) that haunted the Young Pioneers also frustrated officials in both the organization's and the CPP's leadership circles. Officials and even some Young Pioneers themselves went to great lengths to denounce such talk as slanderous and misguided. "Let those people [anti-CPP intellectuals] who know and understand our aims but would deliberately not conform to any of our ideology grumble to their graves," asserted one circa 1961–62 essay professing to have been written by a Young Pioneer. The rumors that plagued the movement, the essay's author insisted, did not reflect reality, but were mere manifestations of the counterrevolutionaries' recognition of the vitality of the Nkrumahist revolution and the last-shall-be-first societal norms it claimed to be constructing. The Young Pioneers, the essay further asserted, had already dismantled the "gangsterism," "child-delinquencies," and "hooliganism" that had afflicted the country and youth of Ghana by instilling in the youth a sense of "courage and optimism in the face of difficulties." As a result, the essay's author proclaimed, "We are undoubtedly aware that since every fruit tastes bitter before it ripes [*sic*]; we shall have to stack-in a lot of patience until those illiterate within the literate class come to understand us."[48] Meanwhile, the *Evening News* unleashed a prominent offensive against the gossip-mongering purportedly undermining the movement, describing those who believed "that the Movement was to spy [on] the private lives of individual citizens" as consumed by "vicious thought." The Nkrumah-founded newspaper argued that the Young Pioneers, four years into its existence, had proven these allegations false, as the movement had "produce[d] young men and women with a sense of civic responsibility, moral integrity, love for work and [introduced] a systematic scheme for training them to know, understand and apply the ideology of Nkrumaism."[49]

At both the national and local levels, the institutional and administrative challenges facing the operation and institutional framework of the Nkrumahist revolution therefore cultivated an environment characterized by personal and community risk. If the CPP and its various wings, as the party regularly maintained, was commissioned with the task of decolonizing and rebuilding Ghana and, by extension, its image, then challenges to and questions about the efficacy of its social and cultural mission had profound political and ideological implications. Herein lay the essence of the CPP's reading of Nkonwa's character and, as such, his assumed guilt. The revolution at its foundation was to be a community-building project, one defined through its own communal ethos rooted in a necessary pan-African unity that was dialectically formed out of a shared African heritage and an anticolonial and socialist future. The result was an increasingly authoritarian and, for many, personally devastating political environment in the country, in which violators of the norms of the Nkrumahist community had the potential of becoming cancerous and were to be dealt with swiftly.

FIGURE 6.1. Hear no evil, see no evil, talk no evil, print no evil. *Source: Evening News*, 28 November 1961.

If engagement with the Nkrumahist state carried with it such risks, the question must be asked: What would motivate one to connect with the state? What engagement—both willing and otherwise—did bring was the potential for a place in the political community of the foreseeable future, and, perhaps more importantly for those who successfully navigated this unpredictable terrain, the benefits and protections that came with that place. For instance, in the case of the Bureau of African Affairs typists discussed earlier, all of whom were already employed in one of the Nkrumah government's most controversial and ideologically driven institutions, the logic underpinning the decisions they made to approach the institution's management is largely clear. The adjustments they sought in their respective pay scales carried with them economic as well as other potential benefits. Furthermore, as discussed above, the methods, discourse, and performance of their requests also conveyed deeper meanings based in the ethical infrastructure of the Nkrumahist project. If the CPP's socialist and pan-African project was a communal one, as the party proclaimed, it thus demanded the party and government's unwavering commitment to the social contract promised in the days of the anticolonial struggle and seemingly reaffirmed in the first months of self-rule via the creation of institutions like the Builders Brigade. As a result, it was not only the party and government that recognized the inseparability of this social contract from the realization of the utopian ambitions and ideals of the Nkrumahist pan-African state. Many in the populace did as well. Petitions such as those deriving from this group of bureau workers thus served as acts of citizenship—claims on the government—in the broadest sense of the term.[50]

The question of engagement, however, becomes murkier when taken outside of the context of institutions like the Bureau of African Affairs and placed into the political, social, and cultural environments of differing Ghanaian communities. Returning to James Kofi Nkonwa, for instance, the case against him originated out of a September 1962 conversation between Nkonwa and a local Jachie farmer named Kwame Kwakwa. According to Kwakwa, who made the initial report on Nkonwa to the CPP's Jachie branch chairman, Nkonwa made significant disparaging remarks about Nkrumah and, in doing so, questioned the government's account of the August attack on the Ghanaian president in Kulungugu. In his report of Kwakwa's statement, Francis Emmal Osei Kofi—the district Young Pioneer official who launched the initial investigation into the matter—explained that, on the morning of 11 September, Kwakwa and Nkonwa met as Kwakwa was on the way to his farm. During the meeting, the two reportedly exchanged pleasantries, after which Nkonwa is said to have made his denunciation of the Jachie Town Development Committee. Nkonwa, then, reportedly shifted the conversation to a discussion of the incident at Kulungugu and the arrest of three prominent CPP officials for planning the attack on Nkrumah by asking, "after all, is Kwame Nkrumah God to know that it was [Tawia] Adamafio, Ako Adjei, and [Coffie] Crabbe who threw the Bomb at Kulungugu?" Nkonwa, then, purportedly further questioned the believability of the government's position by reminding Kwakwa that, even as these men languished in prison awaiting trial, bombs were still going off in Ghana.[51]

At the political level, Kwakwa's reference to the Kulungugu attack was central to the case against Nkonwa. Undertaken just weeks shy of the first anniversary of the 1961 strike, the attack occurred as Nkrumah made an unexpected stop in the far northern town of Kulungugu in order to greet a group of schoolchildren. As Nkrumah prepared to receive a bouquet of flowers from a local child, an unidentified individual threw a grenade into the crowd gathered near the president.[52] As Nkrumah explained in his radio address following the incident, "Suddenly there was a deafening blast and the force of it seemed to lift me right off my feet. The explosive may have fallen only about two-and-a-half yards away from me, for there was a blinding flash, followed immediately by a violent explosion." As a result, the Ghanaian president continued, "the gay cheering crowds had suddenly, in a matter of a few seconds, become a frenzied screaming mass of people, blood-streaked, limping, disfigured."[53] The young child with the bouquet was killed, along with at least one other individual, although some reports note up to a handful of deaths.[54] The government also reported that nearby Bawku Hospital—approximately thirteen kilometers away—had treated an additional seventy-seven individuals for injuries related to the attack. Nkrumah himself received extensive shrapnel wounds, which, at the time, went unreported to the public and would subsequently be rumored as the cause of the cancer that would kill him a decade later.[55]

It is difficult to overstate the importance of the Kulungugu bombing to Nkrumah and the CPP's reading of the Ghanaian political scene in the early 1960s. As with the events accompanying the 1961 strike, the bombing led to a purge within the CPP with the arrest of Coffie Crabbe, Ako Adjei, and Tawia Adamafio. At the time of the bombing, Adamafio was perhaps the second most influential individual in the Ghanaian government. Similarly, Adjei, whose relationship with Nkrumah extended back to the 1945

Manchester Pan-African Congress, had been instrumental in orchestrating Nkrumah's return to the Gold Coast in 1947.[56] As would be hashed out both nationally and internationally in the coming years, the evidence of the group's culpability was spotty at best. In its main, it rested on Adamafio's uncharacteristic absence from Nkrumah's side as the grenade went off and his post-explosion exhortation asking if Nkrumah was dead.[57] As detailed by many of Nkrumah's closest confidants, few events affected the Ghanaian president as deeply and personally as those at Kulungugu. Writing, for instance, in her 1984 memoir, Nkrumah's private secretary Erica Powell explained that, after the event, "I saw what seemed a shrunken, smaller version of [the president] seated at that enormous desk, his eyes gazing sadly into the distance."[58] Both American and British officials observing the Ghanaian political scene at the time echoed Powell's appraisal, with one CIA memo noting that the attack had "affected [him] much more mentally than physically," while the British commented on how the bombing "made [Nkrumah] even more suspicious of those around him."[59]

In the event's aftermath, as claims of an antisocialist and anti-African counterrevolution drove the political environment at the national level, cases like Nkonwa's represented their expression at the local level. Local and regional party offices utilized the attack to frame how they chose to address the perceived threats to the state posed by those who did not fit within the increasingly rigid ideal of party loyalty. In the case against Nkonwa, Nkonwa's alleged questioning of the government's charges against the Kulungugu suspects ultimately provided local and regional party officials the opportunity to reframe local disputes (e.g., Nkonwa's critique of the Jachie Town Development Committee) through the national and international lens of potential neocolonial subversion. For those set on accusing others of such crimes, as Kwakwa did with his allegations against Nkonwa, the narratives surrounding events like Kulungugu were instrumental, in that, at least in part, they provided disgruntled Ghanaians a language through which to couple their own personal grievances against an individual or set of individuals with the interests and fears motivating the CPP. In doing so, they grounded individuals like Kwakwa within the shifting ethical paradigm of the Nkrumahist one-party state.

As discussed earlier in reference to the Young Pioneers and in the broader academic and popular narratives of Nkrumahist rule, decisions to report on neighbors, family members, and others were fraught with a range of ethical and moral concerns linked to idioms of betrayal and self-promotion.[60] However, more may have been going on in the case of

Kwakwa and Nkonwa. In reporting on Nkonwa, Kwakwa was not simply presenting a neighbor and fellow Ghanaian to the party and government. He was ultimately distinguishing himself from his neighbor by linking himself to the political and ethical regimes and narratives of the CPP-led state. Here, the initial report's connection to disputes surrounding the government's narratives of the Kulungugu assassination attempt proves particularly important. In their conversation, at least as presented by the third parties writing on the incident, Nkonwa and Kwakwa's interaction did not reflect a mere difference of opinion or dispute over the facts of the case, as a cursory reading of the reports may suggest. Rather, it was a conflict over narratives of the nation and the moral and ethical responsibilities of the citizenry in regard to self-government and the state's interpretations of these narratives.

Through his alleged comments, Nkonwa had thus challenged not only Nkrumah's judgment, but, more importantly, the authority of the state. Moreover, he did so by expressing his critique in a language of censure that actively ridiculed Nkrumah himself. Here, he alluded to a range of narratives and critiques of the cult of personality that the CPP had constructed around the Ghanaian president as he mocked the limits of Nkrumah's supposed God-like omniscience concerning events in all parts of the country. At the heart of such a critique was also a direct challenge to the intellectual and ideological conceits of the Nkrumahist state, as Nkonwa, if we are to accept the charges against him, broke from the policed unity of the state to hint at a broader dissatisfaction with Nkrumahist rule. Such antistate actions, party ideology maintained, could not organically arise from within the Ghanaian citizenry itself, but instead were the products of a set of externally driven neocolonial powers and their bourgeois allies in Ghana. In this reading of the brief archival record of the event, Kwakwa—as the presumed "staunch member of the Party" the 1962 security report described the Jachie resident to be—was not only distancing himself from such views, but openly aligning himself with the ethical system of policed unity and state security that characterized the increasingly powerful political community of the CPP.

A version of this ethical model also seems to have driven the political framework outlined by former Shama-based Young Pioneers S. Atta-P. Anamon, Lawrence Bessah, Francis D. Hayford, and Joseph Yawson in a 2008 interview. These individuals represented a cohort of Young Pioneers, with some—most notably Bessah, who traveled to the Eastern Bloc in 1965 as part of a Young Pioneer youth exhibition—gaining significant prestige during their time in the movement.[61] As seen in chapter 3, in discussions of their experiences in the Young Pioneers, each of these now upper-middle-aged men expressed dismay at the popular narratives of familial espionage that surrounded the movement, while countering these narratives with a discussion of parental frustrations over the time and energy their school-age children devoted to the organization. In Anamon's case in particular, he spoke of how his father lamented that his son's schooling and participation in the Young Pioneers led him to neglect his duties on the farm. These issues of time management and childhood responsibilities, Anamon asserted, were really "why parents were protesting." However, in what came across almost as a throwaway phrase in the interview, Anamon and his colleagues pointed out that, albeit not as spies, Young Pioneers "were being trained to protect the state," and that those who witnessed activities that went against the state had an obligation to "go directly to report you."[62]

As noted in my initial discussion of these individuals' perceptions of spying and the Young Pioneers, their reflections on the necessity of reporting in certain circumstances exemplified, at least in part, the ontological shift demanded of an Nkrumahist pan-African and socialist citizenry. Their revolutionary spirit, as the principles guiding the Young Pioneers stated, required of them not only the patriotism, discipline, and order emblematic of the movement, but also a diligence in serving and protecting the state and the state's interests.[63] In the case of this interview group of former Young Pioneers specifically, the casualness with which they presented the possibility of what others would have likely referred to as potential reporting, while simultaneously denouncing such popular perceptions, hinted at an assumed everydayness and legitimacy to the actions taken by some Young Pioneers. What emerges, then, is a reference by the interviewees to the broader ethical framework of the Nkrumah-led state in their attempts to reflect on some of the alleged activities of past Young Pioneers. What was important to them was not that some children might have reported on their parents or others, but rather the societal role the Young Pioneers played as a movement in advancing and securing the ideals, mission, and ethics of the Nkrumahist revolution at all levels of Ghanaian society.

THE PAN-AFRICANISM OF DETENTION

The political and social ethos governing the Ghanaian one-party state was not without its counterparts elsewhere in early postcolonial Africa, nor were its effects on those living under single-party rule. In allied Guinea, for instance, Sékou Touré and the Parti Démocratique de Guinée (PDG) engaged in their own revolutionary socialist project built around many of the same principles of one-party democracy and revolutionary citizenship that guided Nkrumah and the CPP. Touré, for example, spoke of an inseparable trilogy ("*trilogie indissociable*") of the people, party, and state guiding the Guinean revolution and the shared obligations of state and citizen in the postcolonial era.[64] As in Ghana, the maintenance and preservation of the Guinean revolution at home and abroad was manifested through an intricate performance and logic of self-presentation, constructed around the assumed universality of the revolutionary experience.[65] The result, as former PDG official Mohamed Mancona Kouyaté explained, was a revolutionary agenda aimed at "the normalization of relationships of every kind, governing, at the heart of every collectivity, individuals among themselves."[66]

Again as in Ghana, those who did not fit into the revolutionary ideal of the PDG faced the potential of severe sanction, including the possibility of detainment. The need for such tools of political control as arrest and detention, if we are to follow the prominent Guinean historian and former PDG cabinet official Sidiki Kobélé Keita, was the direct result of a sustained neocolonial plot against the Touré regime. According to Keita, this plot manifested itself not only in French-led subversive activities within the country, but also in Ivoirian, Senegalese, and other French-allied West African support for Guinean rebels inside and outside the country.[67] By extension, the on-the-ground realities of Guinea's first decade of self-rule reflected a period of increasing political and social repression linked to the centralization of political power. As historian Elizabeth Schmidt argues, "In a marked departure from the past, mobilization for national development became a top-down affair [in the 1960s], with only token input from the grassroots."[68] Between 1969 and 1976, Mairi MacDonald notes, an estimated four thousand people would be arrested for politically related crimes, with approximately a hundred of them sentenced to death. Even more troubling, while a thousand had been released by 1981, "the fate of the rest remained a mystery." Moreover, during their detention, these political prisoners endured "cruel, inhuman, and degrading [treatment], including deliberate starvation . . . and near starvation, extreme overcrowding in unsanitary conditions, refusal of medical attention, and denial of any communication with the world outside the prison."[69]

Numerous other newly independent African countries, including Senegal, Cameroon, Niger, and Tanzania, followed similar paths to varying degrees, sacrificing individual political and social liberties in favor of increased state control.[70] In Ghana, many of the country's most notable political figures would be held under the CPP's preventative detention orders. By the mid-1960s, for instance, J. B. Danquah—the doyen of Gold Coast nationalism—was serving his second stint in prison. E. O. Obetsebi-Lamptey, another prominent former UGCC politician who went into exile in 1961, was arrested in 1962 after returning to Ghana following a promise of amnesty. Following a cancer diagnosis, Obetsebi-Lamptey died in prison in 1963.[71] Danquah, too, would die in prison approximately two years later. As reported by the post-coup commission of enquiry convened to investigate the prominent politician's death, the elderly and ill Danquah endured the last year of his life in Ghana's notorious Nsawam Prison in an "approximately 9 feet by 6 feet area, secured by a solid door with a small open grille in the top half of the door and a barred window high up in the rear wall." Even more damning, the report continued, "The cell contained no bed or other furniture other than a chamber pot." Furthermore, when the prison's medical officials recommended dietary changes to try and revive the UGCC founder's health, they were "overruled by the Director of Prisons."[72]

Other prominent politicians with long histories connected to Nkrumah, including Joe Appiah and Ako Adjei, both of whom were active participants in the 1945 Manchester Pan-African Congress, spent the final years of Nkrumahist rule in prison. Appiah later wrote in his autobiography of how, in the immediate aftermath of the Kulungugu bombing, life in the prison deteriorated dramatically, as "almost every warder turned aggressive and insulting and every little privilege was withdrawn."[73] As one of the alleged coconspirators in the 1962 Kulungugu attack, Adjei faced a potential death sentence. As the trial against Adjei, Adamafio, and Crabbe got under way, most outside observers questioned the government's narrative of the attack, with American officials and others largely holding the opinion that it had originated in nearby Togo among Ghanaian dissidents exiled there.[74] After an initial acquittal, Nkrumah vacated the verdict and replaced the country's chief justice before having the case retried, with a guilty verdict forthcoming. Shortly after the 1965 verdict, Nkrumah commuted the sentences of the three former CPP officials and two other subsequently added coconspirators to twenty years of imprisonment. Nkrumah ultimately explained his decision to the National Assembly by reassuring his fellow politicians that "our clemency . . . [is not] a sign of weakness. On the contrary, it should be taken as a warning and assurance that our security forces will be even more vigilant and ever ready to deal swiftly and effectively with any anti-State activities."[75]

ON THE EVE OF THE COUP

By the time Nkrumah made his declaration commuting the Kulungugu defendants' sentences, an overarching sense of uncertainty and unpredictability undergirded Nkrumahist rule at both the popular and national levels. Internationally, American frustration with Nkrumah and the CPP had begun to grow in 1962 and 1963.[76] The November 1963 assassination of John F. Kennedy and the elevation of Lyndon Johnson to the presidency further intensified the anti-Nkrumah sentiments within the American government.[77] Meanwhile, as one late-1963 US intelligence report indicated, Nkrumah was facing increasing resistance in Africa itself to his political objectives—most notably the creation of a united Africa—as "other leaders have forced him off center stage." The report further cited significant political and economic difficulties in the CPP's attempts to create "a strong socialist state in Ghana." These difficulties included the rapid depletion of the country's foreign reserves and "an ever-widening budgetary gap" that could only be resolved through what the Americans described as "the adoption of politically undesirable austerity measures and . . . a [threatened] cutback in [Nkrumah's] showcase development program." What this meant for Ghana—and, in turn, for American foreign policy in the country—the report maintained, was a likely tightening of the West African country's relationships with the Soviet Union and the rest of the Eastern Bloc.[78]

The shifting nature of American policy toward Ghana between 1962 and 1964 also came to influence Nkrumah and the CPP's own readings of the political upheaval dominating the post-Kulungugu Ghanaian political scene, particularly in relation to additional assassination attempts that occurred in the bombing's aftermath. In September 1962, for instance, just a month after Kulungugu, another grenade went off near Nkrumah's residence and office at Flagstaff House in Accra. By the beginning of 1963, four more bombings would kill at least thirty people and leave approximately three hundred injured.[79] In 1964, there was another attempt on Nkrumah's life when a policeman shot at him from near point-blank range inside Flagstaff House, killing the residence's chief security guard. According to Erica Powell's account of the incident, after failing to shoot the president, the would-be assassin charged at Nkrumah, threatening him with the butt of the gun, but the "extremely fit and fleet of foot" president "easily out-ran the man and led him right round the front of his residence to the kitchens where he [Nkrumah] turned to face him [his assailant] and managed to overpower him."[80] The party- and state-run press provided similarly heroic narratives in the immediate aftermath of the attempted assassination, with several of the newspapers prominently featuring a photograph of Nkrumah pinning his attacker to the ground.[81] According to the *Ghanaian Times*, Nkrumah "rushed on him [his attacker], and after disarming him and throwing his .303 rifle away, pinned him to the ground" with a "ju-jitsu grip" from which the assailant could not escape.[82]

Narratives around the "indestructib[ility]" of Nkrumah, to use the American embassy's description of the *Ghanaian Times*'s account of the incident, circulated in the midst of a broader popular (and, in certain cases, even CPP-led) apprehension concerning the emergent political realities of Ghanaian single-party rule.[83] In his study of the CPP, for instance, political anthropologist Maxwell Owusu points to popular denunciations of the CPP as the "Corrupt People's Party."[84] Others similarly lamented a betrayal of their trust under Nkrumah. Kofi Ampadu, the former Eastern Region Young Pioneer who joined the movement against his parents' wishes, recalled in a 2008 interview that "we thought he [Nkrumah] came to help Ghana, but instead he sold out Ghana." At the root of Nkrumah's duplicity, in Ampadu's opinion, was his pan-Africanism: "He was saving in Egypt. All his money went there." At the time, Ampadu explained, "We didn't know [what it was for], but he was saving up so he would finally go and live with his [Egyptian] wife there."[85] Others further emphasized this theme of betrayal. Eden Bentum Takyi-Micah, a former Central Region pupil-teacher and fervent opponent of the CPP during the 1950s and 1960s, ultimately insisted that it was the British who carried the moral authority of decolonization; it was their vision of a prosperous, democratic Ghana that Nkrumah and the CPP shattered.[86]

Meanwhile, stories of political upheaval surrounding the presidency and party persisted in what would prove to be the final years of Nkrumahist rule, providing, for some, new openings to connect to the state as they countered narratives of turmoil with their own, often fanciful stories of their personal acts of state loyalty. In one December 1965 incident, for example, a security guard at the Bureau of African Affairs approached his supervisors days before Nkrumah was scheduled to visit the institution to tell them that he had been fasting on behalf of Nkrumah and that he had had a vision in which "there was a plot to harm the President." In his account of the vision, the guard, Daniel K. Ohemeng, told of how Nkrumah would be on a "sea journey" when assailants from the country's security forces would attack the president's vessel. Luckily, though, Ohemeng reported to his superiors that, "through certain supernatural efforts," Nkrumah's boat would speed away from the "fatal event." However, he warned, Nkrumah would not be safe yet, for he would encounter at least two additional assassination attempts, including one where a "pillar or other appendage . . . [would] fall on the President in the presence of Madam Fathia," Nkrumah's wife, and another where he would be "submerged into water." On each occasion, though, supernatural or spiritual forces would connect Ohemeng with Nkrumah, bringing the bureau security guard to the president and delivering Nkrumah from danger in a way that would "cheer up the masses who stood by." Ohemeng, then, concluded his account with a note on Nkrumah and the pursuit of African unity, commenting on how he recognized that, while "the President . . . devoted his life for the unification of Africa," in doing so he had alienated many other African leaders. As a result, Ohemeng reported seeing in his vision "blood before a throne with two horses at each side and a glittering star affixed to the Throne depicting confusion." Once again, this time through prayer, Ohemeng claimed to have "solved the situation."[87]

The bureau's leadership dismissed their security guard's claims as "fanatical," "woeful," and "funny unrealistic." Bureau director E. Ofori-Bah even suggested that Ohemeng was "a psychological case that needs watching" and "should be allowed to go on leave."[88] Yet, Ohemeng was not alone in predicting a volatile future for Nkrumah in late 1965 and early 1966. Reflecting on his time in the United States, for instance, Nkrumah's longtime confidant Kofi Duku spoke of an encounter he reportedly had with an official from a prominent American chocolate company about Nkrumah's future in Ghana. As Duku—a former member of the Ghana Cocoa Marketing Board—explained, the people at the company had heard that he was completing a program in business administration at Harvard, so they purportedly invited him to a party at their American headquarters. Duku recalled that, at the party, the official took him aside to warn him that "Nkrumah was going too fast," and "some people don't like it, the way he is going too fast." Thus, "If he goes too fast like that," as Duku interpreted the conversation, "then somebody will make a coup in his country." Duku claimed to have flown immediately after the encounter back to Accra, where he met Nkrumah as he was preparing to fly to Hanoi to help mediate the American-Vietnamese conflict. Shortly thereafter, and against Duku's advice, Nkrumah boarded the plane for Hanoi. Duku concluded the anecdote with a reflection on what he felt was lost with what turned out to be Nkrumah's ill-fated trip abroad: "The man was too radical, but I think it was good for the whole of the world, because changes must come and changes must go through to come. . . . That's why Jesus Christ came and they beat him down until he died. So if Nkrumah died, it is the same thing. . . . They have all come and gone. So Kwame Nkrumah comes and now has gone. What is the difference? He's saving people and bringing forth new people too. So the world goes on."[89]

⌐

Finding overarching patterns in the accounts and anecdotes that comprise this chapter can seem like a fool's errand. The source material for most is often highly limited and nearly always deeply fragmented. In several cases, it is also filtered through at least one third-party source. The aim here has been to contextualize the archival fragments that comprise these anecdotes and thus to make sense of the desires, emotions, motivations, and consequences underlying these and other Ghanaians' engagements with the increasingly ossifying infrastructure of the Nkrumahist one-party state in the early and mid-1960s. It would be saying too much to suggest that Nkrumahist or CPP politics became an ultimately defining feature of Ghanaians' relationships to their various communities during the period. However, in certain ways and in many instances, it is not saying too much to suggest that the political and social repertoire of Nkrumahist pan-Africanism and socialism did become a mechanism for many to expand and redefine their networks of belonging, at a time when other, more established networks were under threat. For some, such actions had to do with the pursuit of personal or professional gain. For others, deeper meanings linked their personal and professional desires to what they saw and possibly accepted as the emerging ethical paradigm of the Nkrumahist state. In either of these circumstances—and many others—both uncertainty and ambitions for belonging became vacillating features of life during the period. It is in these attempts at belonging (successful or otherwise) that the one-party state and Nkrumahist rule itself comes into focus, as they embody, for all involved, the optimism, frustrations, and even dangers that accompanied Africa's decolonization and the first decade of self-rule.

Conclusion

"Forward Ever, Backward Never"

ON 21 February 1966, Kwame Nkrumah boarded a plane for a diplomatic mission to Hanoi. Traveling at the invitation of the North Vietnamese government, Nkrumah, in his mind, was set to help negotiate a peace between the United States and the Vietnamese.[1] He never made it to Hanoi. On 24 February 1966, while the Ghanaian delegation was en route to a stopover in Peking (Beijing), Accra's residents awoke to the sound of gunfire in the streets surrounding Flagstaff House and other key sites in the city. Having traveled from as far as Tamale over the course of the previous day and having taken their positions the night before, groups of soldiers under the command of A. A. Afrifa, A. K. Ocran, and Emmanuel Kwasi Kotoka began the process of arresting prominent figures in the Ghanaian military, security, and intelligence forces. At Flagstaff House, Nkrumah's primary residence and the center of his government, a firefight ensued. Blocking the busy thoroughfare connecting the Accra city center to the airport and the University of Ghana, among other key sites north of the city center, security forces and rebel soldiers battled throughout the morning and afternoon, with both sides suffering shortages of ammunition and manpower. By late afternoon, however, as dusk began to fall over the city, the soldiers finally made their way through the gates of Flagstaff House, signaling the end of the Nkrumah government.[2]

The destruction and confusion left in the wake of the day's occurrences were palpable. As Accra resident Ben Nikoi-Oltai recalled, he was on his way home on the morning of the 24th when he "saw a soldier with a gun running" through the city's industrial area. The longtime CPP supporter assumed that the soldier was trying to break into one of the area's various factories in an attempt to "get money from them." It was only after asking around that Nikoi-Oltai learned that a coup was taking place and that there was fighting throughout the city. As a result of this fighting, he emphasized, many "people had been killed."[3] Historian Kevin Gaines provides a similar account of the violence of the coup as he relays the African American expatriate Preston King's description of the day. According to Gaines, on the morning of the 24th the din of gunfire pulled King and his wife from their bed. After a failed attempt to make their way to Flagstaff House, the couple went to wait out the affair at another expatriate's home, only to venture out later in the day to find a scene of widespread destruction: burning cars and military vehicles, others riddled with bullets, "abandoned rifles, submachine guns, helmets, and shoes," and the bodies of civilians caught in the crossfire.[4]

Over the ensuing months, the new military government of the National Liberation Council (NLC) undertook the intricate process of dismantling the Nkrumahist state. Prominent party leaders, ministers, and officials were arrested, including many expatriates.[5] Nkrumah advisor and Ghana's first attorney general Geoffrey Bing, for his part, spent approximately a month in Ussher Fort Prison following the coup before returning to his native Great Britain.[6] Shirley Graham Du Bois, similarly, suffered repeated interrogations before the military government permitted her to leave the country for the United Kingdom, albeit only after it had ransacked the late W. E. B. Du Bois's library in Accra.[7] Even more troublingly, the military tortured Ideological Institute instructor S. G. Ikoku before returning him, in a canvas sack, to Nigeria, where he was subsequently imprisoned.[8] At the same time, the new government dissolved many of the most controversial Nkrumah-era programs and institutions, most notably the Bureau of African Affairs, the Young Pioneers, the Ghana Muslim Council, and the Kwame Nkrumah Ideological Institute.[9] Despite significant skepticism from the NLC, the Ghana Workers (Builders) Brigade maintained a relatively long afterlife in the aftermath of the coup amid fears of mass unemployment should it be closed.[10]

Meanwhile, in the country's cities and towns, Ghanaians perceived to be CPP loyalists and Nkrumahists endured regular harassment from the military and police. In the case of Ben Nikoi-Oltai, for instance, who was a student at the Ideological Institute at the time of the coup, worries over military and police persecution forced him and many in his cohort to burn their textbooks out of fear of getting caught with now-illegal material (e.g., Marxist texts).[11] Former Shama Young Pioneer Lawrence Bessah—who at the time of the coup was approximately fourteen—recounted how the local police would bring him to the police station every few days for questioning in the weeks following the coup. Seen as a potential spy and Nkrumahist radical on account of his travels with other Young Pioneers in the Eastern Bloc (see chapter 6), Bessah endured persistent demands for a passport never given to him, interrogation regarding his Young Pioneer group's activities during its voyage, and insistence that he turn over any "subversive things" obtained in his travels. According to Bessah, the whole episode so traumatized his grandmother that she took, hid, and eventually burned all the documents from the trip—photographs, letters to his parents, postcards, his journal—and other souvenirs.[12]

On the streets, however, the public image of the coup was one of widespread jubilation. Images of razed Nkrumah statues, vandalized party and government offices, and crowds of Ghanaians apparently of all classes taking to the country's streets with songs of praise for the coup leaders and ridicule of Nkrumah dominated local and international coverage. Accra resident Thomas Daniel Laryea, who at the time of the coup was attending school in Akropong, recalled mock funerals held in Nkrumah's honor, as parades of people carried effigies of the deposed president and sang about their intention to "bury Kwame Nkrumah."[13] Likewise, in Kwahu Praso, Kofi Ampadu told of how, in celebrations following the coup, he and his colleagues in the Young Pioneers took the scarves of their uniforms—a key symbol of Nkrumahist power and prestige—and tied them around their legs in order to show how Nkrumah "disappointed us."[14]

HISTORY, DECOLONIZATION, AND NKRUMAH'S GHANA

By the time of the 1966 coup, the heady days of the 1950s and early 1960s had come to a close in not only Ghana, but much of Africa. Pressures from the Cold War, waves of coup attempts (successful and otherwise), and the seemingly stalled liberation of the southern African settler states had tempered many of the radical hopes and ambitions that shaped the politics of the previous decade. Few continued to talk of a new world, at least in the same way and with the same vibrancy as they had done just several years earlier. In Ghana, neither the NLC nor its civilian successor, the Progress Party (PP) government of longtime CPP rival K. A. Busia, envisioned anything along the lines of the all-encompassing political, social, and economic revolution pursued by Nkrumah and the CPP. Rather, both the NLC and the PP positioned their governments as ushering in a return to order and respectability. The corruption, nepotism, and internal backbiting of the Nkrumah regime, they argued, was thus to give way to the measured progress of a government rooted in parliamentary-style democracy, a mixed economy, and closer political and economic relations with Great Britain, the United States, and their allies.[15] However, over the course of the 1970s and early 1980s, Ghanaians witnessed four more coups as new military leaders, frustrated by the failures of both military and civilian governments, continuously came forward and promised to right the course of a country increasingly in political and economic distress. By the early 1990s, as the neoliberal fervor for elections that followed in the wake of the Soviet Union's demise swept the continent, Ghana—at least on the surface—finally appeared to right its course as the country embarked upon its much celebrated multiparty democracy in 1992. However, the governments led by both of contemporary Ghana's major parties—like so many of their counterparts across the continent—continued, and continue, to preside over escalating levels of youth unemployment, a rapidly weakening currency, limited infrastructure, uneven terms of trade, and vast inequalities in the distribution of wealth. That is, they have not been able to eliminate the same scourges of social injustice that Nkrumah tirelessly denounced and whose revolution ostensibly sought to eliminate during the CPP's decade and a half in power.

In Ghana today, there is a tendency to focus on questions of whether Nkrumah and the CPP succeeded or failed in their nation-building project, with accompanying, related debates over whether he and the country's first mass party were good or bad for Ghana. These debates, while on their face appearing to be normative assessments of the Nkrumahist regime and the costs and benefits of CPP rule, are, at their root, moral discussions related to the exercise of political power and the neoliberal limits placed, after Nkrumah, on the national and continental imagination in the late twentieth and early twenty-first centuries. Many Ghanaians, though, especially those who lived through both the tumult and the revolutionary vibrancy of the 1950s and 1960s, tend to have much more nuanced readings of, and relationships to, the Nkrumah era and the potential it represented. Many recognize the technological and industrial achievements of the regime. It was Nkrumah and the CPP, they rightfully recount, who built Tema, constructed the Akosombo Dam, and provided many of them with the means by which to attend school and find full-time employment. As Koforidua resident and former brigader Yaa Fosuawaa matter-of-factly asserted, "People say Kwame Nkrumah failed, but I had no problem. . . . Nkrumah really helped us. We have not yet gotten any other like him."[16] However, alongside statements such as those by Fosuawaa are often tragic accounts of the political violence, disappointment, economic decline and uncertainty, palpable fear, and deep-seated contradictions instigated or cultivated by the Nkrumah regime. These, too, were the realities of life under CPP rule and they continue to shape how wide swaths of this aging generation of Ghanaians still relate to the Nkrumah regime and its legacy. Yet, these reminiscences do not come without their own challenges as a historical source base.

The challenge for the academic historian is one of how to make sense of this contemporary discourse in a systematic study of the past. The deeply fragmented nature of the postcolonial archival record in Ghana further complicates matters as, in many ways, it helps to maintain the assumption of an artificial coherence to many of the CPP's actions and to what Nkrumahism meant in both thought and practice.[17] Moreover, at times even the oral record of the Nkrumahist past tends to fall into the same ersatz legibility and inherent vagaries of the archive in its articulations of life under midcentury Nkrumahism. As a result, the diversity of responses, beliefs, emotions, values, and personal histories recounted by many Ghanaians tend to become subsumed within the artifice of Nkrumahist homogeneity. As Frederick Cooper has noted in his opus on labor and African decolonization, one of the key challenges facing the study of decolonization is that we already know what happens.[18] We know that, by the mid-1960s, much of the continent achieved its independence, with new nation-states positioning themselves as actors on the international stage. We also know that, in the same period, the forms of citizenship and civic engagement that characterized much of the continent's decolonization had mutated into the gatekeeper politics that still comprise large segments of the continent's political culture.[19]

In Ghana specifically, we know that Nkrumah and the CPP led the country to its internationally celebrated independence in 1957. We also know that, by the mid-1960s, popular discontent was rife in the country, and that the military overthrew Nkrumah and the CPP in 1966: an event that, at least initially, appeared to be met with widespread jubilation on the country's streets. However, our informants in this study know this narrative, too, and at times embedded the assumptions associated with this knowledge into often teleological discussions about why Nkrumah was overthrown, and even about the inevitability of the 1966 coup. This should not come as a surprise when asking people about Nkrumahism, an ideology (or set of principles) so inextricably linked to the midcentury Ghanaian state. What lies in between these framings of midcentury Ghana, however—that is, the aspirations and tensions involved in living with Nkrumahism—often gets lost in such discussions, as well as in many historical reflections on the political, social, and personal complexities elicited by the first decade of self-rule. As a result, what has largely emerged is an approach to the political lives of postcolonial Ghana in which the realities of living with Nkrumahism—with all their ambitions, aspirations, challenges, and contradictions—have given way, at least in many narrative formulations, to the assumed clarity of narratives of either authoritarianism and corruption induced by a perceived un-African ideology, or, perhaps blindly, of a revolution lost.

Living with Nkrumahism has sought to bring to the fore the complications and tensions embedded in writing the history of African decolonization. Few things have more fundamentally shaped the book and its own narratives than the question of how best to position the very real hopes and ambitions brought forth by the prospects of self-rule alongside the broader structural realities—most notably the Cold War and clear disparities in the global economy—that constrained the realization of these ambitions. It may appear overly facile to say it so explicitly, but it is necessary: decolonization and all that it entailed was a historical process that ought to be historicized without the weight of later decades. What people expected of the parties and governments that claimed to represent them changed over time, as did the structural realities governing them both locally and internationally. By the 1960s, for instance, what a decade earlier had appeared to many in Africa and elsewhere as a still-malleable postwar world order had consolidated itself into a bipolar arrangement on the international stage. For those with visions of an alternative future for the postwar world, such a calcifying reality greatly constrained the political and social choices available to them as they sought to construct the postcolonial societies they imagined. This had strong ripple effects on the local stage, as new governments sought to address both the great diversity of interests, experiences, and histories of those whom they were to represent—not to mention their own—in an international environment that was uncertain at best and potentially dangerous at worst.

What is meant by Nkrumahism in this book is thus necessarily a reflection of and on the moving target of decolonization. As the CPP sought to create and consolidate an orthodoxy around the philosophy and politics of "Nkrumahism"—beginning to an extent before independence, but accelerating rapidly in the early 1960s—it was in many ways reacting to a set of local and international realities that the party and government viewed as threatening its vision for not only Ghana's but, just as importantly for many, Africa's future. While many, if not most, studies of Nkrumah-era Ghana have positioned this transition in Ghanaian politics as simply part of a CPP-administered power grab, this study insists that such a move was only part of the equation. Just as importantly, if not more so, changes internationally, continentally, locally, and structurally within Ghana struck at the heart of the Nkrumah-led government's radical anticolonial, pan-African, and socialist vision for a country and continent liberated from all of the vestiges of colonial rule. From the perspective of the CPP (rightly or wrongly), these changes promised a future of continued colonial exploitation—this time, under the guise of a false independence. This, according to Nkrumah and the CPP, was simply unacceptable and had to be avoided at all costs. As a result, both Nkrumah and the CPP responded by arguing for a tightening of control by the state, which ended up having severe repercussions for those who did not fit within the increasingly narrow definition of the Nkrumahist citizen.

Thus, the changing nature of the Ghanaian state itself in turn continuously forced Ghanaians to adapt to evolving political realities. For many, this included finding new ways to engage with or disengage from a changing Nkrumahism during the 1950s and 1960s. In doing so, they had little choice but to find ways to negotiate a political arena comprised at once of the many promises of modernization, social uplift, and belonging that had featured so prominently in the CPP's message since the late 1940s, and, for many, of the growing potential for detention and dislocation caused by Nkrumah's and the CPP's policies. However, it is key to remember that most Ghanaians were not idle spectators as these changes took place. Rather, they made choices, and the choices they made were often strategic and almost invariably historically contingent. As such, their choices were representative of their individual interests, ambitions, and options. Yet, like the Nkrumahist state itself, they too were often constrained by global structural realities and their articulation on the local stage, as well as by the state's readings of and reactions to these changing realities over the course of the 1950s and 1960s.

As a result, it is the question of what lies in between the conventional narrative formulations of Ghana's decolonization that has guided this book. Ultimately, what was there was a moment of exploration and experimentation. Debates and disputes—implicit and explicit—over interpretations of African liberation, pan-Africanism, African socialism, modernization, and mass mobilization in turn all found themselves embedded in a broad process of continental redefinition. After the end of the Second World War opened up the possibilities for African decolonization, decolonization processes themselves unleashed torrents of enthusiasm and popular imaginings for what the future held—for what could be—that must be understood on their own terms. For, in places like Nkrumah's Ghana, it was these imaginings—for better or worse, and often through their incompleteness and inconsistencies—that came to serve as the political and social edifice and legacy of Africa's transition to self-rule.

Notes

INTRODUCTION:
DECOLONIZATION AND THE PAN-AFRICAN NATION

1. Kwame Nkrumah, undated speech, excerpted in Nkrumah, *Axioms of Kwame Nkrumah* (London: Panaf Books, 1969), 82.

2. Howard University Moorland-Spingarn Research Center (hereafter cited as MSRC), Manuscript Division, Kwame Nkrumah Papers (hereafter cited as Nkrumah Papers), Box 154-41, Folder 13, Report by George Padmore, 21 July 1952.

3. This book will adopt the contemporaneous terminology of distinguishing the Gold Coast (as a colony) and Ghana (as the country) from each other. Thus, in discussions of events prior to 6 March 1957, the geographic territory and polity will generally be referred to as the Gold Coast. For events after independence, I will use Ghana.

4. Yale University Beinecke Rare Book and Manuscript Library, Richard Wright Papers, Box 5, Folder 81, Wright, "The Birth of a Man and the Birth of a Nation," unpublished MS, [1957?]. For a similar analysis of the meaning of Ghanaian independence, see "We Salute Ghana," *Crisis*, March 1957.

5. W. Scott Thompson, *Ghana's Foreign Policy, 1957–1966: Diplomacy, Ideology, and the New State* (Princeton, NJ: Princeton University Press, 1969), 67–73, 150–52; Kwame Nkrumah, *The Challenge of the Congo* (London: Thomas Nelson and Sons, 1967), 30–31.

6. Frederick Cooper, "Possibility and Constraint: African Independence in Historical Perspective," *Journal of African History* 49, no. 2 (2008): 167–96.

7. For a discussion of the role of this group of Africanist scholars, often via their work in the Gold Coast's mass education campaigns, in the growth of Gold Coast/Ghanaian historiography, see Kate Skinner, "Agency and Analogy in African History: The Contribution of Extra-Mural Studies in Ghana," *History in Africa* 34 (2007): 273–96. For the preeminent study on African American expatriates in Ghana, see Kevin K. Gaines, *American Africans in Ghana: Black Expatriates and the Civil Rights Era* (Chapel Hill: University of North Carolina Press, 2006).

8. Thomas Hodgkin, *Freedom for the Gold Coast?* (London: Union of Democratic Control, 1951), 3.

9. Thomas Hodgkin, *Nationalism in Colonial Africa* (New York: New York University Press, 1957).

10. David E. Apter, *The Gold Coast in Transition* (Princeton, NJ: Princeton University Press, 1955), 8–20, 291–324.

11. J. Ayodele Langley, *Pan-Africanism and Nationalism in West Africa, 1900–1945: A Study in Ideology and Social Classes* (Oxford: Clarendon, 1973), 358 and, more broadly, 357–68. See also Hakim Adi, *West Africans in Britain, 1900–1960: Nationalism, Pan-Africanism, and Communism* (London: Lawrence and Wishart, 1998), 128–31.

12. Richard Rathbone, "The Government of the Gold Coast after the Second World War," *African Affairs* 67, no. 268 (1968): 210.

13. Colonial Office, *Report of the Commission of Enquiry into Disturbances in the Gold Coast, 1948* (London: His Majesty's Stationery Office, 1948), 38–39.

14. Dennis Austin, *Politics in Ghana, 1946–1960* (London: Oxford University Press, 1964), 70–73.

15. Amponsah Dadzie to Watson Commission, quoted in D. Austin, *Politics in Ghana,* 72n43.

16. Colonial Office, *Report of the Commission of Enquiry,* 34–35.

17. D. Austin, *Politics in Ghana,* 72–73.

18. David Killingray, "Soldiers, Ex-Servicemen, and Politics in the Gold Coast, 1939–1950," *Journal of Modern African Studies* 21, no. 3 (1983): 532–33.

19. Colonial Office, *Report of the Commission of Enquiry,* 10–14.

20. Interview with Ben A. Nikoi-Oltai, Accra, 28 November 2007. I offer a similar narration of the 28 February march and the resulting riots in Jeffrey S. Ahlman, "'The Strange Case of Major Awhaitey': Conspiracy, Testimonial Evidence, and Narratives of Nation in Ghana's Postcolonial Democracy," *International Journal of African Historical Studies* (forthcoming).

21. For instance, see his treatise on the effects of imperialism and global capitalism on colonized territories, which is discussed in more depth in chapter 1. Kwame Nkrumah, *Towards Colonial Freedom: Africa in the Struggle against World Imperialism* (London: Farleigh, 1947).

22. Ibid.; Kwame Nkrumah, *Ghana: The Autobiography of Kwame Nkrumah* (Edinburgh: Thomas Nelson and Sons, 1957).

23. Richard Rathbone, introduction to *Ghana,* vol. 1, pt. 1, of *British Documents on the End of Empire,* ser. B (London: Her Majesty's Stationery Office, 1992), xlix.

24. Nkrumah, *Ghana,* 100–102; D. Austin, *Politics in Ghana,* 83–85.

25. Frantz Fanon, *The Wretched of the Earth,* trans. Constance Farrington (New York: Grove, 1963), 36. On Fanon's interest and experience in Ghana and its relationship to his own ideas of decolonization, see Jeffrey S. Ahlman, "The Algerian Question in Nkrumah's Ghana, 1958–1960: Debating 'Violence' and 'Nonviolence' in African Decolonization," *Africa Today* 57, no. 2 (2010): 67–84. See also Jeffrey James Byrne, *Mecca of Revolution: Algeria,*

Decolonization, and the Third World Order (Oxford: Oxford University Press, 2016), 69–73, 78–86.

26. Fanon, *Wretched of the Earth*, 315–16. For a historicized analysis of *The Wretched of the Earth*, see Christopher J. Lee, *Frantz Fanon: Toward a Revolutionary Humanism* (Athens: Ohio University Press, 2015), 146–78.

27. See, for example, Frederick Cooper, "Conflict and Connection: Rethinking Colonial African History," *American Historical Review* 99, no. 5 (1994): 1542–45.

28. Kwame Nkrumah, *Consciencism: Philosophy and Ideology for Decolonization and Development with Particular Reference to the African Revolution* (London: Heinemann, 1964), 34.

29. James Ferguson, *Expectations of Modernity: Myths and Meanings of Urban Life on the Zambian Copperbelt* (Berkeley: University of California Press, 1999).

30. Jean Allman, "Nuclear Imperialism and the Pan-African Struggle for Peace and Freedom: Ghana, 1959–1962," *Souls* 10, no. 2 (2008): 85.

31. Ibid.; Gaines, *American Africans in Ghana*; Meredith Terretta, "Cameroonian Nationalists Go Global: From Forest *Maquis* to a Pan-African Accra," *Journal of African History* 51, no. 2 (2010): 189–212; Ahlman, "Algerian Question"; Jeffrey S. Ahlman, "Road to Ghana: Nkrumah, Southern Africa, and the Eclipse of a Decolonizing Africa," *Kronos: Southern African Histories* 37 (2011): 23–40; Klaas van Walraven, *The Yearning for Relief: A History of the Sawaba Movement in Niger* (Leiden: Brill, 2013), esp. 397–507; Meredith Terretta, *Nation of Outlaws, State of Violence: Nationalism, Grassfields Tradition, and State Building in Cameroon* (Athens: Ohio University Press, 2014), esp. 177–216.

32. On Fanon, see David Macey, *Frantz Fanon: A Biography* (New York: Picador USA, 2000), 414–15, 445.

33. MSRC, Nkrumah Papers, Box 154-41, Folder 14, Padmore to Nkrumah, 5 August 1955. See also George Padmore, *The Gold Coast Revolution: The Struggle of an African People from Slavery to Freedom* (London: Dennis Dobson, 1953); Padmore, *Pan-Africanism or Communism? The Coming Struggle for Africa* (New York: Roy Publishers, 1956).

34 See, for instance, Timothy Mitchell, *Rule of Experts: Egypt, Techno-Politics, Modernity* (Berkeley: University of California Press, 2002); Vikramaditya Prakash, *Chandigarh's Le Corbusier: The Struggle for Modernity in Postcolonial India* (Seattle: University of Washington Press, 2002).

35. Donald L. Donham, *Marxist Modern: An Ethnographic History of the Ethiopian Revolution* (Berkeley: University of California Press, 1999), xv, 1–2.

36. Ferguson, *Expectations of Modernity*.

37. Leander Schneider, *Government of Development: Peasants and Politicians in Postcolonial Tanzania* (Bloomington: Indiana University Press, 2014).

38. Ibid., 1–10.

39. Ibid., 2. On the cultural politics of Nyerere's Tanzania and the schisms within the TANU state project, see also Andrew Ivaska, *Cultured States: Youth,*

Gender, and Modern Style in 1960s Dar es Salaam (Durham, NC: Duke University Press, 2011); Paul Bjerk, *Building a Peaceful Nation: Julius Nyerere and the Establishment of Sovereignty in Tanzania, 1960–1964* (Rochester, NY: University of Rochester Press, 2015); Priya Lal, *African Socialism in Postcolonial Tanzania: Between the Village and the World* (Cambridge: Cambridge University Press, 2015).

40. James C. Scott, *Seeing Like a State: How Certain Schemes to Improve the Human Condition Have Failed* (New Haven, CT: Yale University Press, 1998).

41. Apter, *Gold Coast in Transition*.

42. Michael Crowder, "Whose Dream Was It Anyway? Twenty-Five Years of African Independence," *African Affairs* 86, no. 342 (1987): 7–24. See also Jean Allman's recent reflection on the historiographical implications of Crowder's query: Allman, "Between the Present and History: African Nationalism and Decolonization," in *The Oxford Handbook of Modern African History*, ed. John Parker and Richard Reid (Oxford: Oxford University Press, 2013), 231–35.

43. Elizabeth Schmidt, *Mobilizing the Masses: Gender, Ethnicity, and Class in the Nationalist Movement in Guinea, 1939–1958* (Portsmouth, NH: Heinemann, 2005).

44. On the CPP's attempts to control the press, see Clement E. Asante, *The Press in Ghana: Problems and Prospects* (Lanham, MD: University Press of America, 1996), 13–35; Jennifer Hasty, *The Press and Political Culture in Ghana* (Bloomington: Indiana University Press, 2005), 33–35; Baba Galleh Jallow, "Defining the Nation: Censorship in Colonial and Postcolonial Ghana, 1933–1993" (PhD diss., University of California, Davis, 2011), 59–94.

45. Mike McGovern, *Unmasking the State: Making Guinea Modern* (Chicago: University of Chicago Press, 2013), esp. 147–226.

46. Ibid., 5, 227, quote on 227.

47. Jay Straker, *Youth, Nationalism, and the Guinean Revolution* (Bloomington: Indiana University Press, 2009), 206–7.

48. See, for instance, Maxwell Owusu, *Uses and Abuses of Political Power: A Case Study of Continuity and Change in the Politics of Ghana*, 2nd ed. (Accra: Ghana Universities Press, 2006); James A. McCain, "Attitudes toward Socialism, Policy, and Leadership in Ghana," *African Studies Review* 22, no. 1 (1979): 149–69; McCain, "Perceptions of Socialism in Post-Socialist Ghana: An Experimental Analysis," *African Studies Review* 22, no. 3 (1979): 45–63. Studies on Nkrumah-era Ghana have had a resurgence in recent years. Some more recent book-length analyses include Ama Biney, *The Political and Social Thought of Kwame Nkrumah* (New York: Palgrave Macmillan, 2011); Harcourt Fuller, *Building the Ghanaian Nation-State: Kwame Nkrumah's Symbolic Nationalism* (New York: Palgrave Macmillan, 2014); Kate Skinner, *The Fruits of Freedom in British Togoland: Literacy, Politics, and Nationalism, 1914–2014* (Cambridge: Cambridge University Press, 2015), 122–207; Justin Williams,

Pan-Africanism in Ghana: African Socialism, Neoliberalism, and Globaliza-
tion (Durham, NC: Carolina Academic Press, 2016), xvii–57.

49. Mahmood Mamdani, *Citizen and Subject: Contemporary Africa and*
the Legacy of Late Colonialism (Princeton, NJ: Princeton University Press,
1996).

50. Jean-François Bayart, *The State in Africa: The Politics of the Belly,* 2nd
ed. (Malden, MA: Polity, 2009). Relatedly, see also Achille Mbembe, *On the*
Postcolony (Berkeley: University of California Press, 2001).

51. Frederick Cooper, *Colonialism in Question: Theory, Knowledge, His-*
tory (Berkeley: University of California Press, 2005), 17–18, 51–52.

52. Interview with Nikoi-Oltai, Accra, 19 January 2008.

53. For many of these records, see Richard Rathbone's foundational collection of British archival documents on Ghana's decolonization: Rathbone,
ed., *Ghana,* vol. 1, pts. 1 and 2, of *British Documents on the End of Empire,* ser.
B (London: Her Majesty's Stationery Office, 1992).

54. The files in PRAAD-Accra's "Bureau of African Affairs" series have
undergone several renumberings in the past years. In this book, I have utilized
the current (last referenced November 2016) numbering system (RG 17/1/-) as
the material's primary citation. I have also included in these citations references to the previous SC/BAA/- system, which was the dominant cataloguing
system until recently. There was also a previous, never fully implemented
RG 17/1/- system began in the mid to late 2000s that appears to have been
discarded or significantly adjusted in the compilation of the new cataloguing
system. All of my earlier publications have utilized the previous SC/BAA/-
numbering system in their references to this collection as well as included
parallel references to the now discarded RG 17/1/- version.

55. For the richest reflection on the state of the Ghanaian postcolonial
archive and the limitations it imposes on scholars seeking to write Ghana's
early postcolonial history, see Jean Allman, "Phantoms of the Archive: Kwame
Nkrumah, a Nazi Pilot Named Hanna, and the Contingencies of Postcolonial
History-Writing," *American Historical Review* 118, no. 1 (2013): 104–29.

56. Among the most notable examples of this scholarship is Maxwell
Owusu's classic, *Uses and Abuses of Political Power.*

57. Allman, "Phantoms of the Archive."

CHAPTER 1: THE WORLD OF KWAME NKRUMAH

1. Kwame [Francis Nwia-Kofi] Nkrumah, "Education and Nationalism in
Africa," *Educational Outlook* 18, no. 1 (1943): 39.

2. Howard University Moorland-Spingarn Research Center, Manuscript
Division, Kwame Nkrumah Papers, Box 154-41, Folder 14, George Padmore to
Kwame Nkrumah, 7 January 1957.

3. Nkrumah, speech at the independence of Ghana, 6 March 1957, excerpted in Kwame Nkrumah, *I Speak of Freedom: A Statement of African*
Ideology (New York: Frederick A. Praeger, 1961), 107.

4. Tony Ballantyne and Antoinette Burton, *Empires and the Reach of the Global, 1870–1945* (Cambridge, MA: Harvard University Press, 2012), 27–77.

5. For an astute recent reflection on the opportunities for political and intellectual connection created by empire in West Africa, see Stephanie Newell, *The Power to Name: A History of Anonymity in Colonial West Africa* (Athens: Ohio University Press, 2013), esp. 29–43.

6. For surveys of the Gold Coast's nineteenth- and early twentieth-century history, see David Kimble, *A Political History of Ghana: The Rise of Gold Coast Nationalism, 1850–1928* (Oxford: Clarendon, 1963); A. Adu Boahen, *Ghana: Evolution and Change in the Nineteenth and Twentieth Centuries* (London: Longman, 1975).

7. For the fullest study of Asante's nineteenth-century history, see Ivor Wilks, *Asante in the Nineteenth Century: The Structure and Evolution of a Political Order* (Cambridge: Cambridge University Press, 1975).

8. See, for instance, Jean Allman and John Parker, *Tongnaab: The History of a West African God* (Bloomington: Indiana University Press, 2005), 54–105.

9. Jane Burbank and Frederick Cooper, *Empires in World History: Power and the Politics of Difference* (Princeton, NJ: Princeton University Press, 2010), 315–17.

10. See, for instance, Benito Sylvain, *Du sort des indigènes dans les colonies d'exploitation* (Paris: L. Boyer, 1901); W. E. B. Du Bois, *The Negro* (New York: Henry Holt, 1915). See also the discussion of Du Bois below.

11. "In Defence of Our Position," *Gold Coast Methodist Times*, 15 November 1897.

12. Uday Singh Mehta, *Liberalism and Empire: A Study in Nineteenth-Century British Liberal Thought* (Chicago: University of Chicago Press, 1999), esp. 46–114. See also Jennifer Pitts, *A Turn to Empire: The Rise of Imperial Liberalism in Britain and France* (Princeton, NJ: Princeton University Press, 2005).

13. John Stuart Mill, *On Liberty* (Boston: Ticknor and Fields, 1863), 24.

14. Mehta, *Liberalism and Empire*, 51–64. On liberalism and the historical imagination, see Theodore Koditschek, *Liberalism, Imperialism, and the Historical Imagination: Nineteenth-Century Visions of Greater Britain* (Cambridge: Cambridge University Press, 2011).

15. Karuna Mantena in particular notes contestations over questions of universality in imperial liberal thought and details more culturally specific notions of colonial administration that she credits as giving rise to indirect rule. See Mantena, *Alibis of Empire: Henry Maine and the Ends of Liberal Imperialism* (Princeton, NJ: Princeton University Press, 2010).

16. *Lagos Standard*, 6 October 1897, quoted in Philip S. Zachernuk, *Colonial Subjects: An African Intelligentsia and Atlantic Ideas* (Charlottesville: University Press of Virginia, 2000), 58.

17. Zachernuk, *Colonial Subjects*, 58–59.

18. University of Massachusetts Amherst Libraries (hereafter cited as UMass Amherst Libraries), Special Collections and University Archives

(hereafter cited as SCUA), W. E. B. Du Bois Papers (MS 312) (hereafter cited as Du Bois Papers), Pan-African Association, "Report of the Pan-African Conference, Held on the 23rd, 24th and 25th July, 1900, at Westminster Town Hall, Westminster, S.W." (typescript). For a survey of the conference, see Imanuel Geiss, *The Pan-African Movement: A History of Pan-Africanism in America, Europe, and Africa*, trans. Ann Keep (New York: Africana, 1974), 176–98.

19. UMass Amherst Libraries, SCUA, Du Bois Papers, Pan-African Congress, Resolutions, ca. 21 February 1919.

20. Ibid. On the 1919 Pan-African Congress more broadly, see Geiss, *Pan-African Movement*, 234–40.

21. For a brief survey of some of these debates and the political and social contexts surrounding them, see Antoinette Burton, "New Narratives of Imperial Politics in the Nineteenth Century," in *At Home with the Empire: Metropolitan Culture and the Imperial World*, ed. Catherine Hall and Sonya Rose (Cambridge: Cambridge University Press, 2006).

22. For a survey of Hobson's life, see John Allett, *New Liberalism: The Political Economy of J. A. Hobson* (Toronto: University of Toronto Press, 1981), 3–46.

23. J. A. Hobson, *Imperialism: A Study* (London: James Nisbet, 1902). For a critical interrogation and contextualization of Hobson's thesis, see Allett, *New Liberalism*, 131–77.

24. W. E. B. Du Bois, "The African Roots of the War," in *W. E. B. Du Bois: A Reader*, ed. David Levering Lewis (New York: Owl Books, 1995), 642–51; originally published in *Atlantic Monthly* 115, no. 5 (May 1915): 707–14.

25. Du Bois, "African Roots of the War," 642–45.

26. Ibid., 648–50.

27. V. I. Lenin, *Imperialism: The Highest Stage of Capitalism: A Popular Outline*, rev. trans. (Moscow: Co-Operative Publishing Society of Foreign Workers in the USSR, 1934). In reference to Hobson's influence on Lenin, historian Stephen Howe even goes so far as to present the Bolshevik's text as "somewhat derivative" of the British economist; Howe, *Ireland and Empire: Colonial Legacies in Irish History and Culture* (Oxford: Oxford University Press, 2000), 74.

28. Du Bois, "African Roots of the War," 645.

29. Lenin, *Imperialism*, 9.

30. Ibid., 79.

31. Ibid., 73.

32. Alexandre A. Bennigsen and S. Enders Wimbush, *Muslim National Communism in the Soviet Union: A Revolutionary Strategy for the Colonial World* (Chicago: University of Chicago Press, 1979), 42. I thank Sergey Glebov for introducing me to the history of Mirsaid Sultan-Galiev.

33. On Sultan-Galiev's arrest and trial, see Stephen Blank, "Stalin's First Victim: The Trial of Sultangaliev," *Russian History/Histoire Russe* 17, no. 2 (1990): 155–78.

34. Bennigsen and Wimbush, *Muslim National Communism*, 41–45.

35. Jawaharlal Nehru, *Soviet Russia: Some Random Sketches and Impressions* (Bombay: Chetana, 1949), 2. On Nehru's visit to the Soviet Union, see Judith M. Brown, *Nehru: A Political Life* (New Haven, CT: Yale University Press, 2003), 83–84; Benjamin Zachariah, *Nehru* (New York: Routledge, 2004), 60–61.

36. Jawaharlal Nehru, *Toward Freedom: The Autobiography of Jawaharlal Nehru* (New York: John Day, 1941), 229–30.

37. Kwame Nkrumah, *Towards Colonial Freedom: Africa in the Struggle against World Imperialism* (London: Farleigh, 1947), 6.

38. Kwame Nkrumah, *Ghana: The Autobiography of Kwame Nkrumah* (Edinburgh: Thomas Nelson and Sons, 1957), 31–47. For the most detailed accounts of Nkrumah's time in the United States and Great Britain, see Nkrumah, *Ghana*, 26–64; Marika Sherwood, *Kwame Nkrumah: The Years Abroad, 1935–1947* (Legon, Ghana: Freedom Publications, 1996).

39. Nkrumah, *Ghana*, 29.

40. "Declaration to the Colonial Workers, Farmers, and Intellectuals," in George Padmore, ed., *Colonial and . . . Coloured Unity: A Programme of Action: History of the Pan-African Congress* (London: Hammersmith Bookshop, 1963), 6; first published 1947 by the Pan-African Federation, Manchester, UK. For a detailed discussion of the Congress, its roots, and organization, see Hakim Adi and Marika Sherwood, *The 1945 Manchester Pan-African Congress Revisited* (London: New Beacon Books, 1995).

41. "Declaration to the Colonial Workers, Farmers, and Intellectuals," in Padmore, *Colonial and . . . Coloured Unity*, 6.

42. Jomo Kenyatta, "The East African Picture," 17 October 1945, ibid., 40–41.

43. G. Ashie Nikoi, "Imperialism in North and West Africa," 16 October 1945, ibid., 32.

44. J. S. Annan, "Imperialism in North and West Africa," 16 October 1945, ibid., 33; "Gold Coaster Would Not Mind Adopting Revolutionary Methods to Gain Freedom," *West African Pilot*, 19 October 1945.

45. UMass Amherst Libraries, SCUA, Du Bois Papers, W. A. Hunton, Francis N. Nkrumah, Rayford Logan, et al., "Resolution of the Colonial Conference in New York," 6 April 1945; Marika Sherwood, "'There is No New Deal for the Blackman in San Francisco': African Attempts to Influence the Founding Conference of the United Nations, April–July 1945," *International Journal of African Historical Studies* 29, no. 1 (1996): 77.

46. UMass Amherst Libraries, SCUA, Du Bois Papers, Hunton, Nkrumah, Logan et al., "Resolution of the Colonial Conference in New York," 6 April 1945.

47. Kwame Nkrumah, "Imperialism in North and West Africa," 16 October 1945, in Padmore, *Colonial and . . . Coloured Unity*, 32.

48. I. T. A. Wallace-Johnson, "Imperialism in North and West Africa," 16 October 1945, ibid., 34.

49. J. Downes-Thomas, "Imperialism in North and West Africa," 16 October 1945, ibid., 34; "Gold Coaster Would Not Mind Adopting Revolutionary Methods to Gain Freedom," *West African Pilot*, 19 October 1945.

50. Kwame Nkrumah, "Imperialism in North and West Africa," 16 October 1945, in Padmore, *Colonial and . . . Coloured Unity*, 32.

51. Kenyatta, "The East African Picture," 17 October 1945, ibid., 40–42; Ken Hill, E. D. L. Yearwood, and Samuel I. O. Andrews, "The Problem in the Caribbean," 18 October 1945, ibid., 46–47, 51–52.

52. Marko Hlubi and Peter Abrahams, "Oppression in South Africa," 16 October 1945, ibid., 37–39.

53. E. J. Duplan, A. Aki-Emi, and A. E. Moselle, "The Colour Problem in Britain," 15 October 1945, ibid., 27–28; Nikoi, Downes-Thomas and F. O. B. Blaize, "Imperialism in North and West Africa," 16 October 1945, ibid., 32–34.

54. "The Challenge to the Colonial Powers," ibid., 5; "Declaration to the Colonial Workers, Farmers, and Intellectuals," ibid., 6–7. Key to the delegates' attempts to illustrate how colonial rule continued their subjugation were efforts to detail the ways in which poverty was an unambiguous symptom of colonialism. See, for instance, Hlubi and Padmore, "The East African Picture," 17 October 1945, ibid., 42–43; Claude Lushington, "The Problem in the Caribbean," 18 October 1945, ibid., 47–48.

55. Broadly, on the Atlantic Charter, see Douglas Brinkley and David R. Facey-Crowther, eds., *The Atlantic Charter* (New York: St. Martin's, 1994).

56. Blaize, 16 October 1945, "Imperialism in North and West Africa," in Padmore, *Colonial and . . . Coloured Unity*, 34.

57. J. A. Linton, 19 October 1945, "The Problem in the Caribbean," ibid., 53.

58. F. R. Kankam-Boadu, "Reminiscences," in Adi and Sherwood, *1945 Manchester Pan-African Congress*, 35.

59. Joseph Appiah, *Joe Appiah: The Autobiography of an African Patriot* (Accra: Asempa, 1996), 164–66; first published 1990 by Praeger, New York.

60. UMass Amherst Libraries, SCUA, Du Bois Papers, Padmore to Du Bois, 9 August 1946.

61. Leslie James, *George Padmore and Decolonization from Below: Pan-Africanism, the Cold War, and the End of Empire* (New York: Palgrave Macmillan, 2015), 98–100.

62. Ibid. For Makonnen's take on the Pan-African Federation, see [T.] Ras Makonnen, *Pan-Africanism from Within*, recorded and edited by Kenneth King (London: Oxford University Press, 1973), 178–95.

63. LaRay Denzer, "I. T. A. Wallace-Johnson and the West African Youth League: A Case Study in West African Radicalism" (PhD diss., University of Birmingham, 1977), 514.

64. Hakim Adi, *West Africans in Britain, 1900–1960: Nationalism, Pan-Africanism, and Communism* (London: Lawrence and Wishart, 1998), 129 and, more broadly on the WANS, 128–34. Adi notes a direct connection between

some of the WANS's founders and the ARPS and the WAYL, namely via Ashie Nikoi (ARPS) and I. T. A. Wallace-Johnson (WAYL). See also Denzer, "I. T. A. Wallace-Johnson and the West African Youth League"; J. Ayodele Langley, *Pan-Africanism and Nationalism in West Africa, 1900–1945: A Study in Ideology and Social Classes* (Oxford: Clarendon, 1973), 357–68.

65. Yale University Beinecke Rare Book and Manuscript Library (hereafter cited as Beinecke Library), Richard Wright Papers (hereafter cited as Wright Papers), Box 133, Folder 1986, Wallace-Johnson and Nkrumah, "Aims and Objects of the West African National Secretariat," n.d.

66. Bankole Awooner-Renner, *West African Soviet Union* (London: WANS, 1946); see also Adi, *West Africans in Britain*, 129–30.

67. "The Cocoa Monopoly," *New African*, March 1946; Gemini, "Riding on the Lion," *New African*, March 1946; "A Resolution on Imperialists' Colonial Policy," *New African*, March 1946. The latter two articles are reproduced in Sherwood, *Kwame Nkrumah*, 140–41.

68. Beinecke Library, Wright Papers, Box 133, Folder 1986, Wallace-Johnson and Nkrumah, "Aims and Objects of the West African National Secretariat," n.d.; "Congress Resolutions: West Africa," Padmore, *Colonial and . . . Coloured Unity*, 56.

69. See "Sir Arnold, Please Speak," *African Morning Post*, 1 December 1937; Gold Coast United, "Pooling the Pool," *African Morning Post*, 1 December 1937; Ziga Wegbe, "Kill the Pool," *African Morning Post*, 1 December 1937; "Dissolve the Pool," *African Morning Post*, 2 December 1937; "Government & the Pool," *African Morning Post*, 3 December 1937; Lobster, "Farmers & Merchants," *African Morning Post*, 3 December 1937. Quote from "Dissolve the Pool." On the series of cocoa holdups (producers' strikes) in the late 1920s and 1930s, see Gareth Austin, "Capitalists and Chiefs in the Cocoa Hold-Ups in South Asante, 1927–1938," *International Journal of African Historical Studies* 21, no. 1 (1988): 63–95.

70. "The Cocoa Monopoly," *New African*, March 1946.

71. Marika Sherwood provides a detailed rundown of articles on the WANS in the West African press; Sherwood, *Kwame Nkrumah*, 130–50. In the *Ashanti Pioneer*, specifically, see Arthur Thrower, "Three Lovers of Africa Meet in London," *Ashanti Pioneer*, 19 February 1946; Padmore, "Mbadiwe Hits West African Unity," *Ashanti Pioneer*, 9 March 1948.

72. Kwame Nkrumah, "A Call for an All–West African National Congress," *Ashanti Pioneer*, 7 February 1947; Nkrumah, "All West African National Congress Scheduled to Take Place in Second Week of October 1948," *Ashanti Pioneer*, 6 June 1947. On the National Congress of British West Africa, see Langley, *Pan-Africanism and Nationalism*, 107–94.

73. Leslie James, *George Padmore and Decolonization from Below*, 81.

74. As chapter 4 notes, Botsio was briefly cast from the CPP hierarchy following the 1961 strike that began in the Western Region cities of Sekondi and Takoradi. However, Nkrumah brought him back into the fold following

the 1962 attempt on the Ghanaian president's life in the northern border town of Kulungugu. On the context surrounding Botsio's "rehabilitation," see W. Scott Thompson, *Ghana's Foreign Policy, 1957–1966: Diplomacy, Ideology, and the New State* (Princeton, NJ: Princeton University Press, 1969), 265–66.

75. Sherwood, *Kwame Nkrumah*, 127–50. See also Ama Biney, *The Political and Social Thought of Kwame Nkrumah* (New York: Palgrave Macmillan, 2011), 32–33.

76. UMass Amherst Libraries, SCUA, Du Bois Papers, Padmore to Nehru, 2 December 1946.

77. Sherwood, *Kwame Nkrumah*, 136, 138–39.

78. Cranford Pratt, "Colonial Governments and the Transfer of Power in East Africa," in *The Transfer of Power in Africa: Decolonization, 1940–1960*, ed. Prosser Gifford and Wm. Roger Louis (New Haven, CT: Yale University Press, 1982), 250–54; Frederick Cooper, *Decolonization and African Society: The Labor Question in French and British Africa* (Cambridge: Cambridge University Press, 1996), 215.

79. Colonial Office, *Report of the Commission of Enquiry into Disturbances in the Gold Coast, 1948* (London: His Majesty's Stationery Office, 1948); National Archives of the United Kingdom, Colonial Office, 879/157, W. H. Ingrams, "Communist Prospects in East and Central Africa," African no. 1180 (1953); Adi, *West Africans in Britain*, 134.

80. See Lord [William Malcolm] Hailey, *Native Administration and Political Development in British Tropical Africa* (Nendeln, Liechtenstein: Kraus Reprint, 1979), 50–51; Pratt, "Colonial Governments and the Transfer of Power in East Africa," 250–59.

81. Adi, *West Africans in Britain*, 134.

82. Richard Wright, *The Color Curtain: A Report on the Bandung Conference* (Cleveland, OH: World Publishing, 1956), 208 (emphasis in original).

CHAPTER 2: FROM THE GOLD COAST TO GHANA

1. Kwame Nkrumah, *Towards Colonial Freedom: Africa in the Struggle against World Imperialism* (London: Farleigh, 1947), 36.

2. *Gold Coast Independent*, 24 October 1947, quoted in Marika Sherwood, *Kwame Nkrumah: The Years Abroad, 1935–1947* (Legon, Ghana: Freedom Publications, 1996), 193. See also "Kwame Nkrumah: An Appreciation," *Gold Coast Observer*, 24 October 1947. Leslie James kindly directed me to the *Gold Coast Observer* article.

3. Interview with M. N. Tetteh, Accra, 8 March 2008.

4. On Nkrumah's imprisonment, see Dennis Austin, *Politics in Ghana, 1946–1960* (London: Oxford University Press, 1964), 90.

5. Interview with Ben A. Nikoi-Oltai, Accra, 28 November 2007.

6. Interview with Kofi Duku, Accra, 13 May 2008.

7. D. Austin, *Politics in Ghana*, 103, 141.

8. Jean Allman, *The Quills of the Porcupine: Asante Nationalism in an Emergent Ghana* (Madison: University of Wisconsin Press, 1993).

9. See, for instance, Richard Wright's description of his 1953 interview with J. B. Danquah in Wright, *Black Power: A Record of Reactions in a Land of Pathos* (New York: Harper and Brothers, 1954), 220.

10. See, for instance, "Educate Our Women," *Evening News*, 3 September 1948; "Teachers with Broken Service," *Evening News*, 22 September 1948; "The Rising Cost of Living," *Evening News*, 28 May 1949; Trade Unionist, "Working Class Politics," *Evening News*, 6 October 1949.

11. Elizabeth Schmidt, *Mobilizing the Masses: Gender, Ethnicity, and Class in the Nationalist Movement in Guinea, 1939–1958* (Portsmouth, NH: Heinemann, 2005); Schmidt, *Cold War and Decolonization in Guinea, 1946–1958* (Athens: Ohio University Press, 2007).

12. For the CPP, see Takyiwaa Manuh, "Women and Their Organizations during the Convention Peoples' Party Period," in *The Life and Work of Kwame Nkrumah: Papers of a Symposium Organized by the Institute of African Studies, University of Ghana, Legon*, ed. Kwame Arhin (Trenton, NJ: Africa World, 1993), 106–8; Jean Allman, "The Disappearing of Hannah Kudjoe: Nationalism, Feminism, and the Tyrannies of History," *Journal of Women's History* 21, no. 3 (2009): 13–35. On the RDA and TANU, see Susan Geiger, *TANU Women: Gender and Culture in the Making of Tanganyikan Nationalism, 1955–1965* (Portsmouth, NH: Heinemann, 1997); Schmidt, *Mobilizing the Masses*, 113–43.

13. See Dorthea E. Lokko, "The Women's Part," *Evening News*, 26 February 1949; Akua Assaabea, "Awake! Women of Ghana," *Evening News*, 28 May 1949; Manuh, "Women and Their Organizations," 107; Mabel Dove, *Selected Writings of a Pioneer West African Feminist*, ed. Stephanie Newell and Audrey Gadzekpo (Nottingham, UK: Trent, 2004), 98–113.

14. C. L. R. James, *Nkrumah and the Ghana Revolution* (London: Allison and Busby, 1977), 56. Established in the 1920s, Achimota Secondary School was one of the premier educational institutions in British West Africa. Nkrumah was a member of one of the first classes to attend the institution, graduating in 1930. For Nkrumah's account of his time at Achimota, see Kwame Nkrumah, *Ghana: The Autobiography of Kwame Nkrumah* (Edinburgh: Thomas Nelson and Sons, 1957), 15–22.

15. Interview with Duku, Accra, 7 May 2008.

16. The colonial government estimated that in the late 1940s there were over four hundred million cocoa trees in the Gold Coast and approximately fifty million that were already infected with the disease. Moreover, it predicted that, at the current rate the disease was spreading, the Gold Coast cocoa industry would "have practically disappeared in 20 years." Colonial Office, *Report of the Commission of Enquiry into Disturbances in the Gold Coast, 1948* (London: His Majesty's Stationery Office, 1948), 48 and, more broadly, 48–51.

17. Francis Danquah, *Cocoa Diseases and Politics in Ghana, 1909–1966* (New York: Peter Lang, 1995), 102.

18. See "The Spirit of the Nation," *Evening News*, 26 July 1949; "Commentary of H. E.'s Legco Address (6)," *Evening News*, 26 July 1949; "Beware of Those Wolves in Sheep Skin," *Evening News*, 15 September 1949. Similarly, it referenced external reports that supported such a view; see George Padmore, "African Chiefs Instruments of British Colonial Rule, says Fabian Colonial Bureau Report," *Evening News*, 1 June 1950.

19. George Padmore, *The Gold Coast Revolution: The Struggle of an African People from Slavery to Freedom* (London: Dennis Dobson, 1953), 67–68; Bankole Timothy, *Kwame Nkrumah: His Rise to Power* (London: George Allen and Unwin, 1955), 88–93; interview with Duku, Accra, 7 May 2008. Estimates vary on the number of these schools, with the onetime director of them, Kofi Duku, recalling that there were approximately eighteen to twenty. Padmore, writing in 1953, counted a dozen, while Richard Wright insisted that approximately a hundred such schools existed at their height, with an estimated fifty still in operation in 1953. Yale University Beinecke Rare Book and Manuscript Library (hereafter cited as Beinecke Library), Richard Wright Papers (hereafter cited as Wright Papers), Box 22, Folder 343, Wright, Travel Journal, 24 July 1953.

20. "Education in a Slave State," *Evening News*, 19 March 1949, reproduced in Timothy, *Kwame Nkrumah*, 88–89.

21. Extreme teacher shortages at all levels in the Northern Territories forced a less aggressive program for that region. Gold Coast, Education Department, *Accelerated Development Plan for Education, 1951* (Accra: Government Printing Department, 1951), 1, 7–8.

22. Ibid., 1.

23. See the speech given in Parliament on 13 June 1957 by Minister of Education C. T. Nylander, in Government of Ghana, National Assembly, *Parliamentary Debates*, vol. 6, cols. 820–23. See also Betty Stein George, *Education in Ghana* (Washington, DC: Government Printing Office, 1976), 43. There is a slight discrepancy between Nylander and George's numbers for primary school and middle school students. For the 1951 numbers, both place the number of students at approximately 220,000. In contrast, for 1957, Nylander rounds up to "not far short of 600,000," with George offering the more precise total of 571,580.

24. George, *Education in Ghana*, 43.

25. Wright, *Black Power*, 65.

26. See, for instance, Yaw Asare, "Ghana Educational Programme," *Evening News*, 26 July 1949.

27. Interview with N. Sifah, Accra, 16 February 2008.

28. For a discussion of the ideological importance of the CPP's emphasis on science and technology, see Jeffrey S. Ahlman, "Africa's Kitchen Debate: Ghanaian Domestic Space in the Age of Cold War," in *Gender, Sexuality, and*

the Cold War: A Global Perspective, ed. Philip E. Muehlenbeck (Nashville, TN: Vanderbilt University Press, 2017).

29. Gold Coast, Education Department, *Accelerated Development Plan*, 5, 7.

30. Ibid., 8. As Lacy S. Ferrell has shown, schools were in such short supply in the Northern Territories that, for much of the early twentieth century, students who attended them often comprised a class of "educational migrants" who were selected by colonial officials to attend schools—in some cases—up to 200 kilometers from their homes; Ferrell, "'We Were Mixed with All Types': Educational Migration in the Northern Territories of Colonial Ghana," in *Children on the Move in Africa: Past and Present Experiences of Migration*, ed. Elodie Razy and Marie Rodet (Suffolk, England: James Currey, 2016).

31. Nylander, in Government of Ghana, National Assembly, *Parliamentary Debates*, vol. 6, cols. 825–26.

32. Jonathan Zimmerman, "'Money, Materials, and Manpower': Ghanaian In-Service Teacher Education and the Political Economy of Failure, 1961–1971," *History of Education Quarterly* 51, no. 1 (2011): 1–27. See also Abena Dove Osseo-Asare, "Scientific Equity: Experiments in Laboratory Education in Ghana," *Isis: A Journal of the History of Science Society* 104, no. 4 (2013): 713–41. Osseo-Asare, for her part, is more generous in her assessment of the achievements of midcentury Ghanaian science education than Zimmerman.

33. Naaborko Sackeyfio[-Lenoch], "The Politics of Land and Urban Space in Colonial Accra," *History in Africa* 39 (2012): 293–329. On Accra's population boom, see Ioné Acquah, *Accra Survey: A Social Survey of the Capital of Ghana, Formerly Called the Gold Coast, Undertaken for the West African Institute of Social and Economic Research, 1953–1956* (London: University of London Press, 1958), 31; Bill Freund, *The African City: A History* (Cambridge: Cambridge University Press, 2007), 66.

34. R. J. H. Pogucki, *Gold Coast Land Tenure*, vol. 3, *Land Tenure in Ga Customary Law* (Accra: Government Printer, 1955), 11; S. S. Quarcoopome, "Urbanisation, Land Alienation and Politics in Accra," *Research Review*, n.s., 8, nos. 1–2 (1992): 42.

35. Quarcoopome, "Urbanisation, Land Alienation and Politics in Accra," 40–54; Quarcoopome, "A History of the Urban Development of Accra: 1877–1957," *Research Review*, n.s., 9, nos. 1–2 (1993): 20–32. See also chapter 3.

36. Kwame Nkrumah, in Republic of Ghana, National Assembly, *Parliamentary Debates*, 28 May 1957, vol. 6, col. 279.

37. Mark Crinson, "Nation-Building, Collecting and the Politics of Display: The National Museum, Ghana," *Journal of the History of Collections* 13, no. 2 (2001): 232. See also Government of Ghana, Ministry of Housing, Town and Country Planning Division, *Accra: A Plan for the Town: The Report for the Minister of Housing* (Accra: Government Printer, 1958), 73.

38. Janet Berry Hess, "Imagining Architecture: The Structure of Nationalism in Accra, Ghana," *Africa Today* 47, no. 2 (2000): 48, 54; Rhodri Windsor

Liscombe, "Modernism in Late-Imperial British West Africa: The Work of Maxwell Fry and Jane Drew, 1946–1956," *Journal of the Society of Architectural Historians* 65, no. 2 (2006): 194. The focus on a cosmopolitan architectural modernity continued well into the 1960s, as seen in Łukasz Stanek's analysis of the Ghana National Construction Corporation, which Stanek shows had a vibrant collaboration with architects and others from a range of Eastern Bloc countries. See Łukasz Stanek, "Architects from Socialist Countries in Ghana (1957–67): Modern Architecture and *Mondialisation*," *Journal of the Society of Architectural Historians* 74, no. 4 (2015): 416–42.

39. Nkrumah, in Government of Ghana, National Assembly, *Parliamentary Debates*, 28 May 1957, col. 279.

40. Keith Jopp, *Tema: Ghana's New Town and Harbour* (Accra: Ministry of Information and Broadcasting, 1961), 26, 30.

41. Ibid.; "New Gateway to Africa," *Evening News*, 8 February 1962. See also Brenda Chalfin, "La rénovation du port de Tema: Économie politique de la frontiére maritime du Ghana," *Politique Africaine* 116 (2009): 64–67.

42. Gold Coast, Census Office, *Census of Population, 1948: Reports and Tables* (Accra: Government Printing Department, 1950), 92; Republic of Ghana, Census Office, *1960 Population Census of Ghana*, vol. 1, *The Gazetteer* (Accra: Census Office, 1962), 368; Republic of Ghana, Census Office, *1970 Population Census of Ghana*, vol. 2, *Statistics of Localities and Enumeration Areas* (Accra: Census Office, 1972), 204. The 1960 and 1970 census figures include the new industrial city, the relocated fishing town (Tema Manhean), Sakumono (only listed as part of Tema District in 1970 census), and neighboring Ashaiman, where the government relocated residents of the old town not entitled to housing in Tema Manhean.

43. Jopp, *Tema*, 8. Jopp's predictions for Tema far exceeded the government's initial projections of seventy-five thousand for the new city; Public Records and Archives Administration Department (hereafter cited as PRAAD), Accra, Administrative Files (hereafter cited as ADM) 13/2/4, Minister of Housing and Town and Country Planning, "Acquisition of the Land for Tema Township," 28 February 1952.

44. David Hilling, "The Evolution of the Major Ports of West Africa," *Geographical Journal* 135, no. 3 (1969): 375, 377.

45. PRAAD-Accra, Record Group (hereafter cited as RG) 17/2/496M, Memo 15, "Policy Regarding Further Housing and Ancillary Development at Akosombo," 20 January 1962; PRAAD-Accra, RG 17/2/496I, Volta River Authority Quarterly Report, 30 July 1963; Stephan F. Miescher, "Building the City of the Future: Visions and Experiences of Modernity in Ghana's Akosombo Township," *Journal of African History* 53, no. 3 (2012), 371–76.

46. Miescher, "Building the City of the Future," 377.

47. Ibid., 378–81; Margaret Peil, "Unemployment in Tema: The Plight of the Skilled Worker," *Canadian Journal of African Studies* 3, no. 2 (1969): 409–19; Brenda Chalfin, "Public Things, Excremental Politics, and the

Infrastructure of Bare Life in Ghana's City of Tema," *American Ethnologist* 41, no. 1 (2014): 92–109.

48. PRAAD-Accra, RG 17/1/34 (Special Collections [hereafter cited as SC]/Bureau of African Affairs [hereafter cited as BAA]/114), unknown to Nkrumah, 20 July 1960.

49. Jane Drew, "Recent Work by Fry, Drew & Partners and Fry, Drew, Drake, & Lasdun in West Africa," *Architectural Design* 25 (1955): 139. See also Maxwell Fry and Jane Drew, *Tropical Architecture in the Humid Zone* (New York: Reinhold Publishing, 1956); Liscombe, "Modernism in Late-Imperial British Africa," esp. 193–204. On the continued influence of Fry and Drew's text in the 1960s, also see Stanek, "Architects from Socialist Countries in Ghana (1957–67)."

50. Hess, "Imagining Architecture."

51. Nate Plageman, "'Accra Is Changing, Isn't It?': Urban Infrastructure, Independence, and Nation in the Gold Coast's *Daily Graphic*, 1954–57," *International Journal of African Historical Studies* 43, no. 1 (2010): 148.

52. Tony Killick, "The Economics of Cocoa," in *A Study of Contemporary Ghana*, vol. 1, *The Economy of Ghana*, ed. Walter Birmingham, I. Neustadt, and E. N. Omaboe (London: George Allen and Unwin, 1966), 367. Despite changes in the currencies used in the Gold Coast/Ghana and West Africa more broadly during the period, Birmingham and his coeditors presented all their values in Ghanaian pounds. Accordingly, they note that, until the creation of the cedi in 1965, the Ghanaian pound (£G) exchanged with equivalency to the pound sterling; Birmingham, Neustadt, and Omaboe, *Study of Contemporary Ghana*, 1:8. All prices, revenues, or expenditures cited in the book will use the currency expressed in the particular source unless otherwise noted.

53. Beinecke Library, Wright Papers, Box 133, Folder 1990, Gold Coast, *Report on the Mines Department for the Year 1951–1952* (Accra: Government Printing Department, 1953); Robert L. Tignor, *W. Arthur Lewis and the Birth of Development Economics* (Princeton, NJ: Princeton University Press, 2006), 112–13.

54. Tignor, *W. Arthur Lewis*, 112. Harcourt Fuller makes a similar comparison to Nigeria; see Harcourt Fuller, *Building the Ghanaian Nation-State: Kwame Nkrumah's Symbolic Nationalism* (New York: Palgrave Macmillan, 2014), 55.

55. Tignor, *W. Arthur Lewis*, 109–43; David E. Apter, *The Gold Coast in Transition* (Princeton, NJ: Princeton University Press, 1955); Kevin K. Gaines, *American Africans in Ghana: Black Expatriates and the Civil Rights Era* (Chapel Hill: University of North Carolina Press, 2006). More broadly, the literature on midcentury modernization projects and the "development concept" is voluminous, but see in particular Frederick Cooper, "Modernizing Bureaucrats, Backward Africans, and the Development Concept," in *International Development and the Social Sciences: Essays on the History and Politics of Knowledge*, ed. Frederick Cooper and Randall Packard (Berkeley: University

of California Press, 1997); David Ekbladh, *The Great American Mission: Modernization and the Construction of an American World Order* (Princeton, NJ: Princeton University Press, 2010), esp. 153–89. For a contrasting focus historicizing community-based development ideology, see Daniel Immerwahr, *Thinking Small: The United States and the Lure of Community Development* (Cambridge, MA: Harvard University Press, 2015).

56. Howard University Moorland-Spingarn Research Center (hereafter cited as MSRC), Manuscript Division, Kwame Nkrumah Papers (hereafter cited as Nkrumah Papers), Box 154-41, Folder 13, Padmore to Nkrumah, 22 November 1951.

57. MSRC, Nkrumah Papers, Box 154-41, Folder 13, Padmore to Nkrumah, 15 November 1951.

58. For an idea of the financial and technical scale of some of the Gold Coast's major development projects (both singularly and when combined with the government's broader development agenda), see, for instance, Tema Development Corporation, *Report and Accounts for the Period Ended 31st March 1954* (Accra: Government Printer, 1955); International Bank for Reconstruction and Development, *Economic Report on Ghana*, Report No. EA-72b, 26 June 1957 (Washington, DC: Department of Operations, Europe, Africa, and Australia); PRAAD-Accra RG 17/2/992, Doxiadis Associates, *Accra-Tema-Akosombo: Final Programme and Plan for the Metropolitan Area: Summary of Report DOX-GHA 12*, 24 February 1961.

59. [Arthur] Creech Jones to V. Tewson, 31 January 1950, in Richard Rathbone, ed., *Ghana*, vol. 1, pt. 1, of *British Documents on the End of Empire*, ser. B (London: Her Majesty's Stationery Office, 1992), 240, 241. The CPP was, at least to an extent, successful in this endeavor to alleviate some of the Colonial Office's concerns about the party and Nkrumah himself, albeit namely through Nkrumah's close relationship with the Gold Coast governor, Charles Arden-Clarke; see, for example, National Archives of the United Kingdom (hereafter cited as NAUK), Cabinet Papers 129/49, Secretary of State for the Colonies, "Amendment to the Gold Coast Constitution," 9 February 1952.

60. G. W. Amarteifio, D. A. P. Butcher, and David Whitham, *Tema Manhean: A Study of Resettlement* (Accra: Ghana Universities Press, 1966), 5.

61. For Tema's earliest history in relation to the broader history of the Ga and the Gold Coast, see Carl Christian Reindorf, *History of the Gold Coast and Asante: Based on Traditions and Historical Facts, Comprising a Period of More than Three Centuries from About 1500 to 1860* (Basel: privately printed, 1895); John Parker, *Making the Town: Ga State and Society in Early Colonial Accra* (Portsmouth, NH: Heinemann, 2000), xxvi–xxvii, 2, 8–16.

62. Ivor Wilks, *Akwamu, 1640–1750: A Study of the Rise and Fall of a West African Empire* (Trondheim: Department of History, Norwegian University of Science and Technology, 2001); David K. Henderson-Quartey, *The Ga of Ghana: History and Culture of a West African People* (London: David K. Henderson-Quartey, 2002), 133, 178–203, 307–46.

63. New York Public Library (hereafter cited as NYPL), Schomburg Center for Research in Black Culture (hereafter cited as Schomburg Center), St. Clair Drake Papers (hereafter cited as Drake Papers), Box 68, Folder 2, Ernest Breakspeare Okyne, "Practical Work Report: Summer Holidays—1965–66, University of Ghana-Legon."

64. Ibid.; Amarteifio, Butcher, and Whitham, *Tema Manhean*, 29–30.

65. Gold Coast, Census Office, *Census of Population, 1948*, 92; Amarteifio, Butcher, and Whitham, *Tema Manhean*, 25.

66. Margaret J. Field, *Social Organization of the Gã People* (London: Crown Agents for the Colonies, 1940), 113–14; Madeline Manoukian, *Akan and Ga-Adangme Peoples* (London: Oxford University Press, 1950), 86–87.

67. Field notes that, at least in the 1930s, Tema maintained a "land committee" largely comprised of the town's priests and others with both secular and religious responsibilities; Field, *Social Organization of the Gã People*, 114. As Parker notes, in nearby Accra, tensions often arose between the chiefs and the priests over each other's claims to their respective rights to land, particularly as the stool holders gained greater political influence in the nineteenth century; Parker, *Making the Town*, 98–99.

68. Field, *Social Organization of the Gã People*, 113–14.

69. Parker, *Making the Town*, 5; Naaborko Sackeyfio-Lenoch, *The Politics of Chieftaincy: Authority and Property in Colonial Ghana, 1920–1950* (Rochester, NY: University of Rochester Press, 2014), 25–26.

70. Margaret J. Field, *Religion and Medicine of the Gã People* (1937; repr., London: Oxford University Press, 1961), 15. Quote from unnamed individual interviewed by Field.

71. Ibid., 14–24. As John Parker has argued, Field's treatment of Ga society largely excises political and social conflict, change, and interaction from its analysis in search of a traditional and purportedly authentic Ga way of life. The result, according to Parker, is a particularly static representation of Ga life and belief systems, as Field attempts to construct an image of an authentic Ga society in Tema founded upon a "democratic gerontocracy of priests and elders." However, in the context of midcentury Gold Coast politics and as with the work of many colonial anthropologists, key aspects of Field's representations of Ga relationships to land, religion, and social and cultural life would gain a sense of orthodoxy in the Gold Coast and among many Ga by the early 1950s. Parker, *Making the Town*, xxvii, 17, quote on xxvii.

72. Amarteifio, Butcher, and Whitham, *Tema Manhean*, 6.

73. Field, *Religion and Medicine of the Gã People*, 11.

74. Amarteifio, Butcher, and Whitham, *Tema Manhean*, 6, 21–22; Field, *Religion and Medicine of the Gã People*, 11.

75. Amarteifio, Butcher, and Whitham, *Tema Manhean*, 6.

76. PRAAD-Accra, ADM 13/2/4, Minister of Housing and Town and Country Planning, "Acquisition of the Land for Tema Township," 28 February 1952.

77. In the Legislative Assembly's debates on the initial compensation plan, members pointed to vagueness in the bill's wording as to whether the annual payment would be 3 percent of the land value in perpetuity, or only until the payments reached the £10,000 valuation; Gold Coast, Legislative Assembly, *Legislative Assembly Debates*, 1 July 1952, issue 2, cols. 343–71.

78. "Tema Lands Now Crown Property," *Daily Graphic*, 2 July 1952.

79. Peter Du Sautoy, "Administrative Problems of the Resettlement of Tema," *Journal of Management Studies* 1, no. 1 (1961): 10; Amarteifio, Butcher, and Whitham, *Tema Manhean*, 55.

80. Amarteifio, Butcher, and Whitham, *Tema Manhean*, 58–60, 62, quote on 59. Architect David Whitham estimates, from descriptions and designs, that most of Tema Manhean's residents were living two to four to a room, and many up to six or seven (62).

81. William Ofori Atta, in Gold Coast, Legislative Assembly, *Legislative Assembly Debates*, 1 July 1952, cols. 347, 348.

82. Ibid., col. 348.

83. Nii Kwabena Bonne II, in Gold Coast, Legislative Assembly, *Legislative Assembly Debates*, 1 July 1952, col. 349.

84. "Tema Harbour Not Necessary—Aduamah," *Daily Graphic*, 22 July 1952.

85. "Tema Chief was Not Consulted," *Daily Graphic*, 9 July 1952.

86. E. W. Adjaye, "Tema People to Sell Land," *Daily Graphic*, 8 August 1952.

87. For the most succinct narrative of the protests, see Amarteifio, Butcher, and Whitham, *Tema Manhean*, 5–20; Du Sautoy, "Administrative Problems in the Resettlement of Tema," 10–13. See also interview with Samuel Kofi Kotey, Tema, Greater Accra, 14 February 2009; interview with Seth Laryea Tettey, Tema, Greater Accra, 19 February 2009.

88. Interview with Kotey, Tema, Greater Accra, 14 February 2009.

89. Du Sautoy, "Administrative Problems of the Resettlement of Tema," 11.

90. Ibid., 10–11.

91. Amarteifio, Butcher, and Whitham, *Tema Manhean*, 25.

92. Du Sautoy, "Administrative Problems of the Resettlement of Tema," 11.

93. Interview with Kotey, Tema, Greater Accra, 14 February 2009.

94. Interview with Tettey, Tema, Greater Accra, 19 February 2009.

95. Amarteifio, Butcher, and Whitham, *Tema Manhean*, 18.

96. See, for instance, I. Neustadt and E. N. Omaboe, *Social and Economic Survey of Tema: Report* (Accra: Office of the Government Statistician, 1959); Doxiadis Associates, *Tema: A Social Survey* (Tema: Doxiadis Associates, Ghana Offices, 1962); NYPL, Schomburg Center, Drake Papers, Box 68, Folder 2, Okyne, "Practical Work Report"; Amarteifio, Butcher, and Whitham, *Tema Manhean*.

97. Otto Koenigsberger, foreword to Amarteifio, Butcher, and Whitham, *Tema Manhean*, v.

98. Beinecke Library, Wright Papers, Box 22, Folder 343, Wright, Travel Journal, 17 July 1953.

99. Ibid. The emphasis Wright places on the centrality of modernization to the decolonization process was also central to his analysis of the politics underpinning the 1955 Bandung Conference. See the journal he kept during his travels to Bandung; Beinecke Library, Wright Papers, Box 29, Folder 417, Wright, Travel Journal, 3 February to 15 April 1955. See also Gaines, *American Africans in Ghana*, 52–76.

100. NYPL, Schomburg Center, Drake Papers, Box 66, Folder 1, Drake interview with J. B. Danquah (notes), 1 February 1955. On Drake's academic appointment, see Gaines, *American Africans in Ghana*, 90–91.

101. NYPL, Schomburg Center, Drake Papers, Box 66, Folder 1, Drake interview with J. B. Danquah (notes), 1 February 1955. Richard Wright provided a similar view of Danquah after meeting him in 1953. According to Wright, Danquah "does not like the modern world and, disliking it, he wants none of it. . . . I outlined the role of industry, its impact upon the lives and personalities of man, and he was wary and skeptical, [and] wanted to know if that was really what was behind all the upheaval in the world." Beinecke Library, Wright Papers, Box 22, Folder 344, Wright, Travel Journal, 29 July 1953.

102. "A New Gold Coast," *Evening News*, 3 April 1956.

103. Amarteifio, Butcher, and Whitham, *Tema Manhean*, 59.

104. Ibid., 59–65. On Gold Coast/Ghanaian cooking habits, see Faye Woodard Grant, *The Nutrition and Health of Children in the Gold Coast* (Chicago: University of Chicago Press, 1955), 6; Ioné Acquah, *Accra Survey*, 47. On the CPP's idealization of the modern kitchen, see Ahlman, "Africa's Kitchen Debate."

105. NYPL, Schomburg Center, Drake Papers, Box 70, Folder 3, E. A. Colecraft, "Daybook-Tema," 12 July 1960.

106. Interview with Kotey, Tema, Greater Accra, 14 February 2009.

107. Interview with Tettey, Tema, Greater Accra, 19 February 2009.

108. Ibid.

109. Ibid.; interview with Kotey, Tema, Greater Accra, 14 February 2009. For the perspective of an individual who arrived to Tema with his family in the 1950s, see, among the many surveys and interviews conducted by teams from the University of Ghana Department of Sociology, NYPL, Schomburg Center, Drake Papers, Box 69, Folder 1, E. A. Colecraft, "Tema Diary," 31 July 1959. See also interview with Benjamin Dodoo, Tema, Greater Accra, 18 February 2009.

110. NYPL, Schomburg Center, Drake Papers, Box 69, Folder, 4, Alfred A. Mensah, "What I Think the City of Tema Will be Like Five Years from Now," Tema New Town, 1959.

111. NYPL, Schomburg Center, Drake Papers, Box 70, Folder 2, P. K. Arhin, "Interviewing Associational Leaders," 1959.

112. NYPL, Schomburg Center, Drake Papers, Box 69, Folder 6, E. W. Okyere-Boakye interview with Reverend Minister Mr. Bannerman, "No. 2 Interview on Associational Structure," [1959?].

113. Jean Allman, "'Hewers of Wood, Carriers of Water': Islam, Class, and Politics on the Eve of Ghana's Independence," *African Studies Review* 34, no. 2 (1991): 2.

114. Kate Skinner, "Reading, Writing, and Rallies: The Politics of 'Freedom' in Southern British Togoland, 1953–1956," *Journal of African History* 48, no. 1 (2007): 123–47; Skinner, *The Fruits of Freedom in British Togoland: Literacy, Politics, and Nationalism, 1914–2014* (Cambridge: Cambridge University Press, 2015), 122–67. See also D. E. K. Amenumey, *The Ewe Unification Movement: A Political History* (Accra: Ghana Universities Press, 1989); Paul Nugent, *Smugglers, Secessionists, and Loyal Citizens on the Ghana-Togo Frontier: The Lie of the Borderlands since 1914* (Athens: Ohio University Press, 2002), 176–98. Relatedly, for the development of Ewe politics in French Togoland and their periodic reaches beyond the border, also see Benjamin N. Lawrance, *Locality, Mobility, and "Nation": Periurban Colonialism in Togo's Eweland, 1900–1960* (Rochester, NY: University of Rochester Press, 2007).

115. Northern People's Party, *The Constitution* (1954), in Commonwealth Political Ephemera from the Institute of Commonwealth Studies, University of London, Phase I: Africa, Part 4: West Africa, Ghana, PP7, Fiche 10. See also Carola Lentz, "'The Time When Politics Came': Ghana's Decolonisation from the Perspective of a Rural Periphery," *Journal of Contemporary African Studies* 20, no. 2 (2002): 245–74.

116. Killick, "Economics of Cocoa," 369; Allman, *Quills of the Porcupine*, 26–27. The producer price for cocoa reached its high of 149 shillings per load in the 1951–52, 1955–56, and 1956–57 fiscal years.

117. Allman, *Quills of the Porcupine*, 26–28.

118. Kwame Nkrumah, "Movement for Colonial Freedom," *Phylon* 16, no. 4 (1955): 400–1; Allman, *Quills of the Porcupine*, 26, 39. See also Björn Beckman, "Government Policy and the Distribution of Cocoa Income in Ghana, 1951–1966," in *The Economics of Cocoa Production and Marketing: Proceedings of the Cocoa Economics Research Conference, Legon, April 1973*, ed. R. A. Kotey, C. Okali, and B. E. Rourke (Legon: Institute of Statistical, Social, and Economic Research, University of Ghana, 1973), 277–85.

119. Untitled song reproduced in Allman, *Quills of the Porcupine*, 38. The literature on the Gold Coast cocoa revolution is vast, but see, for example, Gwendolyn Mikell, *Cocoa and Chaos in Ghana* (New York: Paragon House, 1989).

120. Allman, *Quills of the Porcupine*, 38 and, more broadly, 28, 36–40.

121. Richard Rathbone, "The Government of the Gold Coast after the Second World War," *African Affairs* 67, no. 268 (1968): 210.

122. T. C. McCaskie, "Asante Origins, Egypt, and the Near East: An Idea and Its History," in *Recasting the Past: History Writing and Political Work in*

Modern Africa, ed. Derek R. Peterson and Giacomo Macola (Athens: Ohio University Press, 2009), 125–34.

123. Ibid., 128–29. See also Philip Curtin, *The Image of Africa: British Ideas and Actions, 1780–1850*, 2 vols. (Madison: University of Wisconsin Press, 1964), 257.

124. McCaskie, "Asante Origins, Egypt, and the Near East," 134–37.

125. B. F. Kusi, in Gold Coast, Legislative Assembly, *Legislative Assembly Debates*, 9 November 1953, issue 3, col. 220. Kusi's declaration remains one of the most cited pronouncements in the late-colonial Gold Coast Legislative Assembly, including in D. Austin, *Politics in Ghana*, 178, and Allman, *Quills of the Porcupine*, 22.

126. Kusi, in Gold Coast, Legislative Assembly, *Legislative Assembly Debates*, 9 November 1953, issue 3, col. 219.

127. Allman, *Quills of the Porcupine*, 16–50. For Allman's discussion of the social category of *nkwankwaa*, which largely denotes a class in a state of "uneasy subordination to elder or chiefly authority," see 28–36, quote on 29.

128. Ibid., 61–65, quote on 63. For the most complete analysis of the evolution of the NLM's political message and agenda, see Allman, *Quills of the Porcupine*.

129. R. J. Vile, Memorandum on Visit to Gold Coast, 4 October 1955, in Rathbone, *Ghana*, vol. 1, pt. 2, 113.

130. PRAAD-Accra, RG 17/1/30 (SC/BAA/327), Kofi Akowuah to Nkrumah et al., Bekwai, 30 November 1955; PRAAD-Accra, RG 17/2/689, Isaac Kwakye to Nkrumah, Kumasi, 15 May 1956; Allman, *Quills of the Porcupine*, 51–83.

131. Allman, *Quills of the Porcupine*, 64.

132. For a description of what this meant for families divided by this political conflict, see interview with Kwasi Assiore, Accra, 28 April 2008. Looking at party registration and polling numbers, Richard Rathbone casts doubt on the reliability of both the archival record and people's memories of the intensity and effects of these rivalries on families and communities; Rathbone, *Nkrumah and the Chiefs: The Politics of Chieftaincy in Ghana, 1951–1960* (Athens: Ohio University Press, 2000), 93–94.

133. Interview with K. S. P. Jantuah (formerly J. E. Jantuah), Accra, 26 April 2008; Allman, *Quills of the Porcupine*, 18.

134. PRAAD-Accra, RG 17/1/30 (SC/BAA/327), Ahantahene to Nkrumah, Busua, 27 October 1955.

135. PRAAD-Accra, RG 17/1/485 (SC/BAA/147), S. Okoh to Nkrumah, "Memorandum on the Political Situation in Wassaw South & Central Constituencies," [1955/1956?].

136. Maxwell Owusu, *Uses and Abuses of Political Power: A Case Study of Continuity and Change in the Politics of Ghana*, 2nd ed. (Accra: Ghana Universities Press, 2006), 215, 226.

137. PRAAD-Accra, RG 17/2/689, unknown to Nkrumah, Anloga, 23 March 1956. Emphasis in original. Austin traces the rumors of Nkrumah's

supposed Liberian roots to a reference in the prime minister's autobiography about his father being a goldsmith; Austin, *Politics in Ghana*, 376n16.

138. PRAAD-Accra, RG 17/1/53 (SC/BAA/115), Kwaku Duah to Arthur Creech Jones, Kumasi, 9 March 1955.

139. PRAAD-Accra, RG 17/1/53 (SC/BAA/115), Chairman of the Conference to Nkrumah, "Resolution on the Ashanti Secession Idea," Sunyani, 11 March 1956. See also interview with Owusu Brempong, Legon, Greater Accra, 7 July 2008; Owusu Brempong, "Oral Tradition in Ghana: The History of Bonokyempim and Techiman Politics," *Research Review*, supplement 13 ([1998?]): i–73. More broadly, on the political tensions (traditional and national) surrounding the creation and governance of the Brong Ahafo Region, specifically as it relates to pro- and anti-Asante chieftaincy disputes in Ahafo, see John Dunn and A. F. Robertson, *Dependence and Opportunity: Political Change in Ahafo* (Cambridge: Cambridge University Press, 1973).

140. Paul André Ladouceur, *Chiefs and Politicians: The Politics of Regionalism in Northern Ghana* (London: Longman, 1979), 124. See also Skinner, *Fruits of Freedom in British Togoland*, 157–59.

141. Enid Schildkrout, *People of the Zongo: The Transformation of Ethnic Identities in Ghana* (Cambridge: Cambridge University Press, 1978), 208 and, more broadly, 206–14.

142. "Policy Statement of Dr. Nkrumah at West End Arena on June 12, 1955," *Ashanti Sentinel*, 17 June 1955.

143. MSRC, Nkrumah Papers, Box 154-41, Folder 14, Padmore to J. G. (Markham?), ca. April 1953.

144. Beinecke Library, Wright Papers, Box 103, Folder 1522, Padmore to Wright, 12 April 1956. See also Folder 1522, Padmore to Wright, 5 March 1956.

145. W. Arthur Lewis, *Report on Industrialisation and the Gold Coast* (Accra: Government Printing Department, 1953); Tignor, *W. Arthur Lewis*, 123–27.

146. Princeton University Archives, W. Arthur Lewis Papers, Box 10, Folder 3, Lewis to Nkrumah, 13 April 1956. On the Volta River Project, see Stephan F. Miescher, "'Nkrumah's Baby': The Akosombo Dam and the Dream of Development in Ghana, 1952–1966," *Water History* 6, no. 4 (2014): 341–66.

147. NAUK, Dominions Office (hereafter cited as DO) 201/6, United Kingdom High Commissioner in South Africa to Captain Crookshank, "Financial and Economic Report," 19 September 1955. The South African authorities, for their part, tended to blame the Gold Coast, which they viewed as being caught up in an "experiment" they dismissively referred to as "Socialist Utopianism," with "the whole of Africa to-day being in a turbulent state." NAUK, DO 201/5, "South African Views on United Kingdom Policy in British Territories," ca. 1954.

148. "Now is the Hour: Crush Imperialism Now," *Evening News*, 16 July 1956. See also Convention People's Party, "Operation Independence: Convention People's Party for the General Election, July 1956," in Documents

on African Political History, 1938–1970, comp. Ruth Schachter Morgenthau (Waltham, MA: Cooperative Africana Microfilm Project), reel 5.

149. "Which Path? (4)," *Ashanti Pioneer*, 2 July 1956.

150. Kwame, "Vote N.L.M.: Ashantis and the Election," *Ashanti Pioneer*, 2 July 1956. For detailed analyses of both the NLM and CPP's arguments in the buildup to the election (to which this account owes a heavy debt), see D. Austin, *Politics in Ghana*, 323–40; Allman, *Quills of the Porcupine*, 147–52.

151. Allman, in her analysis of the election results, emphasizes the surprise felt by many by the lack of violence accompanying the election; Allman, *Quills of the Porcupine*, 152.

152. D. Austin, *Politics in Ghana*, 354.

153. Interview with Jantuah, Accra, 26 April 2008.

154. D. Austin, *Politics in Ghana*, 354; Allman, *Quills of the Porcupine*, 152. For their broader discussions of the election results and the vote's aftermath, see Austin's analysis, 347–55, and Allman's, 5, 152–60.

155. PRAAD-Accra, ADM 13/1/25, Cabinet Minutes, 19 September 1956.

156. See, for instance, Allman's treatment of the NLM's post-election activism and the Colonial Office's response; Allman, *Quills of the Porcupine*, 162–75.

157. Ibid., 157–58.

158. Rathbone, *Nkrumah and the Chiefs*, 93–94.

159. For a reflection on the centralization of CPP power in the 1950s with a focus on local government, see Richard Rathbone, "Things Fall Apart: The Erosion of Local Government, Local Justice and Civil Rights in Ghana, 1955–60," in *The British Empire in the 1950s: Retreat or Revival?*, ed. Martin Lynn (New York: Palgrave Macmillan, 2006).

CHAPTER 3: A NEW TYPE OF CITIZEN

1. Public Records and Archives Administration Department (hereafter cited as PRAAD), Kumasi, Ashanti Regional Archives (hereafter cited as ARG) 17/11/3, "Speech Delivered by Comrade Mary Osei, District Commissioner Kumasi North at the Opening of the Young Pioneers Cadre Instructors Course, Asawase, 21st June, 1963."

2. "Pan-Africa: International Confab Here," *Evening News*, 18 April 1957. As noted in the *Evening News* article, the conference was originally intended to occur in October 1957.

3. On the Conference of Independent African States, see PRAAD-Accra, Record Group (hereafter cited as RG) 8/2/772, Conference of Independent African States, *Confidential Report* (1958). See also the selection of files on the conference's planning held in the file folder PRAAD-Accra, RG 17/1/118 (Special Collections [hereafter cited as SC]/Bureau of African Affairs [hereafter cited as BAA]/136), "Conference of Independent African States." An invitation to participate was also sent to South Africa. However, the apartheid government refused to do so without further representation

from Europe. For a broader discussion of the diplomatic planning of the conference, see W. Scott Thompson, *Ghana's Foreign Policy, 1957–1966: Diplomacy, Ideology, and the New State* (Princeton, NJ: Princeton University Press, 1969), 31–34.

4. For a partial list of the AAPC delegations and attendees, see PRAAD-Accra, Administrative Files (hereafter cited as ADM) 16/11, "All-African People's Conference News Bulletin, vol. 1, no. 5: List of Delegations, Heads of Delegations, and Delegates."

5. On the AAPC, see Edwin S. Munger, *All-African People's Conference: Africa for Africans Only Demanded by 240 Delegates from 28 African Countries*, West Africa Series, vol. 3, no. 1 (New York: American Universities Field Staff, 1959); Jan-Bart Gewald, *Hands Off Africa!! An Overview and Analysis of the Ideological, Political, and Socio-Economic Approaches to African Unity Expressed at the First All-African People's Conference held in Accra, Ghana, in December 1958* (n.p.: n.p., 1990); Jeffrey S. Ahlman, "The Algerian Question in Nkrumah's Ghana, 1958–1960: Debating 'Violence' and 'Nonviolence' in African Decolonization," *Africa Today* 57, no. 2 (2010): 73–76.

6. On the much under-researched Ghana-Guinea Union, see Thompson, *Ghana's Foreign Policy*, 67–73.

7. Ako Adjei, in Republic of Ghana, National Assembly, *Parliamentary Debates*, 1 May 1957, vol. 6, col. 110.

8. For the National Assembly debates defining Ghanaian citizenship, see Government of Ghana, National Assembly, *Parliamentary Debates*, 30 April 1957, vol. 6, cols. 60–100; *Parliamentary Debates*, 1 May 1957, cols. 109–19; *Parliamentary Debates*, 2 May 1957, vol. 6, cols. 167–200.

9. Government of Ghana, National Assembly, *Parliamentary Debates*, 1 July 1957, vol. 6, cols. 1537, 1661–68; *Parliamentary Debates*, 3 July 1957, vol. 6, cols. 1668–81; *Parliamentary Debates*, 8 July 1957, vol. 6, cols. 1844–46.

10. Ashanti Command to Nkrumah, "The Unknown Warriors," Kumasi, 26 July 1962, in Ivor Wilks–Phyllis Ferguson Collection of Materials on Ghana (hereafter cited as Wilks-Ferguson Collection), Reel 1. See also Jean Allman, *The Quills of the Porcupine: Asante Nationalism in an Emergent Ghana* (Madison: University of Wisconsin Press, 1993), 190.

11. Ashanti Command to Nkrumah, "The Unknown Warriors," Kumasi, 26 July 1962, in Wilks-Ferguson Collection, Reel 1.

12. Ako Adjei, in Government of Ghana, National Assembly, *Parliamentary Debates*, 3 May 1957, vol. 6, cols. 127–28.

13. Dennis Austin, *Politics in Ghana, 1946–1960* (London: Oxford University Press, 1964), 373–77; S. S. Quarcoopome, "Urbanisation, Land Alienation and Politics in Accra," *Research Review*, n.s., 8, nos. 1–2 (1992): 47–49.

14. Quarcoopome, "Urbanisation, Land Alienation and Politics in Accra," 47.

15. Jennifer Hart, "'One Man, No Chop': Licit Wealth, Good Citizens, and the Criminalization of Drivers in Postcolonial Ghana," *International Journal*

of African Historical Studies 46, no. 3 (2013): 381–83. See also J. Hart, *Ghana on the Go: African Mobility in the Age of Motor Transportation* (Bloomington: Indiana University Press, 2016).

16. D. Austin, *Politics in Ghana*, 375–76.

17. On the CPP's ambitions and their effects on individuals and families who had lived in the Gold Coast for at least more than one generation, see Richard Rathbone, *Nkrumah and the Chiefs: The Politics of Chieftaincy in Ghana, 1951–1960* (Athens: Ohio University Press, 2000), 100–12.

18. Kate Skinner, *The Fruits of Freedom in British Togoland: Literacy, Politics, and Nationalism, 1914–2014* (Cambridge: Cambridge University Press, 2015), 170.

19. Paul Nugent, *Smugglers, Secessionists, and Loyal Citizens on the Ghana-Togo Frontier: The Lie of the Borderlands since 1914* (Athens: Ohio University Press, 2002), 215–16.

20. Skinner, *Fruits of Freedom in British Togoland*, 168–207.

21. D. Austin, *Politics in Ghana*, 376n17. Such vigilantism is not dissimilar to that analyzed by James Brennan in the TANU Youth League in Dar es Salaam; Brennan, "Youth, the TANU Youth League and Managed Vigilantism in Dar es Salaam, 1925–73," *Africa* 76, no. 2 (2006): 221–46.

22. PRAAD-Accra, ADM 13/1/26, Cabinet Minutes, 30 April 1957.

23. See, for instance, "Aspire to be True Leaders of Africa — Osagyefo Tells Youth," *Evening News*, 2 October 1961; "All African Youth Conference: Africa Needs a Dynamic Youth Movement — Osagyefo," *Evening News*, 13 October 1961.

24. For related debates in Tanzania, see Andrew Burton, "Raw Youth, School-Leavers and the Emergence of Structural Unemployment in Late-Colonial Urban Tanganyika," *Journal of African History* 47, no. 3 (2006): 363–87. On the cultural politics of youth in Ghana, see Stephan F. Miescher, *Making Men in Ghana* (Bloomington: Indiana University Press, 2005), esp. 1–83; Nate Plageman, *Highlife Saturday Night: Popular Music and Social Change in Urban Ghana* (Bloomington: Indiana University Press, 2012), 6–13.

25. PRAAD-Accra, ADM 13/2/1, Minister of Health and Labour, "Registration and Direction of Labour," Cabinet Memorandum, 5 July 1951; Gold Coast, Department of Social Welfare and Community Development, *Problem Children of the Gold Coast* (Accra: Department of Social Welfare and Community Development, 1955); PRAAD-Accra, ADM 13/2/40, Minutes of Cabinet Committee on the Proposed Builders Brigade, 2 August 1957, appendix to Minister of Labour, Cooperatives, and Social Welfare, "The Builders Brigade," Cabinet Memorandum, 20 August 1957. The literature on colonial and postcolonial discourse surrounding the "youth problem" in Africa is growing rapidly. See, for example, Andrew Burton, "Urchins, Loafers and the Cult of the Cowboy: Urbanization and Delinquency in Dar es Salaam, 1919–61," *Journal of African History* 42, no. 2 (2001): 199–216; Chloe Campbell, "Juvenile Delinquency in Colonial Kenya, 1900–1939," *Historical Journal* 45, no. 1

(2002): 129–51; Laurent Fourchard, "Lagos and the Invention of Juvenile Delinquency in Nigeria, 1920–60," *Journal of African History* 47, no. 1 (2006): 115–37; Paul Ocobock, "'Joy Rides for Juveniles': Vagrant Youth and Colonial Control in Nairobi, Kenya, 1901–52," *Social History* 31, no. 1 (2006): 39–59; Abosede A. George, *Making Modern Girls: A History of Girlhood, Labor, and Social Development in Colonial Lagos* (Athens: Ohio University Press, 2014).

26. PRAAD-Accra, ADM 13/2/37, Minister of Trade and Labour, "National Builders Brigade," 30 April 1957; PRAAD-Accra, ADM 13/2/38, "Draft White Paper," appendix to Minister of Trade and Labour, "National Builders Brigade," 23 May 1957; PRAAD-Accra, ADM 13/2/38, Minister of Commerce and Industry, "National Workers Brigade," 31 May 1957; PRAAD-Accra, ADM 13/2/38, "Draft White Paper: National Workers Brigade," appendix to Minister of Commerce and Industry, "National Workers Brigade," Cabinet Memorandum, 31 May 1957.

27. PRAAD-Accra, ADM 13/2/38, Minister of Commerce and Industry, "National Workers Brigade," Cabinet Memorandum, 31 May 1957.

28. Ibid.; PRAAD-Accra, ADM 13/2/38, "Draft White Paper: National Workers Brigade," appendix to Minister of Commerce and Industry, "National Workers Brigade," Cabinet Memorandum, 31 May 1957.

29. PRAAD-Accra, ADM 13/2/37, Minister of Trade and Labour, "National Builders Brigade," 30 April 1957.

30. PRAAD-Accra, ADM 13/2/38, "Draft White Paper: National Workers Brigade," appendix to Minister of Commerce and Industry, "National Workers Brigade," Cabinet Memorandum, 31 May 1957.

31. PRAAD-Accra, ADM 13/2/44, Minister of Labour and Co-operatives, "Recommendations by the I.C.A. Advisor regarding the Principles to be Adopted with the Expansion of the Builders Brigade," Cabinet Memorandum, 14 January 1958; PRAAD-Accra RG 14/1/15, Gersbacher, "Report on the Ghana Workers Brigade/Foundation and Progress," 1965.

32. PRAAD-Accra, ADM 13/2/43, Minister of Labour and Cooperatives, "The Builders Brigade: Progress Report," Cabinet Memorandum, 3 December 1957.

33. For a survey of the relatively short-lived relationship between the Nkrumah government and Israel, which persisted until 1961 when Ghana joined Egypt and several other radical North African states as part of the Casablanca Group of African states, see Zach Levey, "The Rise and Decline of a Special Relationship: Israel and Ghana, 1957–1966," *African Studies Review* 46, no. 1 (2003): 155–77. Additionally, as Paul Bjerk and Priya Lal separately show, in Tanzania in the 1960s the government of Julius Nyerere also looked to Israel for guidance and support for its villagization project; Paul Bjerk, *Building a Peaceful Nation: Julius Nyerere and the Establishment of Sovereignty in Tanzania, 1960–1964* (Rochester, NY: University of Rochester Press, 2015), 127–30; Priya Lal, *African Socialism in Postcolonial Tanzania: Between the Village and the World* (Cambridge: Cambridge University Press, 2015), 48–51.

34. PRAAD-Accra, RG 17/1/80 (SC/BAA/121), Ben-Gurion to Nkrumah, Jerusalem, 16 August 1957.

35. Adjingboru A. Syme, *Salute to Israel: The Story of the Ghana Youth Delegation to Israel, 1957* (Accra: Guinea Press, 1958), 32, 33.

36. Ibid., 12.

37. Ibid., 17–19, quote on 17.

38. PRAAD-Accra, RG 17/1/80 (SC/BAA/121), "Youth and Nahal Department of Zahal (Israel's Defence Army)," n.d.; PRAAD-Accra, RG 17/1/80 (SC/BAA/121), "Educational Activities of Zahal (Israel's Defence Army)," n.d.; PRAAD-Accra, RG 17/1/80 (SC/BAA/121), "Farming Near the Aqaba Border," appendix to Chanan Yavor to Nkrumah, 11 May 1957.

39. PRAAD-Accra, ADM 13/2/43, Minister of Labour and Cooperatives, "The Builders Brigade," Cabinet Memorandum, 3 December 1957.

40. See, for instance, Nate Plageman's discussion of the Builders Brigade Band in *Highlife Saturday Night*, 168–69.

41. Interview with E. B. Mensah, Accra, 8 June 2008.

42. Interview with Yaa Fosuawaa, Koforidua, Eastern Region, 25 May 2008. See also interview with Ben A. Nikoi-Oltai, Accra, 19 January 2008; interview with Samuel Kofi Kotey, Tema, Greater Accra, 14 February 2009.

43. Interview with Fosuawaa, Koforidua, Eastern Region, 25 May 2008.

44. Ibid.; interview with Owusu Brempong, Legon, Greater Accra, 7 July 2008.

45. Interview with Fosuawaa, Koforidua, Eastern Region, 25 May 2008.

46. Ibid. See also Jeffrey S. Ahlman, "A New Type of Citizen: Youth, Gender, and Generation in the Ghanaian Builders Brigade," *Journal of African History* 53, no. 1 (2012): 96–98.

47. For the politics and tensions surrounding women's work in Nkrumah-era Ghana and its relationship to other midcentury socialist regimes, see chapter 5 and Jeffrey S. Ahlman, "Africa's Kitchen Debate: Ghanaian Domestic Space in the Age of Cold War," in *Gender, Sexuality, and the Cold War: A Global Perspective*, ed. Philip E. Muehlenbeck (Nashville, TN: Vanderbilt University Press, 2017).

48. Interview with Brempong, Legon, Greater Accra, 7 July 2008.

49. Interview with Mensah, Accra, 8 June 2008.

50. PRAAD-Accra, RG 14/1/3, A. J. Dowuona-Hammond, "Speech by the Minister of Labour and Co-operatives at the Builders Brigade Board Meeting," 24 April 1958.

51. PRAAD-Accra, RG 14/1/2, "Builders Brigade, Development Plan (Draft)," [1958?]; PRAAD-Accra, RG 14/1/1, "Notes Regarding Co-operation by the Builders Brigade with the Liquidators of the Gonja Development Company and the Ministry of Agriculture in a Tobacco Farming Scheme," 1958.

52. Such imagery also laid the basis for today's largely nostalgic memory of the agricultural potential and output of the brigade. For such representations of the Builders/Workers Brigade, see, for instance, interview with Nikoi-Oltai,

19 January 2008; interview with S. Kofi Asiedu, Accra, 16 March 2008; interview with Fosuawaa, Koforidua, Eastern Region, 25 May 2008; interview with Emmanuel Darko, Koforidua, Eastern Region, 25 May 2008.

53. PRAAD-Accra, ADM 13/2/44, Minister of Labour and Cooperatives, "Recommendations by the I.C.A. Advisor Regarding the Principles to be Adopted with the Expansion of the Builders Brigade," Cabinet Memorandum, 16 January 1958.

54. Dowuona-Hammond, in Government of Ghana, National Assembly, *Parliamentary Debates*, 18 June 1959, vol. 15, col. 203.

55. Dowuona-Hammond, in Government of Ghana, National Assembly, *Parliamentary Debates*, 4 March 1959, vol. 14, col. 186; Dowuona-Hammond, *Parliamentary Debates*, 18 June 1959, col. 224.

56. PRAAD-Accra, RG 14/1/15, Gersbacher, "Report on Ghana Workers Brigade/Foundation and Development," [1965?]; PRAAD-Accra, RG 14/1/15, "Workers Brigade—Notes Taken at a Meeting in the Principal Secretary's Office—Ministry of Defence," Minutes, 14 March 1966; PRAAD-Accra, RG 14/1/15, "The Workers Brigade," n.d. In his report, likely undertaken in 1965, Gersbacher places the number of camps at fifty-two. However, another report on the Brigade—undated but clearly from the late Nkrumah period—notes thirty-eight camps in the country.

57. "Work Harder, Gambrah Enjoins School Children," *Ashanti Pioneer*, 14 March 1957; Kofi Akrasi, "School Girls," *Ashanti Pioneer*, 13 May 1957; Cyprian Asare Bediakoh, "School Pupils," *Ashanti Pioneer*, 28 May 1957; "Essence of Independence is Self-Help," *Evening News*, 3 December 1957. The themes of national service and social support became particularly prominent in the Ghanaian press post-1960; see, for instance, "The Youth Must be Made to Appreciate Our Culture," *Evening News*, 16 March 1962; "Children Should Have Good Training," *Evening News*, 3 June 1964.

58. PRAAD-Accra, ADM 13/1/26, Cabinet Minutes, 12 November 1957. See also Jeremy Pool, "Now Is the Time of Youth: Youth, Nationalism and Cultural Change in Ghana, 1940–1966" (PhD diss., Emory University, 2009), 221–22.

59. Pool, "Now Is the Time of Youth," 222. For the wording of the pledge of loyalty, see PRAAD-Accra, ADM 13/1/27, Cabinet Minutes, 5 August 1958.

60. Howard University Moorland-Spingarn Research Center, Manuscript Division, Kwame Nkrumah Papers, Box 154-41, Folder 14, Padmore to Nkrumah, 5 August 1955.

61. Interview with M. N. Tetteh, Accra, 8 March 2008. See also M. N. Tetteh, *The Ghana Young Pioneer Movement: A Youth Organisation in the Kwame Nkrumah Era* (Tema: Ghana Publicity, 1999), 49–52. As with the East African experience studied by Timothy H. Parsons, the Boy Scouts in the Gold Coast and Ghana remained incredibly popular among Gold Coast/Ghanaian boys in the mid- and late 1950s, in many ways delaying the Nkrumah government's formation of its own Ghanaian youth organization; Parsons, *Race*,

Resistance, and the Boy Scout Movement in British Colonial Africa (Athens: Ohio University Press, 2004). See also below for popular comparisons between the Boy Scout and Young Pioneer experience.

62. Interview with M. N. Tetteh, Accra, 8 March 2008. See also PRAAD-Accra, RG 3/5/2115, P. K. K. Quaidoo, "Draft Cabinet Memorandum: Legislation to Provide for the Establishment of the Ghana Young Pioneer Authority (GYPA)," 19 August 1960.

63. Syme, *Salute to Israel*, 17–19; Catriona Kelly, *Children's World: Growing Up in Russia, 1890–1991* (New Haven, CT: Yale University Press, 2007), 62, 547–55; Matthias Neumann, *The Communist Youth League and the Transformation of the Soviet Union, 1917–1932* (New York: Routledge, 2011), 87–88. See also Alexei Yurchak, *Everything Was Forever, Until It Was No More: The Last Soviet Generation* (Princeton, NJ: Princeton University Press, 2006).

64. On the Soviet uniforms, see Merle Fainsod, "The Komsomols—A Study of Youth under Dictatorship," *American Political Science Review* 45, no. 1 (1951): 28; Kelly, *Children's World*, 551. The Ghanaian uniform distinguished itself from the Soviet one with its use of khaki-colored materials, whereas the Soviet uniform included a white shirt, red neckerchief, and dark blue skirts and trousers. The Ghanaian uniform also contained a scarf, "which," according to the *Evening News*, was "red bordered with white and green [to] remind members of their affiliation to the Party, loyalty to the Government and duty to the nation." See "The Role of Ghana Young Pioneers," *Evening News*, 14 June 1962.

65. Kwame Nkrumah, "Memorandum on the Young Pioneers," 4 August 1959, quoted in Emily Watts Card, "The Politics of Underdevelopment: From Voluntary Associations to Party Auxiliaries in Ghana" (PhD diss., Columbia University, 1972), 227.

66. PRAAD-Accra, RG 3/5/2115, Prime Minister, "Financial Provisions for Young Pioneers," Cabinet Memorandum, 17 June 1960.

67. PRAAD-Accra, RG 3/5/2115, Quaidoo, "Ghana Young Pioneers Authority Draft Instructions," 19 August 1960. See Jay Straker, *Youth, Nationalism, and the Guinean Revolution* (Bloomington: Indiana University Press, 2009); Mike McGovern, *Unmasking the State: Making Guinea Modern* (Chicago: University of Chicago Press, 2013).

68. PRAAD-Accra, RG 3/5/2115, Prime Minister, "Financial Provisions for Young Pioneers"; "Pioneers to Have 4 Grades," *Daily Graphic*, 28 April 1962; Charles A. Ballard Jr., "A Contemporary Youth Movement: The Ghana Young Pioneers" (master's thesis, University of Ghana, Legon, 1967), 29–30, 104.

69. Charles A. Ballard Jr., "A Contemporary Youth Movement," 29.

70. PRAAD-Accra, RG 3/5/2115, Prime Minister, "Financial Provisions for Young Pioneers"; Ballard, "Contemporary Youth Movement," 29–30, 104.

71. For a breakdown of the training program for Young Pioneer instructors, see PRAAD-Accra, RG 3/5/2115, "Programme for Senior Officers' Course of the Ghana Young Pioneers," n.d. Relatedly, also see interview with M. N. Tetteh, 8 March 2008.

72. PRAAD-Sunyani, Brong Ahafo Regional Archives (hereafter cited as BRG), 1/12/3, G. A. K. Bansah, "Osagyefo," 1965; PRAAD-Kumasi, ARG 17/5/9, S. Geoffrey Boateng, "Kwame Atoapoma," May 1964.

73. PRAAD-Kumasi, ARG 17/1/36, "Osagyefo Dr. Kwame Nkrumah— The Initiator of African Freedom & Personality," n.d.

74. Interview with Kwasi Assiore, Accra, 24 April 2008.

75. PRAAD-Kumasi, ARG 17/1/20, "Ghana Young Pioneers Code and Me," n.d.

76. Interview with Assiore, Accra, 24 April 2008.

77. PRAAD-Kumasi, ARG 17/6/6, R. O. Frimpong Mansa, "Address by the Regional Organizer of the Ghana Young Pioneers to Asanteman Secondary School: Socialism versus Capitalism," 26 January 1962.

78. PRAAD-Kumasi, ARG 17/6/6, Charlotte Mensah, "Osagyefo and His Budjet [sic]," January 1962. See chapter 4 for a discussion of the 1961 budget.

79. PRAAD-Kumasi, ARG 17/6/6, Opoku Afiriyie, "How We Celebrate Positive Action Day in Kumasi," [1962?].

80. Thomas Burgess, "The Young Pioneers and the Rituals of Citizenship in Revolutionary Zanzibar," Africa Today 51, no. 3 (2005): 5.

81. Interview with Assiore, Accra, 24 April 2008.

82. Interview with Mensah, Accra, 8 June 2008.

83. Interview with S. Atta-P. Anamon, Lawrence Bessah, Francis D. Hayford, and Joseph Yawson, Shama, Western Region, 1 May 2008.

84. PRAAD-Kumasi, ARG 17/11/3, "Speech Delivered by Comrade Mary Osei, District Commissioner Kumasi North at the Opening of the Young Pioneers Cadre Instructors Course, Asawase, 21st June 1963."

85. For a broader discussion of this trend in African nationalist politics, see Mamadou Diouf, "Engaging Postcolonial Cultures: African Youth and Public Space," African Studies Review 46, no. 2 (2003): 3–4.

86. On expectations regarding adult masculinity, see Emmanuel Akyeampong, Drink, Power, and Cultural Change: A Social History of Alcohol in Ghana, c. 1800 to Recent Times (Portsmouth, NH: Heinemann, 1993), 153; Miescher, Making Men in Ghana, 124–33.

87. Interview with Fosuawaa, Koforidua, Eastern Region, 25 May 2008; interview with Mensah, Accra, 8 June 2008.

88. PRAAD-Accra, RG 14/1/15, Gersbacher, "Report on Ghana Workers Brigade/Foundation and Development," [1965?]. Gersbacher reports that, in 1960, most young women who entered the Brigade were between 16 and 20. They were slightly younger than their male counterparts, who were between the ages of 16 and 24 when they entered.

89. Interview with Fosuawaa, Koforidua, Eastern Region, 25 May 2008.

90. Kojo Botsio, in Government of Ghana, National Assembly, Parliamentary Debates, 6 June 1957, vol. 6, cols. 562–64.

91. J. E. Ababio, speech reproduced in "A Nation's Worth Is Measured by Her Youth," Evening News, 16 August 1961. To an extent, such emulation did

occur. In the mid-1960s, for instance, the Tanzanian government established its own politicized youth brigade—Jeshi la Kujenga Taifa (Army to Build the Nation)—in the image of the Builders Brigade; Bjerk, *Building a Peaceful Nation*, 156–57 and, more broadly, 155–79.

92. Ababio, speech reproduced in "A Nation's Worth Is Measured by Her Youth," *Evening News*, 16 August 1961.

93. Interview with Mensah, Accra, 8 June 2008.

94. Jean Allman, "Modeling Modernity: The Brief Story of Kwame Nkrumah, a Nazi Pilot Named Hanna, and the Wonders of Motorless Flight," in *Modernization as Spectacle in Africa*, ed. Peter J. Bloom, Stephan F. Miescher, and Takyiwaa Manuh (Bloomington: Indiana University Press, 2014), 229–43. See also M. N. Tetteh, *The Ghana Young Pioneer Movement: A Youth Organisation in the Kwame Nkrumah Era* (Tema: Ghana Publicity, 1999), 79–83.

95. PRAAD-Kumasi, ARG 17/1/11, J. P. K. Appiah, "A Report of the Ghana Young Pioneers Delegation to the International Work Camp at Wade el Natroun [sic], United Arab Republic from 12th August, 1962 to 15th September, 1962." With the exception of Appiah, who represented the Young Pioneers, this delegation was largely composed of Ghanaian students already based in Cairo, not Young Pioneers traveling abroad.

96. Interview with Lawrence Bessah, Shama, Western Region, 5 July 2008. For more on the international mission of the Young Pioneers, see the reports on Young Pioneers abroad and other documents relating to these endeavors in the file folder PRAAD-Accra RG 3/1/590, "Ghana Young Pioneer Training Scheme." See also Tetteh, *Ghana Young Pioneer Movement*, 84–91.

97. Interview with Nikoi-Oltai, Accra, 19 January 2008.

98. Alhaji Yakubu Tali, in Government of Ghana, National Assembly, *Parliamentary Debates*, 29 August 1957, vol. 7, col. 385.

99. Jatoe Kaleo, in Government of Ghana, National Assembly, *Parliamentary Debates*, 18 June 1959, col. 204.

100. S. G. Antor, in Government of Ghana, National Assembly, *Parliamentary Debates*, 18 June 1959, col. 212–13; *West Africa* (London), 19 September 1959; Peter Hodge, "The Ghana Workers Brigade: A Project for Unemployed Youth," *British Journal of Sociology* 15, no. 2 (1964): 118.

101. PRAAD-Accra, RG 14/1/59, Opanin Kofi Juantuah to Lord Listowel, "United Party Youth League, Ashanti, Resolution Passed on 28th July 1959 at Kumasi, Ashanti." As with the CPP-organized Ga Ekomefeemo Kpee (see above), such allegations against the Brigade paint a picture of an organization in which political vigilantism played a significant role in popular imaginings of the organization and, at least to some degree, in actuality. Again, comparisons with the situation in Tanzania are appropriate; see Brennan, "Youth, the TANU Youth League and Managed Vigilantism."

102. Interview with Nikoi-Oltai, Accra, 19 January 2008. See also interviews with Nikoi-Oltai, Accra, 14 November 2007, 28 November 2007, and

6 June 2008. For a discussion of some of the most significant attempts on Nkrumah's life, see chapters 5 and 6.

103. Interview with Kofi Ampadu, Koforidua, Eastern Region, 26 May 2008.

104. Interview with Nicholas Budu, Accra, 17 December 2007.

105. Interviews with Eden Bentum Takyi-Micah, Accra, 17 March 2008 and 10 May 2008. Quotes from 17 March 2008 interview.

106. Interview with Lawrence Asamoah, Koforidua, Eastern Region, 26 May 2008.

107. Interviews with Jacob Sesu Yeboah, Accra, 24 February 2008 and 13 April 2008.

108. Interview with Anamon, Bessah, Hayford, and Yawson, Shama, Western Region, 1 May 2008.

109. Interview with Yeboah, Accra, 24 February 2008.

110. Interview with Anamon, Bessah, Hayford, and Yawson, Shama, Western Region, 1 May 2008. For further discussion of this group's reflections on accounts of Young Pioneers as child spies, particularly as they pertain to the ethical and civic obligations of the one-party state, see chapter 6.

111. Interview with Assiore, Accra, 24 April 2008.

112. Interview with Budu, Accra, 17 December 2007.

113. PRAAD-Kumasi, ARG 17/2/1, "Soon Ghana Will Be a Country of Paradise," Ejisu, 5 February 1962.

114. Interviews with Takyi-Micah, Accra, 17 March 2008 and 10 May 2008.

115. Ibid.; Hodge, "Ghana Workers Brigade," 118, 127–28, 128n15. I also want to thank Professor Robert Addo-Fening for sharing some of these stories with me in March 2009, after I delivered a paper on the Builders Brigade in the Department of History at the University of Ghana.

116. For a regionally diverse and representative collection of Brigade-related land disputes, see PRAAD-Accra, RG 14/1/59, Mamn Grunshie Maigon to Kwame Nkrumah, "Petition for Compensation in Respect to My Farm Unlawfully Destroyed by the Ghana Builders Brigade Headquarters, Kanda Camp at 37, Military Hospital, Cantonments, Accra," Accra, 2 September 1959; PRAAD-Sekondi, Western Regional Archives, 8/1/156, Kobina Arhin, Kwesi Akumah, et al. to National Organiser of the Builders Brigade, "Petition Against the Anaji Builders Brigade," Sekondi, 11 September 1959; PRAAD-Sunyani, BRG 1/11/13, Acting Regional Organiser to Secretary to the Regional Commissioner, "Worries and Threats on Brigaders at Proposed Sunyani Camp Site," Sunyani, 23 July 1962; PRAAD-Accra, RG 14/1/60, Yaw Sarfo, Akobeahene Bafuor, Akyeampong Kwasi, et al. to Ministry of Defence, Accra, 30 March 1964; PRAAD-Accra, RG 14/1/60, K. Acheampong to Commanding Officer, Workers Brigade, "Acquisition of Site at New Edubiase," Kumasi, 21 March 1966.

117. PRAAD-Accra, RG 14/1/60, Anani Gbenyo to unknown, Accra, 24 January 1965; PRAAD-Accra, RG 14/1/60, "A Citizen" to Chairman, Expediting

Committee, "Complaint about Pay Anomalies in the Workers Brigade," Omankope, 20 May 1968.

118. PRAAD-Kumasi, ARG 17/1/5, Z. B. Shardow to All Regional Organisers, "Non-Alignment with Local Disputes or Differences by Ghana Young Pioneers," Accra, 24 February 1962; PRAAD-Kumasi, ARG 17/1/5, R. O. Frimpong-Mansa to All District Organisers-Ashanti, "Persons Posing as Officers of the Movement," Kumasi, 21 June 1961; PRAAD-Accra, RG 3/1/502, J. Addo Ankrah to Principal Secretary of the Ministry of Education, "Kwame Nkrumah Youth," 12 January 1965.

119. PRAAD-Accra, RG 3/1/502, J. Addo Ankrah to Principal Secretary of the Ministry of Education, "Kwame Nkrumah Youth," Koforidua, 12 January 1965.

120. New York Public Library (hereafter cited as NYPL), Schomburg Center for Research in Black Culture (hereafter cited as Schomburg Center), St. Clair Drake Papers (hereafter cited as Drake Papers), Box 70, Folder 5, St. Clair Drake, "A Talk with a Young Pioneer," 30 July 1965.

121. For discussion of the Guinean "demystification campaigns," see Straker, *Youth, Nationalism, and the Guinean Revolution*; McGovern, *Unmasking the State*.

122. Interview with M. N. Tetteh, Accra, 7 May 2008. Also, see Tetteh, *Ghana Young Pioneer Movement*, 67, 85–86.

123. Plageman, *Highlife Saturday Night*, 67–146.

124. Ibid., 147–82, quote on 148.

125. NYPL, Schomburg Center, Drake Papers, Box 70, Folder 5, J. K. Haywood-Dadzie, "Students on Vacation in Tema," 23 July 1965.

126. Ibid.; NYPL, Schomburg Center, Drake Papers, Box 70, Folder 5, H. K. Addison, "A Pick-Pocket Caught Red-Handed," n.d.; NYPL, Schomburg Center, Drake Papers, Box 70, Folder 5, "Case 4: (Literate) Indirect," n.d.; H. K. Addison, "Profile 4 (Illiterate Boy): Washerman Apprentice," n.d.

127. PRAAD-Kumasi, ARG 17/1/5, J. Kemisey-Yankson to Ghana Young Pioneers Security Officer, "Ghana Young Pioneers-Ashanti Region: Intelligence Report," Kumasi, 14 November 1962.

128. Interview with Assiore, Accra, 24 April 2008.

129. "Guevara Praises Workers Brigade," *Ghanaian Times*, 21 January 1965.

130. PRAAD-Sunyani, BRG 2/9/8, *The Ghana Young Pioneers: Monthly Newsletter from Brong Ahafo Region*, vol. 19 (November–December 1963).

131. See, for instance, National Archives of the United Kingdom, Prime Minister's Office Files 11/2587, Pole (?) to T. J. Bligh, 1 July 1959.

132. PRAAD-Kumasi, ARG 17/11/3, P. K. Adjei to Regional Organiser, Ashanti Region Young Pioneers, Kumasi, 27 December 1962.

133. Nicholas Anane-Agyei, quoted in "Exhibit Good Citizenship, Youths Told," *Evening News*, 16 January 1961.

CHAPTER 4: "WORK AND HAPPINESS FOR ALL"

1. Anoma Okore, "Labour in a Socialist Society," *People's Vanguard*, 29 May 1963.

2. E. B. Mac-Hardjor, "Increased Productivity: What It Means for Our Prosperity," *Ghanaian*, January 1965. For a discussion of the Seven-Year Development Plan, see Ghana Planning Commission, *Seven-Year Development Plan: A Brief Outline* (Accra: Government Printing Department, 1963).

3. Kofi Bannerman, "The Road to Cheaper Prices . . . : Workers' Responsibility in the Socialist State," *Evening News*, 1 February 1964. Emphasis in original.

4. This literature is vast. See, for instance, William H. Worger, *South Africa's City of Diamonds: Mine Workers and Monopoly Capitalism in Kimberley, 1867–1895* (New Haven, CT: Yale University Press, 1987); Frederick Cooper, *On the African Waterfront: Urban Disorder and the Transformation of Work in Colonial Mombasa* (New Haven, CT: Yale University Press, 1987); John Higginson, *A Working Class in the Making: Belgian Colonial Policy, Private Enterprise, and the African Mineworker, 1907–1951* (Madison: University of Wisconsin Press, 1989); Keletso E. Atkins, *The Moon Is Dead! Give Us Our Money! The Cultural Origins of an African Work Ethic, Natal, South Africa, 1843–1900* (Portsmouth, NH: Heinemann, 1993); Cooper, *Decolonization and African Society: The Labor Question in French and British Africa* (Cambridge: Cambridge University Press, 1996).

5. Worger, *South Africa's City of Diamonds*, 110.

6. Unattributed quote in Atkins, *The Moon Is Dead!*, 2. For the precolonial precedents for such a discourse with a particular focus on West Africa, see Klas Rönnbäck, "The Idle and the Industrious—European Ideas about the African Work Ethic in Precolonial West Africa," *History in Africa* 41 (2014): 117–45.

7. Worger, *South Africa's City of Diamonds*, 110–46.

8. Cooper, *On the African Waterfront*, 13.

9. Ibid., esp. 13–41.

10. John Noon, *Labor Problems of Africa* (Philadelphia: University of Pennsylvania Press, 1944), 14–22, quote on 15.

11. Cooper, *On the African Waterfront*, 8, 124–25, quote on 8.

12. Ibid., 114–93. See also Frederick Cooper, "Industrial Man Goes to Africa," in *Men and Masculinities in Modern Africa*, ed. Lisa A. Lindsay and Stephan F. Miescher (Portsmouth, NH: Heinemann, 2003), 128–37.

13. See Karl Marx, *Capital*, vol. 1, *A Critique of Political Economy*, ed. Friedrich Engels, trans. Samuel Moore and Edward Aveling (Mineola, NY: Dover, 2011), 255–59.

14. Jeff Crisp, *The Story of an African Working Class: Ghanaian Miners' Struggles, 1870–1980* (London: Zed Books, 1984), 14–34. See also Raymond E. Dumett, *El Dorado in West Africa: The Gold-Mining Frontier, African Labor, and Colonial Capitalism in the Gold Coast, 1875–1900* (Athens: Ohio University Press, 1998).

15. Crisp, *Story of an African Working Class*, 26.

16. *Mining Journal*, 16 May 1885, quoted in Crisp, *Story of an African Working Class*, 18.

17. "Note of a Meeting between the Representatives of the Gold Coast Chamber of Mines, and the Delegates of the Gold Coast Mines Employees' Union, held at Tarkwa, on Friday, 9th August, 1946," appendix to J. Benibengor Blay, *The Gold Coast Mines Employees' Union* (Ilfracombe, UK: Arthur H. Stockwell, 1950), 48–54. See also "The Arbitration Proceedings," appendix to Blay, *Gold Coast Mines Employees' Union*, 156–297.

18. On the Trades Union Ordinance, see Paul S. Gray, *Unions and Leaders in Ghana: A Model of Labor and Development* (Owerri, Nigeria: Conch Magazine, 1981), 14. On the miners' strike actions, see Crisp, *Story of an African Working Class*, 56–93, esp. 58–59.

19. Kwame Nkrumah, Foreword to Blay, *Gold Coast Mines Employees' Union*, 9.

20. Kwame Nkrumah, quoted in "Nkrumah: Task after S.G. Freedom from Want," *Evening News*, 29 October 1956.

21. Richard Jeffries, "The Evolution of the Ghana Trades Union Congress under the Convention People's Party: Towards a More Radical Re-Interpretation," *Transactions of the Historical Society of Ghana* 14, no. 2 (1973): 280.

22. John K. Tettegah, *Why the New Structure? Speech Delivered at the 14th Annual Delegates Conference of the Ghana TUC, Cape Coast, 25th–26th January, 1958* (Accra: Publicity/Information Department, Ghana Trades Union Congress, [1958]), 10. See also E. A. Cowan, *Evolution of Trade Unionism in Ghana* (Accra: Ghana Trades Union Congress, [1960?]), 91–111.

23. Richard Jeffries provides perhaps the fullest and most powerful analysis of the effects of the CPP's attempted takeover of the Gold Coast/Ghanaian labor movement on the labor movement itself, particularly as it related to the country's railway and harbor workers; Jeffries, "Evolution of the Ghana Trades Union Congress"; Jeffries, *Class, Power, and Ideology in Ghana: The Railwaymen of Sekondi* (Cambridge: Cambridge University Press, 1978), esp. 58–70. For a more policy-oriented analysis, see Gray, *Unions and Leaders in Ghana*, 22–42.

24. Pobee Biney, quoted in Frank Wudu, *The Man Pobee Biney: A Fallen Labour Hero of Ghana* (Accra: State Publishing Corporation, 1968), 4. Also quoted in Jeffries, *Class, Power, and Ideology in Ghana*, 61–62.

25. Anthony Woode, quoted in David E. Apter, *Ghana in Transition*, 2nd rev. ed. (Princeton, NJ: Princeton University Press, 1972), 238–39.

26. "Brother Culture," "TUC & CPP," *Ashanti Pioneer*, 1 April 1957.

27. Kwame Nkrumah, *Towards Colonial Freedom: Africa in the Struggle against World Imperialism* (London: Farleigh, 1947), 17–18, 35–36.

28 George Padmore, *The Gold Coast Revolution: The Struggle of an African People from Slavery to Freedom* (London: Dennis Dobson, 1953), 199. For a more nuanced interpretation of Gold Coasters' relationships and interactions with the United Africa Company and of Gold Coast/Ghanaian consumer culture more broadly, see Bianca Murillo, "'The Devil We Know': Gold Coast Consumers, Local Employees, and the United Africa Company, 1940–1960," *Enterprise &*

Society 12, no. 2 (2011): 317–55; Murillo, *Market Encounters: Consumer Cultures in Twentieth-Century Ghana* (Athens: Ohio University Press, 2017).

29. Cecil Forde, cited in "Ghana Heading towards Socialist State: NASSOISTS Told," *Evening News*, 9 May 1960.

30. Public Records and Archives Administration Department (hereafter cited as PRAAD), Sunyani, Brong Ahafo Regional Archives (hereafter cited as BRG) 1/14/1 (vol. 4), Minutes of the Party Committee of the Regional Office, Sunyani, 13 August 1964.

31. Kofi Baako, "Ghana's Conception of Socialism," enclosure to John P. Meagher to the Department of State, Washington, no. 588, 21 March 1961, in Confidential U.S. State Department Central Files, Ghana, 1960–January 1963: Internal and Foreign Affairs (hereafter cited as Confidential US State Department Files), Reel 1.

32. Ibid.

33. Amilcar Cabral, *Return to the Source: Selected Speeches of Amilcar Cabral*, ed. Africa Information Service (New York: Monthly Review, 1973).

34. Baako, "Ghana's Conception of Socialism." For detailed surveys of the nuanced meanings of concepts of wealth, accumulation, and power in the Gold Coast and Ghana, see T. C. McCaskie, "Accumulation, Wealth, and Belief in Asante History: I. To the Close of the Nineteenth Century," *Africa* 53, no. 1 (1983): 23–43, 79; McCaskie, "Accumulation: Wealth and Belief in Asante History: II. The Twentieth Century," *Africa* 56, no. 1 (1986): 3–23; Sara S. Berry, *Chiefs Know Their Boundaries: Essays on Property, Power, and the Past in Asante, 1896–1996* (Portsmouth, NH: Heinemann, 2001).

35. Michael Burawoy, *The Politics of Production: Factory Regimes under Capitalism and Socialism* (London: Verso Books, 1985), 156. See also Stephen Kotkin, *Magnetic Mountain: Stalinism as a Civilization* (Berkeley: University of California Press, 1995), 202.

36. Burawoy, *Politics of Production*, 156–57.

37. Kwame Nkrumah, quoted in "Serve Ghana Now . . . Replaces . . . Self-Govt Now!," *Evening News*, 26 February 1957.

38. Nkrumah, quoted in Editorial, *Evening News*, 1 January 1960.

39. Ako Adjei, in Government of Ghana, National Assembly, *Parliamentary Debates*, 17 December 1958, vol. 12, col. 546; Douglas Rimmer, "The New Industrial Relations in Ghana," *Industrial and Labor Relations Review* 14, no. 2 (1961): 212–18. The act originally proposed the creation of sixteen national unions. That number was amended to twenty-four by the time of the act's 1958 passage, only to be amended back down to sixteen in 1959.

40. Jeffries, *Class, Power, and Ideology in Ghana*, 24–25.

41. Ghana Trades Union Congress, *An Outline of the Rights and Duties of Members and Officials of the Trades Union Congress (Ghana)* (Accra: Education and Publicity Department of the Trades Union Congress, [1960?]), 2.

42. A. J. Dowuona-Hammond, in Government of Ghana, National Assembly, *Parliamentary Debates*, 18 December 1958, cols. 639, 641.

43. Tettegah, *Why the New Structure?*, 6.

44. Ghana Trades Union Congress, *What Economic Security Does the Ghanaian Worker Enjoy?* (Accra: Education and Publicity Department of the Trades Union Congress, n.d.), 3.

45. Ibid., 3–4. See also "TUC's First Anniversary: Secretary-General Makes Policy Statement," *Information Bulletin of the Trades Union Congress (Ghana)*, March 1960.

46. P. B. Arthiabah, "The Ghana Trade Union Congress and Workers: Its Relationship with Past Governments and Contribution to National Development," Paper presented at the Symposium on the Life and Work of Kwame Nkrumah, organized by the Institute of African Studies, University of Ghana, Legon, May 27–June 1, 1985, 16.

47. "Increased Productivity Means Higher Standard of Living," *Information Bulletin of the Trades Union Congress (Ghana)*, September 1959.

48. George Padmore Research Library on African Affairs (hereafter cited as GPRL), Bureau of African Affairs (hereafter cited as BAA)/Research Library on African Affairs (hereafter cited as RLAA)/423, National Council for Higher Education and Research, "Development of the Kwame Nkrumah Ideological Institute, Winneba, as the Institute of Political Science (Draft Memorandum)," Accra, 24 January 1962.

49. PRAAD-Sunyani, BRG 1/14/33, Kodwo Addison to Party Regional Secretary, "Re: Citizenship in Higher Institutions," Winneba, 13 April 1964; PRAAD-Sekondi, Western Regional Archives (hereafter cited as WRG), 8/1/248, Matthew Arkhurst, "Report on the Deliberations of the Annual Delegates Conference of the Shama District of the Party," Shama Junction, 22 September 1963; PRAAD-Sekondi, WRG 8/1/368, Osei Owusu-Afriyie, "Party Citizenship and Education," Sekondi/Takoradi, 10 April 1964; PRAAD-Sekondi, WRG 24/2/459, Kodwo Addison to John Arthur, "Field Work in Agriculture," Winneba, 20 July 1964; PRAAD-Sekondi, WRG 8/1/368, G. Y. Tovieku, "Invitation to Pat Sloan Lecture on 'USSR for Peace and Independence' and 'Soviet Democracy,'" Sekondi/Takoradi, 19 October 1964.

50. Princeton University Archives (hereafter cited as PUA), W. Arthur Lewis Papers (hereafter cited as Lewis Papers), Box 21, Folder 7, "Appendix to Extract from the Minutes of a Meeting Held on the 11th July 1958," esp. ch. 1; Republic of Ghana, *Second Development Plan, 1959–1964* (Accra: Government Printer, 1959), 1–3.

51. Kwame Nkrumah, in Government of Ghana, National Assembly, *Parliamentary Debates*, 4 March 1959, vol. 14, col. 189.

52. Ibid., col. 192.

53. Government of Ghana, *Second Development Plan*, 4–16, quotes on 16.

54. See ibid., 21, for the plan's nonexhaustive list of potential industries.

55. Ibid., 16–17.

56. Kwame Nkrumah, quoted in "Give Workers a Fair Deal: A Pointer to Economic Freedom," *Evening News*, 9 July 1960. Nkrumah originally gave

this speech at the laying of the foundation stone of the new TUC Hall of Trade Unions on 17 October 1959.

57. PUA, Lewis Papers, Box 20, Folder 7, Economic Adviser's Office (W. Arthur Lewis), 20 February 1958.

58. International Bank for Reconstruction and Development, *Current Economic Position and Prospects of Ghana*, Report No. EA-121a, 29 August 1961 (Washington, DC: Department of Operations, Europe, Africa, and Australia), 1; Tony Killick, "The Economics of Cocoa," in *A Study of Contemporary Ghana*, vol. 1, *The Economy of Ghana*, ed. Walter Birmingham, I. Neustadt, and E. N. Omaboe (London: George Allen and Unwin, 1966), 369.

59. International Bank for Reconstruction and Development, *The Economy of Ghana*, Report No. EA-110a, 29 June 1960 (Washington, DC: Department of Operations, Europe, Africa, and Australia), 4.

60. PUA, Lewis Papers, Box 21, Folder 7, Lewis, "The Second Development Plan: Note by the Economic Adviser: The Size of the Program," 26 June 1958.

61. See Rimmer, "The New Industrial Relations in Ghana," 215–17.

62. A. Y. Ankomah, interview conducted by Jeffries, 15 August 1971, quoted in Jeffries, *Class, Power, and Ideology in Ghana*, 75.

63. A. B. Essuman, interview conducted by Jeffries, 18 July 1971, quoted ibid., 89.

64. Interview with E. B. Mensah, Accra, 8 June 2008.

65. Ann W. Seidman, *Ghana's Development Experience, 1951–1965* (Nairobi: East African Publishing House, 1978), 114–15, 123, 133. It is important to note that the real numbers of the registered unemployed were very small: for instance, less than 3,000 in Accra and less than 100 in Brong Ahafo. As a result, their use for illustration should be taken with a grain of salt. However, the rise in their numbers year over year does appear to show that, with the exception of Accra (the seat of government) and the Volta Region (where the Akosombo Dam was under construction), the employment prospects for one of the most politically and socially idealized portions of the populace were constricting in the early 1960s. After 1961, Seidman notes, the number of registered unemployed nationally would remain steady at around 15,000 per month until 1965. In all, Seidman notes a total Ghanaian labor pool of 2.7 million people.

66. Interview with Thomas Daniel Laryea, Accra, 6 December 2007.

67. Interview with Eden Bentum Takyi-Micah, Accra, 17 March 2008.

68. Republic of Ghana, Census Office, 1960 *Population Census of Ghana: Advance Report of Volumes III and IV: Demographic and Economic Characteristics of Regions* (Accra: Census Office, 1962), 2.

69. Keith Hart, "Small-Scale Entrepreneurs in Ghana and Development Planning," *Journal of Development Studies* 6, no. 4 (1970): 105.

70. Richard Rathbone perhaps states the inequities in Ghanaian development funding and rewards most bluntly: "They [the political class] achieve their rewards by milking the rural areas of Ghana which constitute in very real terms the major areas of wealth creation." For Rathbone, the real question was

how, even after the CPP was overthrown, Ghanaian politicians were still able to get away with such an arrangement; Rathbone, "Ghana," in *West African States: Failure and Promise: A Study in Comparative Politics*, ed. John Dunn (Cambridge: Cambridge University Press, 1978), 32.

71. For an analysis of Ghanaian rural-urban migration and Ghanaians' reactions to the push-and-pull effects of both the village and town, see John C. Caldwell, *African Rural-Urban Migration: The Movement to Ghana's Towns* (New York: Columbia University Press, 1969), esp. 87–119.

72. On the Builders Brigade, see chapter 3. Furthermore, Keri Lambert's emerging research on the Nkrumah government's attempts to establish a vibrant rubber industry in Ghana's Western Region promises to illuminate how these tensions over land and control over one's productive capabilities played out and are remembered at the local level. Lambert is currently advancing this research as part of a dissertation in progress in the Yale University Department of History.

73. On the cocoa holdups, see Gareth Austin, "Capitalists and Chiefs in the Cocoa Hold-Ups in South Asante, 1927–1938," *International Journal of African Historical Studies* 21, no. 1 (1988): 63–95.

74. Marvin P. Miracle and Ann Seidman, *Agricultural Cooperatives and Quasi-Cooperatives in Ghana, 1951–1965* (Madison: Land Tenure Center, University of Wisconsin, 1968).

75. Kojo Botsio, quoted ibid., 29.

76. Miracle and Seidman, *Agricultural Cooperatives and Quasi-Cooperatives in Ghana*, 28–33. More broadly, see also Seidman, *Ghana's Development Experience*, 146–99, and, on state farms, Marvin P. Miracle and Ann Seidman, *State Farms in Ghana* (Madison: Land Tenure Center, University of Wisconsin, 1968). See also Björn Beckman, *Organising the Farmers: Cocoa Politics and National Development in Ghana* (Uppsala: Scandinavian Institute of African Studies, 1976).

77. A Citizen, "Socialism," *Ashanti Pioneer*, 1 July 1960.

78. Joe Appiah, in Republic of Ghana, National Assembly, *Parliamentary Debates*, 25 August 1960, vol. 20, col. 909.

79. PRAAD-Accra, Administrative Files (hereafter cited as ADM) 13/1/30, Cabinet Minutes, 6 February 1961.

80. PRAAD-Accra, ADM 13/1/30, Cabinet Minutes, 30 and 31 May 1961.

81. Lyrics to a song remembered by Accra trader Victoria Laryea; interview with Victoria Laryea, Accra, 22 April 2008.

82. Interview with Thomas Daniel Laryea, Accra, 6 December 2007.

83. Republic of Ghana, Central Bureau of Statistics, *Economic Survey, 1961* (Accra: Ministry of Information and Broadcasting, 1962), 102–3.

84. J. Harvey Perry, *Taxation and Economic Development in Ghana*, Report No. TAO/GHA/4/Rev. 1, 1 July 1959 (New York: United Nations Commissioner for Technical Assistance, Department of Economic and Social Affairs, 1959), 12.

85. Dennis Austin, *Politics in Ghana, 1946–1960* (London: Oxford University Press, 1964), 400; Beckman, *Organising the Farmers*, 207.

86. Beckman, *Organising the Farmers*, 207.

87. Nicholas Kaldor, "Taxation for Economic Development," *Journal of Modern African Studies* 1, no. 1 (1963): 7, 22.

88. Appiah, in Republic of Ghana, National Assembly, *Parliamentary Debates*, 11 July 1961, vol. 24, cols. 202–23.

89. Victor Owusu, in Republic of Ghana, National Assembly, *Parliamentary Debates*, 10 July 1961, vol. 24, cols. 156–60, 165.

90. St. Clair Drake and Leslie Alexander Lacy, "Government versus the Unions: The Sekondi-Takoradi Strike, 1961," in *Politics in Africa: 7 Cases*, ed. Gwendolen M. Carter (New York: Harcourt, Brace, and World, 1966), 80.

91. Sulemana Ibun Iddrissu, in Republic of Ghana, National Assembly, *Parliamentary Debates*, 10 July 1961, col. 183–85.

92. Ibid., 185. Also quoted in Drake and Lacy, "Government versus the Unions," 80.

93. Kwaku Amoa-Awuah, in Republic of Ghana, National Assembly, *Parliamentary Debates*, 10 July 1961, cols. 166–74, quote on 166; A. E. A. Ofori-Atta, *Parliamentary Debates*, 11 July 1961, cols. 223–30; Kofi Baako, *Parliamentary Debates*, 11 July 1961, cols. 238–47. Quote from Amoa-Awuah.

94. Amoa-Awuah, in Republic of Ghana, National Assembly, *Parliamentary Debates*, 10 July 1961, col. 166.

95. Regina Asamany, in Republic of Ghana, National Assembly, *Parliamentary Debates*, 10 July 1961, cols. 180–82.

96. H. K. Boni, in Republic of Ghana, National Assembly, *Parliamentary Debates*, 11 July 1961, cols. 248, 249.

97. Jeffries, *Class, Power, and Ideology in Ghana*, 93.

98. Drake and Lacy, "Government versus the Unions," 82.

99. For the most detailed accounts of the strike, see Drake and Lacy, "Government versus the Unions," 67–118; Jeffries, *Class, Power, and Ideology in Ghana*, 71–101.

100. PRAAD-Accra, ADM 13/1/30, Cabinet Minutes, 5 September 1961.

101. Jeffries, *Class, Power, and Ideology in Ghana*, 93–94.

102. At the time of the strike, Tema harbor was in the final stages of construction and would not begin full-scale operations until the following year. The cabinet, however, did order the country's cocoa exports to be redirected to Tema for shipment in the hopes of avoiding a complete freeze of the Ghanaian cocoa revenues. See PRAAD-Accra, ADM 13/1/30, Cabinet Minutes, 5 September 1961.

103. PRAAD-Accra, ADM 13/1/30, Emergency Cabinet Meeting, Minutes, 14 September 1961.

104. "Nkrumah Continues Holiday," *Ashanti Pioneer*, 8 September 1961; "Railway Employees Still on Their Stand," *Ashanti Pioneer*, 8 September 1961; "Osagyefo Given Tumultuous Welcome," *Ashanti Pioneer*, 18 September 1961;

"Osagyefo Busy at His Desk," *Ashanti Pioneer*, 22 September 1962; Drake and Lacy, "Government versus the Unions," 93.

105. Yaw Tibo, "Socialism," *Ashanti Pioneer*, 5 September 1961.

106. The University of Iowa Libraries, Special Collections and University Archives, Al M. Lee Papers, Box 4, Al Lee, "How I Joined the Peace Corps and Found Mao," n.d. I want to thank Daniel Horowitz for sharing this document with me.

107. PRAAD-Accra, ADM 13/1/30, Cabinet Minutes, 12 September 1961.

108. Ibid.; PRAAD-Accra, ADM 13/1/30, Emergency Cabinet Meeting, Minutes, 13 September 1961.

109. GPRL, BAA/RLAA/371, Establishment Secretariat, "Payment for Days Lost Due to Strike," 12 September 1961; GPRL, BAA/RLAA/371, Establishment Secretariat, "Payment for Time Lost Due to Strike," 14 September 1961. The government's debates on whether and how to withhold pay from striking civil servants continued until at least mid-October; GPRL, BAA/RLAA/371, Establishment Secretariat, "Payment for Days Lost Due to Strike," 18 October 1961.

110. Drake and Lacy, "Government versus the Unions," 101.

111. American Embassy, Accra, to Department of State, 25 September 1961, encl. "President Nkrumah's Address to the Strikers," 20 September 1961, in Confidential US State Department Files, Reel 6. The American embassy's report of the speech comes from the transcript reported in the *Ghanaian Times*, 21 September 1961.

112. See, for instance, Jitendra Mohan, "Nkrumah and Nkrumaism," *Socialist Register* 4 (1967), 214–15.

113. For instance, see Joe Appiah's and J. B. Danquah's accounts of the strike and what they presented as Nkrumah's attempts to come to terms with the weakening state of the country's economy and political situation; Joseph Appiah, *Joe Appiah: The Autobiography of an African Patriot* (Accra: Asempa, 1996), 252–56; first published 1990 by Praeger, New York. For Danquah's take, see J. B. Danquah, *The Ghanaian Establishment: Its Constitution, Its Detentions, Its Traditions, Its Justice and Statecraft, and Its Heritage of Ghanaism*, ed. Albert Adu Boahen (Accra: Ghana Universities Press, 1997), 63–71.

114. Russell to Secretary of State, Accra, 7 September 1961, Department Telegram 362, in John F. Kennedy National Security Files, Africa: National Security Files, 1961–1963 (Frederick, MD: University Publications of America, 1987) (hereafter cited as JFK National Security Files), First Supplement, Reel 11.

115. D. Austin, *Politics in Ghana*, 401–2.

116. Ibid., 380–81. For further discussion of the Preventative Detention Act, see chapter 6.

117. The most prominent opposition figures imprisoned after the strike included S. G. Antor, Joe Appiah, J. B. Danquah, and Victor Owusu; "Fifty to Be Detained for Subversive Activities," *Ghana Today*, 11 October 1961;

D. Austin, *Politics in Ghana*, 401; Drake and Lacy, "Government versus the Unions," 105; Jeffries, *Class, Power, and Ideology in Ghana*, 99–101.

118. According to at least one American official, by as early as 28 September, Gbedemah had informed the United States that he, along with "some 15 other members of Parliament," intended to form their own party and confront Nkrumah and the CPP when the next parliamentary session opened in October; L. D. Battle, "Memorandum for Mr. McGeorge Bundy: The Volta Project and the Current Political Situation in Ghana," [September/October 1961?], in JFK National Security Files, Reel 7.

119. "Leading Cabinet Members Out!," *Evening News*, 29 September 1961; "Six Asked to Resign," *Ghana Today*, 11 October 1961. See also D. Austin, *Politics in Ghana*, 402–7.

120. Russell to Secretary of State, Accra, 2 October 1961, Department Telegram 557, in JFK National Security Files, Reel 8.

121. Interview with N. Sifah, Accra, 16 February 2008.

122. Karl Marx, "Economic and Philosophic Manuscripts of 1844," in *The Marx-Engels Reader*, 2nd ed., ed. Robert C. Tucker (New York: W. W. Norton, 1978), 70–81. See also Marx, "Alienation and Social Classes," in *The Marx-Engels Reader*, 133–35.

123. There is debate among scholars of Marx and Marxist thought over whether Marx himself introduced the conceptual distinctions in discussions of class. For a survey of these debates, see Edward Andrew, "Class in Itself and Class against Capital: Karl Marx and His Classifiers," *Canadian Journal of Political Science* 16, no. 3 (1983): 577–84.

124. Kwame Nkrumah, *Consciencism: Philosophy and Ideology for Decolonization and Development with a Particular Reference to the African Revolution* (London: Heinemann, 1964), 69.

125. See, by way of comparison, Marx and Engels, *Communist Manifesto*, 39–40.

126. K. Badu-Acquah, "The Reinvigoration of Socialism," *Evening News*, 4 January 1961.

127. "Eternal Glory to the Spirit of Positive Action," *Evening News*, 7 January 1961.

128. "Machinery and Raw Materials are Needed," *Evening News*, 12 January 1961.

129. PRAAD-Sunyani, BRG 3/1/29, "Programme of Work for the Year 1965 by Comrade P. A. C. Atuahene, Party Regional Education Secretary, Sunyani, Brong/Ahafo Region."

130. PRAAD-Kumasi, Ashanti Regional Archives 17/6/7, "Attitude toward Employment of Woman," *Party Chronicle*, 11 December 1963.

131. Ghana Planning Commission, *Seven-Year Development Plan*, 29; PRAAD-Accra, Record Group 8/2/863, Office of the Planning Commission, *First Seven-Year Development Plan*, March 1963, ch. 13.

132. Trade Union Correspondent, "To Understand Nkrumaism, We Must Study Marxism-Leninism," *Evening News*, 23 April 1963.

133. Speech by D. K. Foevie, 20 November 1963, quoted in Crisp, *Story of an African Working Class*, 134.

134. PRAAD-Sekondi, WRG 8/1/170, J. K. Dontoh to District Commissioner, "Challenging the Power of the Govt.," Amanful-Takoradi, 28 December 1964.

135. Ashanti Command to Nkrumah, "The Unknown Warriors," 26 July 1962, in Ivor Wilks–Phyllis Ferguson Collection of Materials on Ghana, Reel 1.

136. Jennifer Hart, "'One Man, No Chop': Licit Wealth, Good Citizens, and the Criminalization of Drivers in Postcolonial Ghana," *International Journal of African Historical Studies* 46, no. 3 (2013): 373–96; J. Hart, "Motor Transportation, Trade Unionism, and the Culture of Work in Colonial Ghana," *International Review of Social History* 59, no. S22 (2014): 185–209. See also J. Hart, *Ghana on the Go: African Mobility in the Age of Motor Transportation* (Bloomington: Indiana University Press, 2016).

137. Perhaps most broadly, see Gwendolyn Mikell, *Cocoa and Chaos in Ghana* (New York: Paragon House, 1989); and, specifically connected to the CPP, Jean Allman, *The Quills of the Porcupine: Asante Nationalism in an Emergent Ghana* (Madison: University of Wisconsin Press, 1993), 16–50.

138. New York Public Library, Schomburg Center for Research in Black Culture, St. Clair Drake Papers, Box 70, Folder 3, "Mr. Odamtten" quoted in E. A. Colecraft, "Daybook—Tema," 11 June 1960.

139. Ayi Kwei Armah, *The Beautyful Ones Are Not Yet Born* (Boston: Houghton Mifflin, 1968), 95, 142.

140. Emmanuel Akyeampong, *Drink, Power, and Cultural Change: A Social History of Alcohol in Ghana, c. 1800 to Recent Times* (Portsmouth, NH: Heinemann, 1993), 148.

141. Crisp, *Story of an African Working Class*, 134–35.

142. State Gold Mining Corporation, "Circular to Shop Stewards," 28 September 1964, quoted in Crisp, *Story of an African Working Class*, 135.

143. John Abakah, interview conducted with Jeffries, 3 September 1971, quoted in Jeffries, *Class, Power, and Ideology in Ghana*, 106.

144. "The Party as the Highest Expression of State Power," *Evening News*, 1 February 1964. Emphasis in original.

145. Mac-Hardjor, "Increased Productivity."

146. Republic of Ghana, Ministry of Information and Broadcasting, *Statement by the Government on the Recent Conspiracy, Monday, 11th December 1961* (Accra: Ministry of Information and Broadcasting, 1961), 3, 11–21, quote on 3.

CHAPTER 5: WORKING FOR THE REVOLUTION

1. Gloria Lamptey, "Women, Help Build African Personality," *Evening News*, 23 July 1960.

2. Interview with Lawrence Asamoah, Koforidua, Eastern Region, 26 May 2008.

3. Mount Holyoke College Archives and Special Collections, Gena L. Reisner Correspondence, Folder 1, Gena L. Reisner to Immediate Family and Aunt Eve, Woamé, Togo, 6 November 1964.

4. C. L. R. James, *Nkrumah and the Ghana Revolution* (London: Allison and Busby, 1977), 179–86.

5. George Padmore Research Library on African Affairs (hereafter cited as GPRL), Bureau of African Affairs (hereafter cited as BAA)/Research Library on African Affairs (hereafter cited as RLAA)/327, Meeting of the Bureau of African Affairs Senior Officers, Minutes, 21 November 1961.

6. For more on the bureau, see Jeffrey S. Ahlman, "Managing the Pan-African Workplace: Discipline, Ideology, and the Cultural Politics of the Ghanaian Bureau of African Affairs," *Ghana Studies* 15–16 (2012–13): 337–71.

7. GPRL, BAA/RLAA/327, Meeting of the Bureau of African Affairs Senior Officers, Minutes, 21 November 1961.

8. On the French response to Guinea's *"non"* vote, see Elizabeth Schmidt, *Cold War and Decolonization in Guinea, 1946–1958* (Athens: Ohio University Press, 2008), 168–78; Mairi S. MacDonald, "The Challenge of Guinean Independence, 1958–1961" (PhD diss., University of Toronto, 2009).

9. On Cameroonian decolonization, see Meredith Terretta, *Nation of Outlaws, State of Violence: Nationalism, Grassfields Tradition, and State Building in Cameroon* (Athens: Ohio University Press, 2014).

10. "Independence of Cameroons: Is It Genuine?," *Evening News*, 2 January 1960.

11. On the political and intellectual underpinnings of the decolonization of francophone Africa, see Frederick Cooper, *Citizenship between Empire and Nation: Remaking France and French Africa, 1945–1960* (Princeton, NJ: Princeton University Press, 2014). For a brief survey of postcolonial French-African relations, see Elizabeth Schmidt, *Foreign Intervention in Africa: From the Cold War to the War on Terror* (Cambridge: Cambridge University Press, 2013), 165–92.

12. See Matthew Connelly, *A Diplomatic Revolution: Algeria's Fight for Independence and the Origins of the Post–Cold War Era* (Oxford: Oxford University Press, 2002), 173–275; Jeffrey James Byrne, *Mecca of Revolution: Algeria, Decolonization, and the Third World Order* (Oxford: Oxford University Press, 2016), 68–112.

13. Jean Allman, "Nuclear Imperialism and the Pan-African Struggle for Peace and Freedom: Ghana, 1959–1962," *Souls* 10, no. 2 (2008): 83–102. See also Bill Sutherland and Matt Meyer, *Guns and Gandhi in Africa: Pan African Insights on Nonviolence, Armed Struggle and Liberation in Africa* (Trenton, NJ: Africa World, 2000), 34–42.

14. Editorial Note, *Foreign Relations of the United States, 1958–1960*, vol. XIV (Washington, DC: State Department, 1958–60), 741–42. More broadly, see Thomas Borstelmann, *The Cold War and the Color Line: American Race Relations in the Global Arena* (Cambridge, MA: Harvard University Press,

2001), 126–28; Tom Lodge, *Sharpeville: An Apartheid Massacre and Its Consequences* (Oxford: Oxford University Press, 2011).

15. On the Ghanaian reaction to Sharpeville, see Jeffrey S. Ahlman, "Road to Ghana: Nkrumah, Southern Africa, and the Eclipse of a Decolonizing Africa," *Kronos: Southern African Histories* 37 (2011): 31–34.

16. Public Records and Archives Administration Department (hereafter cited as PRAAD), Accra, Recording Group (hereafter cited as RG) 17/1/80 (Special Collections [hereafter cited as SC]/BAA/251), A. K. Barden, "Report on the 2nd All-African People's Conference held in Tunis on 25th January 1960," n.d.

17. PRAAD-Accra, Administrative Files (hereafter cited as ADM) 13/1/29, Cabinet Minutes, 28 July 1960.

18. Rosalyn Higgins, *United Nations Peacekeeping, 1946–1967: Documents and Commentary*, vol. 3, *Africa* (Oxford: Oxford University Press, 1980), 88. On the establishment of the United Nations mission in the Congo, see Lise Namikas, *Battleground Africa: Cold War in the Congo, 1960–1965* (Stanford, CA: Stanford University Press, 2013), 62–96.

19. Kwame Nkrumah, *The Challenge of the Congo* (London: Thomas Nelson and Sons, 1967), 30–31.

20. GPRL, BAA/RLAA/392, "Nkrumah Suggests Six-Point Solution to Congo Crisis," *Ghanaian Times*, 10 October 1960.

21. Namikas, *Battleground Africa*, 1–3, 112–16, 118–21. See also Ludo De Witte, *The Assassination of Lumumba*, trans. Ann Wright and Renée Fenby (New York: Verso, 2001).

22. GPRL, BAA/RLAA/370, Barden to Nkrumah, "Ghana's Role in Emergent Africa," 25 July 1960.

23. Kwame Nkrumah, Address on Ghana Radio, 14 February 1961, in Accra (American Embassy) to Secretary of State, No. 936, 15 February 1961, in John F. Kennedy National Security Files, Africa: National Security Files, 1961–1963 (Frederick, MD: University Publications of America, 1987) (hereafter cited as JFK National Security Files), Reel 7.

24. Accra (American Embassy) to Secretary of State, No. 951, 16 February 1961, in Confidential U.S. State Department Central Files, Ghana, 1960–January 1963: Internal and Foreign Affairs (hereafter cited as Confidential US State Department Files), Reel 1.

25. GPRL, BAA/RLAA/802, Alphonse Ebassa to Nkrumah, "Congo's Crisis, Lumumba's Death," Freetown, Sierra Leone, 17 February 1961.

26. Convention People's Party, *Programme of the Convention People's Party for Work and Happiness* (Accra: Central Committee of the Party, 1962), 3–7.

27. Ibid., 5.

28. Yao Boateng, in Republic of Ghana, National Assembly, *Parliamentary Debates*, 11 September 1962, vol. 28, col. 174.

29. PRAAD-Accra, RG 17/1/180 (SC/BAA/150), "Memorandum on Party Organisation and Ideology," n.d.

30. Sulemana Ibun Iddrissu, in Republic of Ghana, National Assembly, *Parliamentary Debates*, 11 September 1962, col. 170.

31. "Draft Programme of the Convention People's Party for Work and Happiness," *Evening News*, 28 July 1962.

32. A. K. Barden, "Evolution of Ghanaian Society," *Voice of Africa*, February 1964.

33. *Evening News*, 11 August 1962, quoted in James B. Engle, American Embassy, Accra, to Department of State, "Ghanaian Press Treatment of the Attempt to Assassinate President Nkrumah" [21 August 1962?], in JFK National Security Files, Reel 8.

34. Roger Hilsman to Acting Secretary, Director of Intelligence and Research, State Department, "Nkrumah Removes British Officers from Army Command," [September 1961], in JFK National Security Files, Reel 8; L.D. Battle to McGeorge Bundy, "The Volta Project and the Current Political Situation in Ghana," [October 1961?], in JFK National Security Files, Reel 7; Accra (American Embassy) to Secretary of State, no. 927, 5 December 1961, in JFK National Security Files, Reel 8; H. T. Alexander, *African Tightrope: My Two Years as Nkrumah's Chief of Staff* (London: Pall Mall, 1965).

35. On the events leading to Sutherland's decision to leave Ghana, see Sutherland and Meyer, *Guns and Gandhi in Africa*, 45–46.

36. Erica Powell, *Private Secretary (Female)/Gold Coast* (New York: St. Martin's, 1984), 184–87, 189–92.

37. Kwame Nkrumah, *Guide to Party Action: Address by Osagyefo Dr. Kwame Nkrumah at the First Seminar at the Winneba Ideological School on 3rd February, 1962* (Accra: Central Committee of the Convention People's Party, 1962), 4.

38. Kwame Nkrumah Ideological Institute, *Prospectus* (Accra: Government Printing Office, [1963/1964?]).

39. GPRL, BAA/RLAA/423, Kwame Nkrumah Ideological Institute Curriculum, 14 September 1961; the first two pages of this document are missing from the archival record. See also GPRL, BAA/RLAA/423, National Council for Higher Education and Research, "Draft Memorandum: Development of the Kwame Nkrumah Institute, Winneba, as The Institute of Political Science," Accra, 24 January 1962.

40. Kwame Nkrumah Ideological Institute, *Prospectus*, 7; GPRL, BAA/RLAA/423, National Council for Higher Education and Research, "Draft Memorandum: Development of the Kwame Nkrumah Institute, Winneba, as The Institute of Political Science," Accra, 24 January 1962.

41. Interview with Ben A. Nikoi-Oltai, Accra, 28 November 2007. Nikoi-Oltai never finished his degree at the KNII given that his program of study was interrupted by the 1966 coup overthrowing Nkrumah, which resulted in the institute's closure.

42. Leslie James, *George Padmore and Decolonization from Below: Pan-Africanism, the Cold War, and the End of Empire* (New York: Palgrave Macmillan, 2015), 169.

43. W. Scott Thompson, *Ghana's Foreign Policy, 1957–1966: Diplomacy, Ideology, and the New State* (Princeton, NJ: Princeton University Press, 1969), 58.

44. GPRL, BAA/RLAA/328, Bright Nyondo to Minister of Education, Accra, 25 October 1961.

45. "Baako Has New Job in Cabinet Switch," *Daily Graphic*, 26 September 1959; Ama Biney, *The Political and Social Thought of Kwame Nkrumah* (New York: Palgrave Macmillan, 2011), 138.

46. PRAAD-Accra, ADM 13/1/28, Cabinet Minutes, 8 December 1958; Thompson, *Ghana's Foreign Policy*, 107.

47. Thompson, *Ghana's Foreign Policy*, 107n241.

48. Ibid., 107; Kofi Batsa, *The Spark: Times Behind Me: From Kwame Nkrumah to Hilla Limann* (London: Rex Collings, 1985), 13.

49. GPRL, BAA/RLAA/335, Schedule of Duties, [1964?].

50. Republic of Ghana, Ministry of Information and Broadcasting, *Nkrumah's Subversion in Africa: Documentary Evidence of Nkrumah's Interference in the Affairs of Other African States* (Accra: Ministry of Information and Broadcasting, 1966), 5.

51. Memorandum of Conversation between Richard Erstein, Fritz D. Berliner, and David B. Bolen, "Ghana Solo Trade Fair," 23 November 1960, in Confidential US State Department Files, Reel 8.

52. See, for instance, GPRL, BAA/RLAA/612, J. A. Asiboje to Ghana High Commissioner, London, 31 January 1960; GPRL, BAA/RLAA/729, Lawrence Uzoma D. Echemazu to Barden, Lagos, 25 February 1961; GPRL, BAA/RLAA/1047A, Ansu Osaio to Nkrumah, Moscow, 26 December 1961; GPRL, BAA/RLAA/25, Ossama el-Tayeb to the BAA, Chicago, 12 March 1962.

53. For a collection of letters requesting these BAA publications, see GPRL, file folder BAA/RLAA/27, "Read about Africa Campaign, 1962."

54. Ahlman, "Managing the Pan-African Workplace," 346–47.

55. GPRL, BAA/RLAA/159, Meeting in the Director's Office, Minutes, 28 September 1964.

56. Batsa, *The Spark*, 37–38.

57. Colin Legum, "Socialism in Ghana: A Political Interpretation," in *African Socialism*, ed. William H. Friedland and Carl G. Rosberg Jr. (Stanford, CA: Stanford University Press, 1964), 135–41, quote on 138.

58. Ibid., 139.

59. GPRL, BAA/RLAA/1A, Padmore to Nkrumah(?), "Establishments Proposal," Accra, 21 January 1959. See also GPRL, BAA/RLAA/1A, Padmore to Nkrumah, Accra, 21 January 1959. I want to thank Leslie James for directing me to the material in the GPRL, BAA/RLAA/1A, "Secretary's Personal Correspondence" file folder.

60. GPRL, BAA/RLAA/1A, Padmore to Nkrumah(?), "Establishment Proposal," Accra, 21 January 1959.

61. GPRL, BAA/RLAA/1A, Padmore to R. K. Gardiner, Accra, 25 March 1959; GPRL, BAA/RLAA/1A, Padmore to A. L. Adu, Accra, 19 May 1959.

62. GPRL, BAA/RLAA/248, [African Affairs Centre?], "African Affairs Centre: Explanation of Draft Estimate Expenditures," [November/December

1959]. See, by way of comparison, GPRL, BAA/RLAA/377, Establishment Secretariat, "Monthly Rate for Daily Rated Workers," 12 December 1963.

63. As several scholars show, most women in the formal sector supplemented their income with labor in the informal sector; Eugenia Date-Bah, "Female and Male Factory Workers in Accra," in *Female and Male in West Africa*, ed. Christine Oppong (London: George Allen and Unwin, 1983), 269; Christine Oppong and Katharine Abu, *Seven Roles of Women: Impact of Education, Migration, and Employment on Ghanaian Mothers* (Geneva: International Labour Office, 1987), 63–64.

64. See, for instance, Christine Oppong, *Middle Class African Marriage: A Family Study of Ghanaian Senior Civil Servants* (London: George Allen and Unwin, 1981), 90–94. Lisa Lindsay, for her part, traces similar practices in Nigeria; Lisa A. Lindsay, *Working with Gender: Wage Labor and Social Change in Southwestern Nigeria* (Portsmouth, NH: Heinemann, 2003), 43–46.

65. Margaret Peil, *The Ghanaian Factory Worker: Industrial Man in Africa* (Cambridge: Cambridge University Press, 1972), 109. For a more varied analysis, see Oppong and Abu, *Seven Roles of Women*, 63–68.

66. Kim England and Kate Boyer, "Women's Work: The Feminization and Shifting Meaning of Clerical Work," *Journal of Social History* 43, no. 2 (2009): 318. For a related study on the gender politics of office work, albeit for an earlier period in the Netherlands, see Francisca de Haan, *Gender and the Politics of Office Work: The Netherlands, 1860–1940* (Amsterdam: Amsterdam University Press, 1998).

67. Stephanie Spencer, *Gender, Work and Education in Britain in the 1950s* (New York: Palgrave Macmillan, 2005), 12, 2.

68. Ann W. Seidman, *Ghana's Development Experience, 1951–1966* (Nairobi: East African Publishing House, 1978), 114.

69. Convention People's Party, *Programme of the Convention People's Party for Work and Happiness*, 34.

70. On the Soviet Union, for instance, see Diane P. Koenker, "Men against Women on the Shop Floor in Early Soviet Russia: Gender and Class in the Socialist Workplace," *American Historical Review* 100, no. 5 (1995): 1438–39.

71. See, for instance, Josephine Sappor, "Careers for Ghana Women: Candid and Explicit Evaluation and Suggestions," *Ghanaian*, September 1961; Victoria Nyarku, "The Role of Women in Ghana," *Evening News*, 27 January 1962; Kate Sey, "Women in Ghanaian Society: They Have Equal Opportunities with Men," *Ghanaian*, April 1964; Ekua Mansa, "The Role of Women in Our Revolution," *Evening News*, 24 July 1964. For a broader discussion of the relationship between nation-building, women in the workforce, and the domestic sphere in the CPP, see Jeffrey S. Ahlman, "Africa's Kitchen Debate: Ghanaian Domestic Space in the Age of Cold War," in *Gender, Sexuality, and the Cold War: A Global Perspective*, ed. Philip E. Muehlenbeck (Nashville, TN: Vanderbilt University Press, 2017).

72. PRAAD-Sekondi, Western Regional Archives 8/1/189, Margaret S. Martei, "National Council of Ghana Women Preamble," 1962.

73. Ibid. See also Smith College, Sophia Smith Collection, Countries Collections (MS 445), Box 13, Folder 9, Ayensu, "Ghana," First Conference of Afro-Asian Women, Cairo, *Women's News* (New Delhi), January 1961.

74. Ahlman, "Africa's Kitchen Debate."

75. Barden, "Evolution of Ghanaian Society."

76. Of the available issues ranging from 1961 to 1965, these included: Sylvia Wynter, "Elegy to the South African Dead," *Voice of Africa*, February 1961; Edith Anderson, "West Germany Wants Territories," *Voice of Africa*, March 1961; Kay Beauchamp, "The Role of African Women," *Voice of Africa*, March 1962; Rosalynde Ainslie, "The Unholy Alliance," *Voice of Africa*, August 1962; Anila Graham, "Conférence du Commonwealth sur le Marché Commun," *Voice of Africa*, October/November/December 1962; Mrs. O. G. Abrahams, "Education in South West Africa," *Voice of Africa*, February 1964; Castro Soromenho, "Queen Nzinga of Angola," *Voice of Africa*, March/April 1964; A Special Correspondent, "Women in Mozambique," *Voice of Africa*, January 1965.

77. C. L. R. James, *Nkrumah and the Ghana Revolution*, 56.

78. Kwame Nkrumah, *Ghana: The Autobiography of Kwame Nkrumah* (Edinburgh: Thomas Nelson and Sons, 1957), 108.

79. See, for instance, Akua Assaabea, "Awake! Women of Ghana," *Evening News*, 28 May 1949; Yaa Asantewaa, "Towards Freedom via Nkrumaism: Positive Action and Tactical Action in Our Struggle," *Freedom: CPP Monthly Magazine*, December 1952.

80. Jean Allman, "The Disappearing of Hannah Kudjoe: Nationalism, Feminism, and the Tyrannies of History," *Journal of Women's History* 21, no. 3 (2009): 13–35.

81. Perhaps the most remarkable exception to this representation was a 1961 political cartoon featuring British prime minister Harold Macmillan dressed in drag as the mother of Katangan separatist rebel Moïse Tshombe, who was represented with a caricatured monkey face. In the cartoon, French president Charles de Gaulle served as Tshombe's father; "Son Tshombe," *Evening News*, 12 December 1961.

82. GPRL, BAA/RLAA/237, Sam to unknown, Accra, 6 February 1962.

83. GPRL, BAA/RLAA/237, Sam to Patterson, Accra, 28 February 1962.

84. GPRL, BAA/RLAA/232, Dzima to Odoom, Accra, 13 December 1965.

85. GPRL, BAA/RLAA/187, E. A. Tetteh-Batsa (?) to Barden, "Misbehaviour of V. Menka," Accra, 6 February 1964.

86. GPRL, BAA/RLAA/729, Williams A. Utchay to Makonnen, Accra, 23 July 1962; National Archives of the United Kingdom, Dominions Office 164/40, "Ghanaian Pan-Africanist Activities," 26 January 1962; GPRL, BAA/RLAA/365, Nancy W. Mungai to Principal Secretary, African Affairs Secretariat, Accra, 15 September 1965. I want to thank Jean Allman for sharing the file from the National Archives.

87. GPRL, BAA/RLAA/365, Mungai to Principal Secretary, African Affairs Secretariat, Accra, 15 September 1965.

88. See, for instance, BAA/RLAA/120, Barden to B. Myers-Biney, "Publication—Circulations by the Bureau," Accra, 16 December 1963.

89. In many ways, Ghana's "modern women"—in terms of their representation and the challenges faced by Ghana's young women in institutions like the BAA—are a midcentury variation of the "modern girl" of the interwar period, as analyzed by the Modern Girl Around the World Research Group; see Alys Eve Weinbaum, Lynn M. Thomas, Priti Ramamurthy, et al., *The Modern Girl around the World: Consumption, Modernity, and Globalization* (Durham, NC: Duke University Press, 2008).

90. See, for instance, the unnamed aspiring nurse quoted in Oppong and Abu, *Seven Roles of Women*, 67–68.

91. Jean Allman, "Fathering, Mothering, and Making Sense of *Ntamoba*: Reflections on the Economy of Child-Rearing in Colonial Asante," *Africa* 67, no. 2 (1997): 296–321; Lisa A. Lindsay, "Domesticity and Difference: Male Breadwinners, Working Women, and Colonial Citizenship in the 1945 Nigerian General Strike," *American Historical Review* 104, no. 3 (1999): 783–812; Lindsay, *Working with Gender*, 105–26; Frederick Cooper, "Industrial Man Goes to Africa," in *Men and Masculinities in Modern Africa*, ed. Lisa A. Lindsay and Stephan F. Miescher (Portsmouth, NH: Heinemann, 2003), 128–37. Allman specifically notes at least a partial change in many fathers' own expectations regarding their rights to their children accompanying rising expectations of paternal care.

92. As Emmanuel Akyeampong has suggested, in Ghana, there was often a gap between the reality and ideal in terms of men's abilities to live up to the role of provider, but, according to him, a man had to at least give the appearance of being able and willing to provide for his wife or wives and children. Emmanuel Akyeampong, *Drink, Power, and Cultural Change: A Social History of Alcohol in Ghana, c. 1800 to Recent Times* (Portsmouth, NH: Heinemann, 1993), 153.

93. See, for instance, Peil, *Ghanaian Factory Worker*, 190–200; Akyeampong, *Drink, Power, and Cultural Change*, 152–53, and, to a different extent, Stephan F. Miescher, *Making Men in Ghana* (Bloomington: Indiana University Press, 2005), 115–52.

94. "There Would Be No Question of Illegitimate Children, They Would All Have Rights," *Evening News*, 26 May 1962; Convention People's Party, *Programme of the Convention People's Party for Work and Happiness*, 34–35; O. Owusu-Afriyie, in *Parliamentary Debates*, 1 April 1963, vol. 31, cols. 576–80; Lucia Mercilene, "A Woman's Eye-View of Maintenance of Children Bill," *Ghanaian*, June 1963.

95. "Is There Equal Work Between the Sexes?," *Ghanaian*, August 1964.

96. V. Kojo Abekwa, "Favouritism Towards Female Employees," *Evening News*, 25 February 1964.

97. PRAAD-Accra, no Record Group number (SC/BAA/40), Nkrumah, "Broadcast by Osagyefo the President on 30th April 1963." This file folder is not listed in the current RG 17/1/- finding aid; it is SC/BAA/40 in the previous list.

98. Kwesi Bonsu, "It Occurs to Me," *Ghanaian*, January 1962; PRAAD-Kumasi, Ashanti Regional Archives 17/6/7, "Attitude Toward Employment of Women," *Party Chronicle*, 11 December 1963.

99. Bonsu, "It Occurs to Me."

100. "Stop Gossiping: Women Told," *Evening News*, 20 October 1964.

101. GPRL, BAA/RLAA/327, Meeting of the Bureau of African Affairs Senior Officers, Minutes, 21 November 1961.

102. Ibid. It is important to note that Barden couched his references to infiltration and proper behavior at parties in relation to the recent sacking of an employee of the bureau's Linguistics Section, discussed at the opening of this chapter.

103. GPRL, BAA/RLAA/159, Meeting in the Director's Office, Minutes, 28 September 1964; Ahlman, "Managing the Pan-African Workplace," 350–51.

104. GPRL, BAA/RLAA/376, "General Office Instructions—All Staff," 5 September 1961; GPRL, BAA/RLAA/337, Republic of Ghana, "Oath of Secrecy," 1964.

105. GPRL, BAA/RLAA/376, Barden, "Schedule of Duties: Receptionist," 6 September 1961.

106. GPRL, BAA/RLAA/376, Barden, "General Office Instructions—All Staff," 5 September 1961.

107. GPRL, BAA/RLAA/215, D. B. Sam to Comfort de Souza, Accra, 19 April 1962. The same letter with different addressees also appears in the personnel files of Dinah Patterson (BAA/RLAA/237), Victoria Cosmas (BAA/RLAA/134), and Felicia Welbeck (BAA/RLAA/217). Other women included in the incident were Kate Kissieh, Gladys Kumah, Mercy Lamptey, Mable Akuffo, and Gloria Lamptey.

108. GPRL, BAA/RLAA/237, Sam to Patterson (2), Accra, 19 April 1962.

109. GPRL, BAA/RLAA/665, "Congo 'Student Administration' Publish Alleged Nkrumah Letter," Reuters, 29 September 1960; Nkrumah, Address on Ghana Radio, 14 February 1961, in Accra (American Embassy) to Secretary of State, No. 936, 15 February 1961, in JFK National Security Files, Reel 7; Nkrumah, *Challenge of the Congo*.

110. See, for instance, GPRL, BAA/RLAA/961, Barden, "Mr. Oliveira Moita de Deus Luis Carlos," n.d.; GPRL, BAA/RLAA/772, "No Ghanaians among Caught Angolans," *Ghanaian Times*, 17 June 1961; Bureau of African Affairs, *The Angola Story: Grim Struggle for Liberation* (Accra: Bureau of African Affairs, [1962]). For Ghana's relations with southern African liberation politics, see Ahlman, "Road to Ghana."

111. Kwame Nkrumah, *Laying the Foundation Stone of the Kwame Nkrumah Institute* (Accra: Ministry of Information and Broadcasting, 1961), 4.

112. GPRL, BAA/RLAA/376, Barden, "General Office Instructions—All Staff," 5 September 1961. On the cultural politics of the telephone in the bureau specifically, see Ahlman, "Managing the Pan-African Workplace," 351–54.

113. GPRL, BAA/RLAA/376, Barden, "Schedule of Duties: Receptionist," 6 September 1961.

114. Memorandum for Mr. McGeorge Bundy, the White House, "Ghanaian Subversion in Africa," 12 February 1962, in JFK National Security Files, Reel 8 ; "Is U.S. Money Aiding Another Communist State? Hearing before the Subcommittee to Investigate Administration of the Internal Security Act and Other Internal Security Laws of the Committee on the Judiciary, United States Senate, Eighty-Seventh Congress, Second Session: Testimony of K. A. Busia, December 3, 1962," in JFK National Security Files, Reel 9; Tawia Adamafio, *By Nkrumah's Side: The Labour and the Wounds* (Accra: Westcoast Publishing House, 1982), 104.

115. Thompson, *Ghana's Foreign Policy*, 308–15.

116. American Embassy, Accra, to Department of State, Washington, "Ghana Celebrates Its Third Anniversary: A Brief Look at Its Past, Present, and Future," Accra, 3 March 1960, in Confidential US State Department Files, Reel 1.

117. American Consulate General, Johannesburg, to Department of State, Washington, "Political and Subversive—Report of Nasser-Trained Ghana-Trained Saboteurs in South Africa," Johannesburg, 27 December 1961, in Confidential US State Department Files, Reel 4; American Embassy, Accra, to Department of State, Washington, "Possibility That Former Workers' Brigade Camp at Ho Now Being Used by Bureau of African Affairs," Accra, 24 January 1963, in Confidential US State Department Files, Reel 2. See also Republic of Ghana, Ministry of Broadcasting and Information, *Nkrumah's Subversion in Africa*, 3–36.

118. United States Embassy in Accra to Secretary of State, Accra, N. 995, 1 February 1963, in JFK National Security Files, Reel 9.

CHAPTER 6: NEGOTIATING NKRUMAHISM

1. American Embassy, Accra, to Department of State, Washington, "Ghana's Future Labor, Employment, and Trade Union Policies," No. 562, 15 May 1962, in Confidential U.S. State Department Central Files, Ghana, 1960–January 1963: Internal and Foreign Affairs (hereafter cited as Confidential US State Department Files), Reel 6.

2. Howard University Moorland-Spingarn Research Center (hereafter cited as MSRC), Manuscript Division, Kwame Nkrumah Papers (hereafter cited as Nkrumah Papers), Box 154-38, Folder 80, Afari-Gyan, "The Task of Mental Decolonisation," n.d.

3. Dennis Austin, *Politics in Ghana, 1946–1960* (London: Oxford University Press, 1964), 414–15.

4. William Tubman, quoted in Philip E. Muehlenbeck, *Betting on the Africans: John F. Kennedy's Courting of African Nationalist Leaders* (Oxford: Oxford University Press, 2013), 143.

5. Nelson Mandela, quoted in W. Scott Thompson, *Ghana's Foreign Policy, 1957–1966: Diplomacy, Ideology, and the New State* (Princeton, NJ: Princeton University Press, 1969), 222.

6. See, for instance, "Nkrumah Does No Wrong," *Times of London*, 8 October 1963; "Right to Quash Decisions by Court," *Times of London*, 24 December 1963; Lloyd Garrison, "Portrait of Nkrumah as Dictator," *New York Times*, 3 May 1964; "Dr. Nkrumah's Socialism," *Times of London*, 18 January 1964; "Ghana Facing Tighter Rule," *New York Times*, 9 February 1964; "Ghana," *Atlantic*, May 1964.

7. J. Kirk Sale, "The Loneliness of Kwame Nkrumah," *New York Times*, 27 June 1965. Emphasis in original.

8. Maxwell Owusu, *Uses and Abuses of Political Power: A Case Study of Continuity and Change in the Politics of Ghana*, 2nd ed. (Accra: Ghana Universities Press, 2006), 337.

9. Dennis Austin, "The Working Committee of the United Gold Coast Convention," *Journal of African History* 2, no. 2 (1961): 285.

10. Moses T. Agyeman-Anane, "National Charges against Mr. Kwame Nkrumah," quoted in Jean Allman, *The Quills of the Porcupine: Asante Nationalism in an Emergent Ghana* (Madison: University of Wisconsin Press, 1993), 35–36, quotes on 36.

11. "National Liberation Movement Membership Card," in Commonwealth Political Ephemera from the Institute of Commonwealth Studies, University of London, Phase I: Africa, Part 4: West Africa, Ghana (hereafter cited as Commonwealth Political Ephemera), PP6, Fiche 10.

12. Kwame Nkrumah, in Government of Ghana, National Assembly, *Parliamentary Debates*, 14 July 1958, vol. 11, cols. 407, 410.

13. J. A. Braimah, in Government of Ghana, National Assembly, *Parliamentary Debates*, 14 July 1958, col. 411.

14. R. R. Amponsah, in Government of Ghana, National Assembly, *Parliamentary Debates*, 14 July 1958, col. 422, 423. In late 1958, Amponsah himself was arrested for purported involvement in a coup designed to overthrow and assassinate Nkrumah, which would ultimately subject him to preventative detention. See Jeffrey S. Ahlman, "'The Strange Case of Major Awhaitey': Conspiracy, Testimonial Evidence, and Narratives of Nation in Ghana's Postcolonial Democracy," *International Journal of African Historical Studies* (forthcoming).

15. United Party, *Ghana at the Cross-Roads: A Statement by the National Executive of the United Party on the Government's Decision to Change Ghana into a Republic* (Accra: United Party Headquarters, [1960]), 1, 3–4, reproduced in Commonwealth Political Ephemera, PP16, Fiche 15.

16. K. A. Gbedemah, *It Will Not Be "Work and Happiness for All": An Open Letter Being Also an Appeal to Dr. Kwame Nkrumah (First President of*

the Republic of Ghana) and Comment on, and Criticism of the Proposed New 7 Year Ghana Development Plan (n.p.: n.p., 1962), 6–8, quotes on 6 and 8.

17. Kwame Nkrumah, *Ghana: The Autobiography of Kwame Nkrumah* (Edinburgh: Thomas Nelson and Sons, 1957), 144.

18. Ndabaningi Sithole, "One-Party versus Two-Party System," *Voice of Africa,* September 1961.

19. Ibid. See also Madeira Keita, "One Party System," *Voice of Africa,* October 1961; Julius Nyerere, "One Party System of Government," *Voice of Africa,* May 1962.

20. Public Records and Archives Administration Department (hereafter cited as PRAAD), Accra, Record Group (hereafter cited as RG) 17/1/180 (Special Collections [hereafter cited as SC]/Bureau of African Affairs [hereafter cited as BAA]/150), "Memorandum on Party Organisation and Ideology," n.d.

21. Kwame Nkrumah, *I Speak of Freedom: A Statement of African Ideology* (New York: Frederick A. Praeger, 1961), 164. Also quoted in Colin Legum, "Socialism in Ghana: A Political Interpretation," in *African Socialism,* ed. William H. Friedland and Carl G. Rosberg Jr. (Stanford, CA: Stanford University Press, 1964), 138, with much of the language also incorporated into PRAAD-Accra, RG 17/1/180 (SC/BAA/150), "Memorandum on Party Organisation and Ideology," n.d.

22. PRAAD-Accra, RG 17/1/180 (SC/BAA/150), "Memorandum on Party Organisation and Ideology," n.d.

23. Nkrumah, *I Speak of Freedom,* 164.

24. George Padmore Research Library on African Affairs (hereafter cited as GPRL), BAA/Research Library on African Affairs (hereafter cited as RLAA)/222, Yumu et al. to Ofori-Bah, Accra, 11 November 1965. See also Jeffrey S. Ahlman, "Managing the Pan-African Workplace: Discipline, Ideology, and the Cultural Politics of the Ghanaian Bureau of African Affairs," *Ghana Studies* 15–16 (2012–13): 364.

25. GPRL, BAA/RLAA/222, Yumu et al. to Ofori-Bah, Accra, 11 November 1965.

26. On the Ghanaian economic situation at the time of the typists' petition, see Republic of Ghana, Central Bureau of Statistics, *Economic Survey,* 1965 (Accra: Central Bureau of Statistics, 1966), esp. 101–3.

27. GPRL, BAA/RLAA/222, Yumu et al. to Ofori-Bah, Accra, 11 November 1965.

28. GPRL, BAA/RLAA/98, Bernard B.C. Akoi to A. K. Barden, Accra, 5 December 1961. Emphasis in original.

29. GPRL, BAA/RLAA/98, Bureau of African Affairs to Ghana News Agency et al., "Press Release," Accra, [1961/1962?].

30. Ibid.; GPRL, BAA/RLAA/98, Barden to Akoi, Accra, 16 December 1961.

31. "These Gallant Activists: Drove the Kumasi-Accra Train during the Strike," *Party: CPP Journal* 12, September 1961.

32. GPRL, BAA/RLAA/98, Akoi to D. B. Sam, "Petition for Salary Review," Accra, 22 April 1963.

33. See, for instance, "New Brigade Camp to Boost Up Agricultural Activities," *Evening News*, 29 January 1962; PRAAD-Accra, RG 17/1/49C (SC/BAA/505), National Organiser of the Ghana Workers' Brigade to Kwame Nkrumah, Accra, 25 November 1965. Former brigader Yaa Fosuawaa, and E. B. Mensah, whose brother was a brigader, hint at this system in their discussions of the Brigade's benefits; interviews with E. B. Mensah, Accra, 29 March 2008 and 8 June 2008, and interview with Yaa Fosuawaa, Koforidua, Eastern Region, 25 May 2008.

34. See, for example, the complaints issued by a 1968 brigader writing under the alias of "A Citizen": PRAAD-Accra, Record Group (hereafter cited as RG) 14/1/60, "A Citizen" to Chairman, Expediting Committee, "Complaint about Pay Anomalies in the Workers Brigade," Omankope, 20 May 1968. In terms of policing discipline, see "'Punishment Cells' to Be Built at Brigade Camps," *Daily Graphic*, 10 July 1959.

35. Nkrumah, *I Speak of Freedom*, 209.

36. On chieftaincy, see Richard Rathbone, *Nkrumah and the Chiefs: The Politics of Chieftaincy in Ghana, 1951–1960* (Athens: Ohio University Press, 2000), esp. 140–49; and Rathbone, "Things Fall Apart: The Erosion of Local Government, Local Justice and Civil Rights in Ghana, 1955–60," in *The British Empire in the 1950s: Retreat or Revival?*, ed. Martin Lynn (New York: Palgrave Macmillan, 2006). On the CPP's relationship to the *asafo* companies, see "Asafo Companies Will Be Public Watch Dogs," *Evening News*, 18 January 1962; Kwesi Jonah, "The C.P.P. and the Asafo Besuon: Why Unlike Poles Did Not Attract," *Transactions of the Historical Society of Ghana*, n.s., 3 (1999): 47–56.

37. Interview with Kwasi Assiore, Accra, 24 April 2008.

38. For a first-hand description of life as a Ghanaian political prisoner, see Joseph Appiah, *Joe Appiah: The Autobiography of an African Patriot* (Accra: Asempa, 1996), 257–68; first published 1990 by Praeger, New York.

39. PRAAD-Kumasi, Ashanti Regional Archives (hereafter cited as ARG) 17/1/19, Assistant Security Officer to Regional Organiser of the Ghana Young Pioneers (Ashanti Region), Kumasi, 20 October 1962. See also PRAAD-Kumasi, ARG 17/1/19, Francis Emmal Osei Kofi to Regional Organiser of the Ghana Young Pioneers (Ashanti Region), "Report against Messrs Kwadwo Nyame, Kwaku Atuahene House Numbers PR. 42 and PR. 22 Pramso Respectively," Jachie-Ashanti, 9 October 1962.

40. PRAAD-Kumasi, ARG 17/1/19, Assistant Security Officer to Regional Organiser of the Ghana Young Pioneers (Ashanti Region), Kumasi, 20 October 1962.

41. MSRC, Nkrumah Papers, Box 154-38, Folder 80, Afari-Gyan, "The Task of Mental Decolonisation," n.d. Relatedly, see Frank Gerits, "The Ideological Scramble for Africa: the US, Ghanaian, French, and British Competition for

Africa's Future, 1953–1963" (PhD diss., European University Institute, 2014), 115–44 and esp. 117–18. Gerits highlights Afari-Gyan's terminology of "mental decolonisation," with its emphasis on the psychological aspects of decolonization and its diagnosis of the dangers of a residual colonial mentality in Ghana, as key to what he refers to as Ghana's Nkrumah-era public diplomacy.

42. MSRC, Nkrumah Papers, Box 154-38, Folder 80, Afari-Gyan, "The Task of Mental Decolonisation," n.d.

43. Interview with N. Sifah, Accra, 16 February 2008.

44. Interview with Kofi Ampadu, Koforidua, Eastern Region, 26 May 2008.

45. Peter Hodge, "The Ghana Workers Brigade: A Project for Unemployed Youth," *British Journal of Sociology* 15, no. 2 (1964): 118, 127–28n15.

46. Commission Appointed to Enquire into the Functions, Operation, and Administration of the Workers Brigade, *Report of the Commission Appointed to Enquire into the Functions, Operation, and Administration of the Workers Brigade* (Accra: Ministry of Information, 1966); P. Peregrino-Peters, "Brigader was Stripped and Whipped Says Probe Witness," *Daily Graphic*, 5 April 1967; Jeffrey S. Ahlman, "A New Type of Citizen: Youth, Gender, and Generation in the Ghanaian Builders Brigade," *Journal of African History* 53, no. 1 (2012): 103.

47. PRAAD-Accra, RG 14/1/15, "The Workers Brigade—Notes Taken at a Meeting in the Principal Secretary's Office—Ministry of Defence," Minutes, 14 March 1966; PRAAD-Accra, RG 14/1/15, "The Workers Brigade," 1966. By way of comparison, in the 1962–63 fiscal year, all of Ghana's defense consumption expenditures totaled £G9.2 million. Likewise, its general administration consumption expenditures were £G10.2 million, and those of justice and the police were £G5.4 million. See Republic of Ghana, Central Bureau of Statistics, *Economic Survey, 1963* (Accra: Ministry of Information and Broadcasting, 1964), 133.

48 PRAAD-Kumasi, ARG 17/6/6, Enoch Akonorh Bah (?), "We Are Neither Spies Nor Soldiers," ca. 1961–62.

49. "Osagyefo's Brainchild: Ghana Young Pioneer Movement 4 Years Old," *Evening News*, 13 June 1964.

50. In many ways, these acts of citizenship were also socialist manifestations of the claim-making modernity analyzed by Frederick Cooper and James Ferguson. See James Ferguson, *Expectations of Modernity: Myths and Meanings of Urban Life on the Zambian Copperbelt* (Berkeley: University of California Press, 1998); Frederick Cooper, *Colonialism in Question: Theory, Knowledge, History* (Berkeley: University of California Press, 2005), 131–35; and, by way of empirical illustration, Frederick Cooper, *Citizenship between Empire and Nation: Remaking France and French Africa, 1945–1960* (Princeton, NJ: Princeton University Press, 2014), 165–213.

51. PRAAD-Kumasi, ARG 17/1/19, Francis Emmal Osei Kofi to Regional Organiser of the Ghana Young Pioneers (Ashanti Region), "Report against Mr. James Kofi Nkonwa a Trader of Jachie House No. J.E. 97," Jachie, 12 September 1962.

52. Some popular accounts report that the bomb had been placed inside the bouquet; see interview with Eden Bentum Takyi-Micah, Accra, 17 March 2008; interview with Mensah, Accra, 29 March 2008. Additionally, accounts differ as to the gender of the child delivering the bouquet to Nkrumah.

53. "Text of President Nkrumah's Radio Address of August 14, 1962: Our Nation Stands United—Death Can Never Extinguish the Flame Which I Have Lit," enclosure to American Embassy, Accra, to Department of State, "President Nkrumah's Radio Address of August 14," 16 August 1962, in Confidential US State Department Files, Reel 1.

54. Ibid. Nkrumah himself seemed to suggest three deaths. An American report stated that the exact number was unknown, but other witnesses claimed approximately six dead; Accra [Embassy] to Secretary of State, Accra, No. 380, 9 September 1962, in Confidential US State Department Files, Reel 2; Accra to Secretary of State, Accra, No. 495, 22 September 1962, in Confidential US State Department Files, Reel 2.

55. Accra [Embassy] to Secretary of State, Accra, No. 180, 3 August 1962, in John F. Kennedy National Security Files, Africa: National Security Files, 1961–1963 (Frederick, MD: University Publications of America, 1987) (hereafter cited as JFK National Security Files), Reel 8; "Text of President Nkrumah's Radio Address of August 14, 1962: Our Nation Stands United—Death Can Never Extinguish the Flame Which I Have Lit," enclosure to American Embassy, Accra, to Department of State, "President Nkrumah's Radio Address of August 14," 16 August 1962, in Confidential US State Department Files, Reel 1; Erica Powell, *Private Secretary (Female)/Gold Coast* (New York: St. Martin's, 1984), 193–94. On the rumors connecting Nkrumah's Kulungugu injuries to his subsequent cancer, see interview with Mensah, Accra, 29 March 2008.

56. D. Austin, "Working Committee of the United Gold Coast Convention," 280.

57. David Rooney, *Kwame Nkrumah: The Political Kingdom in the Third World* (New York: St. Martin's, 1988), 220. Adamafio's question, expressed in Ga, has become central to the popular narrative surrounding the event; see interview with Mensah, Accra, 29 March 2008.

58. Powell, *Private Secretary*, 194.

59. Central Intelligence Agency, "Appraisal of Nkrumah's Mental State," 31 August 1962, in JFK National Security Files, Reel 8; National Archives of the United Kingdom, Dominions Office 201/13, Geoffrey de Freitas, British High Commissioner in Ghana, to Secretary of State for Commonwealth Relations, "Ghana: Kulungugu and After," 27 October 1962.

60. See, for instance, Richard Jeffries, *Class, Power, and Ideology in Ghana: The Railwaymen of Sekondi* (Cambridge: Cambridge University Press, 1978), 106; Owusu, *Uses and Abuses of Political Power*, 317–38; interviews with Takyi-Micah, Accra, 17 March 2009 and 10 May 2008.

61. On Bessah's travels, see interview with Lawrence Bessah, Shama, Western Region, 5 July 2008.

62. Interview with S. Atta-P. Anamon, Lawrence Bessah, Francis D. Hayford, and Joseph Yawson, Shama, Western Region, 1 May 2008. For Anamon's fuller discussion see chapter 3.

63. See, for instance, M. N. Tetteh, *The Ghana Young Pioneer Movement: A Youth Organisation in the Kwame Nkrumah Era* (Tema: Ghana Publicity, 1999), 59–77; interviews with M. N. Tetteh, Accra, 8 March 2008 and 7 May 2008.

64. Ahmed Sékou Touré, *L'Afrique et la révolution* (Paris: Présence Africaine, 1967), 124–25, quote on 124.

65. See Jay Straker, *Youth, Nationalism, and the Guinean Revolution* (Bloomington: Indiana University Press, 2009); Mike McGovern, *Unmasking the State: Making Guinea Modern* (Chicago: University of Chicago Press, 2013).

66. Mohamed Mancona Kouyaté, *Nous sommes tous responsables* (Conakry: Imprimerie Moderne de Kaloum, 1996), 123, quoted in McGovern, *Unmasking the State*, 168.

67. Sidiki Kobélé Keita, *La Guinée de Sékou Touré: Pourquoi la prison du camp Boiro?* (Paris: L'Harmattan, 2014), 129–47, 273–75.

68. Elizabeth Schmidt, *Cold War and Decolonization in Guinea, 1946–1958* (Athens: Ohio University Press, 2008), 184.

69. Mairi S. MacDonald, "Guinea's Political Prisoners: Colonial Models, Postcolonial Innovation," *Comparative Studies in Society and History* 54, no. 4 (2012): 890.

70. See, for instance, James Brennan, "Youth, the TANU Youth League and Managed Vigilantism in Dar es Salaam, Tanzania, 1925–73," *Africa* 76, no. 2 (2006): 221–46; Klaas van Walraven, *The Yearning for Relief: A History of the Sawaba Movement in Niger* (Leiden: Brill, 2013); Meredith Terretta, "From Below and to the Left? Human Rights and Liberation Politics in Africa's Postcolonial Age," *Journal of World History* 24, no. 2 (2013): 389–416; Terretta, *Nation of Outlaws, State of Violence: Nationalism, Grassfields Tradition, and State Building in Cameroon* (Athens: Ohio University Press, 2014); Cooper, *Citizenship between Empire and Nation*, 438–40.

71. Commission of Enquiry into Ghana Prisons, *Mr. Obetsebi-Lamptey: Detention and Death in Nsawam Prison: Extracts from Evidence of Witnesses at the Commission of Enquiry into Ghana Prisons* (Accra-Tema: Ministry of Information and Broadcasting, [1967/1968?]).

72. PRAAD-Accra, Administrative Files 5/3/143, *Dr. J. B. Danquah: Detention and Death in Nsawam Prison: Extracts from Evidence of Witnesses at the Commission of Enquiry into Ghana Prisons* (Accra-Tema: Ministry of Information and Broadcasting, 1967), i, ii.

73. Appiah, *Joe Appiah*, 266.

74. Accra (American Embassy) to Secretary of State, No. 318, 29 August 1962, in Confidential US State Department Files, Reel 2; Accra (American Embassy) to Secretary of State, No. 380, 9 September 1962, in Confidential

US State Department Files, Reel 2; D. Austin, *Politics in Ghana*, 412–13. Even Nkrumah's legal advisor and friend, Ghana's former attorney general Geoffrey Bing, questioned the evidence against the Kulungugu conspirators; Geoffrey Bing, *Reap the Whirlwind: An Account of Kwame Nkrumah's Ghana from 1950 to 1966* (London: MacGibbon and Kee, 1968), 410–12.

75. Nkrumah, in Republic of Ghana, National Assembly, *Parliamentary Debates*, 26 March 1965, vol. 38, col. 1529.

76. Muehlenbeck, *Betting on the Africans*, 92–96.

77. See Mary E. Montgomery, "The Eyes of the World Were Watching: Ghana, Great Britain, and the United States, 1957–1966" (PhD diss., University of Maryland, 2004), 195–213; Robert B. Rakove, *Kennedy, Johnson, and the Nonaligned World* (Cambridge: Cambridge University Press, 2013), 192–93.

78. Thomas L. Hughes to the Secretary [of State], "Nkrumah's Frustration: An Opening for the Communist World," in Lyndon Baines Johnson National Security Files, 1963–1969: Africa National Security Files (hereafter cited as LBJ National Security Files), Reel 8.

79. David J. Finlay, Ole R. Holsti, and Richard R. Fagen, *Enemies in Politics* (Chicago: Rand McNally, 1967), 163–64.

80. Powell, *Private Secretary*, 199–200.

81. "Osagyefo Overpowers the Assassin," *Ghanaian Times*, 3 January 1964; "Osagyefo Battles with Gunman and Conquers!," *Evening News*, 3 January 1964; "Osagyefo Triumphs Over Assailant," *Daily Graphic*, 3 January 1964.

82. "Osagyefo Overpowers the Assassin," *Ghanaian Times*, 3 January 1964.

83. Accra (American Embassy) to Department of State, Secstate 474, 3 January 1964, in LBJ National Security Files, Reel 8.

84. Owusu, *Uses and Abuses of Political Power*, 325.

85. Interview with Ampadu, Koforidua, Eastern Region, 26 May 2008.

86. Interviews with Takyi-Micah, Accra, 17 March and 10 May 2008.

87. GPRL, BAA/RLAA/230, Senior Research Office, "Security Precaution RE: The Visit of Osagyefo the President to the Bureau of African Affairs," Accra, 13 December 1965.

88. Ibid. See Ofori-Bah's comment affixed to the report.

89. Interview with Kofi Duku, Accra, 7 May 2008.

CONCLUSION: "FORWARD EVER, BACKWARD NEVER"

1. "Kwame Off to Hanoi," *Daily Graphic*, 22 February 1966. On the Hanoi trip, see W. Scott Thompson, *Ghana's Foreign Policy, 1957–1966: Diplomacy, Ideology, and the New State* (Princeton, NJ: Princeton University Press, 1969), 409–13; Joe-Fio N. Meyer, *Dr. Nkrumah's Last Journey: The Sensational Viet-Nam U.S. War* (Accra: Advance Press, 1985).

2. For the planning and execution of the coup, see A. A. Afrifa, *The Ghana Coup: 24th February 1966* (London: Frank Cass, 1966), 31–37; A. K. Ocran, *A Myth Is Broken: An Account of the Ghana Coup d'État of 24th February*,

1966 (Accra: Longmans, Green, 1968), 49–84; Peter Barker, *Operation Cold Chop: The Coup That Toppled Nkrumah* (Accra: Ghana Publishing Corporation, 1969), 133–210; Dennis Austin, *Ghana Observed: Essays on the Politics of a West African Republic* (Manchester: Manchester University Press, 1976), 102–6.

3. Interview with Ben A. Nikoi-Oltai, Accra, 28 November 2007.

4. Kevin K. Gaines, *American Africans in Ghana: Black Expatriates and the Civil Rights Era* (Chapel Hill: University of North Carolina Press, 2006), 228–29.

5. In his memoir, for instance, A. A. Afrifa recounts how he found former minister of defence and party ideologue Kofi Baako holed up with a rosary in a church near his home, while the military also reportedly discovered former propaganda minister N. A. Welbeck drunk in "a hiding-place in a remote corner of Accra"; Afrifa, *Ghana Coup*, 33.

6. Geoffrey Bing, *Reap the Whirlwind: An Account of Kwame Nkrumah's Ghana from 1950 to 1966* (London: MacGibbon and Kee, 1968), 372–73.

7. Gerald Horne, *Race Woman: The Lives of Shirley Graham Du Bois* (New York: New York University Press, 2000), 204.

8. Gaines, *American Africans in Ghana*, 233.

9. Public Records and Archives Administration Department, Accra, Record Group 3/5/1636, Office of the NLC, "Special Audit Investigations Ordered by the National Liberation Council," 19 April 1966; Jeffrey S. Ahlman, "Managing the Pan-African Workplace: Discipline, Ideology, and the Cultural Politics of the Ghanaian Bureau of African Affairs," *Ghana Studies* 15–16 (2012–13): 362–65.

10. Jeffrey S. Ahlman, "A New Type of Citizen: Youth, Gender, and Generation in the Ghanaian Builders Brigade," *Journal of African History* 53, no. 1 (2012): 102–4.

11. Interviews with Nikoi-Oltai, Accra, 28 November 2007 and 6 June 2008.

12. Interview with Lawrence Bessah, Shama, Western Region, 5 July 2008.

13. Interview with Thomas Daniel Laryea, Accra, 6 December 2007.

14. Interview with Kofi Ampadu, Koforidua, Eastern Region, 26 May 2008.

15. For instance, see A. A. Afrifa's discussion of what he saw as the future of Ghana after the coup; Afrifa, *Ghana Coup*, 107–20. See also D. Austin, *Ghana Observed*, 129–37, 150–55.

16. Interview with Yaa Fosuawaa, Koforidua, Eastern Region, 25 May 2008.

17. On the fragmented nature of the Ghanaian and, more broadly, African postcolonial archive, see Jean Allman, "Phantoms of the Archive: Kwame Nkrumah, a Nazi Pilot Named Hanna, and the Contingencies of Postcolonial History-Writing," *American Historical Review* 118, no. 1 (2013): 104–29.

18. Frederick Cooper, *Decolonization and African Society: The Labor Question in French and British Africa* (Cambridge: Cambridge University

Press, 1996), 6. Prasenjit Duara has made a similar point; Duara, "Introduction: The Decolonization of Asia and Africa in the Twentieth Century," in *Decolonization: Perspectives from Now and Then*, ed. Prasenjit Duara (New York: Routledge, 2003), 6–7.

19. On the "gatekeeper state," see Frederick Cooper, *Africa since 1940: The Past of the Present* (Cambridge: Cambridge University Press, 2002), 156–90.

Bibliography

ARCHIVES

Ghana

George Padmore Research Library on African Affairs, Accra
Public Records and Archives Administration Department, Accra
Public Records and Archives Administration Department, Cape Coast
Public Records and Archives Administration Department, Kumasi
Public Records and Archives Administration Department, Sekondi
Public Records and Archives Administration Department, Sunyani

United Kingdom

National Archives of the United Kingdom

United States

Howard University, Moorland-Spingarn Research Center
Mount Holyoke College, Archives and Special Collections
New York Public Library, Schomburg Center for Research in Black Culture
Princeton University Archives
Smith College, Sophia Smith Collection
University of Iowa Libraries, Special Collections and University Archives
University of Massachusetts-Amherst, Special Collections and Archives
Yale University, Beinecke Rare Book and Manuscript Library
Yale University Library, Manuscripts and Archives

MICROFILM COLLECTIONS

Commonwealth Political Ephemera from the Institute of Commonwealth
    Studies, University of London, Phase I, Part 4: West Africa, Ghana (West
    Yorkshire, England: Altair, 1990)
Confidential U.S. State Department Central Files, Ghana, 1960–January
    1963: Internal and Foreign Affairs (Bethesda, MD: LexisNexis, 2003)
Documents on African Political History, 1938–1970, compiled by Ruth
    Schachter Morgenthau (Waltham, MA: Cooperative Africana Microfilm
    Project)

Ivor Wilks–Phyllis Ferguson Collection of Material on Ghana (Chicago: University of Chicago, Photopublication Department, 1974)

John F. Kennedy National Security Files, Africa: National Security Files, 1961–1963 (Frederick, MD: University Publications of America, 1987)

John F. Kennedy National Security Files, Africa: National Security Files, 1961–1963, First Supplement (Frederick, MD: University Publications of America, 1987)

Lyndon Baines Johnson National Security Files, Africa: National Security Files, 1963–1969 (Frederick, MD: University Publications of America, 1987)

NEWSPAPERS, MAGAZINES, AND OTHER PERIODICALS

Ashanti Pioneer (Kumasi)
Ashanti Sentinel (Kumasi)
Atlantic Monthly (Boston)
Crisis (New York)
Daily Graphic (Accra)
Evening News (Accra)
Freedom: CPP Monthly Magazine (Accra)
Ghanaian (Accra)
Ghanaian Times (Accra)
Ghana Today (Accra)
Gold Coast Independent (Accra)
Gold Coast Methodist Times (Cape Coast)
Gold Coast Observer (Cape Coast)
Information Bulletin of the Trades Union Congress (Ghana) (Accra)
New African (London)
New York Times
Party Chronicle (Accra)
Party: CPP Journal (Accra)
People's Vanguard (Accra)
Spark (Accra)
Times of London
Voice of Africa (Accra)
West Africa (London)
West African Pilot (Lagos, Nigeria)

INTERVIEWS

All interviews were digitally recorded, except those marked with an asterisk (*), and were conducted in either English or Akan/Twi. Interviews were conducted with the assistance of a research assistant and, in the case of interviews conducted in Akan/Twi, were also translated and transcribed with the assistance of a research assistant.

Abenkwan, Magnet. Koforidua, Eastern Region. 26 May 2008.
Ampadu, Kofi. Koforidua, Eastern Region. 26 May 2008.

Anamon, S. Atta-P., Lawrence Bessah, Francis D. Hayford, and Joseph Yawson. Shama, Western Region. 1 May 2008.

Anonymous. Accra. *1 March 2009.

Asamoah, Lawrence. Koforidua, Eastern Region. 26 May 2008.

Asante, K. B. Accra. 6 May 2008, 30 June 2008.

Asiedu, S. Kofi. Accra. *25 November 2007, 16 March 2008.

Assiore, Kwasi. Accra. 24 April 2008.

Bessah, Lawrence. Shama, Western Region. 1 May 2008, 5 July 2008.

Brempong, Owusu. Legon, Greater Accra. 7 July 2008.

Budu, Nicholas. Accra. 17 December 2007.

Darko, Emmanuel. Koforidua, Eastern Region. 25 May 2008.

Dodoo, Benjamin. Tema, Greater Accra. 18 February 2009.

Duku, Kofi. Accra. 7 May 2008, 13 May 2008, 16 May 2008.

Fosuawaa, Yaa. Koforidua, Eastern Region. 25 May 2008.

Jantuah, K. S. P. (formerly J. E. Jantuah). Accra. 26 April 2008.

Kotey, Samuel Kofi. Tema, Greater Accra. 14 February 2009.

Laryea, Thomas Daniel. Accra. 6 December 2007, 18 March 2008.

Laryea, Victoria. Accra. 22 April 2008.

Mensah, E. B. Accra. 29 March 2008, 8 June 2008.

Mensah, E. B., and S. Kofi Asiedu. Accra. *9 December 2007.

Nikoi-Oltai, Ben A. Accra. *14 November 2007, 28 November 2007, 19 January 2008, 6 June 2008.

Sekyi, Emmanuel. Tema, Greater Accra. 18 February 2009.

Sifah, N. Accra. 16 February 2008, 16 March 2008.

Takyi-Micah, Eden Bentum. Accra. 17 March 2008, 10 May 2008.

Tettegah, John K. Accra. 28 February 2009.

Tetteh, M. N. Accra. 8 March 2008, 7 May 2008.

Tetteh, Moses. Tema, Greater Accra. 14 February 2009.

Tettey, Seth Laryea. Tema, Greater Accra. 19 February 2009.

Yeboah, Jacob Sesu. Accra. 24 February 2008, 13 April 2008.

GOVERNMENT REPORTS AND DOCUMENTS

Bureau of African Affairs. *The Angola Story: Grim Struggle for Liberation.* Accra: Bureau of African Affairs, [1962].

Colonial Office. *Report of the Commission of Enquiry into Disturbances in the Gold Coast, 1948.* London: His Majesty's Stationery Office, 1948.

Commission Appointed to Enquire into the Functions, Operation, and Administration of the Workers Brigade. *Report of the Commission Appointed to Enquire into the Functions, Operation, and Administration of the Workers Brigade.* Accra: Ministry of Information and Broadcasting, 1966.

Commission of Enquiry into Ghana Prisons. *Mr. Obetsebi-Lamptey: Detention and Death in Nsawam Prison: Extracts from Evidence of Witnesses at the Commission of Enquiry into Ghana Prisons.* Accra-Tema: Ministry of Information and Broadcasting, [1967/1968?].

Convention People's Party. *Programme of the Convention People's Party for Work and Happiness.* Accra: Central Committee of the Party, 1962.

Doxiadis Associates. *Tema: A Social Survey.* Tema: Doxiadis Associates, Ghana Offices, 1962.

Ghana, Government of. *Second Development Plan, 1959–1964.* Accra: Government Printer, 1959.

Ghana, Government of, Ministry of Housing, Town and Country Planning Division. *Accra: A Plan for the Town: The Report for the Minister of Housing.* Accra: Government Printer, 1958.

Ghana, Republic of, Census Office. *1960 Population Census of Ghana.* Vol. 1, *The Gazetteer.* Accra: Census Office, 1962.

———. *1960 Population Census of Ghana: Advance Report of Volumes III and IV: Demographic and Economic Characteristics of Regions.* Accra: Census Office, 1962.

———. *1970 Population Census of Ghana.* Vol. 2, *Statistics of Localities and Enumeration Areas.* Accra: Census Office, 1972.

Ghana, Republic of, Central Bureau of Statistics. *Economic Survey, 1961.* Accra: Ministry of Information and Broadcasting, 1962.

———. *Economic Survey, 1963.* Accra: Ministry of Information and Broadcasting, 1964.

———. *Economic Survey, 1965.* Accra: Central Bureau of Statistics, 1966.

Ghana, Republic of, Ministry of Information and Broadcasting. *Nkrumah's Subversion in Africa: Documentary Evidence of Nkrumah's Interference in the Affairs of Other African States.* Accra: Ministry of Information and Broadcasting, 1966.

———. *Statement by the Government on the Recent Conspiracy, Monday, 11th December 1961.* Accra: Ministry of Information and Broadcasting, 1961.

Ghana, Republic of, National Assembly. *Parliamentary Debates: Official Report: First Series.* Accra: State Publishing Company, 1957–1966.

Ghana Planning Commission. *Seven-Year Development Plan: A Brief Outline.* Accra: Government Printing Department, 1963.

Ghana Trades Union Congress. *An Outline of the Rights and Duties of Members and Officials of the Trades Union Congress (Ghana).* Accra: Education and Publicity Department of the Trades Union Congress, [1960?].

———. *What Economic Security Does the Ghanaian Worker Enjoy?* Accra: Education and Publicity Department, [n.d.].

Gold Coast, Census Office. *Census of Population, 1948: Report and Tables.* Accra: Government Printing Department, 1950.

Gold Coast, Department of Social Welfare and Community Development. *Problem Children of the Gold Coast.* Accra: Department of Social Welfare and Community Development, 1955.

Gold Coast, Education Department. *Accelerated Development Plan for Education, 1951.* Accra: Government Printing Department, 1951.

Gold Coast, Legislative Assembly. *Legislative Assembly Debates: Official Report*. Accra: Government Printing Department, 1951–1956.

International Bank for Reconstruction and Development. *Current Economic Position and Prospects of Ghana*. Report No. EA-121a, 29 August 1961. Washington, DC: Department of Operations, Europe, Africa, and Australia.

———. *Economic Report on Ghana*. Report No. EA-72b, 26 June 1957. Washington, DC: Department of Operations, Europe, Africa, and Australia.

———. *The Economy of Ghana*. Report No. EA-110a, 29 June 1960. Washington, DC: Department of Operations, Europe, Africa, and Australia.

Kwame Nkrumah Ideological Institute. *Prospectus*. Accra: Government Printing Office, [1963/1964?].

Tema Development Corporation. *Report and Accounts for the Period Ended 31st March 1954*. Accra: Government Printer, 1955.

US Department of State. *Foreign Relations of the United States, 1958–1960*. Vol. 14, *Africa*. Washington, DC: Government Printing Office, 1992.

PUBLISHED BOOKS AND ARTICLES

Acquah, Ioné. *Accra Survey: A Social Survey of the Capital of Ghana, Formerly Called the Gold Coast, Undertaken for the West African Institute of Social and Economic Research, 1953–1956*. London: University of London Press, 1958.

Adamafio, Tawia. *By Nkrumah's Side: The Labour and the Wounds*. Accra: Westcoast Publishing House, 1982.

Adi, Hakim. *West Africans in Britain, 1900–1960: Nationalism, Pan-Africanism, and Communism*. London: Lawrence and Wishart, 1998.

Adi, Hakim, and Marika Sherwood. *The 1945 Manchester Pan-African Congress Revisited*. London: New Beacon Books, 1995.

Afrifa, A. A. *The Ghana Coup: 24th February 1966*. London: Frank Cass, 1966.

Ahlman, Jeffrey S. "Africa's Kitchen Debate: Ghanaian Domestic Space in the Age of Cold War." In *Gender, Sexuality, and the Cold War: A Global Perspective*, edited by Philip E. Muehlenbeck, 157–77. Nashville, TN: Vanderbilt University Press, 2017.

———. "The Algerian Question in Nkrumah's Ghana, 1958–1960: Debating 'Violence' and 'Nonviolence' in African Decolonization." *Africa Today* 57, no. 2 (2010): 67–84.

———. "Managing the Pan-African Workplace: Discipline, Ideology, and the Cultural Politics of the Ghanaian Bureau of African Affairs." *Ghana Studies* 15–16 (2012–13): 337–71.

———. "A New Type of Citizen: Youth, Gender, and Generation in the Ghanaian Builders Brigade." *Journal of African History* 53, no. 1 (2012): 87–105.

———. "Road to Ghana: Nkrumah, Southern Africa, and the Eclipse of a Decolonizing Africa." *Kronos: Southern African Histories* 37 (2011): 23–40.

——. "'The Strange Case of Major Awhaitey': Conspiracy, Testimonial Evidence, and Narratives of Nation in Ghana's Postcolonial Democracy." *International Journal of African Historical Studies* (forthcoming).

Akyeampong, Emmanuel. *Drink, Power, and Cultural Change: A Social History of Alcohol in Ghana, c. 1800 to Recent Times.* Portsmouth, NH: Heinemann, 1993.

Alexander, H. T. *African Tightrope: My Two Years as Nkrumah's Chief of Staff.* London: Pall Mall, 1965.

Allett, John. *New Liberalism: The Political Economy of J. A. Hobson.* Toronto: University of Toronto Press, 1981.

Allman, Jean. "Between the Present and History: African Nationalism and Decolonization." In *The Oxford Handbook of Modern African History*, edited by John Parker and Richard Reid, 224–40. Oxford: Oxford University Press, 2013.

——. "The Disappearing of Hannah Kudjoe: Nationalism, Feminism, and the Tyrannies of History." *Journal of Women's History* 21, no. 3 (2009): 13–35.

——. "Fathering, Mothering, and Making Sense of *Ntamoba*: Reflections on the Economy of Child-Rearing in Colonial Asante." *Africa* 67, no. 2 (1997): 296–321.

——. "'Hewers of Wood, Carriers of Water': Islam, Class, and Politics on the Eve of Ghana's Independence." *African Studies Review* 34, no. 2 (1991): 1–26.

——. "Modeling Modernity: The Brief Story of Kwame Nkrumah, a Nazi Pilot Named Hanna, and the Wonders of Motorless Flight." In *Modernization as Spectacle in Africa*, edited by Peter J. Bloom, Stephan F. Miescher, and Takyiwaa Manuh, 229–43. Bloomington: Indiana University Press, 2014.

——. "Nuclear Imperialism and the Pan-African Struggle for Peace and Freedom: Ghana, 1959–1962." *Souls* 10, no. 2 (2008): 83–102.

——. "Phantoms of the Archive: Kwame Nkrumah, a Nazi Pilot Named Hanna, and the Contingencies of Postcolonial History-Writing." *American Historical Review* 118, no. 1 (2013): 104–29.

——. *The Quills of the Porcupine: Asante Nationalism in an Emergent Ghana.* Madison: University of Wisconsin Press, 1993.

Allman, Jean, and John Parker, *Tongnaab: The History of a West African God.* Bloomington: Indiana University Press, 2005.

Amarteifio, G. W., D. A. P. Butcher, and David Whitham. *Tema Manhean: A Study of Resettlement.* Accra: Ghana Universities Press, 1966.

Amenumey, D. E. K. *The Ewe Unification Movement: A Political History.* Accra: Ghana Universities Press, 1989.

Andrew, Edward. "Class in Itself and Class against Capital: Karl Marx and His Classifiers." *Canadian Journal of Political Science* 16, no. 3 (1983): 577–84.

Appiah, Joseph. *Joe Appiah: The Autobiography of an African Patriot.* Accra: Asempa, 1996. First published 1990 by Praeger, New York.

Apter, David E. *Ghana in Transition.* 2nd rev. ed. Princeton, NJ: Princeton University Press, 1972.

———. *The Gold Coast in Transition.* Princeton, NJ: Princeton University Press, 1955.

Arhin, Kwame, ed. *The Life and Work of Kwame Nkrumah: Papers of a Symposium Organized by the Institute of African Studies, University of Ghana, Legon.* Trenton, NJ: Africa World, 1993.

Armah, Ayi Kwei. *The Beautyful Ones Are Not Yet Born.* Boston: Houghton Mifflin, 1968.

Arthiabah, P. B. "The Ghana Trade Union Congress and Workers: Its Relationship with Past Governments and Contribution to National Development." Paper presented at the Symposium on the Life and Work of Kwame Nkrumah, organized by the Institute of African Studies, University of Ghana, Legon, May 27–June 1, 1985.

Asante, Clement E. *The Press in Ghana: Problems and Prospects.* Lanham, MD: University Press of America, 1996.

Atkins, Keletso E. *The Moon Is Dead! Give Us Our Money! The Cultural Origins of an African Work Ethic, Natal, South Africa, 1843–1900.* Portsmouth, NH: Heinemann, 1993.

Austin, Dennis. *Ghana Observed: Essays on the Politics of a West African Republic.* Manchester: Manchester University Press, 1976.

———. *Politics in Ghana, 1946–1960.* London: Oxford University Press, 1964.

———. "The Working Committee of the United Gold Coast Convention." *Journal of African History* 2, no. 2 (1961): 273–97.

Austin, Gareth. "Capitalists and Chiefs in the Cocoa Hold-Ups in South Asante, 1927–1938." *International Journal of African Historical Studies* 21, no. 1 (1988): 63–95.

Awooner-Renner, Bankole. *West African Soviet Union.* London: WANS, 1946.

Ballantyne, Tony, and Antoinette Burton. *Empires and the Reach of the Global, 1870–1945.* Cambridge, MA: Harvard University Press, 2012.

Ballard, Charles A., Jr. "A Contemporary Youth Movement: The Ghana Young Pioneers." Master's thesis, University of Ghana, Legon, 1967.

Bankole, Timothy. *Kwame Nkrumah: His Rise to Power.* London: George Allen and Unwin, 1955.

Barker, Peter. *Operation Cold Chop: The Coup That Toppled Nkrumah.* Accra: Ghana Publishing Corporation, 1969.

Batsa, Kofi. *The Spark: Times Behind Me: From Kwame Nkrumah to Hilla Limann.* London: Rex Collings, 1985.

Bayart, Jean-François. *The State in Africa: The Politics of the Belly.* 2nd ed. Malden, MA: Polity, 2009.

Beckman, Björn. "Government Policy and the Distribution of Cocoa Income in Ghana, 1951–1966." In *The Economics of Cocoa Production and Marketing: Proceedings of the Cocoa Economics Research Conference, Legon, April 1973,* edited by R. A. Kotey, C. Okali, and B. E. Rourke, 277–85.

Legon: Institute of Statistical, Social, and Economic Research, University of Ghana, 1974.

———. *Organising the Farmers: Cocoa Politics and National Development in Ghana*. Uppsala: Scandinavian Institute of African Studies, 1976.

Bennigsen, Alexandre A., and S. Enders Wimbush. *Muslim National Communism in the Soviet Union: A Revolutionary Strategy for the Colonial World*. Chicago: University of Chicago Press, 1979.

Berry, Sara S. *Chiefs Know Their Boundaries: Essays on Property, Power, and the Past in Asante, 1896–1996*. Portsmouth, NH: Heinemann, 2001.

Biney, Ama. *The Political and Social Thought of Kwame Nkrumah*. New York: Palgrave Macmillan, 2011.

Bing, Geoffrey. *Reap the Whirlwind: An Account of Kwame Nkrumah's Ghana from 1950 to 1966*. London: MacGibbon and Kee, 1968.

Birmingham, Walter, I. Neustadt, and E. N. Omaboe, eds. *A Study of Contemporary Ghana*. Vol. 1, *The Economy of Ghana*. London: George Allen and Unwin, 1966.

Bjerk, Paul. *Building a Peaceful Nation: Julius Nyerere and the Establishment of Sovereignty in Tanzania, 1960–1964*. Rochester, NY: University of Rochester Press, 2015.

Blank, Stephen. "Stalin's First Victim: The Trial of Sultangaliev." *Russian History/Histoire Russe* 17, no. 2 (1990): 155–78.

Blay, J. Benibengor. *The Gold Coast Mines Employees' Union*. Ilfracombe, UK: Arthur H. Stockwell, 1950.

Bloom, Peter J., Stephan F. Miescher, and Takyiwaa Manuh, eds. *Modernization as Spectacle in Africa*. Bloomington: Indiana University Press, 2014.

Boahen, A. Adu. *Ghana: Evolution and Change in the Nineteenth and Twentieth Centuries*. London: Longman, 1975.

Borstelmann, Thomas. *The Cold War and the Color Line: American Race Relations in the Global Arena*. Cambridge, MA: Harvard University Press, 2001.

Brempong, Owusu. "Oral Tradition in Ghana: The History of Bonokyempim and Techiman Politics." *Research Review*, supplement 13 ([1998?]): i–73.

Brennan, James R. "Youth, the TANU Youth League and Managed Vigilantism in Dar es Salaam, Tanzania, 1925–73." *Africa* 76, no. 2 (2006): 221–46.

Brinkley, Douglas, and David R. Facey-Crowther, eds. *The Atlantic Charter*. New York: St. Martin's, 1994.

Brown, Judith M. *Nehru: A Political Life*. New Haven, CT: Yale University Press, 2003.

Burbank, Jane, and Frederick Cooper. *Empires in World History: Power and the Politics of Difference*. Princeton, NJ: Princeton University Press, 2010.

Burgess, Thomas. "The Young Pioneers and the Rituals of Citizenship in Revolutionary Zanzibar." *Africa Today* 51, no. 3 (2005): 3–29.

Burawoy, Michael. *The Politics of Production: Factory Regimes under Capitalism and Socialism*. London: Verso Books, 1985.

Burton, Andrew. "Raw Youth, School-Leavers and the Emergence of Structural Unemployment in Late-Colonial Urban Tanganyika." *Journal of African History* 47, no. 3 (2006): 363–87.

———. "Urchins, Loafers and the Cult of the Cowboy: Urbanization and Delinquency in Dar es Salaam, 1919–61." *Journal of African History* 42, no. 2 (2001): 199–216.

Burton, Antoinette. "New Narratives of Imperial Politics in the Nineteenth Century." In *At Home with the Empire: Metropolitan Culture and the Imperial World*, edited by Catherine Hall and Sonya Rose, 212–29. Cambridge: Cambridge University Press, 2006.

Byrne, Jeffrey James. *Mecca of Revolution: Algeria, Decolonization, and the Third World Order.* Oxford: Oxford University Press, 2016.

Cabral, Amilcar. *Return to the Source: Selected Speeches of Amilcar Cabral.* Edited by Africa Information Service. New York: Monthly Review, 1973.

Caldwell, John C. *African Rural-Urban Migration: The Movement to Ghana's Towns.* New York: Columbia University Press, 1969.

Campbell, Chloe. "Juvenile Delinquency in Colonial Kenya, 1900–1939." *Historical Journal* 45, no. 1 (2002): 129–51.

Card, Emily Watts. "The Politics of Underdevelopment: From Voluntary Associations to Party Auxiliaries in Ghana." PhD diss., Columbia University, 1972.

Carter, Gwendolen Margaret, ed. *Politics in Africa: 7 Cases.* New York: Harcourt, Brace, and World, 1966.

Chalfin, Brenda. "La rénovation du port de Tema: Économie politique de la frontière maritime du Ghana." *Politique Africaine* 116 (2009): 63–84.

———. "Public Things, Excremental Politics, and the Infrastructure of Bare Life in Ghana's City of Tema." *American Ethnologist* 41, no. 1 (2014): 92–109.

Connelly, Matthew. *A Diplomatic Revolution: Algeria's Fight for Independence and the Origins of the Post–Cold War Era.* Oxford: Oxford University Press, 2002.

Cooper, Frederick. *Africa since 1940: The Past of the Present.* Cambridge: Cambridge University Press, 2002.

———. *Citizenship between Empire and Nation: Remaking France and French Africa, 1945–1960.* Princeton, NJ: Princeton University Press, 2014.

———. *Colonialism in Question: Theory, Knowledge, History.* Berkeley: University of California Press, 2005.

———. "Conflict and Connection: Rethinking Colonial African History." *American Historical Review* 99, no. 5 (1994): 1516–45.

———. *Decolonization and African Society: The Labor Question in French and British Africa.* Cambridge: Cambridge University Press, 1996.

———. "Industrial Man Goes to Africa." In *Men and Masculinities in Modern Africa*, edited by Lisa A. Lindsay and Stephan F. Miescher, 128–37. Portsmouth, NH: Heinemann, 2003.

———. "Modernizing Bureaucrats, Backward Africans, and the Development Concept." In *International Development and the Social Sciences: Essays on the History and Politics of Knowledge*, edited by Frederick Cooper and Randall Packard, 64–92. Berkeley: University of California Press, 1997.

———. *On the African Waterfront: Urban Disorder and the Transformation of Work in Colonial Mombasa*. New Haven, CT: Yale University Press, 1987.

———. "Possibility and Constraint: African Independence in Historical Perspective." *Journal of African History* 49, no. 2 (2008): 167–96.

———. "Urban Space, Industrial Time, and Wage Labor in Africa." In *Struggle for the City: Migrant Labor, Capital, and the State in Urban Africa*, edited by Frederick Cooper, 7–50. Beverly Hills, CA: Sage, 1983.

Cooper, Frederick, and Randall Packard, eds. *International Development and the Social Sciences: Essays on the History and Politics of Knowledge*. Berkeley: University of California Press, 1997.

Cowan, E. A. *Evolution of Trade Unionism in Ghana*. Accra: Ghana Trades Union Congress, [1960?].

Crinson, Mark. "Nation-Building, Collecting and the Politics of Display: The National Museum, Ghana." *Journal of the History of Collections* 13, no. 2 (2001): 231–50.

Crisp, Jeff. *The Story of an African Working Class: Ghanaian Miners' Struggles, 1870–1980*. London: Zed Books, 1984.

Crowder, Michael. "Whose Dream Was It Anyway? Twenty-Five Years of African Independence." *African Affairs* 86, no. 342 (1987): 7–24.

Curtin, Philip. *The Image of Africa: British Ideas and Actions, 1780–1850*. 2 vols. Madison: University of Wisconsin Press, 1964.

Danquah, Francis. *Cocoa Diseases and Politics in Ghana, 1909–1966*. New York: Peter Lang, 1995.

Danquah, J. B. *The Ghanaian Establishment: Its Constitution, Its Detentions, Its Traditions, Its Justice and Statecraft, and Its Heritage of Ghanaism*. Edited by Albert Adu Boahen. Accra: Ghana Universities Press, 1997.

Date-Bah, Eugenia. "Female and Male Factory Workers in Accra." In *Female and Male in West Africa*, edited by Christine Oppong, 266–74. London: George Allen and Unwin, 1983.

de Haan, Francisca. *Gender and the Politics of Office Work: The Netherlands, 1860–1940*. Amsterdam: Amsterdam University Press, 1998.

Denzer, LaRay. "I. T. A. Wallace-Johnson and the West African Youth League: A Case Study in West African Radicalism." PhD diss., University of Birmingham, 1977.

De Witte, Ludo. *The Assassination of Lumumba*. Translated by Ann Wright and Renée Fenby. New York: Verso, 2001.

Diouf, Mamadou. "Engaging Postcolonial Cultures: African Youth and Public Space." *African Studies Review* 46, no. 2 (2003): 1–12.

Donham, Donald L. *Marxist Modern: An Ethnographic History of the Ethiopian Revolution*. Berkeley: University of California Press, 1999.

Dove, Mabel. *Selected Writings of a Pioneer West African Feminist*. Edited by Stephanie Newell and Audrey Gadzekpo. Nottingham, UK: Trent, 2004.

Drake, St. Clair, and Leslie Alexander Lacy. "Government versus the Unions: The Sekondi-Takoradi Strike, 1961." In *Politics in Africa: 7 Cases*, edited by Gwendolen M. Carter, 67–118. New York: Harcourt, Brace, and World, 1966.

Drew, Jane. "Recent Work by Fry, Drew & Partners and Fry, Drew, Drake & Lasdun." *Architectural Design* 25 (1955): 137–74.

Duara, Prasenjit. "Introduction: The Decolonization of Asia and Africa in the Twentieth Century." In *Decolonization: Perspectives from Now and Then*, edited by Prasenjit Duara, 1–18. New York: Routledge, 2003.

Du Bois, W. E. B. "The African Roots of the War." In *W. E. B. Du Bois: A Reader*, edited by David Levering Lewis, 642–51. New York: Owl Books, 1995.

———. *The Negro*. New York: Henry Holt, 1915.

Dumett, Raymond E. *El Dorado in West Africa: The Gold-Mining Frontier, African Labor, and Colonial Capitalism in the Gold Coast, 1875–1900*. Athens: Ohio University Press, 1998.

Dunn, John, ed. *West African States: Failure and Promise: A Study in Comparative Politics*. Cambridge: Cambridge University Press, 1978.

Dunn, John, and A. F. Robertson. *Dependence and Opportunity: Political Change in Ahafo*. Cambridge: Cambridge University Press, 1973.

Du Sautoy, Peter. "Administrative Problems of the Resettlement of Tema." *Journal of Management Studies* 1, no. 1 (1961): 10–13.

Ekbladh, David. *The Great American Mission: Modernization and the Construction of an American World Order*. Princeton, NJ: Princeton University Press, 2010.

England, Kim, and Kate Boyer. "Women's Work: The Feminization and Shifting Meanings of Clerical Work." *Journal of Social History* 43, no. 2 (2009): 307–40.

Fainsod, Merle. "The Komsomols—A Study of Youth under Dictatorship." *American Political Science Review* 45, no. 1 (1951): 18–40.

Fanon, Frantz. *The Wretched of the Earth*. Translated by Constance Farrington. New York: Grove, 1963.

Ferguson, James. *Expectations of Modernity: Myths and Meanings of Urban Life on the Zambian Copperbelt*. Berkeley: University of California Press, 1999.

Ferrell, Lacy S. "'We Were Mixed with All Types': Educational Migration in the Northern Territories of Colonial Ghana." In *Children on the Move in Africa: Past and Present Experiences of Migration*, edited by Elodie Razy and Marie Rodet, 141–58. Suffolk, England: James Currey, 2016.

Field, Margaret J. *Religion and Medicine of the Gã People*. 1937; repr., London: Oxford University Press, 1961.

———. *Social Organization of the Gã People*. London: Crown Agents for the Colonies, 1940.

Finlay, David J., Ole R. Holsti, and Richard R. Fagen. *Enemies in Politics.* Chicago: Rand McNally, 1967.

Fourchard, Laurent. "Lagos and the Invention of Juvenile Delinquency in Nigeria, 1920–60." *Journal of African History* 47, no. 1 (2006): 115–37.

Freund, Bill. *The African City: A History.* Cambridge: Cambridge University Press, 2007.

Friedland, William H., and Carl G. Rosberg Jr., eds. *African Socialism.* Stanford, CA: Stanford University Press, 1964.

Fry, Maxwell, and Jane Drew. *Tropical Architecture in the Humid Zone.* New York: Reinhold Publishing, 1956.

Fuller, Harcourt. *Building the Ghanaian Nation-State: Kwame Nkrumah's Symbolic Nationalism.* New York: Palgrave Macmillan, 2014.

Gaines, Kevin K. *American Africans in Ghana: Black Expatriates and the Civil Rights Era.* Chapel Hill: University of North Carolina Press, 2006.

Gbedemah, K. A. *It Will Not Be "Work and Happiness for All": An Open Letter Being Also an Appeal to Dr. Kwame Nkrumah (First President of the Republic of Ghana) and Comment on, and Criticism of the Proposed New 7 Year Ghana Development Plan.* N.p.: n.p., 1962.

Geiger, Susan. *TANU Women: Gender and Culture in the Making of Tanganyikan Nationalism, 1955–1965.* Portsmouth, NH: Heinemann, 1997.

Geiss, Imanuel. *The Pan-African Movement: A History of Pan-Africanism in America, Europe, and Africa.* Translated by Ann Keep. New York: Africana, 1974.

George, Abosede A. *Making Modern Girls: A History of Girlhood, Labor, and Social Development in Colonial Lagos.* Athens: Ohio University Press, 2014.

George, Betty Stein. *Education in Ghana.* Washington, DC: Government Printing Office, 1976.

Gerits, Frank. "The Ideological Scramble for Africa: The US, Ghanaian, French, and British Competition for Africa's Future, 1953–1963." PhD diss., European University Institute, 2014.

Gewald, Jan-Bart. *Hands Off Africa!! An Overview and Analysis of the Ideological, Political and Socio-Economic Approaches to African Unity Expressed at the First All-African People's Conference held in Accra, Ghana, in December 1958.* N.p.: n.p., 1990.

Gifford, Prosser, and Wm. Roger Louis, eds. *The Transfer of Power in Africa: Decolonization, 1940–1960.* New Haven, CT: Yale University Press, 1982.

Grant, Faye Woodard. *The Nutrition and Health of Children in the Gold Coast.* Chicago: University of Chicago Press, 1955.

Gray, Paul S. *Unions and Leaders in Ghana: A Model of Labor and Development.* Owerri, Nigeria: Conch Magazine, 1981.

Hailey, Lord [William Malcolm]. *Native Administration and Political Development in British Tropical Africa.* Nendeln, Liechtenstein: Kraus Reprint, 1979. First published 1942 by His Majesty's Stationery Office, London.

Hall, Catherine, and Sonya Rose, eds. *At Home with the Empire: Metropolitan Culture and the Imperial World*. Cambridge: Cambridge University Press, 2006.

Hart, Jennifer. *Ghana on the Go: African Mobility in the Age of Motor Transportation*. Bloomington: Indiana University Press, 2016.

———. "Motor Transportation, Trade Unionism, and the Culture of Work in Colonial Ghana." *International Review of Social History* 59, no. S22 (2014): 185–209.

———. "'One Man, No Chop': Licit Wealth, Good Citizens, and the Criminalization of Drivers in Postcolonial Ghana." *International Journal of African Historical Studies* 46, no. 3 (2013): 373–96.

Hart, Keith. "Small-Scale Entrepreneurs in Ghana and Development Planning." *Journal of Development Studies* 6, no. 4 (1970): 104–20.

Hasty, Jennifer. *The Press and Political Culture in Ghana*. Bloomington: Indiana University Press, 2005.

Henderson-Quartey, David K. *The Ga of Ghana: History and Culture of a West African People*. London: David K. Henderson-Quartey, 2002.

Hess, Janet Berry. "Imagining Architecture: The Structure of Nationalism in Accra, Ghana." *Africa Today* 47, no. 2 (2000): 35–58.

Higgins, Rosalyn. *United Nations Peacekeeping, 1946–1967: Documents and Commentary*. Vol. 3, *Africa*. Oxford: Oxford University Press, 1980.

Higginson, John. *A Working Class in the Making: Belgian Colonial Policy, Private Enterprise, and the African Mineworker, 1907–1951*. Madison: University of Wisconsin Press, 1989.

Hilling, David. "The Evolution of the Major Ports of West Africa." *Geographical Journal* 135, no. 3 (1969): 365–78.

Hobson, J. A. *Imperialism: A Study*. London: James Nisbet, 1902.

Hodge, Peter. "The Ghana Workers Brigade: A Project for Unemployed Youth." *British Journal of Sociology* 15, no. 2 (1964): 113–28.

Hodgkin, Thomas. *Freedom for the Gold Coast?* Africa and the Future 2. London: Union of Democratic Control, 1951.

———. *Nationalism in Colonial Africa*. New York: New York University Press, 1957.

Horne, Gerald. *Race Woman: The Lives of Shirley Graham Du Bois*. New York: New York University Press, 2000.

Howe, Stephen. *Ireland and Empire: Colonial Legacies in Irish History and Culture*. Oxford: Oxford University Press, 2000.

Immerwahr, Daniel. *Thinking Small: The United States and the Lure of Community Development*. Cambridge, MA: Harvard University Press, 2015.

Ivaska, Andrew. *Cultured States: Youth, Gender, and Modern Style in 1960s Dar es Salaam*. Durham, NC: Duke University Press, 2011.

Jallow, Baba Galleh. "Defining the Nation: Censorship in Colonial and Postcolonial Ghana, 1933–1993." PhD diss., University of California, Davis, 2011.

James, C. L. R. *Nkrumah and the Ghana Revolution*. London: Allison and Busby, 1977.

James, Leslie. *George Padmore and Decolonization from Below: Pan-Africanism, the Cold War, and the End of Empire*. New York: Palgrave Macmillan, 2015.

Jeffries, Richard. *Class, Power, and Ideology in Ghana: The Railwaymen of Sekondi*. Cambridge: Cambridge University Press, 1978.

———. "The Evolution of the Ghana Trades Union Congress under the Convention People's Party: Towards a More Radical Re-Interpretation." *Transactions of the Historical Society of Ghana* 14, no. 2 (1973): 277–86.

Jonah, Kwesi. "The C.P.P. and the Asafo Besuon: Why Unlike Poles Did Not Attract." *Transactions of the Historical Society of Ghana*, n.s., 3 (1999): 47–56.

Jopp, Keith. *Tema: Ghana's New Town and Harbour*. Accra: Ministry of Information and Broadcasting, 1961.

Kaldor, Nicholas. "Taxation for Economic Development." *Journal of Modern African Studies* 1, no. 1 (1963): 7–23.

Keita, Sidiki Kobélé. *La Guinée de Sékou Touré: Pourquoi la prison du camp Boiro?* Paris: L'Harmattan, 2014.

Kelly, Catriona. *Children's World: Growing Up in Russia, 1890–1991*. New Haven, CT: Yale University Press, 2007.

Killick, Tony. "The Economics of Cocoa." In *A Study of Contemporary Ghana*. Vol. 1, *The Economy of Ghana*, edited by Walter Birmingham, I. Neustadt, and E. N. Omaboe, 365–90. London: George Allen and Unwin, 1966.

Killingray, David. "Soldiers, Ex-Servicemen, and Politics in the Gold Coast, 1939–1950." *Journal of Modern African Studies* 21, no. 3 (1983): 523–34.

Kimble, David. *A Political History of Ghana: The Rise of Gold Coast Nationalism, 1850–1928*. Oxford: Clarendon, 1963.

Koditschek, Theodore. *Liberalism, Imperialism, and the Historical Imagination: Nineteenth-Century Visions of Greater Britain*. Cambridge: Cambridge University Press, 2011.

Koenker, Diane P. "Men against Women on the Shop Floor in Early Soviet Russia: Gender and Class in the Socialist Workplace." *American Historical Review* 100, no. 5 (1995): 1438–64.

Kotkin, Stephen. *Magnetic Mountain: Stalinism as a Civilization*. Berkeley: University of California Press, 1995.

Kouyaté, Mohamed Mancona. *Nous sommes tous responsables*. Conakry: Imprimerie Moderne de Kaloum, 1996.

Ladouceur, Paul André. *Chiefs and Politicians: The Politics of Regionalism in Northern Ghana*. London: Longman, 1979.

Lal, Priya. *African Socialism in Postcolonial Tanzania: Between the Village and the World*. Cambridge: Cambridge University Press, 2015.

Langley, J. Ayodele. *Pan-Africanism and Nationalism in West Africa, 1900–1945: A Study in Ideology and Social Classes*. Oxford: Clarendon, 1973.

Lawrance, Benjamin N. *Locality, Mobility, and "Nation": Periurban Colonialism in Togo's Eweland, 1900–1960*. Rochester, NY: University of Rochester Press, 2007.

Lee, Christopher J. *Frantz Fanon: Toward a Revolutionary Humanism*. Athens: Ohio University Press, 2015.

Legum, Colin. "Socialism in Ghana: A Political Interpretation." In *African Socialism*, edited by William H. Friedland and Carl G. Rosberg Jr., 131–59. Stanford, CA: Stanford University Press, 1964.

Lenin, V. I. *Imperialism: The Highest Stage of Capitalism: A Popular Outline*. Rev. trans. Moscow: Co-Operative Publishing Society of Foreign Workers in the USSR, 1934.

Lentz, Carola. "'The Time When Politics Came': Ghana's Decolonisation from the Perspective of a Rural Periphery." *Journal of Contemporary African Studies* 20, no. 2 (2002): 245–74.

Levey, Zach. "The Rise and Decline of a Special Relationship: Israel and Ghana, 1957–1966." *African Studies Review* 46, no. 1 (2003): 155–77.

Lewis, David Levering, ed. *W. E. B. Du Bois: A Reader*. New York: Owl Books, 1995.

Lewis, W. Arthur. *Report on Industrialisation and the Gold Coast*. Accra: Government Printing Department, 1953.

Lindsay, Lisa A. "Domesticity and Difference: Male Breadwinners, Working Women, and Colonial Citizenship in the 1945 Nigerian General Strike." *American Historical Review* 104, no. 3 (1999): 783–812.

——. *Working with Gender: Wage Labor and Social Change in Southwestern Nigeria*. Portsmouth, NH: Heinemann, 2003.

Lindsay, Lisa A., and Stephan F. Miescher, eds. *Men and Masculinities in Modern Africa*. Portsmouth, NH: Heinemann, 2003.

Liscombe, Rhodri Windsor. "Modernism in Late Imperial British West Africa: The Work of Maxwell Fry and Jane Drew, 1946–56." *Journal of the Society of Architectural Historians* 65, no. 2 (2006): 188–215.

Lodge, Tom. *Sharpeville: An Apartheid Massacre and Its Consequences*. Oxford: Oxford University Press, 2011.

Lynn, Martin, ed. *The British Empire in the 1950s: Retreat or Revival?* New York: Palgrave Macmillan, 2006.

MacDonald, Mairi S. "The Challenge of Guinean Independence, 1958–1971." PhD diss., University of Toronto, 2009.

——. "Guinea's Political Prisoners: Colonial Models, Postcolonial Innovation." *Comparative Studies in Society and History* 54, no. 4 (2012): 890–913.

Macey, David. *Frantz Fanon: A Biography*. New York: Picador USA, 2000.

Makonnen, [T.] Ras. *Pan-Africanism from Within*. Recorded and edited by Kenneth King. London: Oxford University Press, 1973.

Mamdani, Mahmood. *Citizen and Subject: Contemporary Africa and the Legacy of Late Colonialism*. Princeton, NJ: Princeton University Press, 1996.

Manoukian, Madeline. *Akan and Ga-Adangme Peoples*. London: Oxford University Press, 1950.

Mantena, Karuna. *Alibis of Empire: Henry Maine and the Ends of Liberal Imperialism*. Princeton, NJ: Princeton University Press, 2010.

Manuh, Takyiwaa. "Women and Their Organizations during the Convention People's Party Period." In *The Life and Work of Kwame Nkrumah: Papers of a Symposium Organized by the Institute of African Studies, University of Ghana, Legon*, edited by Kwame Arhin, 101–27. Trenton, NJ: Africa World, 1993.

Marx, Karl. "Alienation and Social Classes." In *The Marx-Engels Reader*, 2nd ed., edited by Robert C. Tucker, 133–35. New York: W. W. Norton, 1978.

———. *Capital*. Vol. 1, *A Critique of Political Economy*. Edited by Friedrich Engels. Translated by Samuel Moore and Edward Aveling. Mineola, NY: Dover, 2011.

———. "Economic and Philosophic Manuscripts of 1844." In *The Marx-Engels Reader*, 2nd ed., edited by Robert C. Tucker, 66–132. New York: W. W. Norton, 1978.

Marx, Karl, and Friedrich Engels. *The Communist Manifesto*. London: Verso, 1998.

Mbembe, Achille. *On the Postcolony*. Berkeley: University of California Press, 2001.

McCain, James A. "Attitudes toward Socialism, Policy, and Leadership in Ghana." *African Studies Review* 22, no. 1 (1979): 149–69.

———. "Perceptions of Socialism in Post-Socialist Ghana: An Experimental Analysis." *African Studies Review* 22, no. 3 (1979): 45–63.

McCaskie, T. C. "Accumulation, Wealth and Belief in Asante History: I. To the Close of the Nineteenth Century." *Africa* 53, no. 1 (1983): 23–43, 79.

———. "Accumulation: Wealth and Belief in Asante History: II. The Twentieth Century." *Africa* 56, no. 1 (1986): 3–23.

———. "Asante Origins, Egypt, and the Near East: An Idea and Its History." In *Recasting the Past: History Writing and Political Work in Modern Africa*, edited by Derek R. Peterson and Giacomo Macola, 125–48. Athens: Ohio University Press, 2009.

McGovern, Mike. *Unmasking the State: Making Guinea Modern*. Chicago: University of Chicago Press, 2013.

Mehta, Uday Singh. *Liberalism and Empire: A Study in Nineteenth-Century British Liberal Thought*. Chicago: University of Chicago Press, 1999.

Meyer, Joe-Fio N. *Dr. Nkrumah's Last Journey: The Sensational Viet-Nam U.S. War*. Accra: Advance Press, 1985.

Miescher, Stephan F. "Building the City of the Future: Visions and Experiences of Modernity in Ghana's Akosombo Township." *Journal of African History* 53, no. 3 (2012): 367–90.

———. *Making Men in Ghana*. Bloomington: Indiana University Press, 2005.

———. "'Nkrumah's Baby': The Akosombo Dam and the Dream of Development in Ghana, 1952–1966." *Water History* 6, no. 4 (2014): 341–66.

Mikell, Gwendolyn. *Cocoa and Chaos in Ghana.* New York: Paragon House, 1989.

Mill, John Stuart. *On Liberty.* Boston: Ticknor and Fields, 1863.

Miracle, Marvin P., and Ann Seidman. *Agricultural Cooperatives and Quasi-Cooperatives in Ghana, 1951–1965.* Madison: Land Tenure Center, University of Wisconsin, 1968.

———. *State Farms in Ghana.* Madison: Land Tenure Center, University of Wisconsin, 1968.

Mitchell, Timothy. *Rule of Experts: Egypt, Techno-Politics, Modernity.* Berkeley: University of California Press, 2002.

Mohan, Jitendra. "Nkrumah and Nkrumaism." *Socialist Register* 4 (1967): 191–228.

Montgomery, Mary E. "The Eyes of the World Were Watching: Ghana, Great Britain, and the United States, 1957–1966." PhD diss., University of Maryland, 2004.

Muehlenbeck, Philip E. *Betting on the Africans: John F. Kennedy's Courting of African Nationalist Leaders.* Oxford: Oxford University Press, 2012.

———, ed. *Gender, Sexuality, and the Cold War: A Global Perspective.* Nashville, TN: Vanderbilt University Press, 2017.

Munger, Edwin S. *All-African People's Conference: Africa for Africans Only Demanded by 240 Delegates from 28 African Countries.* West Africa Series, vol. 3, no. 1. New York: American Universities Field Staff, 1959.

Murillo, Bianca. *Market Encounters: Consumer Cultures in Twentieth-Century Ghana.* Athens: Ohio University Press, 2017.

———. "'The Devil We Know': Gold Coast Consumers, Local Employees, and the United Africa Company, 1940–1960." *Enterprise and Society* 12, no. 2 (2011): 317–55.

Namikas, Lise. *Battleground Africa: Cold War in the Congo, 1960–1965.* Stanford, CA: Stanford University Press, 2013.

Nehru, Jawaharlal. *Soviet Russia: Some Random Sketches and Impressions.* Bombay: Chetana, 1949. First published 1928 by Allahabad Law Journal Press.

———. *Toward Freedom: The Autobiography of Jawaharlal Nehru.* New York: John Day, 1941.

Neumann, Matthias. *The Communist Youth League and the Transformation of the Soviet Union, 1917–1932.* New York: Routledge, 2011.

Neustadt, I., and E. N. Omaboe. *Social and Economic Survey of Tema: Report.* Accra: Office of the Government Statistician, 1959.

Newell, Stephanie. *The Power to Name: A History of Anonymity in Colonial West Africa.* Athens: Ohio University Press, 2013.

Nkrumah, Kwame. *Africa Must Unite.* London: Panaf Books, 1963.

———. *Axioms of Kwame Nkrumah.* London: Panaf Books, 1969.

————. *The Challenge of the Congo.* London: Thomas Nelson and Sons, 1967.

————. *Consciencism: Philosophy and Ideology for De-colonization and Development with Particular Reference to the African Revolution.* London: Heinemann, 1964.

————. "Education and Nationalism in Africa." *Educational Outlook* 18, no. 1 (1943): 32–40. Published under the name Francis Nwia-Kofi Nkrumah.

————. *Ghana: The Autobiography of Kwame Nkrumah.* Edinburgh: Thomas Nelson and Sons, 1957.

————. *Guide to Party Action: Address by Osagyefo Dr. Kwame Nkrumah at the First Seminar at the Winneba Ideological School on 3rd February, 1962.* Accra: Central Committee of the Convention People's Party, 1962.

————. *I Speak of Freedom: A Statement of African Ideology.* New York: Frederick A. Praeger, 1961.

————. *Laying the Foundation Stone of the Kwame Nkrumah Institute.* Accra: Ministry of Information and Broadcasting, 1961.

————. "Movement for Colonial Freedom." *Phylon* 16, no. 4 (1955): 397–409.

————. *Towards Colonial Freedom: Africa in the Struggle against World Imperialism.* London: Farleigh, 1947.

Noon, John. *Labor Problems of Africa.* Philadelphia: University of Pennsylvania Press, 1944.

Nugent, Paul. *Smugglers, Secessionists, and Loyal Citizens on the Ghana-Togo Frontier: The Lie of the Borderlands since 1914.* Athens: Ohio University Press, 2002.

Ocobock, Paul. "'Joy Rides for Juveniles': Vagrant Youth and Colonial Control in Nairobi, Kenya, 1901–52." *Social History* 31, no. 1 (2006): 39–59.

Ocran, A. K. *A Myth is Broken: An Account of the Ghana Coup d'État of 24th February, 1966.* Accra: Longmans, Green, 1968.

Oppong, Christine, ed., *Female and Male in West Africa.* London: George Allen and Unwin, 1983.

————. *Middle Class African Marriage: A Family Study of Ghanaian Senior Civil Servants.* London: George Allen and Unwin, 1981.

Oppong, Christine, and Katharine Abu. *Seven Roles of Women: Impact of Education, Migration, and Employment on Ghanaian Mothers.* Geneva: International Labour Office, 1987.

Osseo-Asare, Abena Dove. "Scientific Equity: Experiments in Laboratory Education in Ghana." *Isis: A Journal of the History of Science Society* 104, no. 4 (2013): 713–41.

Owusu, Maxwell. *Uses and Abuses of Political Power: A Case Study of Continuity and Change in the Politics of Ghana.* 2nd ed. Accra: Ghana Universities Press, 2006.

Padmore, George, ed. *Colonial and . . . Coloured Unity: A Programme of Action: History of the Pan-African Congress.* London: Hammersmith Bookshop, 1963. First published 1947 by the Pan-African Federation, Manchester, UK.

——. *The Gold Coast Revolution: The Struggle of an African People from Slavery to Freedom*. London: Dennis Dobson, 1953.

——. *Pan-Africanism or Communism? The Coming Struggle for Africa*. New York: Roy, 1956.

Parker, John. *Making the Town: Ga State and Society in Early Colonial Accra*. Portsmouth, NH: Heinemann, 2000.

Parker, John, and Richard Reid, eds. *The Oxford Handbook of Modern African History*. Oxford: Oxford University Press, 2013.

Parsons, Timothy H. *Race, Resistance, and the Boy Scout Movement in British Colonial Africa*. Athens: Ohio University Press, 2004.

Peil, Margaret. *The Ghanaian Factory Worker: Industrial Man in Africa*. Cambridge: Cambridge University Press, 1972.

——. "Unemployment in Tema: The Plight of the Skilled Worker." *Canadian Journal of African Studies* 3, no. 2 (1969): 409–19.

Perry, J. Harvey. *Taxation and Economic Development in Ghana*. Report No. TAO/GHA/4Rev. 1, 1 July 1959. New York: United Nations Commissioner for Technical Assistance, Department of Economic and Social Affairs, 1959.

Peterson, Derek R., and Giacomo Macola, eds. *Recasting the Past: History Writing and Political Work in Modern Africa*. Athens: Ohio University Press, 2009.

Pitts, Jennifer. *A Turn to Empire: The Rise of Imperial Liberalism in Britain and France*. Princeton, NJ: Princeton University Press, 2005.

Plageman, Nate. "'Accra Is Changing, Isn't It?': Urban Infrastructure, Independence, and Nation in the Gold Coast's *Daily Graphic*, 1954–57." *International Journal of African Historical Studies* 43, no. 1 (2010): 137–59.

——. *Highlife Saturday Night: Popular Music and Social Change in Urban Ghana*. Bloomington: Indiana University Press, 2012.

Pogucki, R. J. H. *Gold Coast Land Tenure*. Vol. 3, *Land Tenure in Ga Customary Law*. Accra: Government Printer, 1955.

Pool, Jeremy. "Now Is the Time of Youth: Youth, Nationalism and Cultural Change in Ghana, 1940–1966." PhD diss., Emory University, 2009.

Powell, Erica. *Private Secretary (Female)/Gold Coast*. New York: St. Martin's, 1984.

Prakash, Vikramaditya. *Chandigarh's Le Corbusier: The Struggle for Modernity in Postcolonial India*. Seattle: University of Washington Press, 2002.

Pratt, Cranford. "Colonial Governments and the Transfer of Power in East Africa." In *The Transfer of Power in Africa: Decolonization, 1940–1960*, edited by Prosser Gifford and Wm. Roger Louis, 249–81. New Haven, CT: Yale University Press, 1982.

Quarcoopome, S. S. "A History of the Urban Development of Accra: 1877–1957." *Research Review*, n.s., 9, nos. 1–2 (1993): 20–32.

——. "Urbanisation, Land Alienation and Politics in Accra." *Research Review*, n.s., 8, nos. 1–2 (1992): 40–54.

Rakove, Robert B. *Kennedy, Johnson, and the Nonaligned World.* Cambridge: Cambridge University Press, 2013.

Rathbone, Richard. "Ghana." In *West African States: Failure and Promise: A Study in Comparative Politics,* edited by John Dunn, 22–35. Cambridge: Cambridge University Press, 1978.

———, ed. *Ghana.* Vol. 1, pts. 1 and 2, of *British Documents on the End of Empire,* ser. B. London: Her Majesty's Stationery Office, 1992.

———. "The Government of the Gold Coast after the Second World War." *African Affairs* 67, no. 268 (1968): 209–18.

———. *Nkrumah and the Chiefs: The Politics of Chieftaincy in Ghana, 1951–60.* Athens: Ohio University Press, 2000.

———. "Things Fall Apart: The Erosion of Local Government, Local Justice and Civil Rights in Ghana, 1955–60." In *The British Empire in the 1950s: Retreat or Revival?,* edited by Martin Lynn, 122–43. New York: Palgrave Macmillan, 2006.

Reindorf, Carl Christian. *History of the Gold Coast and Asante: Based on Traditions and Historical Facts, Comprising a Period of More than Three Centuries from About 1500 to 1860.* Basel: privately printed, 1895.

Rimmer, Douglas. "The New Industrial Relations in Ghana." *Industrial and Labor Relations Review* 14, no. 2 (1961): 206–26.

Rönnbäck, Klas. "The Idle and the Industrious—European Ideas about the African Work Ethic in Precolonial West Africa." *History in Africa* 41 (2014): 117–45.

Rooney, David. *Kwame Nkrumah: The Political Kingdom in the Third World.* New York: St. Martin's, 1988.

Sackeyfio-Lenoch, Naaborko. *The Politics of Chieftaincy: Authority and Property in Colonial Ghana.* Rochester, NY: University of Rochester Press, 2014.

———. "The Politics of Land and Urban Space in Colonial Accra." *History in Africa* 39 (2012): 293–329.

Schildkrout, Enid. *People of the Zongo: The Transformation of Ethnic Identities in Ghana.* Cambridge: Cambridge University Press, 1978.

Schmidt, Elizabeth. *Cold War and Decolonization in Guinea, 1946–1958.* Athens: Ohio University Press, 2007.

———. *Foreign Intervention in Africa: From the Cold War to the War on Terror.* Cambridge: Cambridge University Press, 2013.

———. *Mobilizing the Masses: Gender, Ethnicity, and Class in the Nationalist Movement in Guinea, 1939–1958.* Portsmouth, NH: Heinemann, 2005.

Schneider, Leander. *Government of Development: Peasants and Politicians in Postcolonial Tanzania.* Bloomington: Indiana University Press, 2014.

Scott, James C. *Seeing Like a State: How Certain Schemes to Improve the Human Condition Have Failed.* New Haven, CT: Yale University Press, 1998.

Seidman, Ann W. *Ghana's Development Experience, 1951–1965.* Nairobi: East African Publishing House, 1978.

Sherwood, Marika. *Kwame Nkrumah: The Years Abroad, 1935–1947.* Legon, Ghana: Freedom Publications, 1996.

———. "'There is No New Deal for the Blackman in San Francisco': African Attempts to Influence the Founding Conference of the United Nations, April–July, 1945." *International Journal of African Historical Studies* 29, no. 1 (1996): 71–94.

Skinner, Kate. "Agency and Analogy in African History: The Contribution of Extra-Mural Studies in Ghana." *History in Africa* 34 (2007): 273–96.

———. *The Fruits of Freedom in British Togoland: Literacy, Politics, and Nationalism, 1914–2014.* Cambridge: Cambridge University Press, 2015.

———. "Reading, Writing, and Rallies: The Politics of 'Freedom' in Southern British Togoland, 1953–1956." *Journal of African History* 48, no. 1 (2007): 123–47.

Spencer, Stephanie. *Gender, Work and Education in Britain in the 1950s.* New York: Palgrave Macmillan, 2005.

Stanek, Łukasz. "Architects from Socialist Countries in Ghana (1957–67): Modern Architecture and *Mondialisation*." *Journal of the Society of Architectural Historians* 74, no. 4 (2015): 416–42.

Straker, Jay. *Youth, Nationalism, and the Guinean Revolution.* Bloomington: Indiana University Press, 2009.

Sutherland, Bill, and Matt Meyer. *Guns and Gandhi in Africa: Pan African Insights on Nonviolence, Armed Struggle and Liberation in Africa.* Trenton, NJ: Africa World, 2000.

Sylvain, Benito. *Du sort des indigènes dans les colonies d'exploitation.* Paris: L. Boyer, 1901.

Syme, Adjingboru A. *Salute to Israel: The Story of the Ghana Youth Delegation to Israel, 1957.* Accra: Guinea Press, 1958.

Terretta, Meredith. "Cameroonian Nationalists Go Global: From Forest *Maquis* to a Pan-African Accra." *Journal of African History* 51, no. 2 (2010): 189–212.

———. "From Below and to the Left? Human Rights and Liberation Politics in Africa's Postcolonial Age." *Journal of World History* 24, no. 2 (2013): 389–416.

———. *Nation of Outlaws, State of Violence: Nationalism, Grassfields Tradition, and State Building in Cameroon.* Athens: Ohio University Press, 2014.

Tettegah, John K. *Why the New Structure? Speech Delivered at the 14th Annual Delegates Conference of the Ghana TUC, Cape Coast, 25th–26th January 1958.* Accra: Publicity/Information Department, Ghana Trades Union Congress, [1958].

Tetteh, M. N. *The Ghana Young Pioneer Movement: A Youth Organisation in the Kwame Nkrumah Era.* Tema: Ghana Publicity, 1999.

Thompson, W. Scott. *Ghana's Foreign Policy, 1957–1966: Diplomacy, Ideology, and the New State.* Princeton, NJ: Princeton University Press, 1969.

Tignor, Robert L. *W. Arthur Lewis and the Birth of Development Economics.* Princeton, NJ: Princeton University Press, 2006.

Touré, Ahmed Sékou. *L'Afrique et la révolution.* Paris: Présence Africaine, 1967.

Tucker, Robert C., ed. *The Marx-Engels Reader.* 2nd ed. New York: W. W. Norton, 1978.

van Walraven, Klaas. *The Yearning for Relief: A History of the Sawaba Movement in Niger.* Leiden: Brill, 2013.

Weinbaum, Alys Eve, Lynn M. Thomas, Priti Ramamurthy, et al. *The Modern Girl around the World: Consumption, Modernity, and Globalization.* Durham, NC: Duke University Press, 2008.

Wilks, Ivor. *Akwamu, 1640–1750: A Study of the Rise and Fall of a West African Empire.* Trondheim: Department of History, Norwegian University of Science and Technology, 2001.

——. *Asante in the Nineteenth Century: The Structure and Evolution of a Political Order.* Cambridge: Cambridge University Press, 1975.

Williams, Justin. *Pan-Africanism in Ghana: African Socialism, Neoliberalism, and Globalization.* Durham, NC: Carolina Academic Press, 2016.

Worger, William H. *South Africa's City of Diamonds: Mine Workers and Monopoly Capitalism in Kimberley, 1867–1895.* New Haven, CT: Yale University Press, 1987.

Wright, Richard. *Black Power: A Record of Reactions in a Land of Pathos.* New York: Harper and Brothers, 1954.

——. *The Color Curtain: A Report on the Bandung Conference.* Cleveland: World Publishing, 1956.

Wudu, Frank. *The Man Pobee Biney: A Fallen Labour Hero of Ghana.* Accra: State Publishing Corporation, 1968.

Yurchak, Alexei. *Everything Was Forever, Until It Was No More: The Last Soviet Generation.* Princeton, NJ: Princeton University Press, 2006.

Zachariah, Benjamin. *Nehru.* New York: Routledge, 2004.

Zachernuk, Philip S. *Colonial Subjects: An African Intelligentsia and Atlantic Ideas.* Charlottesville: University Press of Virginia, 2000.

Zimmerman, Jonathan. "'Money, Materials, and Manpower': Ghanaian In-Service Teacher Education and the Political Economy of Failure, 1961–1971." *History of Education Quarterly* 51, no. 1 (2011): 1–27.

Index

Cold War, 125, 187; decolonization and, 150, 209; international order and, 1–3; neocolonialism and, 150, 154, 166, 183

Colonial Conference (1945), 41

Committee on Youth Organization (CYO), 9–10, 53; Ghana National Schools and, 54, 225n19

community, 6, 18, 19, 54, 86, 187–97

Conference of Independent African States (1958), 84, 159

Congo, 36, 151–54, 172, 262n81; Ghana and, 152–53. *See also* Patrice Lumumba

Convention People's Party (CPP), 3; accusations against, 76–77, 135, 177; anticolonialism and, 31; cocoa and, 54, 74–75; corruption and, 130, 148–49, 156, 201; diarchy and, 10, 50–52, 85, 182; dictatorship and, 179–83; education and, 53, 54–57, 167–68; employment and, 53; farmers and, 54; founding of, 10; Ghana's independence and, 84–85, 88–89, 114, 177; historiography of, 6, 20; indiscipline and, 183; institutions of, 17–19; modernization and, 14, 15, 51–52, 59, 69–70, 72, 100, 136; nation-building and, 17–18, 48, 51–52, 56, 59–50, 79, 85, 92, 113; neocolonialism and, 157; 1961 Strike and, 137–38, 139–41, 148–50, 174; NLM and, 78–79, 188, 234n132; one-party state and, 22, 28, 154–57, 177–79, 182–83, 187; on opposition politics, 181–83; opposition to, 73–75, 76–78, 179–81; party press and, 17, 23–24, 52–53, 164–65, 185; relationship to TUC, 121, 126; science and, 56–67; "Self-Government Now" and, 10, 12; socialism and, 4, 17, 26, 110, 112, 123–26, 131, 133, 138, 177; Vanguard Activists and, 183; women and, 53, 164–65, 168–69; work and, 120–21, 122; workers and, 126; youth and, 110

Cooper, Frederick, 5, 20, 117–18, 208

Côte d'Ivoire, 198

Council on African Affairs, 40

Crabbe, Coffie, 194, 199

Crinson, Mark, 57

Crisp, Jeff, 119, 146

Crowder, Michael, 16, 216n42

Curtin, Philip, 75

Daily Graphic, 160, 164, 185, 191

Danquah, Francis, 54

Danquah, J. B., 30, 61, 66, 70, 171, 199, 232n101, 254n117

decolonization, 1–3, 74, 114; Africa and, 149–50, 151; Cold War and, 150; historiography of, 5, 20–21, 209–11; postcolonial imaginings and disappointments and, 4–5, 10–16, 206–11

de Gaulle, Charles, 262n81

democracy, 16, 36, 114; multiparty and, 155–56, 177–78, 207; neocolonialism and, 178, 182; one-party and, 155, 177–78, 182–83, 198

development. *See* modernization

Donham, Donald L., 14

Downes-Thomas, J., 42

Drake, St. Clair, 70, 111, 135, 139

Drew, Jane, 59

Du Bois, Shirley Graham, 14, 205

Du Bois, W. E. B., 14, 44, 205; on imperialism, 35–36, 37, 39, 41, 123; pan-African congresses and, 34–35, 40, 159

Duku, Kofi, 24, 50, 53, 202–3, 225n19

Du Sautoy, Peter, 67

Dzima, D. A., 167

East Germany, 105

education: enrollments and, 55, 225n23; fee-free primary education and, 55, 167; migration and, 226n30; science and, 56–57, 225–26n28, 226n32; women and, 53, 167–68, 173–74

Edusei, Krobo, 137

Egypt, 75, 105, 201

empire, 30–31; benefits of, 33; capitalism and, 35–38, 48, 52, 123–24, 173; critics of, 31, 32–33, 35–39, 40–44; liberalism and, 31, 32–35, 37–38, 40, 42, 48, 218n15; world order and, 31–33, 37–38, 40

employment, 53, 87–88, 251n65. *See also* work

England, Kim, 163

Essuman, A. B., 130–31

Ethiopia, 40, 75

ethnicity, 12, 18, 21

Evening News, 17, 23, 70, 116, 164, 168, 185; accusations against NLM, 81; circulation of, 160; on class, 142–43, 146; democracy and, 156; education and, 54–55, 56; on gossip, 191–92; neocolonialism and, 151, 156; women and, 164, 165, 169–70

Ewe, 74, 87
ex-servicemen, 8–9

family, 6, 12, 18, 19, 21, 27, 77–78, 86, 168,
    187, 188, 190
Fanon, Frantz, 11, 14
Federated Youth Organisations (FYO),
    82
Ferguson, James, 13, 14
Ferrell, Lacy S., 226n30
Field, Margaret J., 63, 64, 65, 69, 230n67,
    230n71
Fifth Pan-African Congress (1945). *See*
    Manchester Pan-African Congress
First Pan-African Congress (1919). *See*
    Paris Pan-African Congress
Flagstaff House, 200, 204–5
Foevie, D. K., 143–44
Fosuawaa, Yaa, 94–95, 103, 207–8, 268n33
France, 1, 39, 151–52, 154, 156
Front de Libération Nationale (FLN), 14
Fry, Drew, Drake & Lasdun, 57

Ga, 62, 78, 87–88, 89–90; land
    ownership and, 64–65. *See also* Accra;
    Ga Ekomefeemo Kpee; Ga Shifimo
    Kpee; Tema
Ga Ekomefeemo Kpee, 89, 244n101
Gaines, Kevin K., 205
Garveyism, 40
Ga Shifimo Kpee, 89
Gbedemah, K. A., 137, 157;
    denunciations of Nkrumah and, 139–
    40, 181, 255n118; expulsion from CPP
    and, 140, 161
gender, 12, 18, 21, 150, 167
generation, 18, 19, 21, 27, 103, 150, 167
generational conflict, 53, 102–3, 105–6
Gerits, Frank, 268–69n41
Ghana: African liberation and, 29,
    158; coups and 204–6, 207, 273n5;
    currency and, 228n52; decolonization
    of (*see* Gold Coast); economy of,
    129–31, 134–35, 168; historiography
    of, 6–7; independence of, 1–4, 29–30,
    82, 151, 177, 208; Israel and, 91–93,
    239n33; Mandela on, 177; nation and
    nationalism and, 17, 48, 51, 70, 87,
    177; nationality and, 86–87; nation-
    building and, 17–18, 48, 73; one-party
    state and, 22, 154–57, 176–203; pan-
    Africanism and, 13, 59–60, 85–86,
    131–32, 135; postcolonial archive of,

22–26, 188, 208, 217nn54–55; republic
    and, 17, 22, 154–55, 180–81, 187; rural
    development, lack of, 132–33, 251–
    52n70, 252n72; terminology and, 213n3;
    urban development and, 57–60, 88,
    132, 226–7n38. *See also* Gold Coast
Ghana Congress Party (GCP), 66, 181
*Ghana Evening News. See Evening
    News*
Ghana-Guinea-Mali Union, 4, 85, 153
Ghana-Guinea Union. *See* Ghana-
    Guinea-Mali Union
Ghanaian (magazine), 17, 23, 115, 164,
    168; on women, 169–70
Ghanaian Times, 17, 23, 201
Ghana Muslim Council, 205
Ghana News Agency, 185
Gold Coast: anticolonialism and, 4, 30–
    31; colonization of, 32; Colony and,
    32; decolonization of, 12, 16; diarchy
    and, 10, 50–52, 85, 182; economy of,
    60, 103, 168; historiography of, 6–7;
    postwar period and, 7–10; South Africa
    and, 235n147; terminology and, 213n3;
    urban development and, 57–60
Gold Coast Independent, 49
Gold Coast Methodist Times, 33
Gold Coast Observer, 46
gossip, 170–71, 191–92
Great Britain, 39, 156, 154, 160, 163, 195,
    201, 205, 207; Asante and, 32, 75–76;
    as colonial power, 1–3, 41–43, 47; CPP
    and, 62, 229n59; gender and, 163; Gold
    Coast and, 3, 8, 10, 32, 50–52, 80–81,
    82, 85, 182; neocolonialism and, 154,
    156; Nkrumah in, 3, 40
Guevara, Che, 14, 113
Guinea, 18, 53, 99, 111, 135, 152, 197–98;
    independence of, 4, 151. *See also*
    Ghana-Guinea-Mali Union

Hammarskjöld, Dag, 154
Hanoi, 202, 204
Hart, Jennifer, 144–45
Hayford, Joseph, 196
Hess, Janet Berry, 59
Hilling, David, 58
Hobson, J. A., 35, 36, 37, 123, 219n27
Hodgkin, Thomas, 6

Iddrissu, Sulemana Ibun, 135–36, 155–56
Ikoku, S. G., 205
Imperialism: A Study. See Hobson, J. A.

Mines Employees' Union, 120
Miracle, Marvin P., 133
modernization, 15, 59, 60, 68, 74, 228–29n55; critics of, 62; gender and, 95; urban development and, 57–60, 88. *See also* CPP; Nkrumahism; Tema
Moumié, Félix, 14
Mouvement National Congolais (MNC), 152–53
Mugabe, Robert, 14, 131
Muslim Association Party (MAP), 74, 76–77, 79
Mussolini, Benito, 40

nation/nationalism, 16, 48, 52, 70, 86; African nationalism and, 20; citizenship and, 12, 16–18, 85. *See also* CPP; Ghana; nation-building
National Association of Socialist Students Organisations (NASSO), 161
National Council of Ghana Women (NCGW), 17, 164–65
National Liberation Council (NLC), 205, 206–7
National Liberation Movement (NLM), 52, 74–78, 181–82, 234n132; accusations against CPP, 76, 81, 179–80; cocoa and, 74–75, 81; federalism and, 76, 78–79, 182; legacy of, 183–84; neocolonialism and, 172; rise of, 76–77
nation-building, 17–18, 48, 73, 74, 85. *See also* CPP; Ghana; modernization
Nehru, Jawaharlal, 38–39
neocolonialism, 13, 157–60, 166, 174, 195, 210; fears of, 15–16, 149–50, 157
New African, 45. *See also* WANS
New Structure. *See* TUC
New York Times, 177
Niger, 198
Nigeria, 34, 46, 47, 151, 160, 174
Nikoi-Oltai, Ben, 50, 105–6, 204–6, 259n41
1951 Development Plan, 129
1951 General Election, 50–51, 54, 187
1956 General Election, 81–83
1960 Plebiscite, 180–81
1964 Referendum, 176–77, 187
1961 Budget, 101, 134–36; national savings plan and, 134–35
1961 Strike, 137–39, 141, 147, 151, 156, 185, 253n102; aftermath of, 139–41, 148–50, 194
1966 Coup, 204–6

Nkonwa, James Kofi, 189, 192, 193–96
Nkroful, 7
Nkrumah, Fathia, 202
Nkrumah, Kwame, 3–4, 91, 185, 224n14; accusations against, 77–78, 148–49, 177, 179, 189; anticolonialism and, 9, 30, 39, 47–48; assassination attempts against, 156, 189, 193–95, 200–201; biography of, 7; birth of, 32; cancer and, 194; class and, 142; coup and, 204, 206; cult of personality and, 106, 196; decolonization and, 11–12; family and, 77–78, 234–35n137; on Ghana's independence, 29–30, 84; imprisonment, 50; Kulungugu and, 156, 189, 193–95, 199–200; labor and, 120, 123; as leader of government business, 10, 50; Lumumba and, 4, 152–53, 154; Manchester Pan-African Congress and, 7, 41–42; modernization and (*see* CPP); neocolonialism and, 172; 1961 Strike and, 138–39; Padmore and, 7, 30, 40; pan-Africanism and, 30, 39–40, 46, 84–85, 201–2; as president, 154; as prime minister, 10; return to Gold Coast, 9, 49–50, 194–95; Second Development Plan and, 128; self-government and, 15, 52; *Towards Colonial Freedom* and, 39, 52, 123; travels abroad, 137–38; Tubman on, 177; UGCC and, 9–10, 49; in United Kingdom, 7, 40; in United States, 39–40; views of colonialism and, 9, 15, 30, 39; WANS and, 7, 45–47; on women, 165, 169–70; on work, 126
Nkrumahism, 16–22, 73, 83; ambitions of, 4, 12–13, 19, 51, 80; BAA and, 161; citizenship and, 4, 12–13, 17–18, 27, 85–86, 88–89, 136, 156, 157–58, 183, 192, 197; conformity and, 189–90, 195–97; definition of, 5; democracy and, 16, 155–56, 178–79; dismantling of, 206–7; gender and, 164–76; Ghanaians' relationship to, 20–22, 24, 28, 184–86, 203; historicization of, 208–11; legacies of, 207–9; modernization and, 12, 52, 58–59, 62, 68; multiples of, 21; nation and, 86; orthodoxy and, 22, 208, 209; relationship to pan-Africanism, 5, 131–32, 149; revolution and, 28, 113–14, 128, 136, 141–43, 149–50, 156, 157–58; revolutionary ethics and, 193–97; socialism and, 17–18, 26, 135–36, 177;

swollen shoot disease. *See* cocoa

Syme, Adjingboru, 92

Takoradi, 137–39, 146, 174

Takyi-Micah, Eden Bentum, 107, 110, 132, 201

Tali, Alhaji Yakubu, 106

Tanganyika African National Union (TANU), 53

Tanzania, 15, 53, 198, 239n33, 243–44n91

Tema, 58–59, 61, 62–73, 74, 75, 88, 96; critiques of Tema project, 61; economy of, 63; Ga population and, 62–63, 72, 230n71; harbor and, 61, 253n102; history of, 62–63; land and, 63, 65–67, 68–69, 230n67; migration to, 67, 72–73; modernization and, 68, 69–73; population and, 58, 227nn42–43; protests in, 66–67, 68–73; resettlement and, 62, 64–68, 68–73, 231n77; spirituality and, 63–65, 68; Tema Manhean, 65, 67, 71–73, 231n80; urban development and, 58–59

Tettegah, J. K., 24, 121, 127

Tetteh, M. N., 24, 49–50, 53, 97, 112

Tettey, Seth Laryea, 67, 71–73

Thompson, W. Scott, 159

Tignor, Robert L., 60

Togo, 89, 174, 199

Togoland, 74, 78, 82, 87, 89

Togoland Congress Party (TCP), 82

Touré, Sékou, 4, 111, 198

Towards Colonial Freedom, 39, 52. *See also* Nkrumah, Kwame

Trades Union Congress (TUC), 17, 19, 129, 135, 158; corruption and, 130; New Structure and, 127, 129–30, 133; 1961 Strike and, 137; relationship to CPP, 121, 126

Trades Union Ordinance (1941), 120

Tshombe, Moïse, 262n81

Tsiboe, Nancy, 77–78

Tubman, William, 177

Uganda, 41

unemployment, 9, 87–88, 89–90, 95, 131, 205, 207, 251n65. *See also* employment

United Africa Company (UAC), 123

United Arab Republic. *See* Egypt

United Ghana Farmers' Cooperative Council (UGFCC), 171

United Gold Coast Convention (UGCC), 9, 52, 74, 179, 198; Ghana

National Schools and, 54; Nkrumah and, 9–10, 49. *See also* CYO

United Nations (UN), 152–53, 154

United Party (UP), 106, 135, 180–81, 188–89

United States (US), 39–40, 124–25, 138, 157, 160, 174, 202, 207; anti-CPP activities and, 139–40, 199, 255n118; Cold War and, 1, 153, 154; gender and, 163; on Kulungugu, 195, 199; neocolonialism and, 154, 156, 166, 172; Sharpeville and, 152

University of Ghana, 204

University of Pennsylvania, 7

Upper Volta (Burkina Faso), 135

Voice of Africa, 156, 160, 165, 182, 186

Volta Region, 131

Volta River Authority. *See* Volta River Project

Volta River Project, 59, 62, 80, 128

Wallace-Johnson, I. T. A., 7, 42, 45, 221–22n64

Watson Commission, 8

Welbeck, N. A., 273n5

West African National Secretariat (WANS), 44–47; Nkrumah and, 7, 9, 44–47, 179; socialism and, 45

West African Pilot, 41, 42, 46

West African Student Union (WASU), 43, 44

West African Youth League (WAYL), 45, 221–22n64

West Germany, 105, 154

Whitham, David, 65

Woode, Anthony, 122

Worger, William, 117, 118–19

work, 6, 12, 117–22, 141–47; casual labor, 117–18; citizenship and, 115–16, 127–28; conceptualization of, 115–16; gender and, 90, 103, 162–66, 168–69, 263nn91–92; modernization and, 115; nationalism and, 120, 123; nation-building and, 121; Nkrumah and, 138; productivity and, 115–17, 118, 124, 143–44, 146, 160–61; socialism and, 19, 27, 115–17, 124–26, 133, 138, 141–47; women and, 143, 162–65, 166–75, 261n63, 263n89

workers, 9, 116–17, 117–22, 141–47; alienation of, 117, 124, 143–46; civic education and, 127–28; class and, 142–44; discipline and, 118; mineworkers, 117, 119–20; railway and harbor workers, 120, 121–22, 130 137–38, 146, 185; relationship to state, 125; resistance of, 117, 118, 119–20; respectability and, 118; stereotypes of, 117

Workers Brigade. *See* Builders Brigade

World War I, 35, 36, 37, 41

World War II, 1–2, 43, 211

Wright, Richard, 6, 10, 14; on colonial education, 56; on Danquah, 232n 101; on decolonization, 48; on Ghana's independence, 3; on Ghana National Schools, 225n19; on modernization, 69, 232n99; on Tema, 69

Yawson, Joseph, 102, 196

"Year of Africa," 151–57, 172, 174

Yeboah, Jacob Sesu, 108

Young Farmers' League, 17

Young Pioneers, 17, 18, 24, 26–27, 49, 57, 97–114, 116, 135, 158, 193; activities of, 98–102, 106, 108, 111, 113, 154, 186; age groups of, 99; Christianity and, 189; citizenship and, 98, 102, 105, 113, 186; corruption and, 111, 191; disappointment and, 108, 190; dissolution and, 205; generational

conflict and, 102, 105–6, 109, 111; growth of, 99; indiscipline and, 111; legacy of, 174; militarization and regimentation of, 98, 104–9; models for, 97–98; officials' frustrations and, 111–13; parental frustrations with, 108–9, 190, 197, 201; revolutionary ethics and, 195–97; schools and, 99; socialism and, 100–101, 102; socialization and, 101–2, 109, 110; songs of, 100; spying and, 19, 108–9, 140, 191–92, 195–97, 206; travels abroad and, 105, 112, 196, 206, 244nn95–96; uniforms and, 21, 98, 105–6, 111–12, 113, 190, 206, 242n64; women and, 167

youth, 9, 12, 26–27, 85, 90; African liberation and, 104; citizenship and, 85, 89–90, 96, 97, 103–4, 110, 112, 113; Cold War and, 104; delinquency and, 191; militarization and regimentation of, 27, 103–9; nation-building and, 96, 102, 103, 107; social independence of, 112; socialization and, 110. *See also* Builders Brigade; Young Pioneers

Yumu, Jacob Tetteh, 184

Zanzibar, 101

zongo, 74, 77, 79